Improve Your Quality of Life and Parenting Skills
The Button Therapy Book has made an incredible difference in my attitude and
my life. I am able to relax more and don't get as uptight or angry as I used to.
I have always been a person who had my "Buttons pushed" fairly easily and
now I understand how to identify my Buttons, address them in a calm and loving way and most importantly, get rid of them. I've also been able to take the
information given in the book and pass it on to my children to help them
overcome their "Buttons." Dr. Goodwin gives the reader all the tools they
need to live happier, healthier lives, starting immediately! I highly recommend
this book, it is a must for any person who is interested in improving his or her
quality of life and getting rid of those buttons!
Jodie Wilkerson from Greenville, NC

Get Ready to Unbutton and Be Free!
Button Therapy, a 'MUST HAVE' for any mental health professional and/or
the lay person. I have found many insights in this book and I have recommended it to just about everyone I know. I think that Dr. Goodwin has hit the
'button on the head', and has loosened it's thread with his insightful, caring
explanation of our 'Buttons' and how to deal with them. I find myself referring to it regularly in my business. Thanks Lloyd, I am happier, my clients are
happier and we all understand others and ourselves better now that we have
read your book. We will all be looking forward to your next work!
Suzanne Osborne, Ph.D., Clinical Psychologist, Forensic Psychologist,
Criminal Profiler, Counselor from North Myrtle Beach, SC

A Model for Personal and Spiritual Growth
The Button Therapy Book is a creative synthesis of Eastern and Western
models for personal and spiritual growth. An incredible compilation and synthesis of psychological self-help techniques. You would have to read 10 books
to get the information and number of self-help techniques presented in this
book. I've personally benefited from applying this practical six-step self-help
model to some of my Buttons. The chapter titled "30 Seeds for Your Mind's
Garden" is worth the price of this book alone. The "30 Seeds" are guidelines
that have been helpful in my journey of personal and spiritual growth.
Planting these "life-enhancing seeds" into the gardens of our minds enables us
to become more conscious, aware, loving, and compassionate. This is simply
the best psychological self-help book I've ever read. I've already recommended
this book to my friends. An excellent read!
Patricia Pollard, M.P.A., Administrator from Health Sciences Personnel,
Brody School of Medicine, East Carolina University, Greenville, NC

D0808974

Button Therapy Book: Good for Self-Helpers and Professionals
Goodwin has written a very readable book, which includes a thorough compilation of respected authors, therapists, and philosophers. Those views, augmented with his many years of counseling experience, provide a useful theoretical and practical book for both the mental health professional as well as the individual seeking a good self-help reference and guide, including inventories in the appendix.
Stephen K. Creech, Ph.D., Mental Health Professional and Musician from Winterville, NC.

Button Therapy
I was excited to see three decades of counseling theories, approaches, and strategies in mind-body therapy, brought together in one resource that is readable and accessible for either the lay-reader or counseling professional. This book is unique because it combines psychological research with very usable self-assessments and self-help techniques that can be applied in the "real world". The element that I found most helpful are the "30 Seeds for Your Mind's Garden" in Chapter 21. This presents a summary and cognitive guideline of living life most effectively to its fullest potential.
Mark Stebnicki, Rh.D., LPC, CRC, CDMS Professor and Director, Rehabilitation Counselor Education Program, East Carolina University, Greenville, NC

A Fantastic Book
A super way to learn how to deal with all the Buttons and Button-Pushers in your life. Learn to be a happier, healthier and hopefully a better person all around.
Ned Petrak, Financial Advisor, Goldsboro, NC

CONGRATULATIONS!!!
Congratulations Dr. Goodwin! You've done a wonderful job. I like the holistic nature of this cognitive behavior therapy model. The vast majority of clients I have worked with, see themselves as pawns in this world being blown from one situation to the other with minimal control. They often experience their emotions and actions as responsive to external forces rather than behavioral choices over which they have control. *The Button Therapy Book* teaches that the locus of most situations is internal and therefore, under our control.
Most of us are spiritually empty. I am very positive that they will be able to fill that spiritual void by reading the Button Therapy Book. I will recommend this book to any mental health professional I know.
AGYENIM A-BOATENG, M.S., CRC, CCAS, LPC, Mental Health Professional from Pinehurst, NC

An Excellent Guide To Feeling Good!
The Button Therapy Book provides techniques that will immediately lift your spirits and help you develop a positive outlook on life. Everyone has Buttons and Button-Pushers. Dr. Goodwin provides a framework to recognize the cognitions (i.e. thoughts, beliefs, etc.) attached to Buttons that produce negative results. Through the 21 Button removal strategies described in the book empowerment is accessible. A great "tool box" for those working in the mental health field as well as for anyone seeking personal growth. If you have the desire to dance to the music of the universe instead of dancing every time somebody pushes your Buttons, buy it, read it, you deserve it!
Sharon Williams from Washington, NC

Tired of Getting Your Buttons Pushed?
The Button Therapy Book is an excellent 'life enhancement manual'. I highly recommend it. Its foundations are based on the teachings of Buddha, Jesus Christ and Ken Keyes Jr. *The Button Therapy Book* also nicely wraps up the 'best of the best' literature from prominent psychologists, philosophers, and modern day shamans. The fewer 'Buttons' (i.e. negative cognitions and attachments) we posses, the happier we will be. This book is a GIANT step in that direction. In its most simple terms, The Button Therapy Book shows us how to identify our 'buttons' and how to remove them. This usually results in our greater ability to lead happier, healthier (i.e. less stressful) lives. Enjoy!
Andy Siegle, M.S., CRC Substance Abuse and Mental Health Counselor, Denver, CO

Button-Therapy
Excellent book! Clear and concise writing with many practical exercises and applications. I highly recommend it as a self-help tool and academic resource.
A reader from Greenville, NC

Great Practical Cognitive Behavioral Book!
At last an outstanding down-to-earth cognitive behavioral book which can be easily used by counselors and clients as well. This is an outstanding guide for all who want to improve our inner peace by gaining better control of our emotional and cognitive selves.
Jerry Lotterhos, M.S.W., Professor, Substance Abuse and Clinical Counselor Education Program, East Carolina University, Greenville, NC

Practical Information for Parents, Teachers, Coaches, and Health Care Workers
This book was easy to read. Many quotes were included which I found helpful

in putting things in perspective. Now when I become stressed I can look at things differently. Lloyd's approach to handling stress is holistic and full of common sense. I highly recommend this book.
Nancy Wentworth, Elementary School Teacher, Cape Elizabeth, Maine

Outstanding
This book is beautifully written. The real-life references and quotes compliment the invaluable information that is easily understood. I have already applied the 6 steps to deal with the 'Button- Pushers' in my life. The results are phenomenal.
Erin Wentworth, Medical Student, Cape Elizabeth, Maine

A Psychological Self-Help Book to Facilitate Becoming Happy, Healthy & Holy
Dr. Goodwin, I finished reading your book. I enjoyed reading it and had a difficult time putting it down. Button Therapy will help me personally get free from my buttons and become a healthy, happy, and just maybe a holy person. Button Therapy will also be a central part of the counseling I do in the future. Thanks and happy gardening to you too!
Bill Lewis, Counselor and Graduate Student, East Carolina University, Greenville, NC

Just Try to Push My Button!
Before reading this book, I thought the best I could do when my emotional buttons were pushed, was to recognize and interrupt the reaction. I never expected that I could possibly eliminate the buttons entirely. I plan to apply this wisdom to my own life and share the lessons with my patients.
Susan P. Farris, PA-C, Physician Assistant, Greenville, NC

Great Tools for Improving Family Relationships
My entire family has read this book and we have improved our relationships by implementing this method. Easy reading and wonderful way to keep the blood pressure down! It has helped me with social and business interactions as well.
Susan Gilgenback, Flight Attendant, Cocoa, FL

Very Practical and Empowering
Being able to help families learn about their 'Buttons' has helped parents of the families I do counseling with view presenting problems systemically, with each family member needing to change, instead of their child or teen being the identified problem.
Keith Montgomery, M.S., LPC, CRC, Mental Health Professional, Wilmington, NC

THE BUTTON THERAPY BOOK

HOW TO WORK ON YOUR BUTTONS
&
THE BUTTON-PUSHERS IN YOUR LIFE

LLOYD R. GOODWIN, JR., PH.D.

2002
Trafford Publishing
British Columbia, Canada

Author's Note

The Button Therapy Book is designed to be utilized by relatively "normal" and mentally healthy people as a global psychological self-help method. It also provides a holistic cognitive counseling model for use by mental health professionals. Button Therapy is not an appropriate self-help approach for individuals with moderate to severe mental disorders, such as schizophrenia. This book is not meant to substitute for professional mental health care. Individuals with moderate to severe mental disorders should seek the services of a qualified mental health professional.

Project Direction, Art Direction and Design
Alston Anderson, Anderson/Griffin, Atlanta, Georgia

Illustration Credits
Alston Anderson: cover
Kristin Goodwin: pages 1, 5, 31, and 102

National Library of Canada Cataloguing in Publication Data

Goodwin, Lloyd R., 1944-
 The button therapy book : how to work on your buttons
and the button-pushers in your life
Includes bibliographical references.
ISBN 1-55212-914-4
 1. Cognitive therapy--Popular works. I. Title.
RC489.C63G662 2002   616.89'142   C2001-902849-0

TRAFFORD

This book was published *on-demand* in cooperation with Trafford Publishing.
On-demand publishing is a unique process and service of making a book available for retail sale to the public taking advantage of on-demand manufacturing and Internet marketing.
On-demand publishing includes promotions, retail sales, manufacturing, order fulfilment, accounting and collecting royalties on behalf of the author.

Suite 6E, 2333 Government St., Victoria, B.C. V8T 4P4, CANADA

Phone	250-383-6864	Toll-free	1-888-232-4444 (Canada & US)
Fax	250-383-6804	E-mail	sales@trafford.com
Web site	www.trafford.com	TRAFFORD PUBLISHING IS A DIVISION OF TRAFFORD HOLDINGS LTD.	
Trafford Catalogue #01-0316		www.trafford.com/robots/01-0316.html	

10   9   8   7   6

ACKNOWLEDGMENTS

A SPECIAL ACKNOWLEDGMENT TO BUDDHA for his introducing the concept of attachment over 2500 years ago, and to Ken Keyes, Jr. for reintroducing this concept in the form of "addictive demand" in 1972 in the *Handbook To Higher Consciousness*. Ken Keyes, Jr., in addition to reintroducing the concept of attachment (i.e. addictions and demands), added self-help methods to help free ourselves from our addictive demands that cause psychological distress and pull us from a loving space.

Besides freeing ourselves from our Buttons (i.e. attachments) that create psychological distress and unhappiness, I believe other meaningful goals include becoming more aware, conscious, loving, and compassionate. The teachings of Buddha, Keyes, and Jesus have been instrumental in my ongoing personal journey of working on my "Buttons" and becoming a more compassionate, conscious, accepting, and loving being. It is interesting how the teachings of Jesus are very similar and parallel to those of Buddha presented 500 years earlier (see Borg, 1997). I have included selected sayings from Buddha, Jesus, Keyes, and other illuminated souls throughout *The Button Therapy Book*. I have found the teachings of Buddha, Jesus, Keyes, and Dr. Carl Rogers especially helpful in developing my understanding of unconditional love and compassion.

Other teachings that I have resonated with in developing the Button Therapy model include those of Ram Dass (Dr. Richard Alpert), Dr. John Lilly, Dr. Wayne Dyer, Dr. Albert Ellis, Dr. Aaron Beck, Dr. Abraham Maslow, Dr. Fritz Perls, and Dr. Eric Berne.

I am grateful to my family for providing me with some of my most important lessons for personal growth. My daughter Kristin, son Justin, and ex-wives have been, and continue to be, my most consistent and best teachers. My family and close friends are also my main source of love and support.

A special thanks to Carol Deakin, M.S., CRC for her editorial assistance in developing this book. On April 29, 1999, not long after Carol helped edit this book, she died suddenly and unexpectedly at the young age of 49 years old. I have lost a very good friend and dedicated colleague. She is missed.

Also, a special thanks to Carol Deakin M.S., CRC, Dawn Ellis, Cheryl Gentile, M.S., LPC, CRC-MAC, Ming Ling, Erin Stover, and Stephen Thomas, Ph.D., CRC, CVE for their assistance and helpful feedback during the development of the *Cognitive Self-Assessment Inventory* which is in the appendix.

A special thanks to Alston Anderson of Anderson/Griffin for her beautiful cover design, type-setting and graphics assistance, and support throughout this arduous book production process. Also, a special thanks to my daughter Kristin for her artwork contributions.

I also want to thank my many colleagues and friends, especially Jerry Lotterhos and Suzie Gilgenback, for their emotional support through my many life changes during the past few years. I also want to recognize John Anema who desperately wants to see his name in print in a book and is willing to do almost anything, including paying me $20, for the honor. It's time to pay up John.

Another special thanks to my children, Kristin and Justin, who have given me their permission to use some excerpts from their life experiences as examples to illustrate certain points in the Button Therapy model. At the risk of making family members and myself vulnerable I have opened up parts of our lives to help illustrate concepts in the Button Therapy model. And, last but not least, I want to acknowledge my internist (pulmonary specialist), pharmacist, and the pharmaceutical company that manufactures prednisone for the inspirational boost to actually sit down and write this book (see chapter one).

Lloyd R. Goodwin, Jr.
Greenville, North Carolina

TABLE OF CONTENTS

AUTHOR'S NOTE.. II

ACKNOWLEDGEMENTS... III

1 INTRODUCTION.. 2
An eclectic cognitive counseling model
The term "Button"
My prednisone book
A self-help cognitive counseling model
Holistic Cognitive counseling vs. cognitive-behavioral therapy
Personal growth and spiritual evolution

2 GUIDELINES FOR MENTAL HEALTH PROFESSIONALS..... 4
Holistic counseling
Cognitive counseling
        Historical roots of cognitive counseling
Cognitive-behavioral therapy (CBT)
        Primary focus of cognitive-behavioral therapy
Cognitive therapy/counseling applications
Major differences between Button Therapy and other CBT models
        Attachments vs. irrational beliefs
        Spiritual dimension
        Inclusion of a variety of cognitive interventions
Principles Underlying Button Therapy
When to use the Button Therapy intervention
Client criteria for utilizing Button Therapy
Empowering clients
How to integrate Button Therapy into the counseling session

3 THE BUTTON THERAPY MODEL................................. 23
A humanistic, transpersonal and holistic model
        Humanistic
        Transpersonal
        Holistic

v

When do I use Button Therapy?
   Definitions
      Biocomputer
      Buttons
      Button-Pushers
      Cognitions
      Cognitive therapy/counseling
      Troublesome cognitions
   Six-Step Button Therapy Method
   Sadhaks and Buttons

4 AWARENESS OF STRESS AND DISTRESS:.................... 32
RECOGNIZING WHEN YOUR BUTTONS GET PUSHED
Listen to your body
   The body's wisdom
Identify your feelings
   Hard to control emotions
Acceptance-rejection continuum

5 BUTTONS 36
Identifying our Buttons being pushed
   Identify the conflict of your desired model of how things should
   be versus what is
Types of Buttons

6 DISTORTED STYLES OF THINKING 40
      1. Black and White Thinking
      2. Blaming
      3. Comparing
      4. Catastrophic Thinking
      5. Fair and Just Thinking
      6. Mind Reading
      7. Negativistic Thinking
      8. Overgeneralizing
      9. Pasting and Futuring
      10. Should Thinking
      11. Perfectionist Thinking
      12. I'm "Right" and You're "Wrong" Thinking

7. DEFENSE MECHANISMS 55
Determining when we are using defense mechanisms
   Assess your defense mechanisms

Which defense mechanisms do people tend to use?

8   PERSONALITY TRAITS AND DISORDERS **67**
Personality
Personality Disorders
Toxic and nourishing people
Can we change our personalities?

9   CORE BELIEFS **74**
Self-defeating core beliefs
Parents: Our imperfect biocomputer programmers

10   ASSESS YOUR COGNITIONS **82**
Cognitive Self-Assessment Inventory

11   EMOTIONS **86**
Identify, experience, release, and channel the
    emotional energy associated with your Buttons
What causes emotions?
Our emotional vs. rational minds
Mind -Body emotions
    Molecules of emotion
    The mobile brain
    Gut feeling
    Stress and the brain
    Body/mind therapies
Can emotions precede thought?
Types of emotions
Emotional games
    Anger
    Boredom
    Guilt
Emotional amperage
    Welcome your feelings
Connecting the emotions to Buttons

12   MODELS OF MOTIVATIONAL STATES **99**
Transactional Analysis
Rational-Emotive Behavioral Therapy
Ken Keyes' Living Love System
Abraham Maslow's Hierarchy of Needs
The Seven Chakras in Yoga

Chakras
Malfunctioning chakras
Six motivational states in the Button Therapy Model
Determining your motivational states

13 SIX MOTIVATIONAL STATES **106**
1. Safety and security
2. Pleasure and sensation-seeking
3. Control and power
4. Love and acceptance
5. Personal growth and self-actualization
6. Spiritual and transcendental
In which motivational states do you spend the most time?
Motivational states and perception
Motivational states influence what we see
Activated Buttons affect perception
Multiple motivational states
With which motivational states are most of our Buttons associated?
Determining the motivational states associated with your Buttons

14 BUTTON POWER: **129**
   THE CONSTRUCTIVE AND DESTRUCTIVE POWER OF
   BUTTONS
The constructive power of Buttons
The destructive power of Buttons
My morality Button
The Moral Control Patrol
Consequences of the Moral Control Patrol to society
   Our country's schizophrenic and hypocritical pleasure morality
      policies
   Our morality laws (related to victimless crimes) make criminals
      out of otherwise law-abiding citizens
   Overburdening our criminal justice system
   Moral prohibition laws help make "criminals" rich
   Wasting financial and manpower resources
   Diversion of law enforcement resources from protecting citizens
      from real Criminals
   Corruption
   Disrespect for the law and police
How the Moral Control Patrol maintains it control
"The times they are a changin"
Libertarian backlash

Moral rehabilitation
  The five-step moral rehabilitation process
  Moral rehabilitation in the criminal justice system
The Shadow

15 Button Removal and Cognitive Restructuring 151

Making a conscious choice to keep, modify, or eliminate your Buttons
Choosing to keep your Buttons
  Stress Junkies
  Smiling Sufferers
  Low Self-Esteem
  Magical Thinkers
"I have so many Buttons - I'm hopeless"
Games people play
  Object games
  A neutral game
  Nonplayers
  Metagames
Deciding whether to eliminate the Button or change it to a preference

16 Cognitive Interventions 159

17 Portable Self-Help Cognitive Interventions 164

Changing Demands to Preferences
Self-Talk
Disputing Troublesome Cognitions
Cognitive Thought-Stopping
Flooding
Counting to 10
Here-and-Now
Mad Director Fantasy
Empathy Doubler

18 Scheduled Cognitive Interventions 175

Empty-chair
  Illustration of empty-chair work
The Worry Place
The Scheduled Pity-Pot Technique
Mind-Cleansing
Meditation

19 **COGNITIVE INTERVENTIONS THAT ARE BEST USED IN CONJUNCTION WITH A MENTAL HEALTH PROFESSIONAL** ···················· 185

    Injunctions and Redecision Work
    Inner Child and Reparenting Work
        Cosmic consciousness illumination
        The wounded inner child
        Inner child and reparenting
    Reframing
    Paradoxical Intention
        Advocate for the opposite of what you want
        Scheduling the target behavior you want to change
    Hypnosis
    Self-hypnosis
    Group Button Therapy Empty-chair Technique
    Group Button-Pull

20 **SOME COMMONLY ASKED QUESTIONS ABOUT COGNITIVE INTERVENTIONS** ···················· 202

    "Can I use any of the cognitive interventions described in this book?"
    "Can I combine cognitive interventions?"
    "Do I have to use all six steps of the Six-Step Button Therapy Method every time I work on a Button?"
    "How do I get rid of deeply rooted Buttons that don't want to be uprooted?"
    "Does giving up my Buttons mean I have to give up my wants, desires, and goals and let the people run over me?"

21 **AFFIRMATIONS AND CULTIVATING YOUR MIND'S GARDEN** ···················· 207

    CULTIVATING NEW COGNITIONS WHICH FACILITATE YOUR BECOMING HAPPIER AND MORE AWARE, CONSCIOUS, AND LOVING
    Cultivating your mind's garden
    Reprogramming your biocomputer
    Suggestions for the cultivation of your mind
        Planting new seeds
        Affirmations
    30 seeds for the garden of the mind
    Daily cultivation of your mind
    More resources for affirmations
    Daily cultivation of the mind

22 THE SPIRITUAL DIMENSION **217**
    Distinction between Religion and Spirituality
    Why include the spiritual dimension in a cognitive counseling
        and psychological self-help model?
        The Button Therapy model is a holistic cognitive therapy model
        Spirituality is an integral part of most people's lives
        Spirituality and health
    Do the medical and health insurance establishments support the
        inclusion of spirituality in health care?
    The spiritual dimension in medical school and
        counselor education curricula
    Summary

23 BUTTON-PUSHERS **243**
    Reframing our Button-Pushers as our teachers
    "Does this mean I should stay with the Button-Pushers in my life?"

24 THE SIX-STEP BUTTON THERAPY METHOD: AN
OVERVIEW **248**
    ABE's MBA: A mnemonic device for remembering the six steps
    Illustration of application of the Six-Step Button Therapy
        Perfectionist thinking Button.
    Short-cuts to the Six-Step Button Therapy Method
    Spirit Warriors
    Go forth and slay the Button dragons

25 RECOMMENDED READINGS **258**
    Cognitive therapy
    Emotional healing
    Guide to self-help books
    Holistic health and healing
    Inner Child and Reparenting
    Mind/body healing
    Personality
    Spiritual and personal growth
        Hinduism
        Buddhism
    Christianity
        New Age
        Taoism
        General
    Stress Management

Transactional Anaysis
Yoga and chakras

APPENDIX A: *Cognitive Self-Assessment Inventory (CSAI)* **277**

APPENDIX B: *Motivational States Inventory (MSI)* **295**

APPENDIX C: *Study of Cognitions, Buttons, and Motivational States* **304**
Utilizing the *Cognitive Self-Assessment Inventory (CSAI)* and
the *Motivational States Inventory*

REFERENCES **325**

INDEX **334**

OTHER BUTTON THERAPY MATERIALS **339**

ABOUT THE AUTHOR **341**

TABLES

Table 1: How to Integrate Button Therapy into the Counseling Session .. 21
Table 2: 12 Styles of Distorted Thinking................................... 41
Table 3: Top 10 Should Messages 51
Table 4: Top 10 Styles of Distorted Thinking 54
Table 5: Twenty Common Defense Mechanisms 56
Table 6: Top 10 Defense Mechanisms 66
Table 7: Top 10 Personality Traits 72
Table 8: Top 10 Core Beliefs about Self 77
Table 9: Top 3 Core Beliefs about Relationships 77
Table 10: Top 5 Core Beliefs about Life 78
Table 11: Top 4 Core Beliefs about Illness and Disability 78
Table 12: Top 10 Core Beliefs about Alcohol and Other Drugs 79
Table 13: Top 10 Buttons 84
Table 14: Top 10 Fears: 85
Table 15: The Seven Chakras in Yoga 103
Table 16: The Six Motivational States 121
Table 17: Ranked Centers of Consciousness or Motivational States ... 123
Table 18: Cognitive Interventions 160
Table 19: Six-Step Button Therapy Method for Psychological Self-help .. 257

THE
BUTTON THERAPY
BOOK

CHAPTER ONE

INTRODUCTION

What a strange machine man is! You fill him with bread,
wine, fish, and radishes, and out of him come sighs, laughter,
and dreams.

Nikos Kazantzakis
ZORBA THE GREEK

BUTTON THERAPY is a holistic cognitive counseling and self-help model that includes a six-step method to help us identify when we become psychologically distressed and modify or eliminate the troublesome cognitions (e.g. thoughts) responsible for our distress. The Button Therapy model includes strategies to identify our cognitive distortions, Buttons, and associated emotions. After the Button is identified the Button Therapy model provides practical therapeutic cognitive strategies such as cognitive "thought-stopping," "self-talk," "reframing," and other cognitive self-help and counseling interventions to modify or eliminate the Buttons causing the psychological distress. Button Therapy can be used as a cognitive counseling intervention by mental health professionals and as a psychological self-help model by individuals.

AN ECLECTIC COGNITIVE COUNSELING MODEL

The Button Therapy model is an integration of numerous cognitive, personal growth, and spiritual models. Three models that I have drawn from more than most are the Living Love system of personal growth developed by Ken Keyes, Jr. (1972), Yoga, including its model of the seven chakras, and Buddhism. I was fortunate to be one of the first individuals trained by Ken Keyes, Jr. in his cognitively oriented personal growth system in 1972. I have been integrating concepts and methods from Keyes' "Living Love" system of personal growth, and other cognitive models, into my eclectic professional counseling work since 1972.

THE TERM "BUTTON"

I began developing the Button Therapy model and using the term "Button" in 1974. I discovered that many individuals clicked with the term *Button* more readily than the terms "attachment" from Buddhism, "addiction" and "demand" from Keyes' Living Love System, or the concept of "irrational belief" popularized by Dr. Albert Ellis in his rational-emotive therapy. Over the years, colleagues, clients, and friends have suggested that I write a book on this unique brand of cognitive ("Button") therapy. Although I have been using the Button Therapy model in my personal and professional life for many years, it took me 25 years and some prednisone to become motivated to write this book.

MY PREDNISONE BOOK

Being afflicted with asthma and bronchitis has some advantages. My periodic lung problems are constant reminders of my many blessings and to have compassion for others with health, disability, and life problems. Recently, I have experienced some rather severe respiratory problems which prompted my taking a few cycles of the hormone prednisone as part of my treatment regimen. Prednisone triggers a lot of energy in me. I decided to channel some of this prednisone-generated energy into writing this book. Talking my family's, friends', and students' ears off and driving them nuts was the alternative! The rest of my hormone-induced energy went into my university teaching. On more than a few occasions I lost my emotional composure as I recalled incidents and examples of past clients I had worked with in the past to illustrate course content. I tended to recall clients and their life predicaments that made an emotional impact on me over the years and I found myself becoming overly emotional recalling those memorable encounters during class. Often, I would have to stop in the middle of a story because I was emotionally unable to continue for a minute or so until I regained my composure. This was somewhat embarrassing and I appreciate my students who were supportive during my more emotionally vulnerable periods. These students encouraged and allowed the expression of my emotions, telling me that it makes me more human and not just an aloof academic professor. Besides modeling that it is okay for a man to express his emotions (even when they're hormone induced), I'm sure it also provided some memorable entertainment for students in my courses in 1998. So, I sometimes refer to this book as "my prednisone book." In addition, as a result of this hormone induced emotional roller coaster, I have gained a deeper understanding of creative artists with manic-depression (i.e. bipolar disorder) who have utilized their manic phases to write, paint, and dance their way to completion of their projects.

Twenty-three years is a long time before developing a holistic cognitive counseling model and putting it down on paper and publishing it - but some things get better when they are used clinically and percolate awhile. Also, a hormone motivational boost doesn't hurt!

A SELF-HELP COGNITIVE COUNSELING MODEL

Give a man a fish and you feed him for a day;
teach a man how to fish and you feed him for a lifetime.
Japanese proverb

Since I strongly believe that professional counselors should be teaching clients self-help skills as part of their counseling and psychotherapy, *The Button Therapy Book* is primarily a practical self-help and bibliotherapy resource instead of a more academic tome on cognitive-behavioral therapy. *The Button Therapy Book* is also a practical holistic cognitive counseling manual for professional counselors and psychotherapists who want to integrate cognitive interventions into their counseling practice. The Button Therapy model is a revision and elaboration of the "Five-Step Psychological Self-Help Method" originally published in the *Journal of Humanistic Psychology* (Goodwin, 1981).

HOLISTIC COGNITIVE COUNSELING VS. COGNITIVE-BEHAVIORAL THERAPY

Trying to decide on the terminology to use in describing the Button Therapy (BT) model has been a major dilemma for me. Cognitive-Behavior Therapy (CBT) is the current front runner for many mental health professionals when referring to a counseling theory or strategy that primarily focuses on the cognitive dimension. However, even though the BT model can be referred to as a cognitive-behavioral therapy model, I do not believe this is the most accurate description. The BT model is more holistic than current cognitive-behavioral therapy models. The BT model includes an emotional, spiritual, and interpersonal (i.e. systems) dimension as well as the more traditional cognitive and behavioral dimensions. Ideally, the BT model would be referred to as a cognitive-emotional-behavioral-spiritual-systems counseling and self-help model. However, this is too long of a descriptor. Since the essence of the BT model is a focus on *cognitions* from a holistic perspective I have decided to settle on *holistic cognitive counseling* as the shortened descriptor.

PERSONAL GROWTH AND SPIRITUAL EVOLUTION

For those individuals utilizing this book for work on their personal growth it is hoped this Button Therapy model helps you better cope with the stress in your life and facilitates a more satisfying and happy inner experience. For those of you working on a more esoteric transpersonal and spiritual path, it is hoped that freeing yourself from your Buttons facilitates your personal growth and journey into the planes of increased awareness, consciousness, love, and compassion.

❧

The next chapter is primarily for mental health professionals.
You may want to skip chapter two if you are using this book primarily
as a psychological self-help tool.

GUIDELINES FOR MENTAL HEALTH PROFESSIONALS

You cannot teach a man anything. You can only help him discover it within himself.

Galileo

BUTTON THERAPY is a brief holistic cognitive counseling model, which can be used by mental health professionals, as well as a six-step practical psychological self-help method that can be used by individuals to work on emotional distress and improve the quality of their lives. Button Therapy can also help people better cope with the Button-Pushers in their lives. In addition to working on Buttons causing psychological distress, Button Therapy is a vehicle to facilitate personal and spiritual growth.

Both the *Button Therapy Book* and *The Six-Step Button Therapy Method* (Goodwin, 2002) book can be used as bibliotherapy resources for clients after a cognitive intervention has been introduced during a counseling session. These bibliotherapy resources describe a six-step psychological therapeutic method to work on "Buttons" (i.e. attachments, addictions, and demands), stressors (Button-Pushers), and other aspects of cognitive-emotional-behavioral restructuring.

HOLISTIC COUNSELING

The mental health field is gradually accepting the importance of working with the whole person (i.e. physically, psychologically, and spiritually) and not just the presenting disorder or problem. Most counselors now realize that any presenting problem (e.g. psychoactive drug abuse) affects the whole person.

Adopting a holistic perspective suggests that counselors not work exclusively with cognitive interventions. Cognitions are not isolated phenomena. Cognitions are interrelated with our emotions, behaviors, spirituality, and environment. A change in any one of these aspects affects the others. Also, people do not exist in vacuums. We interrelate with our environment, including all living things. We are part of numerous systems in our environment. For example, we are part of a family system. We impact on our families and our families affect us, even after they are deceased. If in school, the school system affects us and we impact the school. If we work, our work environment affects us and we impact our work

environments. There are many other systems that we may be part of such as health care systems, religious organizations, recreational groups, and athletic teams. The subtler aspects of our environment such as color, sound, touch, smell, food, and where we live also influence us. The need for mental health professionals to adopt a holistic perspective is summarized by the author in another publication (Goodwin, 1986):

> The focus of rehabilitation efforts is on the whole person including physical, mental, and spiritual aspects as well as the person's relation ship to his or her total environment...Thus, no matter how convenient it may be for academicians, theoreticians, and clinicians to divide aspects of human beings into categories, this reductionistic perspective bears little resemblance to the dynamic, creative, and synergistic existence of whole people. (p. 30)

Adopting a holistic *perspective* goes against the current wave of brief and solution-focused therapy models driven by the managed health care environment and health insurance industry. However, whether a client has the motivation, time, or resources to complete a more holistic and comprehensive counseling and treatment plan is a separate issue than whether or not the counselor adopts a holistic perspective when helping a client. In adopting a holistic counseling perspective, counselors often take an eclectic approach and utilize different counseling theories and strategies to work on behaviors, feelings, relationships, systems, and cognitions. Cognitive interventions are often utilized at various times throughout the counseling process when it is necessary to help individuals become aware of how their cognitions are creating emotional distress and behavioral dysfunction. Ideally, counselors develop a basic understanding of the whole person they are working with and develop a comprehensive holistic counseling and rehabilitation plan that includes the cognitive dimension.

COGNITIVE COUNSELING

HISTORICAL ROOTS OF COGNITIVE COUNSELING

The concept of thoughts influencing emotions and behaviors (i.e. cognitive counseling) probably had its beginnings with religion. Meditation and prayer are strategies to become aware of, or alter, our beliefs, wants, expectations, and other cognitions. Buddhism was one of the first spiritual paths to develop a system of spiritual and personal growth that is based in large part on cognitions and cognitive counseling.

BUDDHA. Buddha was born Prince Siddartha Gautama in Nepal about 563 BC, the son of a Sakya clan chieftain. He left home and became a wandering holy man, seeking answers to the age-old spiritual questions. Eventually, after years of effort, he achieved enlightenment while meditating under a bo tree. His followers believe that he reached the blissful state of non-being, referred to as *nirvana*. Because he had achieved nirvana his followers believed that he was freed from the necessity of physical incarnation, but voluntarily renounced his ecstasy in order to guide others towards the same goal. Siddartha Gautama died at the age of 80 around 483 BC (Campbell & Brennan, 1994).

BUDDHISM. Siddartha Gautama was called Buddha, or Enlightened One by his followers. Eileen Campbell and J.H. Brennan (1994) provide a brief synopsis of Buddhism:

> The first Buddhist sermon was preached in Benares, India, about 530 BC. By the time Prince Siddhartha Gautama, the Buddha (or Enlightened One) died some 45 years later, the religion he founded had attracted hundreds of monks and thousands of lay followers. It continued to grow and spread, rooting in China, Tibet, Japan, Burma and much of South East Asia. For a time it flourished much more strongly abroad than it did in its native India, although it is currently enjoying a considerable revival on the sub-continent today and is generally accepted to have influenced Hinduism profoundly.
>
> The fundamental pattern of Buddhism, which some consider to be far more of a philosophy than a religion, was set in the Benares sermon, when Gautama proclaimed the Middle Way between extremes of asceticism and thoughtless hedonism. The Middle Way comprised the Noble Eightfold Path of Right Views, Right Intent, Right Speech, Right Action, Right livelihood, Right Effort, Right mindfulness and Right Concentration. The Path was based on Four Noble Truths: that all life is suffering, that the cause of suffering is desire, that suffering will cease when desire ceases and that the Noble Eightfold Path will lead to the cessation of desire. (p.43)

Buddha, besides creating a spiritual and personal growth system, was probably the first cognitive counselor. The concept that "suffering" is a result of attachment to our desires was one of the essential teachings of Buddha over 2500 years ago. He claimed that "it is not life and wealth and power that enslave men but the cleaving [i.e. attachment] to life and wealth and power" (Carus, 1972, p.62). Buddha's concepts of the Four Noble Truths to explain our attachments to cognitions (e.g. desires) and the concepts of the Middle Way and Noble Eightfold Path of Right Views as a cognitive therapy provides a well developed system of therapeutic cognitive counseling.

PHILOSOPHY AND PSYCHOLOGY. The literature of philosophy, psychology, and studies on self-change also provided a basis for modern day cognitive therapy (Arnkoff & Glass, 1992). Early Greek and 17th and 18th century philosophers included the concept that our view of the world shapes the reality that we experience. For example Plato's concept of ideal forms existing within the mind representing what is real in the world. Descartes' concept that "I think, therefore I am" and Kant's idea that the mind makes nature are other examples of how these philosophers built their view of the world around the idea that the mind determines reality (Leahy, 1996; and Collingwood, 1945).

MODERN COGNITIVE THERAPY/COUNSELING. The cognitive counseling and self-help models evolved from Buddhism and early Greek and 17th and 18th century philosophers. Early self-help cognitive models were developed as approaches to achieve personal development in many areas of life such as happiness, positive thinking, wealth, and improved self-image.

One cognitive self-help model that became very popular in the 1960s was Psycho-Cybernetics. Maxwell Maltz, M.D., a plastic surgeon, developed Psycho-Cybernetics in 1960 to help individuals adjust psychologically after altering their physical bodies. Dr. Maltz believed, "...When you change a man's face you almost invariably change his future. Change his physical image and nearly always you change the man—his personality, his behavior—and sometimes even his basic talents and abilities" (pp. v-vi). Dr. Maltz (1967) included many cognitive interventions in his Psycho-Cybernetics model, including learning, practicing, and experiencing, new habits of thinking, imagining, remembering, and acting in order to, "...(1) develop an adequate and realistic Self-image, and (2) use your Creative Mechanism to bring success and happiness in achieving particular goals" (p.13).

Ken Keyes, Jr., developed another popular cognitive self-help model called the "Living Love Way to Happiness and Higher Consciousness" in 1972. Keyes' Living Love model was inspired primarily by the Noble Truths of Buddha. The Living Love model, described in the now classic *Handbook to Higher Consciousness* (Keyes, 1972), provides a cognitive model to explain how we get ourselves upset and cognitive methods for working on our addictive demands (i.e. attachments). There have been over a million copies sold of the self published *Handbook to Higher Consciousness*, in large part through word-of-mouth publicity. Another best selling practical cognitive self-help book in the 1970s was *Your Erroneous Zones* by Wayne Dyer (1976). Both Keyes and Dyer have written numerous other cognitive self-help books.

Within the disciplines of psychology and psychiatry the cognitive approach developed as a reaction to the narrow perspective of behavioral therapy. Behavioral psychology, "... did not attend to, and even rejected, the importance of internal mediating cognitive responses and processes, such as attribution, problem solving and expectancy" (Wanberg & Milkman, 1998, p.11). According to Wanberg and Milkman (1998) the cognitive constructs work of George Kelly (1955) and the study of the structure of thinking by Jean Piaget (1954) provided a firm foundation for the development of the cognitive restructuring therapies. According to Leahy (1996), Kelly (1955) is the "founder" of cognitive therapy in modern times with his development of cognitive constructs. According to Wanberg and Milkman (1998), the work of Kelly and Piaget provided a firm foundation for the development of the cognitive restructuring therapies.

Mahoney and Arnkoff (1978) have organized the contemporary cognitive-behavioral therapies into three major divisions: (1) cognitive restructuring (CR), (2) coping-skills therapies (CS), and (3) problem-solving (PS) therapies. *Cognitive restructuring* therapies assume that emotional distress is the consequence of maladaptive thoughts. Thus these clinical interventions seek to establish more adaptive thought patterns. *Coping skills* therapies include a variety of techniques that tend to focus on developing stress management skills. *Problem-solving* therapies include a combination of cognitive restructuring techniques and coping-skills training procedures (Dobson, 1988).

The following is an abbreviated historical outline of some of the better-known cognitive self-help and therapy models:

500 BC Buddhism by Siddhartha Gautama (Buddha)
1955   Psychology of Personal Constructs by George Kelly
1960   Psycho-Cybernetics by Maxwell Maltz
1962   Rational-Emotive Therapy by Albert Ellis
1963   Cognitive Therapy by Aaron Beck
1971   Self-Instructional Training by Donald Meichenbaum
1972   Living Love Way to Happiness and Higher Consciousness by
        Ken Keyes, Jr.
1974   Systematic Rational Restructuring by Marvin Goldfried
1981   Psychological Self-Help: A Five-Step Model
        by Lloyd Goodwin, Jr.
2002   The Button Therapy Model by Lloyd Goodwin, Jr.

COGNITIVE-BEHAVIORAL THERAPY

BEHAVIORAL THERAPY. Behavioral therapy focuses on current determinants of behavior with an emphasis on observable overt behavior. It utilizes principles from learning theory and social and experimental psychology (Wanberg & Milkman, 1998). The common intervention approaches used in behavioral therapy are coping and social skills training, contingency management, modeling, anxiety reduction and relaxation methods, self-management methods and behavioral rehearsal (Glass & Arnkoff, 1992).

COGNITIVE THERAPY. The underlying principle of "...cognitive therapy is based on the simple idea that your thoughts and attitudes – and not external events – create your moods" (Burns, 1989, p. xiii). The common interventions used in cognitive therapy are the cognitive restructuring methods of

Rational Emotive Therapy; restructuring of cognitive distortions of negative schemas, maladaptive assumptions, and automatic thoughts; self-instructional training; problem solving; coping skills training; relaxation therapy; modeling strategies; thought stopping; and covert conditioning (Wanberg & Milkman, 1998).

COGNITIVE-BEHAVIORAL THERAPY. Although cognitive and behavioral therapies seemed to develop in parallel paths, over time the two approaches merged into what is now referred to as cognitive-behavioral therapy. As Alan Marlatt has noted, "cognitive therapy a la Ellis and Beck has over the years become progressively more behavioral and that behavioral therapy a la Bandura, Goldfried, Kanfer, Mahoney, Michenbaum, etc. has over the years become progressively more cognitive – together creating contemporary CBT" (Wanberg & Milkman, 1998, p. 12).

PRIMARY FOCUS OF COGNITIVE-BEHAVIORAL THERAPY

The primary underlying assumption of the cognitive-behavioral therapy (CBT) model is that cognitions cause emotions and behavior. Rosenhan and Seligman (1995) break down the cognitive processes that become the focus of CBT treatment into short-term and long-term processes. They identify the short-term cognitive processes as expectations, appraisals, and attributions. The long-term cognitive processes are beliefs and attitudes.

COGNITIVE THERAPY/COUNSELING APPLICATIONS

Cognitive therapy has been extensively tested (Beck, 1995). Controlled studies have demonstrated the efficacy of Cognitive Therapy in the treatment of: major depressive disorder; generalized anxiety disorder; panic disorder; social phobia; substance abuse; eating disorders; couples problems; and inpatient depression. Cognitive Therapy is currently being applied as the sole treatment or as an adjunctive for other disorders such as: obsessive-compulsive disorder; posttraumatic stress disorder; personality disorders; recurrent depression; chronic pain; hypochondriasis; and schizophrenia.

Cognitive therapy is being applied to populations with other than mental disorders including prison inmates, school children, medical patients with a wide variety of illnesses, among many others. Cognitive therapy has been modified for group therapy, couples problems, and family therapy (Beck, 1995).

MAJOR DIFFERENCES BETWEEN BUTTON THERAPY AND OTHER COGNITIVE-BEHAVIORAL THERAPY MODELS

The Button Therapy Model differs from other cognitive-behavioral therapy models in a number of key areas including the etiology of Buttons (e.g. attachments vs. irrational beliefs), adding the spiritual dimension, and including an eclectic array of cognitive interventions.

ATTACHMENTS VS. IRRATIONAL BELIEFS

Interventions based on Aaron Beck's Cognitive Therapy model and Albert Ellis's Rational-Emotive Behavior Therapy (REBT) model attempt to reduce excessive emotional reactions and self-defeating behavior by modifying the faulty or erroneous thinking and maladaptive or irrational beliefs that underlie these reactions (Beck, 1979,1993; Ellis, 1975; Ellis, McInerney, DiGiuseppe & Yeager, 1988).

One major difference between the Button Therapy (BT) model and REBT model is that the BT model focuses on attachments and the REBT model focuses on irrational beliefs as the major way to conceptualize cognitions that are the major etiological culprit (i.e. Buttons) in causing psychological distress. The BT model differs primarily in that the main focus is on the concept of *attachment* and not whether the cognition triggering the psychological distress is rational or *irrational*, or adaptive or maladaptive. The main consideration in the BT model is whether or not the Button (e.g. attachment) is triggering stress, especially emotional distress, not whether the cognition is rational or irrational.

When confronted about the rationality of our beliefs our rational minds tend to go into high gear coming up with many reasons to justify the rightness of our beliefs and that we are justified in feeling and behaving the way we do. In BT, people do not have to judge their beliefs, or other cognitions, as rational or irrational, or right or wrong. They are simply taught to become aware of what they are attached to (e.g. demanding, clinging to, addicted to) whenever they experience emotional distress. They need to simply realize that the more they demand their model of how things should be, even if its rational, right, or justified - and it differs from what is currently happening - the more they will create the experience of psychological distress. They are then taught a six-step cognitive self-help model (i.e. Six-Step Button Therapy Method) to become aware of and work through their attachments, demands, addictions, and expectations. However, examining whether or not a cognition is rational or irrational and adaptive or maladaptive can be helpful with some troublesome cognitions (and Buttons) and can be utilized in the Button Therapy model.

SPIRITUAL DIMENSION

Another major difference between the Button Therapy model and other cognitive-behavioral therapy models is the inclusion of the *spiritual* domain. The spiritual dimension is generally not included in other cognitive therapy models. Our Buttons are the primary reason people become sidetracked from their spiritual paths. Every time we get one of our Buttons pushed we are pulled off center and out of harmony. We are pulled out of our accepting, caring, and love space. Becoming more centered, harmonious, accepting, caring, and loving are qualities shared by most spiritual paths. As we become free of our Buttons we can develop our spiritual aspect, if we choose to do so. The first five steps of the Six-Step Button Therapy Method are designed to help people free themselves from their Buttons. The sixth step entails incorporating and reinforcing positive, proactive, and life enhancing guidelines for living that may include spiritual goals.

INCLUSION OF A VARIETY OF COGNITIVE INTERVENTIONS

The BT model is inclusive and integrates conceptual models of how we distort our cognitions and cognitive interventions from other cognitive therapy models into the BT model. For example, a professional counselor working from the BT model may utilize a cognitive intervention from the Transactional Analysis model such as examining "parental injunctions" or "parental messages" and making new decisions about whether to keep, modify, or discard these messages (i.e. cognitions). Other cognitive therapy models have been developed by Meichenbaum (1977, 1985), Dyer (1976, 1979, and 1981), McKay, Davis and Fanning, (1981) and others. Many of these cognitive therapy models are variations of the models developed by Beck and Ellis and have added helpful concepts and cognitive interventions that can be integrated into the more holistic and elective Button Therapy model. The cognitive models that I resonate with the most come from the teachings of Buddha and Ken Keyes, Jr.

As people become free of their Buttons they become less reactive and robot-like in their emotions, behaviors, and relationships and have more choice as to where to focus their energies. When individuals realize they are responsible for creating their own frustration, anger, anxiety, stress, boredom, and other forms of psychological distress by developing attachments to models of how people and life should be, and begin to change their models, it can be a truly liberating experience.

PRINCIPLES UNDERLYING BUTTON THERAPY

Some of the basic principles underlying Button Therapy include the following.

1. Troublesome cognitions and attachments to cognitions, called *"Buttons"*, *are*

the primary cause of emotional distress.

2. *Cognitions, feelings, behaviors, and health are interrelated.*

3. *Assessment of cognitions (e.g. Cognitive Self-Assessment Inventory)*, especially troublesome cognitions and Buttons, is an ongoing process.

4. *Changes in perceptions, emotions, and behaviors occur primarily through changes in cognitions (e.g. thinking).*

5. We can best influence change in our *Button-Pushers* by first becoming more conscious and getting free from our activated Buttons.

6. Button Therapy initially *focuses on the here-and-now* and can change to a past or future focus as needed.

7. *Button Therapy incorporates a variety of different models* to view the etiology and motivational states associated with Troublesome Cognitions (TC's) and Buttons. BT also incorporates a wide variety of cognitive interventions, including those from other cognitive-behavioral therapy (CBT) models. Button Therapy is an eclective cognitive therapy/counseling model that can accommodate existing CBT models.

8. The Button Therapy model can be used for *spiritual* growth. We can achieve a love and acceptance motivational state, and other higher states of consciousness, by modifying or eliminating TC's and Buttons that trigger reactions that create separateness from God and others.

9. Effective professional mental health practitioners have an eclectic *holistic* counseling perspective that takes into account the whole person. Cognitive therapy is frequently utilized to examine and work with the cognitive dimension of a client during a counseling session. Button Therapy is only one model of cognitive-behavioral therapy (CBT) from which to choose.

10. Button Therapy requires a *good therapeutic climate* including a strong rapport and trust between the counselor and client. Counselor characteristics of warmth, caring, genuineness, acceptance, compassion, empathy, and competence are helpful to developing a good therapeutic climate.

11. Button Therapy requires *active participation* by individuals pursuing BT as a self-help model and *by clients during counseling sessions* including identifying and learning Button Therapy strategies to modify or eliminate troublesome cognitions (TC's) or Buttons.

12. Button Therapy requires *active participation between counseling sessions* including completing "homework" assignments, completing the *Cognitive Self-Assessment Inventory*, monitoring TC's and Buttons, utilizing cognitive interventions, and reinforcing newly acquired life enhancing affirmations.

13. There is an educational aspect of Button Therapy. *Psychological self-help skill training* is an important goal of Button Therapy sessions. Clients are taught how to utilize the Six-Step Button Therapy Method anytime and anywhere to identify and then modify or eliminate TC's and Buttons that are creating emotional distress. This educational process takes place during

the counseling session and is followed up with the brief and practical *Six-Step Button Therapy Method* book, a bibliotherapy resource. Subsequent counseling sessions include follow-up reviews and applications of the Six-Step Button Therapy Method to newly uncovered Buttons.

WHEN TO USE BUTTON THERAPY

The most opportune time to introduce the six-step Button Therapy cognitive intervention into the counseling session is when the individual is experiencing mild to moderate levels of emotional distress. Preferably, when the emotions are recurrent and sufficiently distressful so as to motivate the individual to modify or eliminate the cognitions (i.e. Buttons) causing the distress.

Another opportune time for introducing the need for cognitive work is when the Button-Pusher triggering the distressful emotions is a "significant other" such as a spouse, ex-spouse, or boss. When individuals realize they are giving Button-Pushers (e.g. spouse) control over their emotions and inner experience, they often quickly gain the motivation to work on their Buttons in order to gain control of their feelings and personal inner experience.

CLIENT CRITERIA FOR UTILIZING BUTTON THERAPY

Characteristics of individuals who can benefit most from Button Therapy include:

- **Average to above average intelligence.**
- **No significant cognitive impairments.** Some individuals with chronic alcoholism and other psychoactive drug abuse disorders (e.g. PCP abusers), Alzheimer's, traumatic brain injury, mental retardation, and other conditions that limit cognitive functioning, especially the capacity for abstract reasoning, may not be appropriate for cognitive counseling interventions.
- **Have a capacity for abstract reasoning.** Some individuals, because of cognitive impairments, or lack of abstract reasoning ability, are concrete thinkers and have difficulty identifying and exploring the often fleeting thoughts, beliefs, expectations, models of how things should be, and other subtle aspects of their inner cognitive domain.
- **Have the ability to identify feelings and thoughts.** Few people have difficulty understanding behavioral interventions. However, not everybody has the ability to identify the cognitive and feeling components of a life situation which are necessary for cognitive counseling and self-help interventions.
- **Mild to moderate levels of emotional distress.** Individuals with over-

whelming emotional distress need to reduce the intensity of their emotional experience to a level where their rational mind can be effectively utilized before utilizing cognitive counseling interventions. These individuals need an empathic ear and supportive counseling in order to let enough "steam out of the kettle" before any cognitive intervention is appropriate.

- **Lucid and not experiencing a psychotic episode or emotional crisis.**
- **Appreciates the value of introspection.** Individuals must value rational analysis of themselves, especially the exploration of the models, scripts, programming, expectations, and other cognitions we carry around in our minds.
- **Motivated to assume personal responsibility for their lives.** Individuals must express a willingness to take responsibility for their thoughts and other cognitions. They must also be willing to take responsibility for creating their own feelings and the quality of their inner experience and stop blaming other people for their feelings.
- **A desire to improve the quality of their lives.** Individuals are ready for Button Therapy when they are sick and tired of being mentally, emotionally, and spiritually sick and tired and recognize there's more to life. When individuals want to spend less time psychologically distressed and more time content, happy, aware, conscious, and loving they are prime candidates for Button Therapy.

EMPOWERING CLIENTS

He helps others most, who shows them how to help themselves.
A. P. Gouthey

Teaching self-help skills to individuals is an integral part of professional counseling. Many individuals can benefit from a simple structured model from which to view, understand, and work on their problems and psychological distress. Often, anxiety and stress is reduced simply by having a concrete structured perceptual framework from which to view emotional distress and life's predicaments. As Murray and Jacobson (1971) point out, once clients come to believe that they can cope with a situation, anxiety declines. "Furthermore, a patient's uncertainties and self-fulfilling prophecies of failure in such situations may also decline" (Liberman, 1978, p.64).

Liberman (1978) reviewed several studies in attribution theory which demonstrate that behavior changes, which are self-attributed, are maintained to a greater degree than those which are believed to be due to external causes. In Liberman's own research "...reliance on an external agent for improvement tends to cause its effectiveness to end when it ends. Improvement through successful self-reliance, on the other hand, may be more easily renewable" (p. 64).

In my own clinical experience, most individuals have little difficulty relating to the cognitive concepts and interventions presented through the structure of the Six-Step Button Therapy Method. Individuals learn to utilize the relevant parts of this method rapidly with minimal assistance. I have found that the rate of personal growth accelerates considerably when individuals undergo a transition from other-directed locus of control and support to a more authentic inner-directed locus of control and support system, and assume responsibility for their feelings and inner experience.

How to Integrate Button Therapy into the Counseling Session

The best time to introduce the Six-Step Button Therapy Method is when the individual is experiencing mild to moderate emotional distress and is motivated to end the psychological suffering. Experiencing distressing emotions repeatedly over time often help increase readiness for cognitive counseling interventions. The following are guidelines for utilizing the Six-Step Button Therapy Method during a counseling session:

1. TIMING. Before introducing the Button Therapy (BT) intervention there needs to be enough time in the session to complete this cognitive counseling intervention. Usually, at least 30 minutes is necessary to introduce and utilize the Button Therapy intervention with a client during a counseling session the first time. In subsequent sessions, less time may be needed to utilize the BT intervention because the client will already have a basic understanding of the BT model and how cognitions influence emotions and behavior and have some personal experience with the six-steps of the BT method. Also, once the six steps are learned, any single step or combination of steps in the Six-Step Button Therapy Method can be utilized in a few seconds time without going through all six steps.

2. EMOTIONS. The experience of mild to moderate emotional distress provides an opportunity to introduce the Button Therapy model. Begin by paraphrasing or summarizing what the client has told you about the emotional distress, followed by identification and reflection of the emotions back to the individual. You need to let clients know that you understand them and can empathize with them. The discomfort of the emotional distress provides much of the motivation to engage in cognitive therapy and work on the Button causing the emotional distress.

3. DEVELOP MOTIVATION TO WORK ON BUTTONS. Ask the client if he or she would like to work on getting free from the emotional distress as well as the Button that keeps triggering these feelings. If the emotional distress is related to another person, which is often the case, it is usually helpful to point out to the client that:

> "...you are giving that other person (e.g. boss, coworker, spouse) a lot of power over you.
> ...the other person is the 'Button-Pusher' and all that person has to do is push your Buttons and watch you dance! You are like a puppet on a string.
> ...you go into a robot-like reaction whenever your Buttons get pushed and you have no conscious choice in the matter, it is an automatic unconscious reaction. If you want to give the power to control your feelings and inner experience to the Button-Pusher (e.g. spouse) that's okay. But at least be aware of what you are doing."

4. ASK THE CLIENT IF THEY ARE READY TO WORK ON THEIR BUTTONS CAUSING EMOTIONAL DISTRESS. If the client has experienced enough psychological suffering and emotional distress, and appears motivated to work on his or her Buttons, then ask the client if he or she would like to learn a six-step method to get free from the Button(s) that triggered the emotional distress. It may be obvious to the mental health professional that the individual needs to work on a particular Button. However, the skill of the professional counselor is often necessary to help the individual gain insight and identify the Buttons causing emotional distress and motivate the individual to want to work on modifying or eliminating them. Unless the counselor can help individuals gain the insight and motivation to work on their Buttons, and having them set a goal of modifying or eliminating the specific Buttons, the counselor is pursuing the counselor's goals and not necessarily the client's goals. Working on the counselor's goals without the individual accepting them as his or her goals can result in a lot of wasted time and frustration for both counselors and clients. It is always important to make sure the individual is motivated to work on a particular Button before proceeding to implement the Six-Step Button Therapy Method. The counselor may say something like, "Are you ready to work on your anger Button that is causing you so much emotional pain and pushing your spouse and children away? Or, do you need to stew, suffer, and alienate them some more?"

5. DEVELOP MOTIVATION TO MODIFY OR ELIMINATE TROUBLESOME COGNITIONS OR BUTTONS. Helping the individual understand the *consequences of certain cognitions* (e.g. Core beliefs, thought distortions, and expectations) can be an effective strategy for developing motivation to change. Help the individual see how attachments to cognitions cause his or her emotional distress. Help them connect the adverse consequences related to their relationships with family, co-workers, boss, friends, and impaired physical and mental health to their troublesome cognitions and Buttons. For example, you might say something like, "Can you see how your jealousy Button is harming your relationship with your spouse and actually pushing her away instead of bringing you closer together as you say you want." Then make sure the individual becomes aware of past events, especially recent examples, where his jealousy Button created problems in his relationship with his wife. Then ask, "Are you ready to work on your jealousy Button now?"

6. PROVIDE A BRIEF OVERVIEW OF THE SIX-STEP BUTTON THERAPY METHOD. If the individual indicates he or she is ready for a cognitive intervention then give a brief overview of cognitive counseling and the Six-Step BT Method. Make sure clients understand the concept of "Buttons" (i.e. attachment or addictive demand) and how troublesome cognitions and Buttons cause feelings. You might say something like:

> How we interpret events, situations, and what other people do and say usually determines how we feel about them. And, no two people are going to experience or feel the exact same way about a given event or situation. This is because we are all unique human beings with unique life histories. We each have unique life experiences that influenced the development of our current cognitions (i.e. thoughts, beliefs, expectations, and models of how things should be). Thus, even though a group of people may all view the same event, such as your wife telling you she wants a divorce, each of us will interpret and experience that event differently. How we view any given event depends upon a variety of factors including our past life experiences; cognitions; expectations; personality styles, traits, and disorders; defense mechanisms; cultural programming; and a host of other factors.
>
> Thus, if you want to change your negative emotions, improve the quality of your inner experience, and become happier, healthier, and holier then you need to work on your troublesome cognitions and Buttons, which cause your psychological distress. I would like you to learn a psychological self-help method to help you identify and work on your troublesome cognitions and Buttons. It's called the Six-Step Button Therapy Method. Would you like to give it a try?

7. APPLY THE SIX-STEP BUTTON THERAPY INTERVENTION TO THE CURRENT DISTRESSING PROBLEM. After a brief explanation of the Six-Step Button Therapy Method, begin applying it to the presenting problem and/or emotional distress that the client is currently experiencing or relating during the counseling session.

8. FOLLOW-THROUGH AND CHECK-OUT. Following the BT intervention, process the intervention with the client, and make sure the client has grasped the basic concepts of the Six-Step Button Therapy Method, especially the concept of how our cognitions and Buttons create our feelings, before ending the session. The client will most likely not be able to remember all six steps but should be able to grasp the basic concept of how our troublesome cognitions and attachments (Buttons) create our emotional distress. As a result of this Button Therapy intervention, clients should become motivated to assume more responsibility for creating their own inner experiences, including their emotions. Hopefully, they begin to realize that if they are not happy with the current state of their inner experience it is up to them to assume responsibility for changing it. Hopefully, they now have a better understanding of how they create most of their feelings and their inner experience and have some tools to change it.

9. BIBLIOTHERAPY AND HOMEWORK. Following the BT cognitive intervention give the client *The Six-Step Button Therapy Method* book as a bibliotherapy resource which provides a brief overview of the six steps and reinforces what was learned during the counseling session. The Button Therapy book will allow for review of the Six-Steps in the Button Therapy Method outside of the counseling session. Individuals seldom remember all six of the steps following the first time use of the BT method in a counseling session. Ask the client to read the Six-Step Button Therapy book between counseling sessions. In the following session, ask the client to share his or her reactions to the book. Also, review and further process the previous session, if necessary, by asking if he or she had any more insights into the Button that was worked on in the previous session in light of reading the book. Also, inquire as to whether the client had the time or opportunity between sessions to do any continuing work on that Button or other Buttons.

If the client clicks with *The Six-Step Button Therapy Method* book then refer the client to this more comprehensive *Button Therapy Book*. If the client relates positively to the Button Therapy model then it can be used in future sessions when a cognitive counseling intervention is the treatment of choice. When this cognitive intervention is used on subsequent occasions both the counselor and client will already be tuned in to the same model, concepts, and language of the Button Therapy model. Most individuals relate readily with the concept of Buttons and they find that the Six-Step Button Therapy Method makes sense to them.

10. COGNITIVE SELF-ASSESSMENT INVENTORY (CSAI). At this point if they have read The Button Therapy Book and can relate comfortably with this cognitive counseling model, then you may want to introduce the *Cognitive*

Self-Assessment Inventory (Goodwin, 2002a) described in chapter ten and available in Appendix A. Ask the client to complete the *CSAI* before the next session. The *CSAI* will help identify the client's most troublesome cognitions and Buttons that can be explored in future counseling sessions. Also, the *CSAI* can be administered at the beginning of the counseling process as part of a genenral psychological assessment.

11. PRACTICE USING THE SIX-STEP BUTTON THERAPY METHOD. Ask individuals to apply the Six-Step Button Therapy Method the next time they become upset or distressed between counseling sessions and share the results during the next counseling session. Individuals will need to practice utilizing this method in order to utilize it effectively in the marketplace of life. One objective of teaching the Six-Step BT Method to individuals is so they can have a portable psychological self-help tool available to them when they experience emotional distress while in their environment. Like acquiring any new skill it takes time, effort, practice, and patience.

After the Six-Step Method is learned, the processing of many of our Buttons can be worked on within a matter of seconds or a few minutes. However, some Buttons have the force of twenty or thirty years of conditioning behind them and will not easily disappear. These Buttons will require patience and consistent work each time they are activated. These deeply rooted Buttons will most likely take many encounters with Button-Pushers to uproot them.

The remainder of the book presents the Button Therapy model and Six-Step Button Therapy Method. It is presented in easy to understand language and in a self-help manner for individuals to work with alone, with loved ones, or with a mental health professional.

TABLE 1

HOW TO INTEGRATE BUTTON THERAPY INTO THE COUNSELING SESSION

The following is a summary of the guidelines for utilizing the Six-Step Button Therapy Method during a counseling session:

1. TIMING
- Allow enough time in the counseling session before introducing the Button Therapy model (approximately 30 minutes for first time and 5 or 10 minutes for subsequent times).

2. EMOTIONS
- The client's experiencing of mild to moderate distressing emotions provide an opportunity to introduce the Button Therapy model.
- Help the individual identify and experience the feelings (e.g. paraphrase, summarization, and reflect the feelings).
- Demonstrate empathy.

3. DEVELOP MOTIVATION TO WORK ON BUTTONS
- Ask if they are tired of giving control of their feelings over to a Button-Pusher (e.g. spouse or coworker).

4. ASK IF READY TO WORK ON BUTTONS CAUSING EMOTIONAL DISTRESS
- Ask if they have suffered enough yet?
- If yes, ask if they would like to learn a self-help method to better understand how they get themselves upset and how to become happier, healthier, and holier.

5. DEVELOP MOTIVATION TO MODIFY OR ELIMINATE TROUBLESOME COGNITIONS OR BUTTONS
- Connect consequences (e.g. negative feelings) with cognitions such as core beliefs, thought distortions, expectations, defense mechanisms, or personality traits.
- Ask if they are ready to modify or eliminate the troublesome cognitions or Buttons causing the emotional distress.

6. **PROVIDE A BRIEF OVERVIEW OF THE SIX-STEP BUTTON THERAPY METHOD**
   - Make sure they understand how their cognitions and interpretation of events and situations determine how they experience the event.

7. **APPLY THE SIX-STEP BUTTON THERAPY INTERVENTION TO A CURRENT PROBLEM**

8. **FOLLOW-THROUGH AND CHECK-OUT**
   - Following the BT intervention ask individuals to summarize how they would apply the six steps the next time this Button gets pushed.
   - Review the six steps.
   - Give pep talk as to how they now have a tool to better understand how they get themselves uptight and how they now have a six-step method to work on their thoughts and other cognitions in order to change their negative emotions and improve the quality of their lives.
   - Review the six steps again during the summarization at the end of the counseling session.

9. **BIBLIOTHERAPY AND HOMEWORK**
   - Following the BT intervention, give the individual the brief and practical *Six-Step Button Therapy Method* book as a bibliotherapy resource to help the individual remember the Six-Step Button Therapy Method and reinforce using the method after they leave the session.
   - Ask for their reaction the following counseling session. If they clicked with the Button Therapy model and book, refer them to the more comprehensive *Button Therapy Book* and ask them to complete the *Cognitive Self-Assessment Inventory* (see Appendix A).

10. **COGNITIVE SELF-ASSESSMENT INVENTORY *(CSAI)***
    - Have client complete between sessions.
    - The *CSAI* will help identify self-defeating styles of thinking, should messages, core beliefs, personality traits, and defense mechanisms which will provide grist for the personal growth mill for many counseling sessions.

11. **PRACTICE USING THE SIX-STEP BUTTON THERAPY METHOD**
    - Acquiring any new skill requires time, effort, practice, and patience.

The Button Therapy Book: How to Work on Your Buttons and the Button-Pushers in Your Life by Lloyd R. Goodwin, Jr.
© 2002.Published by Trafford Publishing. www.trafford.com

CHAPTER THREE

THE BUTTON THERAPY MODEL

However young, the seeker who sets out upon the way shines bright over the world.
But day and night the person who is awake shines in the radiance of the spirit.
Meditate. Live purely. Be quiet. Do your work, with mastery.
Like the moon, come out from behind the clouds! Shine.

Buddha

BUTTON THERAPY is a six-step holistic cognitive counseling and self-help psychological method to reduce emotional distress and related maladaptive behavior. Button Therapy can improve the quality of your inner experience, increase your happiness, inner peace, and facilitate your personal and spiritual growth. Button Therapy works primarily by utilizing a six-step psychological self-help method to modify or eliminate "Buttons" and other distortions in thoughts, perceptions, and beliefs. Button Therapy can help you become free from your "Buttons" that cause much of the emotional distress in your life and help you become more aware, conscious, and loving. When used to facilitate consciousness growth, the Six-Step Button Therapy Method becomes an existential here-and-now meditation-in-action technique that can be used while interacting in the marketplace of life.

A HUMANISTIC, TRANSPERSONAL AND HOLISTIC MODEL

Button Therapy (BT) is holistic cognitive therapy model and includes a six-step method to work on troublesome cognitions and Buttons. BT places a primary focus on identifying and processing thoughts and other cognitions that trigger emotional distress and restrict inner experiences. BT works with emotions associated with activated Buttons through an innovative Six-Step Button Therapy Method. BT also includes a spiritual aspect that permeates the entire BT model and is the essence of the sixth step.

HUMANISTIC

The Button Therapy model is a humanistic model. It is my belief that people are basically good and have an innate desire to become loving and fully-functioning and self-actualized human beings. Just as an acorn has an innate tendency to become a fully grown oak tree so do humans have an innate tendency to become fully-functioning and self-actualized human beings. Both benefit from a nurturing environment to become fully actualized.

Unfortunately, because of inherited personality or biological factors, environment, parents, friends, or the acquisition of certain beliefs and desires, we sometimes develop cognitions and programming that block our natural growth tendency toward becoming fully functioning self-actualized beings. Many people become dulled and homogenized by the conditioned reality of their existence and have lost touch with the basic goodness of themselves and other people and the natural tendency to become self-actualized. Button Therapy is a tool for awakening the dormant innate personal growth tendency and working on the Buttons that pull us from our natural tendency to become loving, conscious, aware, and spiritual human beings (i.e. self-actualized).

TRANSPERSONAL

The Button Therapy model is a transpersonal counseling model in that I believe part of the natural tendency toward personal growth and self-actualization is to actualize the God-like part of us which is striving to merge with God or the universal life force. It is common for our rational minds and egos to become well developed to the exclusion of our nonmaterial and spiritual aspects. We are often unbalanced in a holistic (i.e. body, mind, and spirit) sense. We are either too rational and not in touch with our feelings, or so emotionally reactive we can't make rational decisions. The programming we have acquired in our biocomputers (i.e. mind) has clouded our innate natural tendency to transcend our egos and rational minds. Many individuals have abandoned the pursuit of transpersonal and spiritual development. Button Therapy can be used to work on the Buttons that create emotional distress, as well as the subtler troublesome cognitions and Buttons that pull us from our spiritual and transcendental journeys.

HOLISTIC

The BT model is a holistic cognitive counseling model. Troublesome cognitions and Buttons keep us from our natural progression toward wholeness. Troublesome cognitions and Buttons keep us stuck in conditioned ways of perceiving, thinking, feeling, behaving, and relating to other people. Troublesome cognitions and Buttons are some of our primary barriers to personal growth and spiritual evolution. The Button Therapy model is holistic in that it is acknowledged that Buttons do not develop in isolation from our biology, environment, family, and life experiences. When individuals identify their Buttons and decide to work on them utilizing the Six-Step Button Therapy Method, they are also encouraged to identify the emotions and motivational states associated with the Buttons. In addition, individuals are encouraged to gain an understanding of how certain cognitions and Buttons developed and how they are maintained in their minds. Also, individuals are encouraged to understand the Button-Pusher's role in their life drama.

The sixth step of the Six-Step Button Therapy Method is the identification and reinforcement of new life-enhancing models, affirmations, and messages. As individuals consciously cultivate new life-enhancing seeds into the garden of their minds they are encouraged to plant seeds that allow for the development of their spiritual aspect.

Button Therapy can play an integral part in our journey towards wholeness, self-actualization, and spiritual development. BT is not a total personal growth system in and of itself. We have cognitive, emotional, behavioral, spiritual, and interpersonal aspects. Also, we are part of other systems including our families, work, and school. We impact on the other people in our systems and they impact on us. There is much inter-relatedness and interdependence with other people who are part of our systems. I believe that, on a subtler level, we are all part of a universal energy system that provides an underlying connectedness between all life. Many people believe there is a divine intelligence that is the source of all universal life energy. This intelligence has been called different names including God, Goddess, Allah, Krishna, Brahman, the Universal Mind, the One, Supreme Being, and the Tao, among others. The universal life force has varied names such as Chi, Ki, Qi, and Prana. A holistic perspective takes into account the whole person (i.e. body, mind, spirit, and interpersonal) including the cognitive aspect, and all the systems with which we interact.

Button Therapy includes the emotional, behavioral, interpersonal, and spiritual dimensions but has a primary focus on our *cognitions*. Button Therapy provides a six-step method to help you get in touch with your cognitions and Buttons that create your emotions, stress, and inner experience. There are many other life activities such as exercise, nutrition, wellness activities, and spiritual practices that are necessary to become a healthy, happy, and holy individual. Button Therapy is simply one potential tool when focusing on cognitive self-help and therapy. The focus of BT is primarily on our Buttons and the resulting emotional distress and cognitive, behavioral, and interpersonal dysfunction. BT also provides for the positive life-enhancing affirmations that help direct our journey of personal growth and self-actualization. Individuals are encouraged to adopt a holistic perspective and work on their whole being, not just the cognitive aspect.

Conscious effort and persistence is required to become free from many of our securely rooted "Buttons." Most of our Buttons did not suddenly appear overnight. Many of our Buttons have the force of twenty or thirty years of programming behind them and are securely rooted in place. Some of our addictive demands or "Buttons" have been learned, reinforced, and cemented in place over a long period of time and will not disappear easily.

WHEN DO I USE BUTTON THERAPY?

The Six-Step Button Therapy Method is a portable method of working on Buttons that can be utilized anywhere and anytime. In the Button Therapy model the best time to work on Buttons is when they are pushed (i.e. activated). This is when we tend to become acutely aware of their existence and can become motivated to work on them. We can also explore and work on Buttons during the quiet and reflective times we set aside for meditation, personal exploration, and inner growth. Many individuals devote some of their meditation time to explore and work on their attachments (i.e. Buttons). Seeking out our Buttons during meditation is fine, but the most opportune time to work on our Buttons is when we encounter the Button-Pusher in the marketplace of life and experience the distressing emotional consequences resulting from having our Buttons pushed.

DEFINITIONS

BIOCOMPUTER

Biocomputer refers to our *mind* that contains our cognitions and all our programming such as beliefs, scripts, expectations, needs, wants, desires, models of how things should be, past learning, and other cognitions. As we can change software in a computer we can change our mind's inner programming to suit our wants and goals.

BUTTONS

Buttons are the *attachments, demands, addictions,* and *needs* that we develop to certain cognitions and models of how things should be. Buttons are our emotionally reactive hot spots when activated. When our Buttons get pushed we unconsciously and instantaneously emotionally react.

For example, let's suppose that I have a belief that I should be able to have a few beers each day after a hard day at the office. However, my drinking behavior becomes a "Button" if I get uptight about not being able to drink on any given day after work. If I become upset and stressed whenever someone threatens my supply of alcohol, I run out of alcohol, or my friends hassle me about drinking beer every night then I have a Button related to my alcohol use. In this example, I have a model in my mind of how I am going to spend my time after work when I get home. If I am attached or demanding that this model be played out in real life then I will get myself uptight when I am unable to actualize this model or whenever I think something or someone is threatening my implementing my model.

Another common example relates to a "religion" Button. If a husband becomes upset whenever his wife starts talking about the virtues of a certain "religion," then he has a "Button" related to personal growth and spiritual pathways. In this example, he is attached (demanding, needing, addicted) to a model that he is carrying around in his mind that people, especially his spouse, share his model of pathways for personal growth and spirituality. When she doesn't agree with his model of how the personal growth and spiritual game is supposed to be played, he gets himself upset. Thus, the "Button" is the *attachment* (i.e. demanding, clinging, needing) to the model (script, expectation, cognition) that he has in his mind (biocomputer) of how people are supposed to work on their personal growth and spiritual paths.

We can become attached to any belief, expectation, or model of how things should be. Whenever we get ourselves upset, it can usually be related to a demand or attachment that we have related to other people, our environment, or ourselves. We also have "Big Monster Buttons" and "Small Annoying Buttons".

BIG MONSTER BUTTONS *(BMB's)*. These are Buttons that when activated can turn us into emotionally reactive lunatics who are ready to kill! When a BMB becomes pushed we temporarily loose control and often say or do things that, in hindsight, we wished we hadn't. When we have a *BMB* activated let's hope the inhibitory centers in the cerebral cortex of our brains which prevent us from automatically acting out our impulses are functioning adequately.

SMALL ANNOYING BUTTONS *(SAB's)*. SAB's are Buttons that don't have a lot of emotion associated with them. So when they become activated we still get ourselves uptight but not to the point of going into a "kill" mode. SAB's are those times when we become disgusted with ourselves because we have gone off a diet, called a boyfriend when we swore we would never see him again, or have a flat tire going to work. These events can get us uptight because we are carrying around models of how we want these events to happen. We want to stay on the diet, we don't want to give in and call the boyfriend after an argument, and we want to get from our home to our office without having a flat tire. However, the reality is that these events can happen and if we get ourselves uptight when they happen we have a Button related to them. In other words we are attached to a model in our heads of how these events were supposed to happen. Most of our Buttons are of the SAB variety.

In order to determine if you have a Button related to some specific person or situation ask yourself if you could take it or leave it without becoming upset. For example, "Would I be upset in the slightest if this person left me." Or, "If I couldn't have a beer at that party Saturday night would I be upset?" If your answer to these types of questions is "yes" then you have a Button related to that person or situation. How much emotion you are backing up the attachment or demand with will determine whether your Button is a *"Big Monster Button"* or a *"Small Annoying Button"*.

If you relate better to another term for Button such as *attachment, demand, clinging, or needs* then feel free to do so. At varying times I have used all these terms depending on the situation and type of Button.

BUTTON-PUSHERS

The Button-Pusher is the person, thing, or situation that is not following your script of how this particular scene in your life should be played. It is the Button-Pusher who activates (i.e. pushes) your Buttons. In the example above, the husband's spouse was his "Button-Pusher" when she didn't buy into his model of appropriate personal growth and spiritual paths. We can become attached or addicted to all kinds of things including beliefs, people, scripts of how people should behave, material things, psychoactive drugs, pets, our cars operating without breaking down, being treated fairly, and virtually anything else. In a stress and coping model the Button-Pusher is the stressor that triggers the stress response also known as the "fight or flight response."

COGNITIONS

Cognitions refer to our thoughts, beliefs, "needs," wants, desires, expectations, programming, scripts, and models that we carry around in our minds of how things should be.

COGNITIVE THERAPY/COUNSELING

The essential assumption underlying all cognitive therapy models is that thoughts cause feelings. As Drs. McKay, Davis, and Fanning (1997) explain:

> All of the cognitive techniques that have been developed and refined in the last half of the twentieth century flow out of this one simple idea: that thoughts cause feelings, and many emotions you feel are preceded and caused by a thought however abbreviated, fleeting, or unnoticed that thought may be.
> In other words, events by themselves have no emotional content. It is your interpretation of an event that causes your emotions. This is often represented as the 'ABC' model of emotions:
> A. Event————> B. Thought ————> C. Feeling
> Change the thought and you change the feeling. (p. 17)

TROUBLESOME COGNITIONS

A troublesome cognition (TC) is a cognition (e.g. thought) that is likely to become a Button. A TC is often unrealistic, irrational, and acquired early in life. For example, a troublesome cognition may be an outdated belief or parent message that was appropriate and helpful at age five but is a barrier to personal growth at age thirty. A TC is often self-defeating and can easily lead to psychological distress or become a Button. For example, we may have a "should message" in our mind that says we must do everything perfectly and not make mistakes. This "should message" can be annoying at times and can lead to psychological distress but only if we become attached to it or start demanding it (i.e. turns into a Button). If the should message stays on preferential programming, or we happen to do something perfectly, this cognition will not result in psychological distress and we may even experience satisfaction or pleasure.

SIX-STEP BUTTON THERAPY METHOD

The Six-Step Button Therapy (BT) Method is a clinical cognitive therapy tool that can be used by mental health professionals in counseling or by individuals as a psychological self-help tool. The Six-Step BT Method can be used whenever we become upset or stressed to get in touch with our "Button" that is causing our psychological distress. The Six-Step BT Method can help us understand how we are getting ourselves upset, providing us with specific steps to work through our emotional distress, uproot our Buttons, and encourage us to start consciously increasing our positive self-talk, affirmations, and inner programming of life-enhancing guidelines for living.

The following is an outline of the Six-Step BT Method:

SIX-STEP BUTTON THERAPY METHOD

1. **Awareness of Stress and Distress:** Recognizing the stress when your Buttons get pushed by tuning in to your:
- Body
- Feelings
- Acceptance-rejection of self or others

2. **Button Identification:** Pinpointing your Buttons.

3. **Emotions:** Identifying, experiencing, releasing, and channeling the emotional energy associated with your Buttons to your Buttons.

4. **Motivations:** Determining the motivational states associated with your Buttons.
- Safety & Security
- Pleasure & Sensation-Seeking
- Control & Power
- Love & Acceptance
- Personal Growth & Self-Actualization
- Spiritual & Transcendental

5. **Button Removal and Cognitive Restructuring:** Choosing to keep, modify, or eliminate your Buttons. Utilizing cognitive interventions.

6. **Affirmations and Cultivating the Garden of Your Mind:** Cultivating new cognitions which facilitate your becoming happier and more conscious and loving.

SADHAKS AND BUTTONS

Sadhaks is an Eastern term for individuals who are consciously working on their spiritual development. The current increasing interest in New Age topics in the United States has spawned a new generation of sadhaks. The New Age zeitgeist has also renewed the spiritual search and helped fuel the personal growth journeys of some older sadhaks who have been coasting on a personal growth and spiritual plateau for a number of years. Some older sadhaks, such as myself, have become sidetracked by responsibilities of careers, families, finances, hobbies, athletics, and other concerns.

Buttons are one of the major barriers to our becoming more aware, loving, and entering the subtler planes of energy awareness and higher consciousness. There are many spiritual seekers who focus their efforts toward gaining knowledge, skills, and methods aimed at facilitating their spiritual evolution and completely avoid the inner work necessary to work on their Buttons (i.e. attachments, demands, addictions). Many New Age sadhaks have just as many Buttons that pull them from an aware, conscious, loving, centered, and compassionate here-and-now space as more traditional people going about the business of life. The New Age sadhaks have Buttons from the same motivational states as more traditional people. For example, the New Ager may be trying to force (i.e. power-trip) his or her spiritual path on others just as much as a Christian missionary from a traditional organized religion. The only difference is the form of the Button and Button-Pusher.

The messenger (i.e. Button-Pusher) comes in infinite forms. Buttons are barriers to any meaningful journey toward personal growth and spiritual evolution. The more Buttons we have, the more blocked we are in our personal growth and spiritual development. Thus, an integral part of any serious work on our personal growth and spiritual evolution involves doing our inner work, which includes self-exploration, self-knowledge, and working on our Buttons.

CHAPTER FOUR

AWARENESS OF STRESS AND DISTRESS:

RECOGNIZING
WHEN YOUR BUTTONS GET PUSHED

...Stress-related psychological and physiological disorders have become the number one social and health problem in the last decade...Most standard medical textbooks attribute anywhere from 50 to 80 percent of all disease to psychosomatic or stress-related origins.

Kenneth R. Pelletier, Ph.D.
MIND AS HEALER, MIND AS SLAYER

Awareness in itself is healing.
Fritz Perls, M.D., Ph.D.

THERE ARE SIX STEPS for working on troublesome cognitions and Buttons in the Button Therapy model. The first step is awareness. The earlier we can recognize when we are stressed or upset the better. Our tendency is to ignore the early signs of stress and distress in our lives until it becomes so obvious and overwhelming that we become physically ill, mentally unhealthy, or inappropriately act it out (e.g. anger outburst). We can best work on our Buttons by early recognition of cues that are associated with being stressed. Three good ways to recognize the early signs of stress include tuning into your body, feelings, and acceptance-rejection continuum.

LISTEN TO YOUR BODY

Body is that portion of Soul that can be perceived by the five senses.
William Blake

These bodies are perishable; but the dwellers in these bodies are eternal, indestructible, and impenetrable.
THE BHAGAVAD GITA (500? B.C.)

Become aware of when your body tenses and feels tight. Many people first "hear" their bodies in their shoulder, neck, stomach, and head muscles.

Also, breathing patterns tend to change and become shallower when under stress. Unfortunately, many people have experienced chronic distress for so long that they have developed much chronic muscle tension or "body armor" as Dr. Wilhelm Reich called it. This body armor makes it difficult, if not impossible, to "hear" our bodies when we tense under stress because we are already in a state of chronic muscle contraction. There are many effective bodywork, touch, and energy therapies that can help us release muscle tension, break free from our body armor, and facilitate physical, mental, and spiritual healing such as acupuncture, biofeedback, body manipulation (e.g. osteopathic and chiropractic treatments), massage therapy, Reiki, therapeutic touch, and yoga postures.

Once we have reduced our muscle tension and some of the bound up energy in our bodies we are more able to "hear" our bodies when our bodies communicate to us. We can become aware of activated Buttons sooner when we can hear the messages being sent from our bodies.

THE BODY'S WISDOM

As you release your body armor, quiet your body, and become more centered and harmonious, you will be able to hear your body when it communicates subtler messages. For example, the use of touch in healing practices has been a part of medicine from ancient times to the present. The skilled and sensitive hands of some health care professionals and other healers are one of their most important diagnostic and therapeutic tools. Also, utilizing touch, some sensitive healers can detect or "sense" subtle physical cues in their hands during assessment and therapy. For example, Dr. Delores Krieger, a nurse, healer, professor, and co-founder of the "therapeutic touch" healing modality points out that, during a "therapeutic touch" healing session, the healer most frequently picks up one, or a combination, of the following cues in the healee's energy field during the assessment:

- Temperature differentials, such as a sense of heat or cold.
- Pressure, or feelings of congestion in the energy flow.
- Changes in or lack of synchronization in the intrinsic rhythmicity of the healer's energy field.
- Localized weak electric shocks or tingly feelings as you move the energy cen
- ters in the palms of your hands through the healee's energy field. (Krieger, 1993, p. 46)

Physician and author Deepok Chopra, M.D. (1998a) points out that we should listen to our body's wisdom, which expresses itself through signals of comfort and discomfort. "When choosing a certain behavior, ask your body, 'how do you feel about this?' If your body sends a signal of physical or emotional distress, watch out. If your body sends a signal of comfort and eagerness, proceed" (p. 1).

IDENTIFY YOUR FEELINGS

The body begins to form around the feelings that animate it, and the feelings, in turn, become habituated and trapped within the body tissue itself.
Ken Dychtwald, Ph.D.
BODY-MIND

When you experience negative or distressing emotions such as anxiety, depression, frustration, and anger, know that a Button is being pushed. A "negative" emotion is a subjective experience and what is "negative" must be defined by each individual. Identify and "own" your feelings. Instead of ignoring, suppressing, or denying your negative feelings, readily accept them and view them as the emotional energy associated with your Buttons. Your negative emotions are cues to begin the inner work of modifying or eliminating the cognition (e.g. thought) associated with your Button triggering the negative feelings.

HARD TO CONTROL EMOTIONS

Sometimes we experience emotions that we have little control over. For example, our emotions, behavior, and inner experience can be dramatically influenced by such biological factors as brain tumors, hormones, blood sugar levels, systemic infections, metabolic disorders, and cognitive-emotional impairments (e.g. autism). Our biology (e.g. brain tumor) and physical aspects (e.g. acute pain from broken bone) are other examples of phenomena that can dramatically influence our cognitions and emotions without being consciously processed through our cognitions. One can make an argument that even these acute physical stressors are interpreted by our cognitive processing, however fleeting, which impacts how we experience the incoming stimuli. However, for the most part there are certain events, usually related to our biology and stress response (i.e. "fight-or-flight response") that are almost always going to evoke a certain predictable response with minor variations no matter what type of cognitive programming we have. For example, everybody would probably experience very similar emotions if they were to fall from a second story window to the ground. They would most likely experience emotions associated with the fight-or-flight stress response such as fear, anxiety, and eventually pain when they hit the ground.

You should have your physical health status checked out by a health care professional before embarking on any self-help mental health approach, especially if you suspect that you may have a biologically based disorder affecting your mental health. Many serious mental disorders, such as schizophrenia, may have a biological basis. A qualified health or mental health professional should be consulted to assess any possible organic etiology for severe or chronic mental illness.

ACCEPTANCE-REJECTION CONTINUUM

Be NOT angry that you cannot make others as you wish them to be...
since you cannot make yourself as you wish to be.

Thomas A. Kempis

Another cue to recognize signs of stress relates to whether or not you can emotionally accept certain behaviors and other aspects of yourself and others. If you are throwing yourself or others out of your acceptance or heart space, then you are experiencing a Button being pushed. On a more subtle level, when you feel out of harmony, off-center, and separate from other people and other life systems, you are probably experiencing a Button being pushed. I say "probably" because it is possible that your emotions and inner experience are being influenced by life events that you have little, if any, control over, such as certain biological events.

CHAPTER FIVE

BUTTONS

An older student came to Otis and said, "I have been to see a great number of teachers and I have given up a great number of pleasures. I have fasted, been celibate and stayed awake nights seeking enlightenment. I have given up everything I was asked to give up and I have suffered, but I have not been enlightened. What should I do?"
Otis replied, "Give up suffering."

Camden Benares
ZEN WITHOUT ZEN MASTERS

THE CONCEPT THAT "SUFFERING" is a result of attachment to our desires was one of the essential teachings of Buddha over 2500 years ago. He claimed that "it is not life and wealth and power that enslave men but the cleaving to life and wealth and power" (Carus, 1972, p.62). In 1972, Ken Keyes, Jr. published the *Handbook To Higher Consciousness* in which he Westernized the concept of "cleaving" or attachment and referred to it as "addiction" or "addictive demand:"

> An addiction is a programming (or operating) instruction to your bio-computer (mind) that triggers uncomfortable emotional responses and excites your consciousness if the world does not fit the programmed pattern in your mind. The identifying characteristic of an addiction is that if your desire is not fulfilled, you respond emotionally in a computer-like way and automatically play out a program of anger, worry, anxiety, jealousy, fear, etc. That which you emotionally avoid is just as much an addiction as is something you desire. (Keyes, 1975, p.19)

Signs of having a Button is *needing* something rather than simply wanting it, or *demanding* something rather than merely preferring it. When we demand life to be other than what it is, we trigger within ourselves feelings of psychological distress.

IDENTIFYING OUR BUTTONS BEING PUSHED

The essence of all cognitive therapy models, including the Button Therapy model, is realizing how our cognitions (i.e. beliefs, scripts, expectations, demands, attachments, clinging, needs) are major determinants of our feelings and how we experience life. We are constantly creating our inner experience. We may not be able to control the people and situations in our lives but we can learn to perceive and interpret these people and events in such a way as to not become distressed, and remain in a conscious, harmonious, accepting, or loving space.

IDENTIFY THE CONFLICT OF YOUR DESIRED MODEL OF HOW THINGS SHOULD BE VERSUS WHAT IS

After recognizing when you are experiencing stress, the second step in the Six-Step BT Method is to connect your stress to a demand that you are making for things to be different than they currently are. See the conflict of life scripts. Become aware of the model, script, or expectation you are demanding versus what life is currently offering you. Tell yourself "I am currently getting myself uptight and out of harmony right here and now by...

- addictively **demanding** that ...(describe the model of how you think this scene in your life should be played out here and now.)"
- **clinging** to ...(describe this demand/Button)"
- being **attached** to ...(describe your model of how things should be)."
- **needing** this script that I carry around in my head of how this life drama is supposed to by played out ...(describe the demand/Button) and the other actors on the stage are simply not playing their parts correctly."
- being **addicted** to ...this person...this drug...this food...etc. (describe the Button)."

Use whatever words click with you (e.g. demanding, clinging, attached, needing, or addicted), depending on the situation at hand, to connect the stress or distress with the Button. From a stress and coping model, the Button-Pusher is the stressor that pushes the Button (i.e. demand or attachment) which triggers the stress response. The stress response is also known as the "fight-or-flight" response. I have found all these terms useful depending on the Button that I'm working on at the time. Usually, when I get myself uptight today, I ask myself "what am I *clinging* to here?" And, that's all it takes. I become aware of what is happening and I can either let go of my *attachment* (Button) completely, or modify my *demand* (Button) to a preference, and regain my inner harmony, consciousness, accepting attitude, or love space.

Sometimes when I have a Button pushed, the *irrationality* of my demand (Button) jumps out at me and I can let go of the Button or modify it to a more rational preference. Sometimes I realize how *addicted* I am to something (e.g. desire to be appreciated) or to somebody agreeing with a certain belief that I have (e.g. that people should treat other people fairly and with respect). When people don't follow these models I have of how things should be, my Buttons get pushed and I get myself uptight. I then realize that I am *addicted* or *needing* versus *preferring* or *wanting* things to go my way. And if I want to free myself from some unpleasant emotions and regain my "center" and sense of harmony in my here-and-now I need to work on my Buttons (i.e. addictions and "needs") that are creating my emotional distress.

Sooner or later I realize that I can make better decisions over how to better deal with the Button-Pushers (i.e. stressors) in my life if I am acting from an aware, proactive, and conscious place instead of an unconscious reactive robot-like place. Plus, it usually doesn't work to try and manipulate and power-trip other people into my models of how things should be. When I react unconsciously to a Button being pushed I oftentimes create more distress in those around me and end up spewing more negative toxins in the air. I have found that I am better able to actualize my wants and goals by acting from a proactive, conscious place instead of a reactive, unconscious place.

In the personal example given above, once aware of my attachment to this model of how people should be treated, I decided to work on freeing myself from this Button. I have decided that this is still a valued want and preference. Thus I will do what I can to actualize it, but I choose to act consciously from a proactive place where I have my conscious awareness working for me in order to increase my chances of these acts happening—instead of an uptight, unconscious, and reactive place where I may not be making the best decisions.

When using the Six-Step Button Therapy Method try using the different terms such as demand, attachment, addiction, clinging, or need and see which one clicks with you with that particular Button. Different terms help us conceptualize the nature of certain Buttons better than others. You will probably gravitate toward one term that resonates with you more than others when working on most Buttons.

After you realize that you have a Button that creates distress when pushed, the next part of step two is to identify the type of demand or cognitive distortion that may be associated with the Button.

TYPES OF BUTTONS

Identifying our troublesome cognitions, cognitive distortions, and Buttons can be confusing. The next few chapters explore some common cognitive distortions such as "should messages" and self-defeating "core beliefs" that can create emotional distress. We can develop Buttons by becoming attached to these types of common cognitions that we carry around in our minds. Also, cognitive distortions can hinder our efforts to uproot Buttons. Troublesome and distorted cognitions can prevent our accurately seeing our cognitions and

Buttons. Also, our distorted cognitions can impede the implementation of strategies to modify or eliminate Buttons causing our negative emotions by minimizing the frequency and intensity of distress they cause. The ways we distort our cognitions (e.g. thoughts) described in the next few chapters include: Twelve Distorted Styles of Thinking; Defense Mechanisms; Personality Traits and Disorders; and Core Beliefs. Some guidelines and methods for assessing your cognitions are also included in these chapters and Appendix A (*The Cognitive Self-Assessment Inventory*).

CHAPTER SIX

DISTORTED STYLES OF THINKING

There is nothing either good or bad but thinking makes it so.
William Shakespeare
HAMLET

The thought manifests as the word;
The word manifests as the deed;
The deed develops into habit;
And habit hardens into character;
So watch the thought and its ways with care,
and let it spring from love, born out of concern for all beings.
Buddha

MUCH OF OUR STRESS AND PSYCHOLOGICAL SUFFERING comes from the way we process information through our biocomputers (minds). How we interpret the incoming stimuli or information will determine how we experience it and feel about it. If your experience of life is full of stress, distress, frustration, anger, depression, anxiety, or other unpleasant experiences, then you may want to look at how you are processing the incoming information in your mind.

Here are 12 common distorted styles of thinking that can develop into Buttons and generate emotional distress: (1) Black and White Thinking (2) Blaming (3) Comparing (4) Disaster Thinking (5) Fair and Just Thinking (6) Mind Reading (7) Negativistic Thinking (8) Overgeneralizing (9) Pasting and Futuring (10) Should Thinking (11) Perfectionist Thinking, and (12) Right and Wrong Thinking. The following are descriptions of these common cognitive distortions. Table 2 provides a summary of the 12 styles of distorted thinking which can be utilized as a quick reference when working the second step of the Six-Step Button Therapy Method.

TABLE 2

1 2 STYLES OF DISTORTED THINKING

1. **Black and White Thinking.** Processing everybody and everything as either good or bad, or right or wrong.
2. **Blaming.** Blaming other people or events for our feelings. And, failing to take responsibility for our behavior and the quality of our inner experience.
3. **Comparing.** Comparing ourselves to others.
4. **Catastrophic Thinking.** Thinking of all the possible things that could go wrong and imagining them turning into a disaster. Also, called "disaster thinking."
5. **Fair and Just Thinking.** When we have beliefs related to what is fair and what constitutes justice for people who do the "wrong" thing.
6. **Mind Reading.** A type of thinking whereby a person thinks he or she knows the intention of someone else's actions or inaction without them verbally telling them.
7. **Negativistic Thinking.** When we focus on the negative aspect of any person or situation, ignoring any strengths or assets.
8. **Overgeneralizing.** From one observation, it is assumed that it will always be the same.
9. **Pasting and Futuring.** Ruminating about distressing events in the past or worrying about the future.
10. **Should Thinking.** Carrying around models of how things should be.
11. **Perfectionist Thinking.** Belief that one should do everything perfectly, preferably the first time around.
12. **I'm "Right" and You're "Wrong" Thinking.** Individuals with a strong need (i.e. have a Button) to always be "right."

The Button Therapy Book: How to Work on Your Buttons and the Button-Pushers in Your Life by Lloyd R. Goodwin, Jr.
© 2002. Published by Trafford Publishing. www.trafford.com

BLACK OR WHITE THINKING

Black or white thinkers tend to process everything and everybody as either good or bad or right or wrong. There is no middle ground in this type of polarized thinking. Individuals who think this way tend to be very judgmental, critical, authoritarian, and moralistic. Even a relatively conscious and high functioning individual with a healthy style of "continuum thinking" can decompensate under stress and revert back to "black and white thinking." For example, parents, when confronted by a teenager who regularly tests the boundaries of acceptable behavior, often revert in times of stress to saying something like, "Look - these are the rules in this house. And as long as you live under this roof you will abide by my rules. If you don't like it — too bad. It's my way or the highway!" Discussing the problem behavior, listening to explanations, and exploring the options described so well in the guide to good parenting books may all go out the window when a teenager constantly pushes the limits. Goodbye Dr. Spock and hello Major Dad!

Teenagers pushing the parameters of acceptable behavior are good examples of how "black and white thinking" often prevails after a sufficient number of typical teenage acting-out behaviors have worn down the patience of the most together, understanding, empathic, and loving parent. Another common example relates to correctional staff in the criminal justice system. The most "together," humanistic, and caring correctional staff member will often decompensate into "black and white" thinking after enough inmates, parolees, and probationers repeatedly test the limits of their relationship and the rules. Finally the probation officer will elicit a response like, "Look, you broke a condition of your probation. You've been warned before. I'm revoking your probation! It's back to prison for you. End of discussion. Tell it to the Judge."

Black and white thinkers are more likely to develop alcohol and other drug abuse problems, possibly because they are trying to cope with the constant distress created by this mode of thinking. In reality, there are few, if any, absolutes. It is more realistic and accurate to think in terms of continuums, probabilities, risk factors, and shades of gray.

BLAMING

This type of thinking involves blaming other people or events for our feelings and actions (or inaction) and failing to take responsibility for the general quality of our inner experience. This results in statements like: "You made me angry...sad...jealous...happy...etc." "It's your fault I didn't pursue college... my career...my dreams...etc."

We are responsible for the choices we make concerning our lives as well as how we choose to think about the people and events in our lives. The constant blaming of others for our negative feelings and life predicaments prevents us from taking responsibility for our lives and keeps us stuck in the illusion that other people and situations control our feelings and inner experience.

One of the signs of progress on our personal growth journey is going from an external to an internal locus of control. Once we begin taking responsibility for our thoughts, feelings, and behaviors, we tend to enter the fast track of personal and spiritual growth.

COMPARING

Comparing yourself to others in terms of personal appearance, money, intelligence, and qualities of your spouse is a guaranteed way to give yourself an "I'm not ok" negative stroke. There will always be someone who is smarter, prettier, more handsome, has more money, and has a spouse who is more understanding, supportive, better looking, and sexier. Playing the comparing game is a guaranteed way to accumulate negative strokes for your ego. If your goal is to create chronic emotional distress and lower self-esteem, this cognitive style is a sure way to get there.

To counteract this cognitive style of thinking, utilize the cognitive thought-stopping technique described in chapter ten to stop yourself from comparing as soon as you realize you are doing it. Replace your comparing with a positive "self-talk" message such as, "I have accumulated enough negative 'I'm not ok' strokes over the years and choose not to beat myself up any more. I'm an 'ok' person and my self-esteem and happiness does not depend on what other people do, have, or believe." Chapter 21 provides some positive affirmations and life-enhancing guidelines for living.

CATASTROPHIC THINKING

Catastrophic thinking is a type of thinking whereby the person thinks of all the possible things that could go wrong and imagines them turning into a disaster. This thinking style is guaranteed to generate anxiety and fear. In reality, few situations turn out to be disasters. The cognitive thought-stopping technique described in chapter ten can help you switch your focus from the possible outcome (i.e. disaster scenario) to the here-and-now existential process of your life.

FAIR AND JUST THINKING

Fair and just thinking refers to when we have beliefs related to what is fair and what constitutes justice for people who do the "wrong" thing. A variation of "right or wrong" thinking, this style of thinking involves determining whether or not something is "fair and just." It's not an easy task to sit down and list what constitutes "fair and just" actions or behaviors. This list could go on forever. However, we are able to quickly determine when, others or we have been wronged. Most of us were raised with models of right and wrong and what's fair and unfair. However, everybody has their own variations of these fairness models. Also, some peoples' fairness models are simply overruled periodically by opportunities for money, sex, power, and pure greed. Oftentimes, it comes down to the way I satisfy my want or need is "fair" and the way you satisfy your wants or needs is "unfair." As a result, life is not always fair and just.

CRIMINAL JUSTICE SYSTEM. When somebody transgresses one of our fairness models, which has been codified into societal law, we expect the offender to be arrested, prosecuted, and punished. We expect them to receive their "just deserts" for their legal transgression. We want justice. However, our criminal justice system is seldom "just."

Crime routinely appears at or near the top of surveys asking Americans to name the most important issues facing the country (Johnson, 1997). According to government surveys in 1994, U.S. residents aged 12 or older experienced approximately 42.4 million crimes. Thirty-one million (73 percent) were property crimes, 10.9 million (26 percent) were crimes of violence, and approximately a half million (1 percent) were personal thefts (Perkins & Klaus, 1996). Many people are convinced that the crime problem is getting worse, not better. Sixty-seven percent think that violent crime in the country is increasing according to a survey by Louis Harris and associates in May of 1997. Half of Americans think the amount of crime in their own community will be worse in the year 2000 according to a Yankelovich Partners survey commissioned by Time/CNN in January, 1997 (Johnson, 1997).

Most crimes are not reported to the police. According to government surveys approximately two-thirds of personal and household crimes (Meddis, 1986) and 58 percent of all violent crimes, including 68 percent of completed rapes, are not reported to police (Perkins & Klaus, 1996).

Also, most people who commit crimes are not arrested. Many offenders who are caught are not prosecuted. Those offenders who are prosecuted typically receive minor consequences because of defense attorneys' legal maneuvering and plea bargain arrangements. According to the Administrative Office of the U.S. Courts (1967) in 1967 there were 26,344 convictions and 5,191 dismissed or acquitted cases in the United States District Courts. Of the total, 86.7 percent were disposed of without trial. People tried by the court without a jury constituted 4.6 percent, while 8.7 percent had jury trials. "Society could not and would not tolerate the prosecution of every person who violated even those laws which are perfectly clear" (Sax,1969, p. 2). According to Dr. Vernon Fox (1985), a noted criminologist and professor of criminology at Florida State University, "Plea bargaining is the making of a 'deal' between the prosecution and the defense with the consent of the judge for a lesser charge or a lesser sentence in exchange for a guilty plea, thereby avoiding a trial that might be lengthy. Because of this practice, the criminal justice system has sometimes been referred to as the 'criminal negotiating system' ...The public attitude is the same today: It would be too expensive" (pp.36 & 41).

Eighty-six percent of Americans say the court system does too much to protect the rights of the accused and not enough to protect the rights of the victims according to an ABC News survey in February, 1994. Only 3 percent of Americans say the courts deal too harshly with criminals and 85 percent say they are not harsh enough according to the National Opinion Research Center in May, 1994 (Johnson, 1997). Those offenders who are arrested, convicted, and incarcerated seldom serve their entire sentences and are let out of prison early because of overcrowding and "good behavior."

Most people have lost faith in the "fairness of justice" of our criminal justice system. In a 1995 Gallup Survey, only 20 percent report having "a great deal or quite a lot of confidence" in the criminal justice system. African-Americans and other minority groups are more concerned than whites about their chances of being treated fairly by police and the criminal justice system. Sixty-one percent of whites, compared to 19 percent of African-Americans, say that racial and other minorities receive equal treatment in the criminal justice system (Johnson, 1997).

RELATIONSHIPS. The fairness models involving criminal behavior and the criminal justice system represent only a few of our fairness models we carry around in our biocomputers. How about your fairness models related to "right" behavior in interpersonal relationships? You probably have a fairness model as to what constitutes the "right" and decent way to behave, interact, and treat other people. Possibly your fairness model is similar to the golden rule which advises us to treat other people the way that we would like to be treated. How about our fairness models related to "right" livelihood. How about the business person who over charges you or misrepresents his or her products? How about certain industries (e.g. oil, automotive, military-industrial) that manipulate whole economies, countries, politics, legislation, and wars to accommodate their business interests?

POLITICS. How about our political system that is primarily controlled by the economic interests of special interest groups, certain large corporations, and wealthy individuals? How many politicians are wealthy, if not going into public office, then retiring from political office? What chance does the average person with average financial means have of being elected to a state or national public office? In a recent survey of adults conducted for Bruskin Goldring by Kirshenbaum, Bond, and partners (Hall & Jerding, 1998), only 43 percent of adults believe that totally honest politicians can get elected. According to Walter Williams, a nationally syndicated newspaper columnist, "The dramatic decline in the public's trust of the federal government from a high of 76 percent in 1964 to 20 percent in 1994 elicited the argument that citizens had moved from healthy skepticism about Washington to a deep anger and a paranoid distrust of the federal government. Trust now stands above 30 percent and the deep anger has receded" (Williams, 1998, p.A10). This survey was before the President Clinton sex scandal with a White House intern. It appears the public has resigned itself to the inevitability of "politics as usual."

The business as usual machinations of political life are so questionable and viewed so negatively (i.e. "unfair") that I suspect many sane, honest, conscious, aware, and mentally healthy people do not want to become involved with politics. Individuals motivated to seek a major political office often appear to be either naïve, morally righteous, and idealistic people, or individuals with strong power and control needs. Sometimes, apparently sane and altruistically motivated individuals enter politics thinking they can change the system for the better and "make a difference." However, most people have given up on our political system and no longer even play this game any longer (i.e. they don't run for office and they no longer vote in elections). The most recent United States Census Bureau report (Shepard, 1998) indicates that only 54 per cent of the voting age population voted in the 1996 presidential election. Primary voter turnout in nonpresidential years has been steadily declining since a high of 32 percent in 1962. The 1998 record low turnout of 17 percent was attributed to general satisfaction with the economy and an adverse reaction to the increasing coarseness and incivility of partisan politics (Benedetto, 1998a). Sometimes, people get sufficiently upset about some specific issue and write their political representative. Most people don't even take time out of their lives to do this political act, questioning whether or not this will "make a difference."

The commonly used phrase "it was a political decision" is used regularly by people to connote that a decision was unfair. The word "political" is used synonymously with "unfair" in today's usage.

ILLNESS AND DEATH. How about our fairness models related to disease, death, and dying? What do your fairness models say about the 43-year-old mother with two young children who has been a good, caring, and nurturing mother to her children then is diagnosed with terminal cancer? While down the street there is a 43-year-old child molester with a record of four child-molesting convictions who is currently out on probation and enjoying freedom from prison and good health. Many individuals have definite "fairness and justice" models related to this scenario.

OUR WORK WORLDS. We carry around many models in our heads as to what is fair and just in our work worlds. For example, have you ever felt that:
- Somebody else with less qualifications was hired for a job instead of you?
- A coworker was unfairly promoted over you?
- You did not receive the pay raise you deserved?

- You are not receiving the salary you deserve for the work you do?
- That it's not fair that movie stars and professional athletes receive higher salaries than you do?
- Because you have a disability, employers discriminate against you?
- Because you are a minority, you are being discriminated against?
- You are not receiving the recognition you deserve for your professional accomplishments?

It is not hard to see that we carry around in our minds many fairness and justice models and that much of life is neither fair nor just! Carrying around fairness and justice models in our biocomputers is inevitable, and probably a good thing. However, if you are *demanding* that your fairness and justice models always be followed (i.e. you have a fairness Button) you will experience much suffering in your life. Because life is full of unfairness and injustices. And life will continually offer you Button-Pushers to help you become aware of these fairness and justice Buttons you need to work on if you want to change your emotions, inner experience, and become more conscious, aware, loving, and compassionate.

You will be better off *preferring* life to be fair and just. Also, it is important to "walk your talk." That is, you do the "right thing" in your life and hopefully you can influence your children, friends, coworkers, and others by your example. When confronted with the unfairness of life's injustices, do what you can to right the wrong from a centered, conscious, and loving place where you can increase the probability of "making a difference." Avoid reacting from an unconscious, reactive, and emotionally upset place where you are likely to spew out more negative toxins in the air and make things worse.

MIND READING

A type of thinking, often with a twinge of paranoia, whereby a person thinks he or she knows the intention of someone else's actions or inaction without being verbally told. Mind reading is one of the most common triggers for marital disputes. One partner gets angry when their partner does something "wrong" (i.e. didn't play out the scene the way the first partner had expected it to go), even though the "right" script was not verbally expressed. We make many assumptions about what other people, especially those closest to us, know about our cognitive models (e.g. expectations and scripts) of how things should be without our verbally letting them know exactly what these models are. And, we are quick to "jump on" someone, often a loved one, when they do not fit into our models of how things should be.

When I catch myself getting uptight because of "mind reading," I ask myself, "Did I verbally express my want or script of how I want this person to behave?" Verbally letting my wants and expectations of what I expect of other people two years ago, or even two months ago, doesn't count. People live in their own present moment realities with their own daily dramas, issues, problems, crises, joys, and circle of friends, and are not always cognizant of my models for this particular scene in their lives. The desired model of what we want needs to be verbally expressed repeatedly and recently.

Stop reading for a minute and try to get into the mind frame of your spouse (boyfriend, girlfriend, child, or close friend):

- What are they currently thinking or concerned about?
- What are their long range and short term goals they are currently trying to achieve?
- What are they currently thinking about their job and work life?
- What are they planning to do today...tonight...tomorrow?

Hopefully, you can gain an increased appreciation of how people are caught up in their own worlds, realities, and life dramas. They are seldom able to remember your wants, unless you've just verbalized them. So before you express your emotional distress (e.g. anger) at someone ask yourself, "Did I clearly communicate my want for how this scene is supposed to be played out to this person?" Also, you may want to ask yourself, "Is this person consciously trying to push my Buttons just to get a reaction out of me?" Usually the answer is no. You can dissipate much of the emotional energy generated by your Button with this realization. If the Button-Pusher is repeatedly and consciously pushing your Buttons just to see you react, then, in addition to working on your Button, you may want to reconsider whether this is the kind of person with whom you want to hang out.

NEGATIVISTIC THINKING

This type of thinking is when we focus on the negative aspect of any person or situation, ignoring their strengths or assets. Negativistic thinking is a popular pastime for chronic complainers and people who like to spend time with "ain't it awful" interpersonal relationships and games. There can be a hundred positive aspects of someone and the negativistic thinker will find the one or two least attractive qualities and focus on those to the exclusion of the many positive qualities. Fun people to be around!

OVERGENERALIZING

From one experience or observation, people who overgeneralize assume that it will always be the same. Your daughter periodically forgets to do some of her chores around the house and you scold her in a disappointing manner, "You never do anything to help out around the house!"

This cognitive distortion is an innate style of thinking with teenagers. The teenage daughter doesn't receive the overpriced new blue jeans she wants from the new specialty store in the mall and she wails at her parents, in that teenage angst style that only teenagers can do, "You never buy me any clothes!" Overgeneralizing has similarities to "Black and White" and "Catastrophic Thinking (exaggeration)." When we are overgeneralizing, we tend to use descriptive words such as always, never, everybody, nobody, and hopeless. To illustrate:

- *Always:* "I always have to drive the kids to their friends house or to their activities. I've had it with doing everything for our children. Why don't you
- spend some time helping me out with parenting duties!"
- *Never:* "You never admit it when you are wrong."
- *Everybody:* "Everybody at school smokes marijuana. Why are you so upset with my smoking a little dope on weekends?"
- *Nobody:* "Nobody plays records or cassette tapes anymore. Get with the CD age!"
- *Hopeless:* "I studied hard for that research exam and I only got a B. I'm hopeless in math and statistics. Are there any graduate schools that don't require the GRE to be admitted?"

Any of these sound familiar? We all have used overgeneralizations at one time or another. If overgeneralizations are one of your commonly used cognitive patterns you might want to work on this cognitive style of thinking and any Buttons you have in this area. I'm sure your family and friends will appreciate your efforts.

PASTING AND FUTURING

Enjoy today and don't waste it grieving over a bad yesterday— tomorrow may be even worse.

Anonymous

Remembering the past and planning for the future can be a very beneficial, emotionally rewarding, and necessary way of thinking. However, focusing your waking hours ruminating about distressing events that occurred in the past or worrying about a potentially stressful situation that may or may not happen in the future are non-productive and distress-producing styles of thinking.

Pasting is a way of triggering a variety of pleasant or distressful emotions. Recalling fond memories can trigger pleasant feelings. Recalling distressing events can trigger unpleasant feelings. Actors use the "pasting" type of thinking to generate certain desired emotions needed for their portrayal of certain characters in movies and plays. Pasting is an effective technique for triggering feelings. Unfortunately, some people unconsciously use this type of thinking resulting in much distress in their lives. So, if you choose to wallow in your negative emotions by "pasting," you have picked an effective technique.

Futuring about some imagined potential disaster is an effective way of triggering anxiety and worry. Dr. Fritz Perls, the founder of Gestalt Therapy, observed that most anxiety is stagefright. We become anxious and worried over what may or may not occur in the future.

LIVING IN THE HERE-AND-NOW. In actuality, the only reality that exists is our present existential "here-and-now" moment. What's past is past. If there is something you can or want to do to resolve, finish, or correct something that occurred in the past then take time here-and-now and do it (e.g. make amends). But don't sit around and ruminate about it. Get off your butt and act now! If you catch yourself worrying about the future, take action "here-and-now" and do what you can to prepare for the future (e.g. a presentation, meeting, romantic date, etc.). The "here-and-now technique," in combination with the cognitive thought-stopping technique described in chapter ten, is an effective strategy for dealing with anxiety, worry, and other negative emotions generated by unproductive pasting and futuring. As physician and author Deepak Chopra (1998) puts it:

> Live in the present, for it is the only moment you have. Keep your attention on what is here and now; look for the fullness in every moment. Accept what comes to you totally and completely so that you can appreciate it, learn from it, and then let it go. This moment is as it is because the universe is as it is. Don't struggle against the infinite scheme of things; instead, be at one with it. (p. 1)

SHOULD THINKING

We tend to carry around many models of how things should be. This "shoulding" style of thinking is very prevalent and potentially distressful. Many of our "should messages" trigger our stress response and may also adversely affect our self-esteem and all other aspects of our lives.

SHOULD MESSAGES. Table 3 provides the top ten "should messages" from a study of adults using the *Cognitive Self-Assessment Inventory (CSAI)* (see Appendix A). Subjects in this study were asked to rate twenty "should messages" on a 1 to 5 scale with 1 indicating "strongly disagree" and 5 indicating "strongly agree." Most (75 percent) of the adults in this study were undergraduate and graduate students at East Carolina University in Greenville, North Carolina. See Appendix C for a description of this study and complete results.

TABLE 3

TOP 10 SHOULD MESSAGES

Rank		Percent Agreeing or Strongly Agreeing
1.	I should live life to its fullest.	89
2.	I should love, or at least like, both of my parents.	77
3.	I should make other people feel better when they are upset.	73
4.	I should be independent and self-sufficient and not have to rely on other people.	68
5.	I should please my parents.	64
6.	I should keep control of my feelings.	60
7.	I should remain centered, balanced, harmonious, and focused on my personal and spiritual growth at all times.	56
8.	Everyone should like and accept me because I'm basically a good and decent person.	52
9.	I should like all of my children equally.	51
10.	I should take more risks with men/women, career, and life in general.	49

The Button Therapy Book: How to Work on Your Buttons and the Button-Pushers in Your Life by Lloyd R. Goodwin, Jr.
© 2002.Published by Trafford Publishing. www.trafford.com

Recognize any of these should messages or beliefs? A few of them are probably securely rooted in your mind. There are more should messages listed in the *CSAI* in Appendix A.

Should messages are neither good nor bad, nor right or wrong. They are simply some common messages, injunctions, and beliefs that we carry around in our minds. Many of these cognitions are positive and life-enhancing. We adopted many of these should messages very early in life from our parents, teachers, clergy, and other adult figures in our environment. These messages and beliefs can become *Buttons* or problems only when we become attached to them and begin demanding them instead of preferring them. Keeping them as worthy goals to work toward achieving is life enhancing.

When exploring your should messages you may want to also determine if your should messages are realistic and rational. If your should messages are not realistic, rational, and life-enhancing they become "troublesome cognitions" that can easily turn into full blown Buttons when the right Button-Pushers come along.

PERFECTIONIST THINKING

Many people hold a belief that they should do everything perfectly, preferably the first time around. Nothing they do seems to please them. Their perfectionist models also apply to other people.

Procrastination is often a consequence of perfectionist thinking. Because procrastinators anticipate failure or are unable to meet their own challenging or unattainable standards, they often procrastinate in important matters by allocating their time poorly and leaving the things that mean most to them to the last. Perfectionist students tend to say things like, "I can't start my term paper now. I need to wait until I have enough time to do it right (i.e. perfect). I think I'll clean the kitchen instead." There are a lot of perfectionists in graduate schools of universities. And although their perfectionist models create a lot of emotional distress, perhaps this cognition helped them do well academically and make it to graduate school. However, perfectionist thinkers often pay the price for good grades and high achievement with excessive stress.

I'M "RIGHT" AND YOU'RE "WRONG" THINKING

Some individuals have a strong need (i.e. have a Button) to always be "right." Individuals who are attached to their "right" models are usually annoying to be around and tend to be poor listeners. During conversations they interrupt constantly or impatiently wait for an opening to express their opinions and views that are presented in a matter of fact manner with no room for discussion. This is the Paul Harvey or Rush Limbaugh type of speaker. Everything they say has a, "...and that's the way it is" tone to it. In reality, most everybody has an opinion or view on certain matters. Oftentimes, the people they are talking with think or feel just as strongly about certain matters as do the "Right and Wrong" and "Black and White" thinkers. However, the person with this cognitive style of thinking is usually not interested in your views.

If you want to combat this maladaptive and alienating type of thinking, simply ask yourself the following question the next time you catch yourself demanding that everyone agree with your point of view (i.e. coming from your "Control and Power" motivational state): "Here and now is it more important for me to try and convince this individual that I am "right" and she is "wrong" knowing that my behavior is alienating this person and pushing her Buttons. Or, is it more important to me to engage in a give and take conversation, realizing it is more important to remain in an accepting love space with this person?"

When I catch myself trying to "power-trip" someone in a conversation with my "right" model of how things are, or should be, I catch myself and switch to an accepting and love "motivational state" (fourth motivational state). I realize that the person with whom I am talking and I are two individuals with different points of view. I get in touch with my control and power needs and reign them in. I realize it's all OK. It's all part of the drama of life. The "I'm right and you're wrong game" is a no-win game. As it is a common way to create separation and disharmony with other people. And, by creating the separating emotions of frustration, anger, superiority, and inferiority we have lost the Master Game of living our lives in love, harmony, higher consciousness, and oneness.

The ten most common cognitions reflecting "styles of distorted thinking" according to the study of cognitions reported in Appendix C are presented in Table 4.

TABLE 4

TOP TEN COGNITIONS REFLECTING STYLES OF DISTORTED THINKING

Rank		Percent Agreeing or Strongly Agreeing
1.	Everything happens for a reason **(Fair & Just Thinking)**.	77
2.	I know what someone (e.g. spouse, boy/girlfriend) is communicating to me without them verbalizing it **(Mind Reading)**.	60
3.	I tend to get very concerned and anxious worrying about what may happen in the future **(Futuring)**.	50
4.	My spouse or good friends know the way I like things to be done without me having to tell them **(Mind Reading)**.	50
5.	I compare myself to other people, especially in terms of appearance, money, intellect, or possessions **(Comparing)**.	47
6.	I know what people "really mean," even if they verbalize something else in their communication **(Mind Reading)**.	45
7.	There is a right way and a wrong way of doing things **(Black & White Thinking)**.	44
8.	Other people (e.g. spouse, boss) make me angry, sad, or happy **(Blaming)**.	44
9.	I want people to admit it when they are wrong and I am right **(I'm "right" and you're "wrong" thinking)**.	43
10.	I spend a lot of time thinking about things I should have said or done in the past **(Pasting)**.	42

The Button Therapy Book: How to Work on Your Buttons and the Button-Pushers in Your Life by Lloyd R. Goodwin, Jr.
© 2002. Published by Trafford Publishing. www.trafford.com

CHAPTER SEVEN

DEFENSE MECHANISMS

The faults of others are easier to see than one's own;
the faults of others are easily seen, for they are sifted like chaff,
but one's own faults are hard to see.
This is like the cheat who hides his dice and shows the dice of his opponent,
calling attention to the other's shortcomings, continually thinking
of accusing him.

Buddha
UDANAVARGA 27.1

Why do you see the speck in your neighbor's eye,
but do not notice the log in your own eye?
Or how can you say to your neighbor,
"Friend, let me take the speck out of your eye,"
when you yourself do not see the log in your own eye?
You hypocrite, first take the log out of your own eye,
and then you will see clearly to take the speck out of your neighbor's eye.

Jesus
HOLY BIBLE Luke 6.41-42

DEFENSE MECHANISMS are used primarily to protect us from overwhelming anxiety, stress, and threats to our ego. Defense mechanisms are additional ways we can distort our thinking. They can result in self-defeating cognitions, emotions, and behavior. Ego-defense mechanisms, sometimes called "coping mechanisms," are relatively unconscious and automatic psychological strategies to protect our self-concept and reduce or avoid stress. Defense mechanisms also help us reduce or avoid anxiety, unacceptable thoughts and impulses, and internal or external conflict. Our defense mechanisms often originate in childhood and adolescence, and become reinforced throughout our life experiences. We all have defense mechanisms. They are necessary for our mental health. Some defense mechanisms are adaptive and helpful. As O'Connell and O'Connell (1980) point out:

> "Defense mechanisms are necessary because they help protect us from pain. Each of us can endure just so much pain. When physical pain becomes too intense, we lose consciousness and

thereby effectively block out further painful stimuli. Physical pain is one such stimulus, anxiety or mental pain is another.

Each one of us can stand only just so much anxiety. When that point is reached, a kind of psychological 'trigger point,' we begin to defend ourselves against further painful stimulation. In short, we begin to use our defense mechanisms." (p. 98)

Although some defense mechanisms effectively help us cope, some defense mechanisms can become self-defeating and block our personal growth. They can distort awareness, perceptions, and impair our ability to hear what others tell us. Also, defense mechanisms can prevent us from experiencing the full consequences of our Buttons. This can result in an inability, or lack of initiative, to modify or eliminate our self-defeating Buttons. Without consciously working on our personal growth we can remain stuck in maladaptive patterns of coping, operating our biocomputers, and interpersonal relationships for a lifetime.

Twenty common defense mechanisms are summarized in Table 5.

TABLE 5

TWENTY COMMON DEFENSE MECHANISMS

1. **Altruism.** Focusing on serving others, partly to fulfill one's own needs.

2. **Attack.** The striking back at Button-Pushers with physical or verbal aggression when pain is experienced.

3. **Compensation.** The protection of self-esteem by masking weaknesses or developing certain positive traits to make up for limitations.

4. **Denial.** A conscious attempt to suppress unpleasant reality.

5. **Displacement.** The redirecting of emotional energy, often angry feelings, triggered from a Button-Pusher to a less threatening and safer target.

6. **Fantasy.** The retreat into daydreams and imagination to escape problems or to avoid conflict

7. **Humor.** The use of humor to reduce anxiety, stress, or fear.

8. **Idealization.** The unwarranted praise of another or oneself by exaggerating virtues.

9. **Identification.** Internalizing the characteristics of others or identifying with a winner in order to overcome fear, inadequacy, low self-esteem or to cope with loss or helplessness.

10. **Intellectualization.** An attempt to avoid painful feelings by escaping to our rational minds.

11. **Isolation of Affect.** The compartmentalization of painful emotions from the events associated with them (e.g. rape victim who can recount details of the rape without recalling the feelings associated with the event).

12. **Projection.** Attributing unacceptable thoughts, feelings, wishes, traits, and impulses to others.

13. **Rationalization.** Providing a plausible, self-serving false reason to justify failure or unacceptable emotions or ideas.

14. **Reaction Formation.** A type of feeling substitution whereby individuals adopt the exaggerated opposite attitude and behavior from the way they really feel and believe.

15. **Regression.** A return to an earlier and less mature coping style when confronted with overwhelming stress.

16. **Repression.** The unconscious exclusion of threatening or painful thoughts, feelings, impulses, and wishes from awareness (e.g. forgetting and amnesia).

17. **Sublimation.** The redirection of unacceptable drives, feelings, and impulses into socially acceptable goals and behaviors.

18. **Substitution.** The substitution of one unavailable option for another available option.

19. **Suppression.** The conscious avoidance or unacceptable thoughts, feelings, and behaviors.

20. **Withdrawal.** Withdrawal when the pain of stress, anxiety, or frustration is too much to bear (e.g. avoiding stress and flight into failure).

The Button Therapy Book: How to Work on Your Buttons and the Button-Pushers in Your Life by Lloyd R. Goodwin, Jr.
© 2002. Published by Trafford Publishing. www.trafford.com

The following are twenty common defense mechanisms adapted from Corey and Corey (1997), Hales and Hales (1995), O'Connell & O'Connell (1980), Rosenhan and Seligman (1995), and Maxmen and Ward (1995).

ALTRUISM

Altruism refers to when people focus excessively on serving others, partly to fulfill their own needs. Some service to others is necessary, therapeutic, and good for the soul. However, some people focus on excessive service to various causes, and because of lack of availability or attention, fail to take care of themselves and their families. While they are out saving the environment, homeless, drug abusers, minorities, and whales, they can avoid dealing with personal, interpersonal, family, and work problems that are too uncomfortable to confront. In their minds they think they are doing the "right thing" or "God's work" and wonder why their spouse and children are not more understanding when they don't spend time with them.

ATTACK

The pain-attack response is the most physical, primitive, and aggressive form of defense. When we experience pain, from a physical or psychological stressor, our tendency is to strike back at the closest object, usually the Button-Pusher. *Verbal aggression* is one way we can strike back at a Button-Pusher. We have all shouted, screamed, or said things to a Button-Pusher that we later regretted. *Sarcasm*, *ridicule*, and *wit* are more sophisticated and indirect ways of striking back at Button-Pushers.

COMPENSATION

Through the defense mechanism of compensation we can protect our self-esteem by masking perceived weaknesses or developing certain positive traits to make up for limitations. The adolescent in a wheelchair with paraplegia who becomes the statistician and runs the scoreboard at the basketball games in high school is one example.

DENIAL

Denial is a conscious effort to suppress unpleasant reality. It is a way of distorting our thinking, feeling, or perception about stressful situations. "Denial is the lack of awareness of external realities that would be too painful to acknowledge. It differs from repression, which is a denial of internal reality" (Maxmen & Ward, 1995, p.75). For example, Craig ignored the reality of his poor performance in graduate school. He continued to party and avoid studying his assignments for his classes. He "closed his eyes" as his Cs and Ds kept accumulating. With his third letter grade of "C", Craig continued to deny there was a problem and was subsequently terminated from graduate school.

DISPLACEMENT

Displacement is the redirecting of emotional energy, often angry feelings, triggered from a Button-Pusher to a less threatening and safer target. People who get their Buttons pushed at work by their boss and, because they might get fired if they express their anger to the boss, come home and express their withheld anger at their spouse, children, or dog with the slightest provocation.

FANTASY

Fantasy is the retreat into daydreams and imagination to escape problems or to avoid conflicts. Fantasy can involve gratifying frustrated desires by imaginary achievements.

HUMOR

Humor is used to reduce anxiety, stress, or fear. An example is when someone makes an amusing, incongruous, or absurd comment in a social situation with a group of people to break the tension and provides an opportunity to release some uncomfortable energy.

IDEALIZATION

"The unwarranted praise of another or oneself by exaggerating virtues. 'Better to idealize a spouse than to see the jerk for what he is and be a very lonely divorcee'" (Maxmen & Ward, 1995, p. 75).

IDENTIFICATION

The internalization of the characteristics of others - their ideas, values, mannerisms, status, and power. A common strategy for overcoming fear and inadequacy. People often rate themselves and each other by the college they attended, where they buy their clothes, or by the car they drive. The identification with athletic teams and celebrities (e.g. autographs) is common in our society. Identification is also "...used to increase one's sense of self-worth, to cope with (possible) separation or loss, or to minimize helplessness, as with 'identification with the aggressor,' as seen in concentration-camp prisoners who assumed the mannerisms of their Nazi guards" (Maxmen & Ward, 1995, p. 75).

INTELLECTUALIZATION

An attempt to avoid painful feelings by escaping to our rational minds. Although excessive intellectualization is annoying to many people, this behavior is especially irritating to the spouse who is trying to get his or her partner to share how he or she feels about some marital concern.

ISOLATION OF AFFECT

The compartmentalization of painful emotions from the events associated with them. Only the affective part of the experience is deleted while the information part is retained. Whereas in repression and denial, both the affective and information components of experience are deleted. People who have experienced traumas such as natural disasters and victims of violent crimes (e.g. raped, mugged), often use this defense mechanism. A soldier may kill someone and compartmentalize the guilt, anxiety, and fear he may otherwise feel. A rape victim may be able to recount the details of the rape to health care professionals and police without recalling any of the intense emotions associated with the rape. Isolation can also be used constructively. For example, the parent who reprimands a child or the orthopedic surgeon who saws off a patient's leg can't be too in touch with their feelings or it may adversely affect the outcome.

PROJECTION

*Confucius said, "When you see a good man, try to emulate his example,
And when you see a bad man, search yourself for his faults."*
Confucius
THE APHORISMS OF CONFUCIUS: WIT AND WISDOM

Projection is attributing unacceptable thoughts, feelings, wishes, traits, and impulses to others. It is substituting "you" for "I." According to research by Halpern (1977), people who deny or repress their own sexual impulses have been shown to project them onto others and to rate others as more lustful than, in fact, they are. Projection often involves seeing clearly in others the unacceptable traits and actions that we don't like about ourselves. When other people exhibit these disowned and unaccepted parts of us they often become our Button-Pushers.

For example, consider the college professor who blames the workaholic colleague for leading an unbalanced life and not spending enough time with his family when, in reality, he is the workaholic and is feeling guilty about not spending enough time with his family, especially his children. He does not even know for sure if his colleague spends time with his family or not. He is projecting his own guilt producing actions onto a colleague.

Scapegoating is a form of projection whereby one blames a particular person or group for the misfortunes of oneself, one's group, or even one's entire nation or race. For example, Adolf Hitler directed his own sense of frustration and failure into anti-Semitism. Another example is the Scapegoating of the black race by white society in the United States. We are left with the residues of Scapegoating a variety of different minority groups in our language as evidenced by such words as nigger, wop, redneck, gook, kike, and spik (O'Connell & O'Connell, 1980).

RATIONALIZATION

Rationalization is providing a plausible, self-serving, false reason to justify failure or unacceptable emotions or ideas. Such excuses help protect our threatened ego. "I could have gotten an A on that exam but...the professor didn't cover the material very well in class...the professor writes really poor exams... I didn't get a good nights sleep before the exam...etc."

The *"sour grapes"* form of rationalization is when we are unsuccessful at achieving a goal. The young man who fails to make the football team may rationalize his failure by telling himself that he did not really want to play on the team and that he would probably get injured anyway.

The *"sweet lemons"* form of repression denies the pain and twists the situation so that it is superficially a positive event. The student who doesn't get the part in the school play who comforts herself by saying that she now has more time to study.

REACTION FORMATION

A type of feeling substitution whereby individuals adopt the exaggerated opposite attitude and behavior from the way they really feel and believe. The mother of a child with a severe disability such as autism becomes supermom spending all her waking hours meeting and anticipating her child's every need in order to counteract a fleeting thought, and resulting guilt feelings, that she wished her child were dead. "Me thinks the lady doth protest too much" is one of the clues of this defense mechanism.

REGRESSION

A return to an earlier and less mature coping style when confronted with overwhelming stress. For example, the university student who doesn't like the grade she receives on an exam and confronts the professor in an emotional tirade. She complains about the poorly written exam, inappropriate scoring of certain items, and throws the exam on the floor in anger and exits the classroom by slamming the door shut with such force that the whole room reverberates. Let's hope she isn't majoring in counseling or psychology! Another example is when parents return from the hospital with a new baby and the older sibling suddenly begins to suck his thumb or have "accidents."

REPRESSION

When we unconsciously exclude threatening or painful thoughts, feelings, impulses, and wishes from awareness. Repression is an unconscious mechanism and *suppression* is a conscious process. Partially repressed conflicts and memories play a significant role in abnormal behavior. "In *multiple personality*, for example, an individual has two or more personalities that are alien to each other. When one personality is dominant, the others are repressed" (Rosenhan & Seligman, 1995, p.87).

Forgetting is sometimes an example of repression. Children may "forget" to have their parents' sign a failed test paper sent home by their teacher. A counseling student "forgets" to bring in her counseling tapes to the counseling practicum seminar the first due date so they can be critiqued by the professor and other practicum students. I've "forgotten" a dentist appointment more than a few times.

Amnesia is another form of "forgetting" and denial in which one clouds one's awareness of a specific event and also keep anything associated with it out of consciousness. A person who has killed someone may not remember the event, since recognizing himself as a murderer may be more than he can integrate into his conscious awareness of himself (O'Connell & O'Connell, 1980, p.109). In my past clinical work with offenders in the criminal justice system, an offender would often relate how during a robbery, "the gun went off and must have hit the victim." I never heard, "When I was robbing the store, I pulled the trigger and shot and killed the store clerk because he wasn't doing exactly as I wanted quickly enough!" It's always, "the gun went off," as if magically of its own volition. It was too much for the person to assume responsibility for killing someone.

SUBLIMATION

The redirection of unacceptable drives, feelings, and impulses into socially acceptable goals and behaviors. Somebody who has sadistic aggressive thoughts becomes a professional boxer instead of a serial killer.

SUBSTITUTION

Substitution refers to exchanging an unavailable option for another available option. An example is the high school student who couldn't get a date with his first choice and finds another to go out with instead. Also, the job seeker who cannot get a job in the organization that is her first choice and finds a similar job in another organization.

SUPPRESSION

The conscious avoidance of unacceptable thoughts, feelings, and behaviors. "I don't want to deal with the end of the year report due at work next week. I'll work on it tomorrow ." "I'll do my income taxes and get them in the mail by April 15, it's only April 14th."

WITHDRAWAL

We can withdraw if the pain of stress, anxiety, or frustration is too much to bear and we cannot cope with it assertively. Children may turn away and pout, cry, or fantasize. We sometimes simply withdraw from people and situations that trigger feelings of inferiority.

Avoiding success and flight into failure are ways of insulating ourselves against the fear of failure. Some students decide in advance to fail, apparently so they will not be disappointed when they do fail. Students who avoid studying for a test is one example of this defense mechanism. "If they pass the test they can congratulate themselves for achieving a passing grade and for knowing that they could have gotten a higher grade if they had studied" (O'Connell & O'Connell, 1980, p. 106).

DETERMINING WHEN WE ARE USING DEFENSE MECHANISMS

Most of our defense mechanisms are automatically triggered without conscious thought or intention. It is not easy becoming aware of when defense mechanisms are activated. O'Connell and O'Connell (1980) offer some clues and suggestions for discovering them underneath the camouflage of rational and orderly behavior:

- When we are doing or saying something that does not fit the situation or the people involved.
- Doing something not characteristic of ourselves.
- Feeling out of control and not acting like oneself. When we make remarks such as: "I was so overwhelmed I didn't know what I was doing." "I knew I was saying the wrong things but I just couldn't help myself." "I don't know what came over me, I just wasn't myself."
- Unable to make a decision or feeling "tied up in knots."
- When we find ourselves in uncomfortable situations and when we sense discomfort and pain.

Defense mechanisms can be adaptive or maladaptive. It depends on the situation, how they are used, and how extensively they are utilized. For example, denial is frequently maladaptive. The drug addict who denies she has a drug problem while she is repeatedly arrested for driving under the influence of too much alcohol, has lost her husband to divorce, has been fired from work, and has impaired physical health is an example of maladaptive use of denial. However, denial can temporarily help the individual with a recent spinal cord injury paralyzed from the neck down lying in a hospital bed immobilized by a "halo" restraining device. Denial can help prevent this individual from experiencing overwhelming feelings of despair, depression, fear, helplessness, and hopelessness. The defense mechanism of denial allows this individual to have hope and muster the motivation to undergo rehabilitation efforts in hopes of someday regaining functional use of his or her body. The question is not whether or not we have defense mechanisms but whether they are adaptive and helpful, or maladaptive barriers to our personal growth.

ASSESS YOUR DEFENSE MECHANISMS

Review the list of defense mechanisms (see Table 5 for a brief summary of the 20 defense mechanisms) or *The Cognitive Self-Assessment Inventory* in Appendix A and determine which ones you tend to rely on. Set a goal to work on eliminating those defense mechanisms that you frequently use which are blocking your personal growth and self-actualization.

WHICH DEFENSE MECHANISMS DO PEOPLE TEND TO USE?

In a 1998-1999 study conducted by the author utilizing the *Cognitive Self-Assessment Inventory (CSAI)*, 293 adults, most of whom were college students, were asked, "Which of the following defense mechanisms do you tend to rely on the most?" Each defense mechanism was briefly described (see the *Cognitive Self-Assessment Inventory* in Appendix A). Each defense mechanism was scored on a one to five scale:

1=Not at all   2=Sometimes   3=Don't know   4=Frequently   5=Very frequently

Table 6 illustrates how the defense mechanisms are ranked according to their mean score. The percentage of subjects who use each defense mechanism "frequently" or "very frequently" is also provided. See Appendix C for more information about the study. Results of this study indicate that adults tend to most frequently use "humor" to deal with anxiety and stressful situations. The next most frequently utilized defense mechanism is "altruism" followed by "compensation," and "rationalization." "Intellectualization" rounds out the top five defense mechanisms utilized by this norming group of 293 adults.

TABLE 6

TOP 10 DEFENSE MECHANISMS

The most "frequently" and "very frequently" used defense mechanisms by the norming group in this study.

Rank	Percentage who use "frequently" or "very frequently"
1. Humor	70
2. Altruism	35
3. Compensation	34
4. Rationalization	21
5. Fantasy	20
6. Attack	18
7. Suppression	18
8. Intellectualization	16
9. Substitution	16
10. Withdrawal	16

The Button Therapy Book: How to Work on Your Buttons and the Button-Pushers in Your Life by Lloyd R. Goodwin, Jr. © 2002.Published by Trafford Publishing. www.trafford.com

CHAPTER EIGHT

PERSONALITY TRAITS, STYLES, AND DISORDERS

No good tree bears bad fruit, nor again does a bad tree bear good fruit;
  for each tree is known by its own fruit.
Figs are not gathered from thorns, nor are grapes picked from a
  bramble bush.
The good person out of the good treasure of the heart produces good,
  and the evil person out of evil treasure produces evil;
  for it is out of the abundance of the heart that the mouth speaks.

Jesus
HOLY BIBLE Luke 6.43-45

PERSONALITY TRAITS, STYLES, AND DISORDERS are another common way we can distort our perception and thinking. According to psychiatrist John Oldham, M.D. and Lois Morris (1995) our personality style, "...represents the orderly arrangement of all your attributes, thoughts, feelings, attitudes, behaviors, and coping mechanisms. It is the distinctive pattern of your psychological functioning—the way you think, feel, and behave—that makes you definitely you" (p. 16).

Your personality most likely helped determine the types of cognitions and Buttons that you currently have. Also, your personality helps determine how you react and cope when one of your Buttons gets pushed. If you are going to become aware of and eliminate some of your troublesome cognitions and Buttons you will find it helpful to better understand your personality.

PERSONALITY

Personality or "character traits" are described by Maxmen and Ward (1995) as:

> ...ingrained, enduring patterns of behaving, feeling, perceiving, and thinking, which are prominent in a wide range of personal and social contexts. Personality is the psychological equivalent of physical appearance: We grow up with both, and although we can adjust each, they remain essentially the same and affect the rest of our lives...Personality features may or may not be adaptive. Compulsiveness in a student is adaptive when it promotes orderly study habits, but it's maladaptive when the student spends hours sharpening pencils instead of studying. Personality traits turn into personality *disorders* when they become (a) inflexible and maladaptive, and (b) significant-

ly impair social and occupational functioning or cause substantial subjective distress. People with personality disorders are
not always in significant emotional distress. Often, the people
they are living or working with are more distressed. (p. 389)

PERSONALITY DISORDERS

Personality disorders affect between 10 and 14 percent of the total
population. Many people with personality disorders do not realize that there is
anything wrong with them. Others see it, though. Individuals with personality
disorders are frequently in conflict with family members, employers, colleagues,
and subordinates (Oldham & Morris, 1995). Personality disorders tend to first
become apparent during adolescence or earlier, persist through life, and become
less obvious by middle or old age. Personality disorders are more pronounced
during periods of high energy (e.g. adolescence) and under stressful conditions
(Maxmen & Ward, 1995). There are ten personality disorders listed in the
Diagnostic and Statistical Manual-Fourth Edition (DSM-IV) (American
Psychiatric Association, 1994), the mental health practitioner's primary resource
for classifying and labeling mental disorders. The following are the essential
features of ten personality disorders from the DSM-I V and four more personality disorders generally recognized by mental health professionals and included in the Appendices of the DSM-IV or the DSM-III-R for future study:

- **Antisocial Personality Disorder** is a pattern of disregard for and violation
  of the rights of others.
- **Avoidant Personality Disorder** is a pattern of social inhibition, feelings of
  inadequacy, and hypersensitivity to negative evaluation.
- **Borderline Personality Disorder** is a pattern of instability in interpersonal relationships, self-image, and affects, and marked impulsivity.
- **Dependent Personality Disorder** is a pattern of submissive and clinging
  behavior related to an excessive need to be taken care of.
- **Histrionic Personality Disorder** is a pattern of excessive emotionality and
  attention seeking.
- **Narcissistic Personality Disorder** is a pattern of grandiosity, need for
  admiration, and lack of empathy.
- **Obsessive-Compulsive Personality Disorder** is a pattern of preoccupation with orderliness, perfectionism, and control.
- **Paranoid Personality Disorder** is a pattern of distrust and suspiciousness
  such that others' motives are interpreted as malevolent.
- **Schizoid Personality Disorder** is a pattern of detachment from social
  relationships and a restricted range of emotional expression.
- **Schizotypal Personality Disorder** is a pattern of acute discomfort in close
  relationships, cognitive or perceptual distortions, and eccentricities of

behavior. (p. 629)

The following are four additional personality disorders. The **Depressive Personality Disorder** and **Passive-Aggressive Personality Disorder** are included as appendices of the DSM-IV as disorders for further study. The **Self-Defeating Personality Disorder** and **Sadistic Personality Disorder** were included as appendices in the DSM-III-R (American Psychiatric Association, 1987). Because many mental health professionals recognize these disorders they are being included in this list.

- **Depressive Personality Disorder** is a pattern of depressive cognitions and behaviors including feelings of dejection, gloominess, cheerlessness, joy-lessness, and unhappiness. These individuals are overly serious, incapable of enjoyment or relaxation, lack a sense of humor, and tend to brood and worry. They tend to have low self-esteem and are pessimistic, negativistic, critical, and judgmental towards others (American Psychiatric Association, 1987).
- **Passive-Aggressive Personality Disorder** (Negativistic Personality Disorder) is a pattern of negativistic attitudes and passive resistance to demands for adequate performance in social and occupational situations. The resistance is expressed by procrastination, forgetfulness, stubbornness, and intentional inefficiency, especially in response to tasks assigned by authority figures. They feel cheated, unappreciated, and misunderstood, and blame their failures on others. They chronically complain and tend to be sullen, irritable, impatient, argumentative, cynical, and skeptical (American Psychiatric Association, 1987).
- **Self-Defeating Personality Disorder** (Masochism) is a pattern of avoiding or undermining pleasurable experiences, being drawn to situations or relationships in which he or she will suffer, and prevents others from helping him or her (American Psychiatric Association, 1987).
- **Sadistic Personality Disorder** is a pattern of cruel, demeaning, intimidating, and aggressive behavior. They will hurt, humiliate, punish, bully, threaten, and intimidate in order to achieve dominance and control the members of their family and those who are subordinate or dependent on them in their work. They may be violent and fascinated by weapons, martial arts, injury, or torture (American Psychiatric Association, 1987; Oldham & Morris, 1995).

In addition to the personality disorders categories described above individuals can also be viewed as either toxic or nourishing.

TOXIC AND NOURISHING PEOPLE

People can be viewed at any given moment on a toxic - nourishing continuum.

Toxic < _______Normal__/_____ > Nourishing

TOXIC BEHAVIORS. When we are toxic we are often caught up in an activated Button. When we have our Buttons pushed it's like having a dark cloud of negative energy surrounding and permeating us. We are reacting unconsciously, experiencing negative emotions, being off-center, being out of harmony, and spewing out negative toxins in the air (e.g. a child or adult throwing a temper tantrum). Some people hang out in a toxic state, not because they are constantly having their Buttons pushed, but because they have toxic personality traits, styles, or disorders. "Toxic" individuals who exude chronic negative energy are like psychic vampires who, when encountered, suck the vital life force right out of our beings, leaving us feeling off-center and out of harmony. When we see a "toxic" person in the grocery store we quickly look the other way to avoid eye contact and go down a different aisle in order to avoid them.

If we accidentally encounter a "toxic" person in public and they snare us with their eye contact and engage us in conversation, we look for the first opportunity to bolt and run like hell. When at a safe distance and physically disengaged from the "toxic" person, we try to clear the negative energy that entered our energy field by vigorously shaking it off like a horse shaking off a swarm of horse flies. We then attempt to return to a more nourishing, centered, and harmonious state of being by deep breathing, repeating a mantra, or practicing some other portable centering technique.

Individuals with toxic personality traits, styles of relating, or personality disorders, as well as individuals who spend a lot of time thinking negatively, have few, if any, intimate friends. Most people avoid toxic people like the plague. Lillian Glass, Ph.D. (1995), a communications specialist, came up with thirty types of "toxic people," whom she also refers to as "Toxic Terrors:" The Cut-You-Downer; The Chatterbox; The Self-Destroyer; The Runner (runs from stress and unpleasant situations); The Silent but Deadly Volcano; The Gossip; The Angry Pugilist; The Gloom and Doom Victim; The Smiling Two-Faced Backstabber; The Wishy-Washy Wimp; The Opportunistic User; The Bitchy, Bossy Bully; The Jokester; The Unconscious Social Klutz; The Mental Case; The Bullshitting Liar; The Meddler; The Penny-Pinching Miser; The Fanatic; The Me, Myself, and I Narcissist; The Eddie Haskell (two-faced); The Self-Righteous Priss; The Snooty Snob; The Competitor; The Control Freak; The Accusing Critic; The Arrogant Know-It-All; The Emotional Refrigerator; The Skeptical Paranoid; and The Instigator.

You may recognize yourself or others in this list of toxic behaviors and people. If you recognize yourself in this list don't come down on yourself. Just see it as more grist for the personal growth mill. Your awareness is the first and most important step to changing unwanted self-defeating cognitive distortions, characteristics, and toxic behaviors. Also, don't waste your time and energy attempting to directly change other people. Instead, work on your own personal growth. We all have room for improvement. I have yet to meet a completely self-actualized person. Self-actualization is a process not an end state. We are always changing and in a state of flux. We are either evolving toward self-actualization, coasting, or regressing toward an earlier state of development. Hanging out in a positive, nourishing, and loving space is the most effective way to positively influence other people and help change the world for the better.

NOURISHING PEOPLE. Nourishing people tend to be centered, caring, and compassionate. They are primarily motivated by the "acceptance and love" motivational state (described in chapter 13). People feel good and uplifted when around nourishing people. Nourishing people have positive energy fields and attract people and animals. Even plants grow and thrive in the presence of nourishing people. We want to be around them because their energy is positive and nourishing to us. Also, "nourishers" remind us of when we were in that place and help motivate us to return there. Nourishing people tend to have as many friends as they want.

Most of us have, at varying times, been toxic and nourishing. As we encounter our Buttons we move toward the toxic side of the continuum. As we eliminate our Buttons we become more centered, conscious, and compassionate. When we come from the motivational states of "acceptance and love," "personal growth and self-actualization," and "spiritual and transcendental" motivational states (described in chapter 13) we move toward the nourishing side of the continuum.

Although we may temporarily jump dramatically from one location to another on the toxic-nourishing continuum, we tend to hang out somewhere on this continuum. And where we hang out on this continuum is how other people generally view us. A worthy goal in life is to move toward the nourishing end of the toxic-nourishing continuum.

The ten most frequently cited personality traits and styles from the study of cognitions in Appendix C are presented in Table 7.

TABLE 7

TOP 10 PERSONALITY TRAITS

Rank	Percentage Agreeing or Strongly Agreeing
1. I like competition and challenges.	78
2. I am devoted to my spouse (girl/boyfriend).	62
3. I get bored quickly with the same old thing.	59
4. I like to serve others and make sure their needs are met.	56
5. I am more competent and capable than the average person.	52
6. I am a natural leader. I feel comfortable taking charge and assuming responsibility and authority.	52
7. I am very sensitive to negative feedback.	43
8. I am very orderly, perfectionistic, and punctual.	42
9. I am very interested in mysticism, paranormal phenomenon, metaphysics, dreams, and "new age" topics.	35
10. I enjoy taking risks, thrill-seeking behavior, and living on the edge.	33
11. I am even-tempered and am seldom extremely sad or happy.	33

The Button Therapy Book: How to Work on Your Buttons and the Button-Pushers in Your Life by Lloyd R. Goodwin, Jr. © 2002. Published by Trafford Publishing. www.trafford.com

CAN WE CHANGE OUR PERSONALITIES?

As with many of our physical traits such as eye color and height, our genes confer a range of personality predispositions. Environment, life experiences, parents, family, culture, and peers then sculpt the final "you" from the possibilities (Oldham & Morris, 1995). Although personality traits are ingrained and enduring, the potential for change always exists. "Intense life pressures and experiences - from the horrors of war to the birth of a child to the rigors of psychotherapy - can exert tremendous force on the personality. To adapt, your personality restructures itself. You can also learn to make certain small changes and adjustments, first by understanding how your personality is structured, and then by knowing how to enter the system and fine-tune it...no matter how rigid or how limited your personality, biologically your fate is never really sealed" (Oldham & Morris, 1995, p. 30).

CHAPTER NINE

CORE BELIEFS

Man is made by his belief. As he believes, so he is.
THE BHAGAVAD GITA (500? B.C.)

All that we are is the result of what we have thought.
Buddha

WE ALL HAVE CORE BELIEFS. These are the messages, injunctions, and models of how things should be that we acquire throughout life. Most of these messages, models, and programming were put into our biocomputers (mind) very early in our lives by our primary caretakers, which for most of us were our parents. We also acquired our programming from a variety of other sources such as other family members, teachers, clergy, the media, and our culture in which we live. Much of our programming is necessary, beneficial, and helps us negotiate the complexities of life. Our lives would be unmanageable if we could not rely on our past learning and memory, and had to relearn things every time we performed daily activities such as driving an automobile.

SELF-DEFEATING CORE BELIEFS

In addition to our life-enhancing core beliefs and programming, many people have certain core beliefs about themselves and others that distort thinking related to their self-esteem and other areas of life. Some of the more common self-defeating core beliefs are:

* I don't deserve to be loved.
* I'm not lovable.
* I'm not sexy.

- I'm not capable of truly loving anybody.
- If I openly and honestly express my love to my spouse (boyfriend/girl friend), I will become vulnerable and he/she will stomp on my heart till my blood fills the streets.
- I am going to wait until Mr./Mrs. Right (i.e. the person of my dreams) comes along before I open up and become intimate with anyone.
- If I feel good for too long something terrible is bound to happen real soon.
- I must please and agree with everybody to be accepted.
- I must follow the life path (i.e. expectations) my parents have set out for me including the type of career, wife/husband, house, and neighborhood I live in - because "they only want what is best for me."
- I'm not as smart, capable, or competent as most people I know.
- If people really knew me they wouldn't like me or find me very interesting.
- The bottom line in life is accumulating money, nice things, and power.
- I'm a loser.
- Divorce is a sign of failure or a sin.
- I'm a toxic person. I have a dark cloud that follows me around and nobody wants to be near me or be friends with me.
- I'm not attractive to other people or myself.
- I don't have very good ideas or opinions.
- I'm a bad person because of some of the things I've done in my life.
- The world owes me a living. I didn't ask to be brought into this world.
- The world is basically an unsafe place.
- Most people are only out for themselves and will screw you the first chance they get.
- Other people make me have negative feelings such as anger, anxiety, and jealousy.
- Most people are better off and doing better than I am.
- I am a victim of life's circumstances.
- I have very little control over my life.

The core beliefs listed above are potentially destructive and self-defeating, especially the ones that are deeply rooted in our psyches. If you are carrying around any of these potentially destructive core beliefs, reflect back on how you acquired them. They were probably acquired very early in your life as a result of unpleasant life experiences. Some counseling theories hold that many of our basic core beliefs, parental injunctions, messages, and life scripts were placed in our minds within the first five or six years of life. We then spend the rest of our lives gravitating toward people and situations that reinforce our core beliefs.

For example, you may believe that you are basically "a bad person" because of numerous negative parental injunctions put into your biocomputer early in life. Your poor self-esteem may have been reinforced with negative strokes (attention) every time you didn't live up to your parents' expectations. If you have this core belief of being a "bad person" then you are likely going to gravitate to people and situations that will reinforce that basic core belief. As a child, you may find yourself constantly in trouble at school, which results in teachers and vice principles giving you constant negative strokes and "not ok" messages through their reprimands, school detentions, and suspensions. You may find yourself attracted to romantic and sexual partners that have trouble loving, focusing on your needs, or giving you positive strokes. You may be attracted to partners who are "jerks," self-centered, and quick to belittle you and maybe even physically hit you or your children. As a result, you receive more than your quota of negative strokes and "I'm not ok messages" which reinforce your basic core belief that "I'm a bad person or I'm not ok."

We are relatively unconscious about which core beliefs we have in our biocomputers, let alone how we acquired them. Also, we seldom realize how our core beliefs affect almost all aspects of our lives. Part of our journey into personal growth and self-actualization is learning about our core beliefs, especially our self-defeating ones, and change those beliefs that are blocking our self-actualization. This often requires the feedback of other knowledgeable individuals (e.g. professional counselors and psychotherapists) who are aware of these psychological phenomena. Mental health professionals can also help you modify or replace self-defeating core beliefs with healthier ways of thinking, feeling, and behaving.

The top ten "Core Beliefs about Self" from the study of cognitions (see Appendix C) are presented in Table 8. The top three "Core Beliefs about Relationships" are presented in Table 9. The top five "Core Beliefs about Life" are presented in Table 10. The top 4 "Core Beliefs about Illness and Disability" are presented in Table 11. The top 10 "Core Beliefs about Alcohol and Other Drugs" are presented in Table 12.

TABLE 8

TOP 10 CORE BELIEFS ABOUT SELF

Rank	**Percentage Agreeing or Strongly Agreeing**
1. If I don't pay any attention to my problems they will go away.	14
2. I am a victim of life's circumstances.	11
3. If I allow myself to feel really excited or good about someone or something it will be followed by something equally terrible.	10
4. Most people are doing better than I am.	9
5. Other people currently control my life.	7
6. I'm not sexy.	6
7. I am not as intelligent or as competent as most of my friends.	6
8. I must please and agree with people to be accepted.	5
9. Most people are better off than I am.	5
10. If people really knew me they wouldn't like me.	5

TABLE 9

TOP 3 CORE BELIEFS ABOUT RELATIONSHIPS

1. I'm waiting for Mr. or Miss Right to come along.	33
2. I resent my spouse (boy/girlfriend) for some things he or she has done to hurt me.	25
3. Divorce is a sign of failure or a sin.	19

The Button Therapy Book: How to Work on Your Buttons and the Button-Pushers in Your Life by Lloyd R. Goodwin, Jr.
© 2002.Published by Trafford Publishing. www.trafford.com

TABLE 10

TOP 5 CORE BELIEFS ABOUT LIFE

Rank   **Percentage Agreeing or
                                                            Strongly Agreeing**

1. There are no coincidences in life – everything happens for a reason. 52

2. The world is basically a fearful and unsafe place. 11

3. Most people are only out for themselves and will cheat or 10
   betray you sooner or later, usually sooner.

4. The bottom line in life is accumulating money, nice things and power. 7

5. I'm entitled to be taken care of – I didn't ask to be brought into 4
   this world with all its problems.

TABLE 11

THE TOP 4 CORE BELIEFS ABOUT ILLNESS AND DISABILITY

Rank   **Percentage Agreeing or
                                                            Strongly Agreeing**

1. If people have enough faith in God and His healing 20
   powers He will cure them of their disabilities.

2. If people have enough faith in God or a higher spiritual power 16
   they can heal themselves from any illness.

3. People have illness or disability because it is part of their 3
   Karma (past deeds in either this life or a past life).

4. People have illness or disability because God is punishing them. 1

The Button Therapy Book: How to Work on Your Buttons and the Button-Pushers in Your Life by Lloyd R. Goodwin, Jr.
© 2002.Published by Trafford Publishing. www.trafford.com

TABLE 12

TOP 10 CORE BELIEFS ABOUT ALCOHOL AND OTHER DRUGS

Rank	Percentage Agreeing or Strongly Agreeing
1. I don't have any major problems with my alcohol and drug use.	82
2. Problem drinkers and other drug abusers can learn to drink/drug responsibly.	43
3. I have no desire to give up alcohol and other drugs.	35
4. People who have the disease of alcoholism or drug addiction will have it the rest of their lives.	34
5. People have a fundamental human right to self-medicate with any drug.	30
6. Alcoholics Anonymous and related 12 step mutual-help groups are the best approaches to help substance abusers.	29
7. There is nothing wrong with psychoactive drugs.	22
8. All drugs should be legalized.	18
9. I shouldn't have to feel any unpleasant feelings or pain.	13
10. Only someone who has experienced alcohol or another drug addiction can help another alcoholic or drug addict.	12

The Button Therapy Book: How to Work on Your Buttons and the Button-Pushers in Your Life by Lloyd R. Goodwin, Jr. © 2002. Published by Trafford Publishing. www.trafford.com

We acquired many core beliefs from our parents. As we become aware of our self-defeating programs, messages, scripts, models, and other cognitions in our mind it is easy to become upset with our parents and other programmers of our biocomputers.

PARENTS: OUR IMPERFECT BIOCOMPUTER PROGRAMMERS

They said to him,
 "Teacher, this woman was caught in the very act of committing adultry.
 Now in the law Moses commanded us to stone such women.
 Now what do you say?
He said to them,
 "Let anyone among you who is without sin be the first to throw a stone at her."

Jesus
HOLY BIBLE JOHN 8. 4-5 & 7

While we can become excited, hopeful, and energized with each new personal insight on our journey of personal growth such as recognizing some of our self-defeating core beliefs. We can also become upset when we realize that up to now we've unconsciously allowed parents, teachers, clergy, politicians, business people, the media, the tobacco industry, the alcohol industry, the pharmaceutical industry, the traditional medical industry, and a host of all kinds of forces in our society to program their beliefs, wants, "needs," expectations, and scripts of how things should be into our biocomputers. We sometimes don't acquire this realization until we are in our 30s, 40s, 50s, or later. Sometimes never. And that is a long time of living our lives according to other peoples' expectations. If, as adults, we are not satisfied with the results of our programming, and we gain an awareness of how most of our programs got into our biocomputers, there is sometimes a sense of betrayal, anger, and distrust that surfaces towards the primary programmers in our lives. We can become sidetracked at this point and waste a lot of time becoming upset with our programmers. Instead of keeping our focus on our goals of where we want to be in terms of our lives, we can become preoccupied with a sense of betrayal and feelings of anger and revenge. Lest we become too harsh on our parents, we need to be mindful that our parents and other programmers were products of their parents and related programmers, and were doing the best they could with their levels of awareness and consciousness. Our parents probably thought the messages they helped program into our biocomputers were in our best interest. They wanted the best for us and went about parenting the best way they knew how. However, some parents may have parented from a very egocentric, selfish, controlling, and hurtful place with no pretensions as to trying to do what was best for their children. Some parents were mentally ill or drug-addicted and were incapable of providing positive nourishing parenting experiences. Perhaps they had an authoritarian, aggressive, and sadistic personality disorder with poor impulse control, a violent temper, and periodically verbally or physically battered their family members.

THE PARENTING BUTTON. Many people have a "Button" related to how they wanted to be parented in their younger formative years. Some people have definite ideas about how they currently want to be parented. If this is one of your Buttons, see it as more grist for the personal growth mill and work on *your* Button that is getting *you* upset. Individuals with a "parenting Button" will often try to force parents into following their script of how they want their parents to parent them. Attempts at manipulating, cajoling, and coercing parents into their parenting script usually don't work. Attempts to change parents from a "control and power" motivational state usually places an increased strain on the parent-child relationship and results in feelings of frustration and anger. After the "parenting" Button gets pushed enough times, we tend to avoid the Button pusher (parent) and think up excuses for why we can't visit this Christmas, thanksgiving, and other times.

Some people were fortunate to have relatively loving, aware, and conscious parents who instilled positive, life-enhancing scripts into their biocomputers beginning at very early ages. If you are one of these individuals, you are probably realizing how fortunate you are and are grateful for your parents' level of personal development and wisdom in parenting. Those individuals are very fortunate to go through life with a relatively happy, conscious, and loving inner experience because of life-enhancing parental programming. However, even though these people start life at a more advantageous place on the personal growth continuum, they will acquire parental injunctions and Buttons throughout life. Many "parental" injunctions and Buttons develop from other surrogate parent sources such as teachers, clergy, and older siblings and can create much stress and disharmony.

CHAPTER TEN

ASSESS YOUR COGNITIONS

I found that the chief difficulty for most people was to realize that they had really heard "new things": that is, things that they had never heard before. They kept translating what they heard into their habitual language. They had ceased to hope and believe there might be anything new.

Ouspensky

IN THE LAST FEW CHAPTERS you have probably recognized a number of your distorted thinking styles, maladaptive defense mechanisms, toxic personality traits or disorders, and self-defeating core beliefs. However, they are usually easier to spot in our spouses, children, bosses, and friends than ourselves.

COGNITIVE SELF-ASSESSMENT INVENTORY

The Cognitive Self-Assessment Inventory (CSAI) is designed to help you gain a better understanding of your core beliefs, "should messages," defense mechanisms, personality traits, thought distortions and Buttons. If you want to gain a better understanding of yourself then complete the *CSAI* in Appendix A and the *Motivational States Inventory (MSI)* in Appendix B.

Answer the questions on the *CSAI* and *MSI* truthfully. There are no right or wrong answers. The goal is to gain a better understanding of yourself, especially how your mind works to create distress, unhappiness, and prevent personal growth. If you want to work on your distorted cognitions and Buttons that are creating psychological distress, and develop a happier and more fulfilling inner experience, then putting blinders on and lying to yourself probably won't get you there. So fill out the *CSAI* and *MSI* honestly and identify where you need to focus your inner work in order to become more aware, conscious, happy, loving, compassionate, and holy (or at least not so uptight all the time!).

In the study of cognitions described in Appendix C it was found that the average number of "agree" responses indicating potentially troublesome cognitions from the norming group of 293 adults was twenty-two. The average number of "strongly agree" responses indicating potential Buttons was eight. The number of "strongly disagree" responses was twenty-eight. Cognitions that individuals strongly agree with or disagree with both indicate potential Buttons. We can be just as "attached" to being against something as we are for something.

Of the distorted styles of thinking, should messages, and core beliefs that you have agreed with, strongly agreed with, or strongly disagreed with — ask yourself if you are demanding, or attached to any of them. The cognitions (e.g. beliefs and thoughts) that you are attached to or demanding are probably some of your *primary* Buttons or major emotional hot spots!

Cognitions that are not listed on the *CSAI* are often variations of the cognitions listed in the *CSAI*. The top ten potential Buttons from the first 117 items on the *CSAI*, excluding items 118-137 related to defense mechanisms, are presented in Table 13.

TABLE 13

TOP 10 POTENTIAL BUTTONS

The rank-ordered top ten combined "agree" and "strongly agree" cognitions from the first 117 items (excluding defense mechanisms) on the *Cognitive Self-Assessment Inventory.* These are the potential top 10 Buttons (i.e. attachments).

Rank	Percentage Agreeing or Strongly Agreeing
1. I should live life to its fullest.	89
2. I don't have any major problems with my alcohol and drug use.	82
3. I like competition and challenges.	78
4. I should love, or at least like both of my parents.	77
5. Everything happens for a reason.	77
6. I should make other people feel better when they are upset.	73
7. I should be independent and self-sufficient and not have to rely on other people.	68
8. I should please my parents.	64
9. I am devoted to my spouse.	62
10. I know what someone (e.g. spouse, boy/friend) is communicating to me without them verbalizing it.	60
11. I should keep control of my feelings.	60

FEARS

We can also learn about our Buttons from our fears. The top ten fears from a sample of adult subjects in the study of cognitions (see Appendix C) are listed in Table 14. The complete list of fears listed by this sample are listed in Appendix C.

What are your main fears? Identifying your fears can help you identify some of your Buttons. When we fear something or somebody, we are clinging (i.e. attached) to something. Utilizing the Six-Step Button Therapy Method you can identify a fear, determine which motivational state it is associated with, the feelings associated with it, and utilize one of the cognitive interventions to uproot the attachment (i.e. Button).

TABLE 14

TOP 10 FEARS

Two hundred and ninety-three adult subjects were asked to list their five main fears as part of the study of cognitions described in Appendix C. Two hundred and seventy-six subjects responded to this question. Some subjects listed fewer than five fears. The subjects' fears fell into the following categories that are rank-ordered with the most frequently reported fear listed first. Each fear is followed by the percentage of respondents reporting that item as a fear.

Fear	Percent Responding
1. **Failure** to achieve goals or not being successful in life (e.g. completing college/ passing licensure exam)	49
2. **Death of loved one** (e.g. family member/ child/ parent)	46
3. **Death and Dying** (includes having a terminal illness=4)	33
4. **Physical illness and diseases** (e.g. cancer/ Burns)	25
5. **Being alone** (e.g. loneliness/not finding a partner/not belonging/ and includes growing old alone=2)	20
6. **Financial problems and being poor** (includes being poor when old=2)	18
7. **Uncertainty of future** (e.g. career choice/ getting a job/ unknown)	13
8. **Becoming disabled** (e.g. head injury/ dementia)	11
9. **Relationship problems** (e.g. not being liked/rejection/betrayal/ divorce or breaking up/problems with friends)	10
10. **Lack of Intimacy** (e.g. not being loved/not getting married)	8

CHAPTER ELEVEN

EMOTIONS

*For human beings, one of the most powerful forces in shaping our world is
the strength of our emotions. Our emotions lead to healing and to killing, to
giving life or taking it. And only when we are aware of, understand, and
know how to balance our emotions, along with our bodies, minds, and spirits,
are we able to truly live in balance.*
> Joel Levey, Ph.D. and Michelle Levey, M.A.
> LIVING IN BALANCE: A Dynamic Approach for
> Creating Harmony & Wholeness in a Chaotic World

❧

*Helping people better manage their upsetting feelings - anger, anxiety,
depression, pessimism, and loneliness - is a form of disease prevention. Since
the data show that the toxicity of these emotions, when chronic, is on a par
with smoking cigarettes, helping people handle them better could potentially
have a medical payoff as great as getting heavy smokers to quit.*
> Daniel Goleman, Ph.D.
> EMOTIONAL INTELLIGENCE

IDENTIFY, EXPERIENCE, RELEASE, AND CHANNEL THE EMOTIONAL ENERGY ASSOCIATED WITH YOUR BUTTONS

THE THIRD STEP of the Six-Step Button Therapy Method is to
identify the emotions associated with the Buttons being pushed. After identifying and taking responsibility for your emotions, experience the emotion, then
release and channel the *emotional energy to the Button that is triggering the negative emotions.* Instead of taking responsibility for our negative emotions and
directing the emotional energy associated with our activated Buttons to our
Buttons causing the emotions, most individuals direct their emotions (e.g.
anger) to the Button-Pushers who activate the Buttons. Try not to direct the
emotional energy associated with an activated Button to the Button-Pusher.
Instead, take responsibility for your emotions and consciously experience your
emotional distress as a direct result of *your* Buttons being pushed. Take responsibility for your feelings. Then channel the activated emotional energy to your
Buttons causing your psychological distress. The focus of step three is to identify
and take responsibility for your emotions, as well as use the energy associated with

your emotions to modify or eliminate troublesome cognitions and Buttons.

It helps to talk to your activated Button. For example, you might say, "I've had it with my need to control everything and everybody around me (i.e. control Button). I am going to let go of my need for my teenage daughter to be a mature adult. She's only sixteen years old. She'll mature eventually and become more responsible as she grows up. I still prefer that she act responsibly but will no longer demand it (i.e. Button). I need to give my daughter and myself a break. I just hope she makes it through her teenage years relatively unscathed."

As a result of experiencing the negative emotional energy triggered by the activated Button and connecting it to the culprit Button, you will begin to break the conditioned link between your programmed expectation, script, or model of how things should be, and your attachment or addiction (i.e. Button) to it. It is important, if you are to become free from your buttons, that you not simply release the emotional energy in a cathartic manner but consciously experience your emotional distress as a direct result of your attachments to your expectations, programs, models, or scripts.

WHAT CAUSES EMOTIONS?

Emotions are triggered by stimuli from both internal and external events. How we choose to interpret these events depends on our mental programming and on situational cues. When events occur which do not conform to our expectations, and we are attached to those expectations, we experience unpleasant emotions. When events occur which do conform to our programmed expectations, we experience satisfaction and sometimes pleasure and happiness. As Albert Ellis (1975), one of the early pioneers of cognitive therapy, put it, "...you make yourself happy or miserable by your perceptions, attitudes, or self-verbalizations about these outside events" (p. 33). Ellis also points out that this principle appeared in the writings of several ancient Greek and Roman philosophers, notably the famous Stoic Epictetus, who in the first century A.D. wrote in the *Enchiridion*: "Men feel disturbed not by things, but by the views which they take of them." William Shakespeare, many centuries later, rephrased this thought in *Hamlet*: "There (exists) nothing either good or bad but thinking makes it so." (p. 33).

Aaron Beck (1967), another pioneer of cognitive therapy, provides evidence from experimental and clinical findings which indicates that depressed and anxious feelings often follow cognitive processes. Schachter and Singer (1962) demonstrated that a vague feeling of arousal may be experienced as euphoria or irritation, depending on external cues. Rokeach (1960) claims that every emotion has its cognitive counterpart.

Our Emotional vs. Rational Minds

Often times our emotions simply appear and it is difficult to understand what triggered them. As Daniel Goleman, Ph.D. (1995) pointed out, our emotions, especially the ones associated with our fight-or-flight stress response, are *associative* by nature.

> "The logic of the emotional mind is associative; it takes elements that symbolize a reality, or trigger a memory of it, to be the same as that reality. That is why similes, metaphors, and images speak directly to the emotional mind, as do the arts - novels, film, poetry, song, theater, opera. Great spiritual teachers, like Buddha and Jesus, have touched their disciples' hearts by speaking in the language of emotion, teaching in parables, fables, and stories. Indeed, religious symbol and ritual makes little sense from the rational point of view; it is couched in the vernacular of the heart" (Goleman, 1995, p. 294).

Because of this associative nature of the emotional mind, things need not be defined by their objective identity. "What matters is how they are *perceived*; things are as they seem. What something reminds us of can be far more important than what it 'is.' Indeed, in emotional life, identities can be like a hologram in the sense that a single part evokes a whole" (Goleman, 1995, p. 294).

The rational mind reasons by objective evidence and new information can change beliefs. However, the emotional mind takes its beliefs to be absolutely true, and so discounts any evidence to the contrary. That is why it is so hard to reason with someone who is emotionally upset, no matter how sound your argument. Feelings are self-justifying, with a set of perceptions and "proofs" all their own (Goleman, 1995). The "associative" type of emotions will tend to dominate our inner experience when triggered. However, we still can activate our rational minds at some point as the energy associated with the emotion subsides. As we gain awareness as to what is happening, we can gradually gain control over how we choose to deal with triggered emotions. We can then channel the emotional energy to the cognition, if the cognition is a Button that we want to modify or eliminate. If the emotions are experienced as pleasant and enjoyable, we may want to simply savor the feelings, sensations, and experience.

Can Emotions Precede Thought?

It is important to point out that many of our emotions seem to precede or be simultaneous with thought and are triggered by association with certain perceptions, objects, smells, sounds, and people. For example, if we are in a car wreck we will probably experience certain emotions such as fear, anger, and possibly pain, if injured. A survival cognition or Button that triggers our stress (i.e. fight or flight) response when we become threatened triggers these emotions. "This rapid-fire emotional reaction takes over in situations that have the urgency of primal survival" (Goleman, 1995, p.293). As Goleman further explains:

> The emotional mind is far quicker than the rational mind...Because it takes the rational mind a moment or two longer to register and respond than it does the emotional mind, the "first impulse" in an emotional situation is the heart's, not the head's...There is also a second kind of emotional reaction, slower than the quick-response, which simmers and brews first in our thoughts before it leads to feeling...But the rational mind usually does not decide what emotions we "should" have. Instead, our feelings typically come to us as a fait accompli. What the rational mind can ordinarily control is the course of those reactions. A few exceptions aside [e.g. professional actors], we do not decide when to be mad, sad, and so on. (p. 291-294)

According to Dr. Goleman (1997), "More recent neurological research suggests that while emotional impulse originates in the limbic centers, how we express our emotions is regulated by structures that are newer in evolution, located in the prefrontal cortex just behind the forehead" (p. 68).

MIND-BODY EMOTIONS

From a holistic perspective, our physical, psychological, and spiritual aspects are interconnected. Emotions help provide a biochemical link between body, mind, and spirit. Dr. Candace Pert (1999), primary discoverer of opiate receptors in the brain, and currently a research professor in the department of physiology and biophysics at Georgetown University Medical Center believes our emotions travel between the two realms of mind and body, as the peptides and their receptors in the physical realm, and as the feelings we experience and call emotions in the nonmaterial realm. In Dr. Pert's (1999) book *Molecules of Emotion* and in an interview with Caren Goldman (1998) for *Intuition* magazine she provides an innovative view of emotions.

MOLECULES OF EMOTION

After years of studying neuropeptides, Dr. Pert (1999) has concluded that they are responsible for our emotions – not only the familiar feelings of anger, fear, sadness, and joy, but also spiritual inspiration, awe, bliss, and other states of consciousness. Neuropeptide receptors are located throughout the nervous system. Dr. Pert's research has shown that the immune system also produces its own. Dr. Pert has come to believe that the brain and nervous, endocrine, and immune systems are interlocked in a "psychoimmunoendocrine" network that serves as a multidirectional, body-wide system in which every part communicates with every other part. This concept varies dramatically with the prevailing view that the mind has power over the body. As Dr. Pert points out, "For a long time, neuroscientists agreed that emotions are controlled by certain parts of the brain – the amygdala, hippocampus, and hypothalamus. This is a big, 'neurocentric' assumption that I now think is either wrong or incomplete....Instead, emotions are the nexus between mind and matter, going back and forth between the two and influencing both" (Goldman, 1998).

THE "MOBILE BRAIN"

Do our cognitions, conscious or unconscious, trigger all emotions? Are emotions controlled by the amygdala, hippocampus, and hypothalamus parts of the brain as traditionally thought? Dr. Candace Pert pushes the frontier of science in speculating on where emotions originate. She points out that,

> "If we accept the idea that peptides and other informational substances are the biochemicals of emotion, their distribution throughout the body's nerves has all kinds of significance...Body and mind are simultaneous. I like to speculate that the mind is the flow of information as it moves among the cells, organs, and systems of the body. The mind, as we experience it, is immaterial, yet it has a physical substrate that is both the body and the brain...The term "mobile brain" is a good way to describe the psychosomatic network. Every one of the zones, or systems, of the network – the hormonal, the gastrointestinal, the neural, and the immune – communicates with the others via the peptides and messenger-specific peptide receptors. As these biochemicals of emotion carry information to the major systems of the body, they link these systems into the Body/Mind...we must see emotions as cellular signals that are involved in the process of translating information into physical reality, literally transforming mind into matter and influencing health. (Goldman, 1998, pp. 24, 49)

GUT FEELING

The mind doesn't control the body and the body doesn't control the mind. The mind and body are one. The gut provides an example of how the "mind" extends throughout the entire body. As Dr. Pert explains,

> The entire lining of the intestines, from the esophagus through the large intestines, and including each of the seven

sphincters, is lined with cells. There are nerve cells and other cells that contain neuropeptides and receptors. To me, it seems entirely possible that the density of receptors in the intestines may be why we have " gut feelings." Studies show that gut motility increases when we're excited or angry and that it decreases when we're content. And then, because this is a two-way network, it's also the case that the movement of the gut as it digests food and excretes impurities can alter your emotional state. The word dyspeptic means grouchy or irritable, but originally it referred to having poor digestion. (Goldman, 1998, p. 49)

The reason we have "gut feelings" about people or situations or feel anxious "butterflies" in our stomachs is because we have a second "brain" in our bowel, according to Michael Gershon, M.D., a neurobiologist at New York's Columbia-Presbyterian Medical Center and author of *The Second Brain* (Gershon, 1999). According to Dr. Gershon an independent network of neurons in the gut not only signals our bodies to stress but causes illness. Actually, 95 percent of all the neurotransmitter serotonin in the body is in the gut, where it triggers digestion. Nerve cells in the gut also use serotonin to communicate with the brain. "The entire nervous system is also a vast chemical warehouse within which is represented every one of the classes of neurotransmitter found in the brain" (P. xiii). Also, the brain in our heads communicates with the "brain" in our gut (*Psychology Today*, May/June 1999).

STRESS AND THE BRAIN

Stress can actually change the shape, size, and number of neurons in the hippocampus, a part of the brain involved with learning and memory. Stress also decreases a nerve growth factor called "brain-derived neurotrophic factor" (BDNF) which strengthens synaptic connections in the hippocampus and enhances the growth of neurons that respond to the neurotransmitter serotonin according to Yale University neurobiologist Ronald Duman, Ph.D. (Marano, 1999). Serotonin plays a role in regulating mood, aggression, sensory perception, pain, eating, sleep, and body temperature.

STRESS-RELATED EMOTIONS EARLY IN LIFE. Early life experiences can establish a lifelong pattern of brain activity. New research demonstrates that stress early in life permanently sensitizes neurons and receptors throughout the central nervous system so that they perpetually overreact to stress. For example, Psychologist Christine Heim, Ph.D. reported at a meeting of the Society for Neuroscience that sexual abuse in girls before puberty creates hyperactivity of the stress-hormone system headquartered in the brain's hypothalamus. And this likely makes them more vulnerable to depression as adults (Marano, 1999).

A NEW MODEL FOR STRESS AND DEPRESSION. New research has reinforced the holistic perspective of physical and mental disorders. Depression is one example where research is demonstrating that it is a whole-body disorder. A new model of depression generated by researchers has been called the diathesis-stress model. Marano (1999) summarizes this model:

> Simply put, some inherited factor—a flawed gene for BDNF, individual differences in PFC [prefrontal cortex] activity—creates the biological vulnerability for major depression. Then some early stressful experience—such as parental neglect or physical or sexual abuse—sets up the brain to permanently overreact to environmental pressures. Then even small degrees of later stress provoke an outpouring of stress hormones, such as CRF [corticotropin-releasing factor] and cortisol, throughout the brain (and body). These hormones act directly on multiple sites to produce the behavioral symptoms of depression—the vegetative state, the sleep disturbances, the cognitive dullness, the loss of pleasure. They push the amygdala into overdrive, churning out the negative emotions that steer the depression's severity and add a twist of anxiety. To boot, they magnify the effects of the neurotransmitter glutamate so that it overstimulates neurons until their dendrites collapse and shrink up. (pp. 72-73)

It appears that both mental health professionals and neurobiologists are reinforcing the notion that the life-long impact of harmful stress, especially stress-provoking early life experiences, helps determine our emotional aspect as adults.

BODY/MIND THERAPIES

This unified Mind/Body concept, "… suggests there are almost infinite pathways the conscious mind can use to access – and modify – the unconscious mind and body," according to Dr. Pert. This Body/Mind unity may help explain the reliving of emotionally laden experiences from early in life during the release of chronically tensed muscles throughout the body during bodywork, including structural integration (i.e. Rolfing) sessions. Or, this may help explain the reliving of past emotionally laden experiences when a neurologist touches certain parts of the cerebral cortex of the brain with a probe. As Dr. Pert adds, "…we need to start thinking about how the mind manifests itself in various parts of the body, and, beyond that, how we can bring that process into consciousness" (Goldman, 1998, p.50).

Good physical and mental health depend on the healthy expression of our emotions. According to Dr. Pert (1999), "…when emotions are expressed—which is to say that the biochemicals that are the substrate of emotion are flowing freely—all systems are united and made whole. When emotions are repressed, denied, not allowed to be whatever they may be, our network pathways get blocked, stopping the flow of the vital feel-good, unifying chemicals that run both our biology and our behavior. This, I believe, is the state of unhealed feeling we want so desperately to escape from" (pp.273-274).

Health and healing requires a holistic approach that includes the unified Mind/Body/Spiritual system. The new holistically oriented health care practitioners realize this reality and attempt to assess and treat the whole person, and not focus exclusively on the presenting problem. "When stored or blocked emotions are released through touch or other physical methods, there is a clearing of our internal pathways, which we experience as energy...The body can and must be healed through the mind, and the mind can and must be healed through the body" (Pert, 1999, pp. 274, 276). It is unfortunate that our traditional health care providers are fearful of touching patients in anything other than a cursory handshake or cold and clinical manner as part of a diagnostic process. Fear of malpractice lawsuits from patients in our litigious society doesn't help the venturing of traditional health care providers into the new mind-body healing. One of the primary reasons holistically oriented health care practitioners are becoming so popular is because many of these practitioners integrate touch through such modalities as massage therapy, Rolfing, Reiki, osteopathic and chiropractic body manipulations, and other mind-body therapeutic clinical counseling approaches into their health care. Also, they recognize the mind-body-spiritual connection treat the whole person, not just the symptom.

TYPES OF EMOTIONS

Clinicians and researchers continue to disagree over the primary categories of emotions. Daniel Goleman, Ph.D. (1995) offers eight basic categories of emotions:

1. *Anger:* fury, outrage, resentment, wrath, exasperation, indignation, vexation, acrimony, animosity, annoyance, irritability, hostility, and, perhaps at the extreme, pathological hatred and violence.
2. *Sadness:* grief, sorrow, cheerlessness, gloom, melancholy, self-pity, loneliness, dejection, despair, and, when pathological, severe depression.
3. *Fear:* anxiety, apprehension, nervousness, concern, consternation, misgiving, wariness, qualm, edginess, fright, terror; as a psychopathology, phobia and panic.
4. *Enjoyment:* happiness, joy, relief, contentment, bliss, delight, amusement, pride, sensual pleasure, thrill, rapture, gratification, satisfaction, euphoria, whimsy, ecstasy, and at the far edge, mania.
5. *Love:* acceptance, friendliness, trust, kindness, affinity, devotion, adoration,

infatuation, and agape.

6. *Surprise:* shock, astonishment, amazement, and wonder.
7. *Disgust:* contempt, disdain, scorn, abhorrence, aversion, distaste, and revulsion.
8. *Shame:* guilt, embarrassment, chagrin, remorse, humiliation, regret, mortification, and contrition.

MULTICULTURAL EMOTIONS. Dr. Paul Ekman has discovered that the facial expressions for at least four main emotions (fear, anger, sadness, enjoyment) are recognized in cultures around the world, suggesting their universality (Goleman, 1975).

EMOTIONAL GAMES

Emotions serve many purposes. One of the ways we can use emotions is to play psychological games. Unfortunately, many of the games people play are played unconsciously and are self-defeating, maladaptive, and hurtful to others. The following are examples of how we sometimes use emotions to manipulate, punish, control, or otherwise derive some conscious or unconscious psychological payoff.

ANGER

• To manipulate, control, or force others into our models of how things should be.
• To punish people who do not follow our models of how things should be.
• To push people away when they violate our "space" or "rights."
• Some people will use anger to push people away who are approaching their intimacy zones. This is a common strategy for individuals with a "border line personality disorder."
• To justify an extra-marital affair, a spouse may manufacture anger at their spouse.
• To generate energy in order to motivate ourselves to action (e.g. sports). Watch some of the top temperamental tennis players during the next U.S. Open tennis tournament.

BOREDOM

• To demonstrate that we are not sufficiently entertained and that we want another person to take responsibility for entertaining us. "It's your responsibility to make my "here-and-now" more interesting. Entertain me."

Common among college students in the classroom, especially undergraduate students, who have been raised on fast-paced multimedia environments.
- To demonstrate our boredom around others can be a passive ploy to encourage people to change what they are currently doing and do something else that we find more entertaining and interesting. Boredom reflects a failure to take responsibility for creating one's own entertainment and satisfaction with life.

GUILT

- To punish self.
- To prevent others from getting angry at us (e.g. "Look I'm already aware that I screwed up and I'm upset with myself. So you don't have to get angry with me I'm already punishing myself)."
- To defy expectations or obligations, after you've made a commitment to self or others to do something. Guilt can then be expressed to prevent others or self from getting angry with us.
- To demonstrate to self or others our good morals or intentions, even though on this occasion we failed to demonstrate them.

There are many emotional games people play either consciously or unconsciously. As we become aware of them we can then choose to continue playing them, knowing that they are self-defeating and seldom increase positive, loving, and nourishing relationships or we can stop our psychological game playing and develop more authentic and rewarding relationships.

Another recommendation in working with the emotional aspect of our Buttons is to fully experience or increase the intensity of emotions being triggered.

EMOTIONAL AMPERAGE

Another part of the third step is to fully experience or increase the intensity of the emotions associated with the Button that was pushed. As Keyes (1975) explains, "since much of your emotional programming was put into you through shock, pain, crying, and suffering, remember that it helps to *consciously build up your present pain, crying, and suffering* so that you can rapidly wipe out this programming" (p. 107).

Hoehn-Saric (1978) provides experimental evidence which supports the clinical observation that emotional arousal is an important ingredient in attitude change. "These results suggest that heightened arousal under conditions of cognitive disorganization helps to unfreeze an attitude, but cognitive reorganization and a supportive environment are needed to change the attitude and to retain it in the new frame" (p. 105).

Since many of our Buttons were associated with intense emotions when they became registered in our minds, it helps to consciously generate the strongest emotional energy possible to increase the electrochemical voltage to affect deep-seated programming associated with the limbic system of our old brain. For example, one day my daughter missed her first class period in high school on the last day of the Fall semester because her ride to school was late. Because she was late, she missed the end of the semester examination that counts for half her grade in her first course. She made it to school on time to take the next exam in the next course. A school official called me and informed me that my daughter had missed her exam. She said that my daughter would be allowed to make up the exam either during the Christmas holidays or at the beginning of next semester, *if* the teacher of the first course agrees. My daughter and this particular teacher do not get along and this incident just added more fuel to the fire.

The teacher did not allow my daughter to take the make-up exam. This event triggered one of my control Buttons. I have this model in my mind that my daughter makes it to school on time, doesn't miss any exams, performs well on the exam, and doesn't further antagonize any teachers with whom she doesn't get along. The reality of the situation didn't fit my model of how my daughter's high school days should go. I was attached, that is, I have a Button related to my model of how my daughter's school behavior is supposed to go. I became angry first at the Button-Pushers (i.e. my daughter missing the exam) and then at the rigid inflexible teacher caught up in her right and wrong models. Then as I became more conscious, instead of unconsciously reacting, I was able to redirect my anger at my Buttons related to my expectation of my daughter and her teacher's school behavior. By identifying and exaggerating my anger and directing it towards my Buttons that were causing my anger I was able to let go of my attachment to my expectations related to this school incident.

After freeing myself from my need to control Button in the above example I was able to realize the bigger picture and process this event from a more centered, conscious, and aware place. In the final analysis, I wanted to get back into a loving, caring, and nourishing relationship with my daughter. And I needed to get free from my Button that was creating a separating emotion (i.e. anger) in order to resume a more loving relationship with her. I looked at my priorities and asked myself, "What is more important, my daughter's performance in one class in high school or maintaining a close, loving, and nourishing father-daughter relationship?" I opted for the loving nourishing relationship with my daughter. I realize it doesn't have to be an either/or situation. But I have given my daughter the traditional father-daughter talk explaining the reasons why high school performance and grade point averages are important, and she still chooses to take a nontraditional career and life path. I have decided to love her no matter which path she chooses to take. I know she has a beautiful, free, and loving spirit, honors all life forms (e.g. she's a vegetarian), has an exceptional talent in music (i.e. singing), art, dance, massage, and energy work.

Unfortunately, these are not attributes valued by most school systems which tend to value a cognitive, rational, linear, analytical mode of teaching, learning, and knowledge. However, with these and many other positive attributes I know she will mature into a beautiful adult who will continue to be valued by her family, friends, and society in general with the right encouragement and nourishing support from her family, friends, and a few understanding, sympathetic, and supporting teachers.

My daughter was so dissatisfied with her high school experience that she passed her GED exam at the local community college, skipped her junior and senior years of high school, and began attending college at age 16. She learned about this educational option on her own by talking to friends and staff at the local community college. She has the full support of her mother and I for taking this shortcut to college. She successfully completed one year of college and then decided to leave at age 17 for California to attend a massage therapy school that included body and energy work. She graduated and became certified as a massage therapist in California.

WELCOME YOUR FEELINGS

Greet all of your feelings, instead of ignoring or suppressing some of them. All of your feelings are okay. *Acting* on some feelings may not be okay. Take responsibility for your feelings as they are yours and yours alone.

Encounter your feelings, especially your unpleasant stress-producing ones, and they can become your teachers for lessons that you need here-and-now for your personal growth. Many of your feelings will be related to the core beliefs listed earlier in step number two (chapters 5-10). Identifying and expressing your feelings helps you free yourself from your Buttons. Working with your feelings can also help you discover your creativity and help you work through interpersonal problems. You can also generate intense emotional energy to place new life-enhancing messages into your mind. Powerful and intense emotions are an important ingredient in attitudinal change.

CONNECTING THE EMOTIONS TO BUTTONS

Connecting the feelings to the event which triggered them is not unique to the Button Therapy model and is emphasized in some other therapeutic and personal growth systems including Psychoanalysis (Freud, 1959),

Primal Therapy (Holden, 1975), and Scientology (Hubbard, 1950). Connecting the feelings to the event that triggered them is an important part of Button therapy. Instead of just identifying and releasing your feelings (i.e. catharsis) from an activated Button, use the energy generated from your emotions to free yourself from your Button that triggered the feelings. For example, if you have a flat tire going to work and become angry, you might say to yourself, "Darn. I am really angry right now because I'm attached to a model in my head that says I get from my home to work with no problems. However, here and now my car has a flat tire. Do I continue to cling to my model of a problem-free trip from home to work and continue to experience anger, or do I let go of my attachment and associated anger and put my energy into fixing the flat tire? I think I'll quit ruining my here and now experience with negative emotions, which isn't helping me or the situation, get back into a better space, and get on with the task of changing the tire."

After you become *aware* of the stress from an activated *Button* (step 1), identify the Buttons being pushed (step 2), and *emotions* (step 4) associated with the Buttons, the next step is to determine the *motivational states* (step 4) associated with your Buttons.

CHAPTER TWELVE

MODELS OF MOTIVATIONAL STATES

The first thing in my teacher's book, the first thing he ever wrote on his slate (because he was silent) was:
> *Desire is a trap*
> *Desire-lessness is moksha (liberation)*
> *Desire is the creator*
> *Desire is the destroyer*
> *Desire is the universe*
And: That applies to the physical plane, the astral plane, and the causal plane.

Baba Ram Dass
BE HERE NOW

THERE ARE MANY counseling theories and related counseling approaches helpful in exploring and understanding motivational states associated with our Buttons. Some counseling and related resources particularly helpful in understanding our motivations for thoughts, emotions, behaviors include Transactional Analysis, Rational-Emotive Behavioral Therapy, Ken Keyes' Living Love System, Abraham Maslow's heirarchy of needs, the seven chakras from Yoga, and the six motivational states from the Button Therapy model.

TRANSACTIONAL ANALYSIS

Transactional Analysis (TA) provides a model to identify, explore, and understand how we develop our scripts, models, and "parental" messages and injunctions that we carry around in our minds. Through "redecision" work, TA also provides a method to modify or eliminate selected "parent" messages, injunctions, and life scripts. Some resources for working with the transactional analysis model and techniques are found in the recommended reading section under "Transactional Analysis" at the end of this book.

RATIONAL-EMOTIVE BEHAVIOR THERAPY

Rational-emotive behavior therapy (REBT) is another helpful model to explore our inner programming. REBT is particularly helpful in examining our beliefs and determining whether they are rational or irrational. Irrational beliefs wreak havoc in our lives and REBT provides a model to identify and dispute irrational beliefs.

KEN KEYES' LIVING LOVE SYSTEM

Another model, which places less emphasis on the rational analysis of how our programming and Buttons developed and more emphasis on determining present centers of consciousness in our "here and now," is found in Ken Keyes's (1975) conception of the "seven centers of consciousness:"

1. Security center
2. Sensation center
3. Power center
4. Love center
5. Cornucopia center
6. Conscious-awareness center
7. Cosmic consciousness center

The Ken Keyes system of personal growth has practical methods to help people become free of their "addictive demands." Ken Keyes' books, videos, and audiotapes related to cognitive interventions, personal growth, and spiritual development are described in the recommended reading section.

ABRAHAM MASLOW'S HIERARCHY OF NEEDS

Abraham Maslow's hierarchy of needs is another excellent model from which to identify and understand our motivational states. Maslow believed that humans are motivated by a number of basic needs that are species-wide, apparently unchanging, and genetic or instinctual in origin.

According to Maslow (1968) it is a basic or instinctoid need if:

1. Its absence breeds illness
2. Its presence prevents illness
3. Its restoration cures illness
4. Under certain (very complex) free choice situations, it is preferred by the deprived person over other satisfactions
5. It is found to be inactive, at a low ebb, or functionally absent in the healthy person (p. 22)

These needs include:

"BASIC NEEDS"
- Physiological needs such as air, water, food, shelter, sleep, and sex.
- Safety and security.
- Love and belongingness.
- Self-esteem and esteem by others.

"GROWTH NEEDS"
- Meaningfulness, self sufficiency, effortless, playfulness, richness, simplicity, order, justice, completion, necessity, perfection, individuality, aliveness, beauty, goodness, and truth. (Goble, 1971, p. 52)

According to Maslow (1968), "the single holistic principle that binds together the multiplicity of human motives is the tendency for a new and higher need to emerge as the lower need fulfills itself by being sufficiently gratified" (p. 55). Thus, it becomes difficult to work on the higher "growth" needs when we are preoccupied with getting or keeping a job in order to earn money to pay for rent, utilities, and food. "So far as motivational status is concerned, healthy people have sufficiently gratified their basic needs for safety, belongingness, love, respect, and self-esteem so that they are motivated primarily by trends to self-actualization (defined as ongoing actualization of potentials, capacities and talents, as fulfillment of mission (or call, fate, destiny, or vocation), as a fuller knowledge of, and acceptance of, the person's own intrinsic nature, as an unceasing trend toward unity, integration or synergy within the person)" (Maslow, 1968, p. 25).

THE SEVEN CHAKRAS IN YOGA

Yoga provides the oldest model from which to view our motivational states. Yoga is a very complex and extensive science. "It [Yoga] includes a science of the body, an understanding of the energy level which governs the body's functions, a study of the mind and higher states of consciousness as well as a whole philosophy of the structure and nature of the universe" (Rama, Ballentine & Ajaya, 1976, p. 216). "The aim of all Yoga practice is to achieve truth wherein the individual soul identifies itself with the supreme soul or God. To do this, it has to transcend different vehicles or bodies of the soul, which bring individual or self-consciousness" (Vishnudevananda, 1960, p. 6).

CHAKRAS
"A chakra is a spinning vortex of energy created within ourselves by the interpenetration of consciousness and the physical body. Through this combination, chakras become centers of activity for the reception, assimilation, and transmission of life energies. Uniting the chakras is what we experience as the

'self.' It is through our chakras that our self grows and changes and interacts with the world" (Judith, 1994, p. 1). There are seven primary chakras. In addition, there are many minor chakras such as the ones in our hands and feet. "Some Hatayogis hold that there are forty-nine chakras while the ancient yogis taught that there are 144 chakras" (Sivananda, 1957, p. 98).

"Chakras are centers of spiritual energy that are located in the astral body. They have corresponding centers in the physical body, which are known as plexuses" (Vishnudevananda, 1960, p.296). The chakra positions correspond, in the physical body, to points along the spinal cord and affect major nerve ganglia, glands of the endocrine system, and various bodily processes, such as breathing, digesting, or procreating. These centers are all in vertical line when we sit erect. This is why it is important to sit erect during meditation. Within each of these chakra centers can be seen the relationship between certain aspects of the physical world, the energy system, the mind, and higher consciousness (Judith, 1994; and Rama, Ballentine & Ajaya, 1976). See Table 15 for a summary of the location and associated life functions of the seven primary chakras.

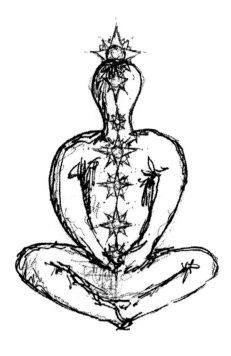

TABLE 15

THE SEVEN CHAKRAS IN YOGA

1. THE ROOT (ANAL) CHAKRA
- Self-survival
- Grounding
- Fear and Paranoia

2. THE GENITAL CHAKRA (SEAT OF LIFE)
- Sensuality, pleasure and sexuality
- Survival of species

3. THE SOLAR PLEXUS CHAKRA
- Power, will, and control
- Domination and submission
- Inferiority complex

4. THE HEART CHAKRA
- Love and emotion
- Empathy and compassion
- Balance

5. THE THROAT CHAKRA
- Communication
- Nurturance
- Creativity

6. THE THIRD EYE CHAKRA
- Intuition and clairvoyance
- Introspection
- Imagination

7. THE CROWN CHAKRA
- Understanding and knowing
- Unity with God consciousness
- Highest state of consciousness

Adapted from Rama, Ballentine & Ajaya (1976) and Judith (1994).

The Button Therapy Book: How to Work on Your Buttons and the Button-Pushers in Your Life by Lloyd R. Goodwin, Jr.
© 2002.Published by Trafford Publishing. www.trafford.com

Malfunctioning Chakras

When a chakra is closed or overactive and out of balance with the other chakras, health problems can develop. Mental and physical health disorders are related to the areas associated with the malfunctioning chakra(s). According to Barbara Brennan (1988), a contemporary healer and expert in chakras, auras, and energy fields:

> Most of us react to unpleasant experiences by blocking our feeling and stopping a great deal of our natural energy flow. This affects the development and maturation of the chakras, resulting in inhibition of a fully balanced psychological func-tion...Whenever a person blocks whatever experience he is having, he in turn blocks his chakras, which eventually become disfigured. The chakras become 'blocked,' clogged with stag-nated energy, spin irregularly, or backward (counterclockwise) and even, in the case of disease, become severely distorted or torn...When the chakras are functioning normally, each will be 'open,' spinning clockwise to metabolize the particular ener-gies needed from the universal field. A clockwise spin draws energy from the UEF [Universal Energy Field] into the chakra...When the chakra spins counterclockwise, the current is flowing outward from the body, thus interfering with metabolism...Most people I observe have three or four chakras spinning counterclockwise at any one time. (p. 71)

For example, the Power (third) chakra represents our "get up and go," our action, our will, our vitality, and sense of personal power. On the physical plane, the third chakra is associated with metabolism, the process whereby we turn food (matter) into energy and action. Digestion and stomach troubles, hypoglycemia, diabetes, ulcers, or addiction to stimulants, such as caffeine, are all related to malfunctioning of the third chakra (Judith, 1994).

> When the third chakra is closed down, one may feel tired, afraid, shaky, quiet, or withdrawn. There is a fear of taking risks, confronting people or issues, taking charge, and with all this, a lack of energy. There may be too much seriousness and not enough laughter, ease or fun, all of which help the third chakra open and relax...If the chakra is too open, then we have a kind of bully archetype-someone who also needs to be in control, to dominate, to seek after power, prestige, ambi-tion...[and] can make a person narcissistically self-centered. (Judith, 1994, p. 26)

Six Motivational States in the Button Therapy Model

The six motivational states in the Button Therapy model were adapted primarily from Ken Keyes' Living Love System, Abraham Maslow's hierarchy of needs, and the seven chakras in Yoga. Each of these counseling and personal growth systems provides a model from which to view motivations for our thoughts, emotions, and behaviors. This fourth step of the Six-Step Button Therapy Method allows for the accommodation of any of the "motivational" models presented above. You may find yourself gravitating to one of these models, or combination of these models, for the fourth step instead of the six motivational states from the Button Therapy model. Use whichever model of motivational states that resonates with you.

Six Motivational States

1. Safety and Security

2. Pleasure and Sensation-Seeking

3. Control and Power

4. Love and Acceptance

5. Personal Growth and Self-Actualization

6. Spiritual and Transcendental

Chapter 13 describes the six motivational states from the
Button Therapy model.

---◎---

SIX MOTIVATIONAL STATES

The mind is its own place, and in it self can make a Heav'n of Hell, a Hell of Heav'n.

John Milton
PARADISE LOST

AS YOU EXPLORE AND WORK on your Buttons, it helps to become aware of the motivational states associated with these Buttons. After you become aware that one of your Buttons has been pushed (step 1), identify your Button (step 2), identify and own the triggered emotions associated with your Button (step 3), the *fourth step* of the Six-Step BT Method is to become aware of the motivational states associated with your Button.

This chapter provides a description of the six motivational states in the Button Therapy model. This will help you determine the motivational states associated with your Buttons and troublesome cognitions.

1. SAFETY AND SECURITY

Security is mostly a superstition.
It does not exist in nature nor do children as a whole experience it.
Avoiding danger is no safer in the long run than outright exposure.
Life is either a daring adventure, or nothing.
To keep our faces toward change and behave like free spirits in the presence of fate is strength undefeatable.

Helen Keller
LET US HAVE FAITH

The following tend to be associated with our safety and security needs:

- Securing food, water, air, and shelter
- Self-survival
- Safety and security
- Egotism and narcissism
- Unsettled, not grounded, off-balance, and lack of stability

- Excessive need for order and routines and avoid novelty
- Eating disorders or preoccupation with food
- Preoccupation with material things, possessions, and money
- Lonely and isolated
- Low energy, tired, and excessive sleep
- **FEELINGS** - insecurity, fear, paranoia, worry, anxiety, panic, hopelessness, shame, embarrassment, and envy.
- **WORK ROLES** - Includes long-tenured governmental workers, teachers, and nontenured university professors.

     INSECURITY. Securing the basic necessities of life such as food, water, shelter, air, and sleep are required to survive and sustain life. Much of our behavior from this motivational state is directed toward securing these necessities. We also develop and protect our basic sense of self and self-concept from this motivational state. Feelings of fear, paranoia, anxiety, and insecurity are triggered when we think our physical or psychological basic "necessities" are jeopardized. Have you ever felt insecure because somebody has verbally attacked you at work? Have you ever felt insecure when you received a low grade on a test in school? Some college students even overreact when they receive a grade of C on a test when they are accustomed to grades of As and Bs. Sometimes, students are so insecure and overreactive they even contemplate dropping out of school after receiving just one test grade that was lower then expected. Anytime someone confronts the view we hold of ourselves, our ego defense mechanisms may be called into action to protect us. When our self-perception is threatened we may withdraw and shore up our protective walls or become aggressive and attack in order to neutralize the stressor or Button-Pusher. Excessive preoccupation with self can result in self-defeating beliefs and behavior that is egotistical and narcissistic.

     Feeling safe and secure is also related to feeling settled, grounded, stable, and balanced. Relying on predictable and stable routines, and avoiding novel and unplanned activities are usually behaviors originating from the safety and security motivational state. Some people live out their entire lives in the same old patterns and routines clinging to the known and familiar, and fear making any major change in their lives.

     EATING DISORDERS. Preoccupation with food and food addictions are sometimes related to maladaptive attempts to be safe and secure. A basic motivation associated with eating disorders is a fear of becoming fat. There is such a concern about self-perception and body image that some individuals will resort to self-starvation (anorexia nervosa) or bingeing and purging (bulimia). People with eating disorders often have conflicted issues related to the "security and sensation" and the "control and power" motivational states. When we spend time securing food, material things, and money we are often motivated by our need to feel safe and secure.

ISOLATION AND LONELINESS. The focus on accumulating an abundance of material wealth can become excessive and an unhealthy compulsive preoccupation in life. Efforts to make ourselves feel safe and secure can be poorly handled to the point that we try to manipulate and control other people to help us achieve our security, or we fight them because they threaten our material possessions or egos. Constant attempts to control and manipulate other people often results in isolation and loneliness.

ENERGY DRAINERS. It takes a lot of energy to try and manipulate or force people into our scripts of how things should be so we can feel more safe and secure. Our troublesome cognitions and Buttons drain us of our energy. We can become drained of our energy, tired, and require more sleep to recharge our energy reserves when we are preoccupied with activities coming from a safety and security motivational state.

JOB LOSS. Feelings of insecurity, fear, worry, and anxiety are often triggered when our food, shelter, transportation, and jobs are threatened or lost. Loosing one's job can be devastating. Many people have much of their self-identity and self-worth associated with their work roles. For these people, a loss of their job means a loss of self-identity, self-worth, and the breadwinner role in the family. These losses along with the loss of income and the ability to provide for basic necessities for self and family has resulted in intense emotional pain and suffering. Suicide has also resulted from the accumulation of these types of losses, especially losing one's job. The loss of a job can also result in anger and paranoia resulting in homicidal actions towards those individuals thought responsible for the loss of job (e.g. work place violence). The threat of a loss of a job can also be extremely anxiety provoking. The anxiety and tension permeates the air and are so thick you can cut it with a knife in an organization that is going through a major reorganization or downsizing. In this era of corporate takeovers and downsizing this source of anxiety and stress is prevalent and very real.

INSECURITY FEELINGS. Feelings of insecurity can be triggered by many life situations including having bad breath or body odor when we are around others, especially someone to whom we are attracted. Or how about wondering if your family will be able to survive in the manner they have become accustomed if you unexpectedly die? Corporations have done enough research to know we are motivated to do many things because of our security needs. It is no accident that the mouthwash, underarm deodorant, and insurance industries are so numerous and successful. The world of business has learned how to push our safety and security Buttons and trigger feelings of insecurity with their advertisements. For example, a man unexpectedly meets the woman of his dreams in an elevator where they are up close and personal. The man becomes anxious and wonders whether his deodorant is working. The advertisement then provides us with the solution for resolving our insecure feelings in up-close-and-personal encounters with the opposite sex: their product.

WORK ROLES. Some work roles such as governmental employees, teachers, and university professors, especially nontenured faculty, often seem to attract individuals with high safety and security needs. Individuals remain in these jobs for much of their professional lives because of the relative security that accompanies these types of jobs. In these types of jobs there is much talk of security related topics such as probationary periods, seniority, and tenure. Rumors of reorganization, downsizing, and program closings can trigger security Buttons resulting in extreme stress and anxiety among the employees in any type of organization, including governmental and educational workers.

2. PLEASURE AND SENSATION-SEEKING

I couldn't help it. I can resist everything except temptation.
Oscar Wilde
LADY WINDERMERE'S FAN

The following tend to be associated with our desire for sensual pleasure:

- Psychoactive drugs
- Sex
- Music, movies, and plays
- Feelings
- Eating food
- Exercise
- Relaxation
- Reproduction and survival of species
- **FEELINGS** - intense emotions or "stuffed" emotions, boredom, frustra-tion, tension, disappointment, and jealousy.
- **WORK ROLES** - Includes musicians, rescue workers (e.g. paramedics), chefs, wine tasters, race car drivers, "extreme" athletes, licit and illicit drug dealers, sex industry performers and distributors, and prostitutes.

Most people enjoy the sensual pleasure derived from a variety of activities. For example, many people enjoy touching or being touched by a loved one or petting their cat or dog. Many individuals increasingly seek the therapeutic touch of the massage therapist. People are learning about the pleasant sensation of therapeutic touch as well as the pleasant feelings and therapeutic effects associated with smell in aromatherapy.

But, as Sobel and Ornstein (1996) point out:

> Today many of us aren't getting our minimum daily require-
> ment of sensory pleasures—pleasures that are vital to our
> health and well-being...many sensual pleasures we're designed
> to experience are thwarted in the modern world. We miss the
> glory of the sunrise and sunset as we hustle in our commute;
> we miss the stars in our city-lit nights. The synthetic foods in
> our markets often bear little resemblance to the natural foods
> we were built to eat. Our ancestors heard the pleasant sound of
> a stream and the wind rustling in the trees, but for us it's the
> din of traffic, jackhammers, and deafening leaf blowers. (p. 57)

DRUGS, SEX AND ROCK-N-ROLL

There are many experiences that trigger "peak experiences."
"Apparently most people, or almost all people, have peak experiences, or
ecstasies...I want to report that the two easiest ways of getting peak experiences...are through music and through sex" (Maslow, 1972, p. 175).

When our thoughts and behavior are directed toward drugs, sex, and
music we are most likely coming from this second motivational state.

PSYCHOACTIVE DRUGS

When we use psychoactive drugs such as coffee (caffeine), soft drinks
(caffeine), tobacco (nicotine), alcohol, marijuana, hallucinogens, cocaine, heroin, and other psychoactive drugs we are triggering the pleasure centers of our
brains. If, after repeated use, we become addicted to these drugs, the primary
motivation for their use may be to avoid the uncomfortable sensations of withdrawal. We are probably motivated from our pleasure and sensation-seeking
motivational state when we play or listen to music and watch movies and plays.
Many musicians combine psychoactive drug use with their musical activities. If
you've ever smoked marijuana or taken hallucinogens and listened to music or
engaged in sexual activity you most likely have an experiential knowledge of
what this motivational state is about.

SEX

It's been so long since I made love I can't remember who gets tied up.
                                                        Joan Rivers

Sex is one of the most common ways we trigger our pleasure centers in
our brains. One survey cited in *New Woman* magazine found 54 percent of men
think sexual thoughts every day or several times a day compared with only 19

percent of women. What was surprising in this survey was that 67 percent of women say they think about sex as little as a few times a month (Jackson, 1996). Another study indicates that the typical male college student thinks about sex about seven times a day, while his female counterpart enjoys about five such thoughts (Doskoch, 1998). Our thoughts about sex don't stop when we enter the work force. A survey of 1,479 Canadians found that 35 percent fantasize about having sex with a co-worker, and 18 percent actually had an affair with a colleague (Psychology Today, March/April 1999).

Researchers studying sexual fantasies confirm that almost everyone has them. About five percent of men and women say they have never had a sexual fantasy. We begin fantasizing between the ages of 11 and 13. Sexual fantasies are most common in teens and young adults and become less common with increasing age. The sexual scenario we most often imagine is ordinary, non-kinky intercourse with a past or current lover. Other common fantasy scenarios include scenes of sexual irresistibility because of their sheer seductive power and animal magnetism. Dominance and submission fantasies are also common. In these, sexual power is expressed either through sadomasochistic ritualistic activities or through rape fantasies. One study reports that 44 percent of men have had fantasies of dominating a partner. Other studies found that 51 percent of women fantasized about being forced to have sex, while a third imagined: "I'm a slave who must obey a man's every wish." Interestingly, women report less jealousy than men do if their partners' fantasies involve another person. Also, researchers find little difference in the fantasies of heter- and homosexuals-except in the gender of participants (Doskoch, 1995).

Much of our behavior is sexually motivated. When you get dressed do you pick out clothes to wear that will be attractive to the opposite sex (or same sex if you are gay)? Have you ever interacted with someone primarily because you enjoy his or her physical appearance (i.e. body)? Have you ever fantasized what someone would look like naked or what it would be like to have sex with him or her? All of these activities are most likely coming from the pleasure and sensation-seeking motivational state.

Music

According to one survey, some people find music more thrilling than sex. Music and other sounds are a powerful part of our lives. Music can powerfully alter our moods, emotions, and physiology. The right music at the right time brings us joy or serenity, soothes our frazzled nerves, or lifts us up when we're feeling down (Sobel & Ornstein, 1996). Some researchers claim listening to music will improve math and science skills. "Proponents say that music therapy can be used to increase the brain's ability to perform tasks that require visualizing spatial relationships between objects and doing tasks in an orderly sequence. These skills are used in math and science" (Yu, 1999).

Also, playing a musical instrument and singing are excellent ways to relieve stress, alter our moods, and experience pleasure.

FEELINGS

Feelings can be very sensual. Have you ever had the desire to cry, partially because it feels good to have a good cathartic cry every now and then? How about going to a scary movie to experience some intense feelings of anxiety, fear, and shock? Have you ever turned a minor annoyance into a full-blown anger outburst just to let it all hang out and experience the intensity of these feelings? Fully experiencing intense emotions can be a sensually satisfying experience. Sex, psychoactive drugs, hormones, and music can also facilitate experiencing intense feelings.

FEELING AVOIDERS. We can also go toward the other end of the emotional continuum and avoid our feelings. Do people experience you as cold and aloof? Are you in touch with your feelings? Can you identify and express your feelings appropriately? Or, do you express your feelings inappropriately and make yourself and people around you uncomfortable (e.g. anger outbursts directed toward your Button-Pushers)? Do you rely on psychoactive drugs to alter your mood and feelings? Many alcohol and other psychoactive drug abusers have learned to avoid unpleasant feelings through the use of psychoactive drugs. Recovering psychoactive drug abusers often need to learn how to deal with feelings they haven't fully experienced in a long time because of their drug use. Feelings of the recovering drug abuser begin to surface in a non-drugged state during the recovery process and oftentimes become frightening and overwhelming to the newly sober individual.

The most common way people avoid their feelings is probably because they are not living in their here-and-now. As Drs. Sobel and Ornstein (1996) point out, "We are often only vaguely aware of what's going on. To fully enjoy your senses, you have to pay attention. Since we often go on automatic pilot, focus on the pleasures your senses can bring. Mindlessness is the enemy of sensual pleasure. Stay tuned in to the moment (p. 58)."

PLEASURE PHOBICS

There is a strong anti-pleasure bias in medicine, psychology, and the mainstream populace in this country. Some people believe they should not experience pleasure and that experiencing pleasure is not healthy. There is a great amount of information about the health hazards of pleasure and a scarcity of details about its health-promoting effects. Clearly, some behaviors that trigger pleasure are injurious to health (e.g. tobacco and cocaine smoking). Also, some pleasure-seeking behaviors can become addictive compulsions, destroying lives, relationships, and the ability to experience pleasure itself. However, there are also healthy ways to experience pleasure and derive its health benefits. "The important point is that worrying too much about anything - including calories, salt, cancer, and cholesterol - can rob your life of vitality, and that living optimistically, with pleasure, zest, and commitment enriches if not lengthens life... feeling good pays off not only in immediate enjoyment but also in better health" (Sobel & Ornstein, 1998, p. 2).

WORK SETTINGS

The types of jobs that people tend to gravitate to with strong pleasure and sensation-seeking motivations include musicians, rescue workers, licit and illicit drug dealers, wine tasters, sex industry performers and distributors, and prostitutes. Individuals with high sensation-seeking or thrill-seeking needs tend to gravitate to such vocations as rescue workers. For some EMTs or paramedics, the adrenaline rush of an alarm bell going off signaling the call to duty, the hurried ambulance ride, and the arrival to the scene of a gory accident can make the day for those individuals with high sensation-seeking and thrill-seeking (T) personality characteristics. These high T-personality individuals are sometimes disappointed when a rescue call is just for an elderly person experiencing cardiac distress. What really makes the day for a T-personality is a messy car wreck with life threatening injuries and lots of blood. There are often many other motivations for gravitating to, EMT and paramedic jobs besides a desire to experience an adrenaline rush and intense sensations, but sensation-seeking is often part of the initial motivation for these types of jobs. The complex psychodynamics and other possible career motivations of prostitutes, musicians and rescue workers is beyond the scope of this book.

3. CONTROL AND POWER

For my own healing, I will only work on myself. It's up to you to work on yourself to reclaim your own loving true-self. If I am in conflict with you, and I blame your repressed unconscious programming, I will just keep myself stuck in my own false-self. The most helpful thing I can do for both of us is to work only on myself!

Ken Keyes, Jr.
YOUR ROAD MAP TO LIFELONG HAPPINESS

The following tend to be associated with the desire to control self and others:

- Control and power
- Aggression and bullying
- Domination and submission
- Manipulation and conning
- Authoritarian personality
- Critical and judgmental
- A "know it all" attitude
- Competitiveness (e.g. athletes, debaters)
- **FEELINGS** - anger, irritation, resentment, hostility, hate, impatience, inferiority, and fear of loss.
- **WORK ROLES** - Includes attorneys, politicians, judges, administrators, salespeople who work on commission (e.g. telemarketers), and health care professionals.

We are sometimes motivated to control others in our environment. Excessive energy from this motivational state can result in aggression and bullying in attempts to force people to follow our model of how things should be. Our attempts to control, dominate, and power-trip others often results in resistance and defensiveness from those we are trying to control. This can result in arguments and uncomfortable feelings and negative energy polluting the air.

Sometimes we abandon the frontal approach and attempt to get people to do our bidding through more subtle manipulation and conning. Some people are really slick and manipulate through extreme kindness, submission, and massaging other peoples' egos: The "you can catch more flies with honey" approach to getting what you want.

Feelings of frustration, irritation, and anger can result from the inability to impose one's will on others. We can also develop feelings of inferiority if we are consistently unable to achieve certain goals.

COMPETITIVENESS

Much of our competitiveness comes from the desire for control, power, and domination. We want to win and be on top. Even if we can't personally win competitions we can identify with winning teams and vicariously be a winner. Notice how peoples' egos become temporarily boosted and they experience feelings of elation when "their" athletic team wins a competition. Also, notice how these same people can become withdrawn, deflated, and disappointed when "their" team loses. Individuals can alternate between being elated, energetic, and talkative — to being deflated, depressed, and withdrawn, all because "their" team won or lost.

Partially because of this powerful influence of athletic events on our mood and egos, our society has placed an incredible value on celebrity athletes. A much higher value is placed on celebrity athletes than almost any other activity in our society. Some star athletes earn annual salaries in the millions of dollars. Many football coaches at major universities earn two and three times the annual salary of university presidents who earn two and three times the salary of university professors. The prioritization of what we value as a society is very interesting and unsettling.

WORK ROLES

The work roles of professional athletes, politicians, judges, administrators, and salespeople who work on commissions appear to attract individuals primarily motivated by the desire for control and power. Also, the avoidance of certain jobs is sometimes motivated by control needs. For example, some individuals have declined promotions to administrative positions at work because they choose not to assume a control position over others or they are insecure or afraid to have control over other people.

4. LOVE AND ACCEPTANCE

...love your enemies, bless those who curse you, do good to those who hate you...
Jesus

❧

Just as a mother would protect her only child at the risk of her own life, even so, cultivate a boundless heart towards all beings.
Let your thoughts of boundless love pervade the whole world.
Buddha

The motivational state of love and acceptance tends to be associated with:

- Acceptance and love of self and others
- Giving and caring
- Nourishing energy which attracts people and animals

- Intimacy
- Healing
- Selfless service
- Understanding and empathy
- Compassion
- Peaceful, tranquil, serene, content, and relaxed
- Balanced, harmonious, and happy
- Sense of belonging
- Responsible
- **FEELINGS** - Love, compassion, and happiness.
- **WORK ROLES** - Includes healers, helping professionals, teachers, and hospice workers.

Some of our actions and thoughts are motivated by love. Most of us want to be accepted and loved. And most of us want to accept and love others and ourselves. Actualizing this state of acceptance and love often entails learning how to separate people from their actions. Behind the annoying personality traits, insensitive and maladaptive behaviors, and unpleasant emotional outbursts there is that universal US place where we are all human and lovable. At the same time, we are currently "perfect," given the current state of our awareness and self-actualization. Nobody is born perfect or completely self-actualized.

PERSONAL GROWTH CONTINUUM

Dysfunctional < ________Normal____/_____ > Self-Actualized
Illness   Wellness

We are all on a personal growth continuum with the potential for total psychological dysfunctionality and physical illness on one end and psychological self-actualization and physical wellness on the other end. Most of us hang out around a certain area on the personal growth continuum, fluctuating from one part of the continuum to another, moment to moment and day to day. We have good days when everything in our lives seems to be going well. And we have bad days when we seem to have every Button we have pushed, creating much emotional distress. Wherever we are on the personal growth continuum is ok and "perfect" for our current level of personal development.

WE ARE PERFECT

Humans are not perfect, especially when measured against some arbitrary standard established by a particular society, group, or individual. The oneness space that can be found in all humans is the humanness that is both imperfect and perfect. We are imperfect because we are never completely self-actualized. There are always higher levels of awareness, consciousness, and states of being to achieve. Yet, we are "perfect" because we are living, making decisions, interacting with family and others, and working from our current levels of consciousness and personal growth depending on where we are on the personal growth continuum. Given our current levels of awareness, consciousness, and number of Buttons, we are living our lives the best that we can. We can learn to separate the person with his or her "perfect" inner oneness and humanness space from his or her "imperfect" behaviors and actions. We can learn to accept and love the "perfect" inner oneness and humanness part of everyone.

LOVE AND ACCEPTANCE ENERGY

We can usually distinguish the people who are coming from an accepting and loving motivational state. They appear warm, caring, understanding, and empathic. They are nourishing and enjoyable people to be around. Also, we can usually tell when acceptance and love are not motivating peoples' thoughts and actions. They seem emotionless and cold. Sometimes people come from a very unloving motivational state and spread negative toxins in their environment. Toxic people can sometimes be viewed as having a dark cloud hovering around them. People often go to great lengths to avoid being around toxic people.

The love and acceptance motivational state is also associated with compassion. Some people can demonstrate exceptional compassion for other people still caught up in their Buttons and experiencing emotional distress. Compassionate people are usually well-liked and respected individuals.

LOVE, INTIMACY AND HEALTH

If scientists suddenly discovered a drug that was as powerful as love in creating health, it would be heralded as a medical breakthrough and marketed overnight—especially if it had as few side effects and was as inexpensive as love.

Larry Dossey, M.D.
HEALING WORDS

Abraham Maslow (1954, 1968 & 1972) has provided evidence that we need love and intimacy in our lives for healthy functioning and to progress on our evolution toward self-actualization. More recently, heart specialist Dean Ornish, M.D. (1998) has written a book titled Love & Survival: The Scientific Basis for the Healing Power of Intimacy in which he describes the many studies that have proven the healing power of love, intimacy, and relationships. In a recent interview for New Age magazine Dr. Ornish (Ostriker, 1998) states,

Love and intimacy are at the root of what makes us sick and what makes us well, what causes sadness and what brings happiness, what makes us suffer and what leads to healing...People who feel lonely, depressed, and isolated have three to five times greater rates of premature death and disease from virtually all causes compared to people who have a sense of love, connection, and community. I don't know anything in medicine, including drugs and surgery which has such a powerful impact on death and disease. Yet these are things that we generally don't learn about in our medical training and we don't value in our culture. (p. 18).

Dr. Ornish points out that people oftentimes deal with feelings of loneliness and isolation, and fill their unfulfilled love and intimacy needs with food, alcohol and other psychoactive drugs, watching TV, surfing the internet, and work. People have found numerous activities that become substitutes for intimacy, relationships, and a sense of community. Many cultures talk about the vital life force (i.e. chi, ki, prana, kundalini, shakti) that connects everyone and everything. When we cut ourselves off from this vital life force with our emotional defenses and when we isolate ourselves, we are literally cutting ourselves off from the source of life (Ostriker, 1998).

In addition, to be happy in life it is essential to give and receive love. As Ken Keyes, Jr (n.d.) states, "Your life can be successful, wealthy, prestigious and influential. But it won't be enough. You will not reach your potential for happiness unless you experience a lot of love for yourself and for other human beings" (p. 103).

5. PERSONAL GROWTH AND SELF-ACTUALIZATION

All the evidence...indicates that it is reasonable to assume in practically every human being, and certainly in almost every newborn baby, that there is an active will toward health, an impulse toward growth, or toward the actualization of human potentialities.

Abraham H. Maslow
THE FARTHER REACHES OF HUMAN NATURE

The following tend to be associated with the motivation to become a more fully functional and self-actualized person:

- Involvement with personal growth activities, holistic health, and personal counseling
- Views and experiences life holistically

- Desires to work on all aspects of self, including "Buttons"
- Enjoys life, playful, and sense of humor
- Curious and Creative
- Aliveness, spontaneity, and few inhibitions
- Insightful, aware, and conscious
- Peak experiences
- Lives in the here and now
- Sees in continuums and probabilities versus black and white (absolutes)
- Increased self-sufficiency, internal locus-of-control, individuality, courage, and resistance to societal and cultural molding
- Open-minded and receptive to feedback
- Has intimate friendships and good interpersonal skills
- Competent and high achiever
- Balanced lifestyle between family, work, personal growth activities and play
- Altruism
- Fair and just
- Honest, truthful, genuine, moral, and clear sense of values
- Environmental sensitivity
- **FEELINGS** - joy, awe, abundance, enthusiasm, excitement, gratitude, completeness, and happiness.
- **WORK ROLES** - Includes mental health professionals, clergy, teachers, and healers.

Much of our behavior is motivated by the desire to work on our personal growth and become more self-actualized. For an increasing number of people this has become an almost full-time personal quest. There are thousands of self-help books, videos, and other resources for helping us on our personal development journeys. Some people become involved in personal growth seminars, workshops, and other activities. Others join mutual-help support groups oriented to some specific problem area such as alcoholism (e.g. Alcoholics Anonymous) or divorce. There are many "new age" and related support groups that have formed around some specific personal growth approach (e.g. meditation groups) or gender (e.g. women's and men's support groups).

6. SPIRITUAL AND TRANSCENDENTAL

Every day, people are straying away from the church and going back to God.
Lenny Bruce
THE ESSENTIAL LENNY BRUCE

The following tend to be associated with the spiritual and transpersonal motivational state:

- Love and compassion
- Transcendental and transpersonal experiences
- Unity with God or higher power
- Cosmic consciousness
- Knows the Truth when encounters it
- Understanding and knowing
- Holistic perspective and sees the interrelationships between all life, energy, and the universe
- Appreciates beauty, nature, and kindness
- Purpose and meaning to life
- Increased frequency of peak experiences
- Meditation and prayer
- Conscious and aware, including the subtler energies
- Intuitive and may have psychic abilities (e.g. telepathic, sees auras, clairvoyant)
- Has well developed "crap detector"
- Wisdom
- Healing
- Views death as transition to another dimension
- **FEELINGS** - love, compassion, joy, and bliss.
- **WORK ROLES** - Includes gurus, clergy, "teachers," healers, and holistic mental and physical health care providers.

When our thoughts and actions are directed toward transcending our egos, and sense of self, in order to merge with God consciousness we are coming from the spiritual and transcendental motivational state.

TABLE 16

THE SIX MOTIVATIONAL STATES

1. **SAFETY AND SECURITY**
- Survival
- Gathering material things
- *Feelings:* Insecurity, worry, anxiety, fear, and paranoia

2. **PLEASURE AND SENSATION-SEEKING**
- Sex, drugs and rock-n-roll
- *Feelings:* Boredom, tension, and jealous

3. **CONTROL AND POWER**
- Aggression
- Domination and submission
- *Feelings:* Anger, impatience, and inferiority

4. **LOVE AND ACCEPTANCE**
- Giving, caring and nurturance
- Compassion
- *Feelings:* Love, compassion, and happiness

5. **PERSONAL GROWTH**
- Humanistic/holistic growth activities and counseling
- Open-minded, open to feedback and willing to take risks
- Introspective and creative
- *Feelings:* Joy, awe, enthusiasm, and happiness

6. **SPIRITUAL AND TRANSCENDENTAL**
- Intuitive
- Understanding and knowing
- *Feelings:* Love, compassion, peace, serene, content, joy, and bliss

The Button Therapy Book: How to Work on Your Buttons and the Button-Pushers in Your Life by Lloyd R. Goodwin, Jr.
© 2002. Published by Trafford Publishing. www.trafford.com

IN WHICH MOTIVATIONAL STATES DO YOU SPEND THE MOST TIME?

Review the six motivational states and determine which motivational states you tend to most frequently come from. Are you frequently worried about your job security and spending an inordinate time in the "safety and security" motivational state? Are you constantly thinking about sex and spending an inordinate amount of time in the "pleasure and sensation-seeking" motivational state? Are you constantly angry from constantly trying to control other peoples' beliefs and behaviors from the "control and power" motivational state? Or, perhaps you are hanging out in a peaceful "acceptance and love" motivational state with yourself and people in your environment. Maybe the majority of your time is spent consciously working on your personal growth or spiritual progress.

As part of the study of cognitions, Buttons, and motivational states referred to earlier in this book and described in Appendix C, a sample of adults were asked to rank the time they spend coming from each of the six motivational states using the Motivational States Inventory (see Appendix B). Table 17 provides a rank-order of the time spent in the six motivational states or "centers of consciousness" in a typical day with the subjects indicating that they spent the most time in the "control and power" motivational state.

TABLE 17

RANKED CENTERS OF CONSCIOUSNESS OR MOTIVATIONAL STATES

How 106 adults rank-ordered the time they are spending in the six "motivational states" or "centers of consciousness." A rank of one indicates that this sample of subjects as a whole are spending most of their time in the "Control and Power" motivational state or "center of consciousness" followed by the "Spiritual and Transcendental," etc.

Rank

1. **CONTROL AND POWER:** Spending time judging, criticizing, or trying to control other people in your life.

2. **SPIRITUAL AND TRANSCENDENTAL:** Spending time experiencing love, compassion, transcendental states, and a sense of connectedness and unity with God and all living things. Spending time on spiritual development.

3. **PLEASURE AND SENSATION-SEEKING:** Spending time seeking or con cerned with sex, food, mood altering drugs, music, and exercise.

4. **SAFETY AND SECURITY:** Spending time seeking or being concerned with such things as job, relationships, and money.

5. **LOVE AND ACCEPTANCE:** Spending time seeking or concerned with gaining and/or giving acceptance, love, and compassion.

6. **PERSONAL GROWTH AND SELF-ACTUALIZATION:** Spending time enjoying or concerned with life, feeling alive, acting spontaneously and seeking personal growth and self-actualization.

The Button Therapy Book: How to Work on Your Buttons and the Button-Pushers in Your Life by Lloyd R. Goodwin, Jr.
© 2002. Published by Trafford Publishing. www.trafford.com

MOTIVATIONAL STATES AND PERCEPTION

Everything has its beauty, but not everyone sees it.
Confucius

The quality and accuracy of our perception varies moment to moment depending upon our cognitions, emotions, motivational states, and Buttons. How we filter life events through our programming, expectations, memories, core beliefs, distorted thinking styles, defense mechanisms, and other cognitive distortions determines how we perceive ourselves and the world around us. If I am an alcoholic utilizing the defense mechanism of denial, I do not accurately perceive the consequences of my abusive drinking. I selectively perceive what I accept and screen out what I don't.

Also, our mood and emotions affect our perception. If I am depressed, I am probably selectively perceiving more of the negative aspects of my life situation and myself and not sufficiently seeing the positive aspects. If I am depressed it is difficult to get up in the morning, walk outside, and appreciate the beauty of the sunshine, trees, and plants as I get in my car to drive to work. If I were depressed I would selectively screen in more of the unpleasant aspects of my life. This is why cognitive therapy is the counseling treatment of choice for clinical depression.

MOTIVATIONAL STATES INFLUENCE WHAT WE SEE

When the highest type of men hear Tao,
They diligently practice it.
When the average type of men hear Tao,
They half believe in it.
When the lowest type of men hear Tao,
They laugh heartily at it.
Lao-Tzu
TAO TE CHING

The motivational state that we are coming from at any given moment influences our perceptions. For example, if I drive down the main street of town and I am hungry (i.e. safety and security motivational state) I will selectively perceive restaurants. I will see and smell some of them. And I will not notice or pay any attention to the bank, photo shop, or the optometrist's office. If I drive down the same Main Street and I'm horney, (i.e. pleasure and sensation-seeking motivational state) I start noticing foxy ladies. The sexier the better. That becomes the focus of my attention and the other stores and people become the "background." If I drive down Main Street and I am running for mayor (i.e. control and power motivational state), I selectively screen in places on Main Street where I can put one of my campaign posters. I'm driving down the same Main Street but I selectively perceive and pay attention to the aspects that will satisfy my wants, needs, and Buttons related to specific motivational states that I am experiencing at that particular moment.

ACTIVATED BUTTONS AFFECT PERCEPTION

Activated Buttons, especially those that trigger intense emotions like anger, fear, and jealousy, tend to dominate our consciousness and influence how we perceive our environment and ourselves. Thus the phrase, "I was so angry at her I couldn't see straight!" It's pretty hard to accurately perceive the music playing on the stereo, smell the incense burning, or notice other aspects of your world when you've just been told by your spouse that she's having an extramarital affair and your activated Button has catapulted you into a jealous rage. To the degree we eliminate our Buttons and other cognitive distortions, we increase the accuracy of our perceptions of our environment and ourselves.

MULTIPLE MOTIVATIONAL STATES

Most behaviors and activities can be approached from any of the six motivational states. For example, when we eat food primarily because we are hungry and need nutrients to survive and maintain health, we are probably coming from the "safety and security" motivational state. When we eat food primarily because it smells and tastes good and not because we are hungry, we are probably motivated by the "pleasure and sensation-seeking" motivational state. Thus the motivation for eating behavior can arise from either motivational state either singularly or in combination.

SEX AND MOTIVATIONAL STATES. Another example relates to sexual behavior. We can have sex with somebody not because we want to have sex but because we think it will make us more secure (i.e. from the "safety and security motivational state). A fifteen-year-old girl in high school may have sex with her boyfriend for fear of losing him if she doesn't "put out." Or, an adult has sex primarily because he or she simply enjoys triggering the pleasure centers of his or her brain (i.e. from the "pleasure and sensation-center" motivational state). Sex can also be experienced from the "control and power" motivational state as in a sadomasochism form of sexual encounter. There's the "controller" who derives pleasure by dominating and restraining his or her sex partner and the "controlled" who enjoys being subjugated and restrained. Sex can also be experienced by two people simultaneously from the "love and acceptance" motivational state. A person may have sex while primarily working on a sexual dysfunction such as impotence or frigidity (i.e. from the "personal growth and self-actualization" motivational state). Using sex with a partner to achieve spiritual and transcendental states can be the motivational state for some people (e.g. tantra yoga). We can also have sex from many different motivational states at the same time. We could become sexually aroused (i.e. pleasure motivational state) by being bound or handcuffed (i.e. power-tripped and controlled motivational state) to the bedposts. And we could engage in such sexual escapades because we love (i.e. love motivational state) or feel insecure and fear losing our partner (i.e. security motivational state). However, existentially, at any given moment one of the six motivational states will be primary and dominant. The motivational states may shift moment to moment but at any given moment one motivational state will be primary.

Another common example of how we can come from multiple motivational states and create havoc with society relates to the "Moral Control Patrol." The moral control patrol described in the next chapter illustrates how we can become involved, preoccupied, and even obsessed with the need to control other people's beliefs and behaviors, especially those beliefs and behaviors related to spirituality and how people derive their pleasure.

WITH WHICH MOTIVATIONAL STATES ARE MOST OF OUR BUTTONS ASSOCIATED?

One hundred and six subjects completed the *Motivational States Inventory* (see Appendix B) in the study of cognitions, Buttons, and motivational states described in Appendix C. This 106 subset of the total 293 subjects indicated that their Buttons were associated with the following rank-ordered motivational states. Their Buttons (i.e. attachments) tended to be most frequently associated with the "Love and Acceptance" motivational state, followed by "Personal Growth and Self-Actualization," "Pleasure and Sensation-Seeking," etc.:

- "Love and Acceptance"
- "Personal Growth and Self-Actualization"
- "Pleasure and Sensation-seeking"

- "Safety and Security"
- "Spiritual and Transcendental"
- "Control and Power"

DETERMINING THE MOTIVATIONAL STATES ASSOCIATED WITH YOUR BUTTONS

It is likely that you will have Buttons related to all six of the motivational states. However, at different stages in your life you will probably discover that most of your activated Buttons relate to one or two motivational states. When you have a Button pushed, determine which of the motivational states is associated with the demand or attachment (i.e. Button). There are many possible motivations for your wants, behaviors, feelings, cognitions, and Buttons. It is not unusual when you begin looking at the possible motivational states associated with your Buttons to discover that there is more than one motivational state or intention associated with your Button at the time it is pushed. Even though there may be more than one motivational state associated with an activated Button, there is usually one motivational state that is predominate at any given moment.

Usually when we want something it is related to a few basic motivations. We want or do things because we think it will bring us security, sensations (either gain pleasure or avoid pain), control (power), acceptance and love, personal growth, or spirituality. Whenever we get ourselves upset it is usually related to Buttons related to one or more of the first four motivational states in the Button Therapy Model:

1. *Safety and security* - our desire to feel safe and secure.
2. *Pleasure and sensation-seeking* - to obtain or maintain pleasure.
3. *Control and power* - to control self, other people, or situations.
4. *Love and acceptance* - to love and be loved and accepted.

In determining which motivational state(s) the Button is associated with, it is sometimes helpful to ask yourself one of the following questions:

- "Why am I demanding this particular script in my life drama to be different than it is?" "If this life script happens the way I want - will it make me feel more secure (1st motivational state)?... will it bring me pleasure (2nd motivational state)?... will it make me feel more in control of my life or other people (3rd motivational state)?... will it allow me to accept or love this person (4th motivational state)?
- "Why do I have a need for this scene to go my way?" "If this scene in my •

life goes my way will it make me feel more secure (1st motivational state)?...
will it bring me pleasure (2nd motivational state)?...etc.

- "Why am I demanding this person to behave a certain way?"
- "Why is it so important to me that this person I'm talking to agree with me?"
- "Why am I so addicted to this person...belief...drug...music...food...pleasure...sensation?"

CONNECTING FEELINGS WITH MOTIVATIONAL STATES. If you have difficulty determining which motivational states your Button is associated with, try identifying the *feelings* that are generated when your Button was pushed. Then refer to the summary of "The Six Motivational States" and related feelings in Table 16, or check the "motivational states" section earlier in this section, to help determine which motivational state(s) are associated with your feelings. Sometimes, by first identifying the feelings we can immediately recognize which motivational state we are coming from.

Very often our Buttons that get pushed repeatedly are associated with a specific motivational state. For example, if you have a high need to control the people and situations in your life, you will be confronted by many people and situations that will push your "control" Buttons. The control Button will take many different forms such as needing other people to behave and believe a certain way. Life will provide you with many opportunities (i.e. "teachers") to work on your control and power Buttons. Also, with a control Button, you will be spending a lot of your waking hours feeling frustrated, irritated, angry, and hostile. Life has an uncanny way of getting us in touch with our Buttons that we need to work on in order to experience happiness and proceed along our journey of personal growth. Life will continue to offer you "teachers" (i.e. Button-Pushers) until you get the message (i.e. teaching).

SUMMARY OF FIRST FOUR STEPS OF THE SIX-STEP BUTTON THERAPY METHOD. After you become *aware* that you are stressed (Step 1), identify the *Button* (Step 2), identify, "own," experience, and utilize the *emotions* triggered by your Button to begin freeing yourself from your Button (Step 3), the fourth step is to become aware of the *motivational states* associated with your Button. The next step is involves choosing to keep, modify, or eliminate the Button (Step 5).

CHAPTER FOURTEEN

BUTTON POWER
THE CONSTRUCTIVE AND DESTRUCTIVE POWER OF BUTTONS

Mystics and schizophrenics find themselves in the same ocean, but the mystics swim whereas the schizophrenics drown.
R. D. Laing
THE POLITICS OF EXPERIENCE AND THE BIRD OF PARADISE

THE POWER of beliefs, expectations, and wants, as well as our attachments to them (i.e. Buttons), can be either a very constructive or destructive force in our lives.

THE CONSTRUCTIVE POWER OF BUTTONS

BUTTONS CAN HELP US ACHIEVE OUR GOALS. Strong attachments to our beliefs, expectations, values, and models of how things should be have helped many of us attract our love partners, raise our families, and achieve our education, careers, material things, personal growth, and spiritual goals. The attachment a parent develops for a healthy life for his or her child can result in heroic efforts to save a drowning daughter or lift a car off a trapped son. The attachments we develop for positive life-enhancing beliefs help us live healthy, conscious, productive, and spiritual lives. Attachment to God or a creative universal life force can literally transform us into conscious and compassionate beings who periodically experience moments of peak experience, grace, and bliss. Unless we develop an unhealthy preoccupation with living forever, our attachment-to-life Button can be a positive force in our lives and help us live a long and healthy life.

BUTTONS CAN MOTIVATE US TO PROTECT LOVED ONES. Buttons that trigger unpleasant experiences can also result in constructive change. For example, parents have Buttons pushed when their young children engage in life-threatening behavior such as crossing a street without looking both ways. The parental distress triggered by these Buttons can be directed toward impressing upon the child the seriousness of the situation and the necessity of using safer street-crossing skills. Parental discipline of a child often arises from activated Buttons that scare the dickens out of them.

Unfortunately, having an addiction-to-life Button also means that we will experience stress and distress when we perceive our lives or the lives of our loved ones threatened in some way. However, in many people this addiction-to-life Button is so infrequently pushed and creates such infrequent distress that they may feel no need to work on it. However, people dealing with chronic or terminal illnesses, either personally or in loved ones, may want to work on their addiction-to-life Button if they are spending too much of their waking consciousness experiencing stress and distress. If they continue to cling to a healthy, illness-free, and disability-free model for their loved one, and are not able to accept with love and compassion a loved one with a handicapping condition or chronic illness, or the inevitability of death, they will experience much emotional distress throughout these periods of their lives.

BUTTONS CAN MOTIVATE US TO CHANGE. Our Buttons that trigger the experience of anger can motivate us to action such as contact the authorities or our political representative about some injustice. Anger can provide the motivation and fuel to go out of our way to help save our polluted earth, assist less fortunate people, and rescue endangered species. Jealousy, or the fear of losing a love interest, can motivate us to lose a few pounds, improve our appearance, be a little less egocentric, and give our love interest more attention.

THE DESTRUCTIVE POWER OF BUTTONS

Toward no crimes have men shown themselves so cold-bloodedly cruel as in punishing differences in belief.

James Russell Lowell
WITCHCRAFT, volume 2

Buttons can not only motivate us for positive goals but can also trigger the most destructive force known to mankind. Human history is full of people killing in the name of God, a political system, or some other belief. Throughout history people attached to their religious beliefs have terrorized, tortured, subjugated, and killed other people who hold different religious beliefs. Almost as prevalent, virulent, and destructive is our long history of nations going to war over differing political systems. The body count from Buttons related to differing religious and political beliefs continues to mount in contemporary times from killing abortion doctors to terrorist bombings of government buildings. Activated moral, religious, and political Buttons can be extremely dangerous and deadly.

MY MORALITY BUTTON

I find good people good
And I find bad people good
If I am good enough.
> Lao-Tzu
> THE WAY OF LIFE

One of my beliefs to which I am attached (i.e. Buttons) relates to the belief that people have the right to their own spiritual, political, and personal beliefs, even if they differ from the majority of other people. I believe that people should adopt a "live and let live" philosophy and not impose their physical space, beliefs, values, and models of how things should be on others. I believe people should treat other people, animals, and other life forms with respect and love and allow people to live life as they choose. Also, I expect other people to treat me the same way. I try to live by the Golden Rule and treat other people, as I would like to be treated. So, one of my major Buttons that I get myself angry with is when people attempt to power-trip their morality on others including myself. I am still judging others against my model of how people should treat each other. I am still attached to this model and when this "judgmental" Button gets pushed I create periodic distress within myself. I am aware of this Button and I am continually working on upleveling this model of how things should be from addictive to preferential programming.

I believe that most destructiveness, pain, and distress in life is related primarily to people aggressively acting from their "control and power" motivational state. And the most common beliefs, values, and models of how things should be that controlling people are trying to force on other people relate primarily to the pleasure and spiritual domains. The following example of the "Moral Control Patrol" demonstrates how our "need-to-control" Button can trigger misery, hate, and destructiveness to people and society in general.

THE MORAL CONTROL PATROL

Granting that you and I argue. If you get the better of me, and not I of you, are you necessarily right and I wrong? Or if I get the better of you and not you of me, am I necessarily right and you wrong? Or are we both partly right and partly wrong? Or are we both wholly right and wholly wrong? You and I cannot know this, and consequently we all live in darkness.
> Chuang Tzu (369-286 B.C.)
> ON LEVELING ALL THINGS

People in the Moral Control Patrol (MCP) have strong needs (i.e. Buttons) related to convincing, and if need be, coercing other people to adopt their values, beliefs, and behaviors related to all aspects of life, especially those beliefs and behaviors related to the pleasure and spiritual domains. The MCP are self-appointed guardians of morality and values. The MCP attempt to determine how things should be. People in the MCP have decided what is morally "right" and "wrong" not only for themselves, but also for you and me. The MCP believe they are blessed with an ability to discern right and wrong ways to experience pleasure and God. This unique and exclusive ability of MCP moral discernment usually has the benefit of religious insight and guidance.

CONSEQUENCES OF THE MORAL CONTROL PATROL TO SOCIETY

Men never do evil so completely and cheerfully as when they do it from religious conviction.

Blaise Pascal
PENSEES

The following is a sampling of just how devastating people with strong control needs (i.e. "control and power motivational state") can be to individuals, families, and society when they are attached (i.e. have Buttons) to their beliefs, values, and models of how things should be, especially their beliefs related to pleasure, politics, and spirituality. Some of the destructive consequences to our society when one group of people (i.e. the MCP) force their beliefs related to morality and the right and wrong ways to experience pleasure and spirituality include the following:

- Schizophrenic and hypocritical legislation related to pleasure and morality
- Criminalizing a large segment of our country's otherwise law-abiding population
- Overburdening and overcrowding our criminal justice system
- Morality laws help make "criminals" rich
- Wasting limited financial resources that are drastically needed elsewhere in society
- Diverting law enforcement resources from protecting citizens from real criminals (i.e. crimes where there is a victim)
- Corruption of law enforcement officers, attorneys, judges, bankers, accountants, and others
- Disrespect for the law

Our Country's Schizophrenic and Hypocritical Pleasure and Morality Policies

The MCP-inspired morality legislation has reeked havoc in our country. Our country has legislation that is schizophrenic and hypocritical when it comes to legal and illegal ways to experience pleasure. For example, we legally permit adults to use certain recreational psychoactive drugs such as alcohol, nicotine (tobacco), and caffeine (coffee, tea, and soft drinks). We also permit the use of certain other psychoactive drugs (e.g. prescription mood altering drugs) for health promotion purposes with the written permission (i.e. prescription) from a surrogate parent (i.e. state licensed physician). However, we prohibit adults' self-recreating, self-exploring, and self-medicating with certain other psychoactive drugs such as marijuana, hallucinogens, cocaine, and heroin. Physicians may give us permission to use certain psychoactive drugs medically, like marijuana for treating the side effects from cancer chemotherapy or morphine and heroin (in England) to treat pain. However, even physicians can not give permission to use drugs for pleasure or self-exploration.

Our hypocritical laws also affect many other areas of life such as sexual and gambling behavior. We prohibit having sex in "unnatural" ways (e.g. sodomy laws) — unless one lives in one of the states that has no sodomy laws and is more accepting of homosexuals. We prohibit having sex for money (e.g. prostitution laws) — unless one lives in certain counties in Nevada. We prohibit people from gambling — unless we are gambling in approved state run lotteries and casinos. Attempts have also been made by the MCP to restrict certain types of literature, movies, videos, and music over the years. Our public policies and laws concerning how we trigger the pleasure centers of our brains is extremely hypocritical, irrational, and schizophrenic.

Our Morality Laws (Related to Victimless Crimes) Make Criminals out of Otherwise Law-Abiding Citizens

Our country's morality laws related to victimless crimes proscribe criminal penalties for those who violate them. Deviating from MCP-approved ways of triggering the brain's pleasure centers can bring on the full wrath of the MCP and law enforcement officials. These legal restrictions on ways to experience pleasure are often implemented under the guise of helping guide those poor heathens who don't have proper religiously-based morals from harming themselves or others.

Overburdening our Criminal Justice System

Our MCP-backed legislative and criminal justice systems have already incarcerated so many people that our jails and prisons are bursting at the seams. The United States incarcerates more of its citizens than any other country except Russia. Congress is increasingly allocating more of our tax dollars to build additional prisons. The MCP-backed police and criminal justice system appears to operate under the prison construction motto, "You build them and we'll fill them." How much longer can we clog our courts, prisons, and probation and parole caseloads with the MCP-offenders who have harmed no one, except possibly themselves? Shouldn't those drug users who do become drug abusers be helped and treated with compassion by skilled health, mental health, and substance abuse professionals, not by police and the criminal-justice system? Shouldn't prostitutes who want to get out of the business receive counseling services as to healthier ways to make a living and be treated for any existing physical or mental health problems?

How much longer will we allow the MCP to continue to emotionally and financially destroy individuals, families, and society because they were caught using (i.e. possessing) a non-MCP and non-governmentally approved drug or got caught receiving money for sex?

MORAL PROHIBITION LAWS HELP MAKE "CRIMINALS" RICH

Our drug prohibition laws provide lots of tax-free money for "criminals." The illicit drug market in the U.S. is estimated at $150 billion a year. One group of cocaine distributors sold 37,500 kilos a month for gross sales of almost $20 million a month according to a federal judge (Sweet, 1996). Drug prohibition is the main source of revenue for organized crime. Drug prohibition, like alcohol prohibition, has made a lot of people rich and politically powerful. Drug prohibition equals lots of tax-free money and an underground economy. Drug prohibition is one area where the MCP and organized crime agree and support each others' efforts to maintain drug prohibition laws albeit for different reasons.

Drug prohibition has made the sale and distribution of certain drugs so financially lucrative that there is no way this form of commerce will disappear as long as we have drug prohibition laws. For example, the pharmaceutical cost of cocaine and heroin is approximately 2 percent of the street price of those drugs (Buckley, 1996). The markup on cocaine and heroin is 20,000 per cent according to *The Economist* (Sweet, 1996). About $500 worth of heroin and cocaine in a source country will bring in as much as $100,000 on the streets of an American city (McNamara, 1996).

In commenting on why drug prohibition isn't working, Dr. Joseph D. McNamara (1996), former police chief in Kansas City, Missouri and San Jose, California comments, "It's the money stupid. After 35 years as a police officer in three of the country's largest cities, that is my message to the righteous politicians who obstinately proclaim that a war on drugs will lead to a drug-free America... All the cops, armies, prisons and executions in the world cannot impede a market with that kind of tax-free profit margin. It is the illegality that permits the obscene markup, enriching drug traffickers, distributors, dealers, crooked cops, lawyers, judges, politicians, bankers, and businessmen" (p.42).

It is not only the illicit drug growers and distributors making big bucks on drug prohibition. There are a host of governmental agencies and workers and other industries that have a vested economic interest in keeping drug prohibition on the books. As Dr. McNamara (1996) points out, "President Eisenhower warned of a military-industrial complex that would elevate the defense budget unnecessarily. That military-industrial complex pales in comparison to the host of industries catering to our national puritanical hypocrisy – researchers willing to tell the government what it wants to hear, prison builders, correction and parole officers' associations, drug-testing companies, and dubious purveyors of anti-drug education" (p.42). Drug prohibition is big business and financially supports both the "good guys" (i.e. government, drug enforcement agencies, and the MCP) and the "bad guys" (i.e. illicit drug users, dealers, and gangsters).

WASTING FINANCIAL AND MANPOWER RESOURCES

Perhaps one of the most devastating consequences of morality Buttons and the MCP to society is the diversion of limited financial and manpower resources to a hopeless cause. Spending financial and personnel resources attempting to enforce morality laws (i.e. victimless crimes), especially sex and drug prohibition laws are analogous to throwing billions of dollars into a big insatiable black hole in space. The money is totally wasted in terms of making a dent in the sex and drug business. And, as more and more people have finally realized, only makes things worse.

If moral prohibition laws (i.e. victimless crimes) were repealed, our government could probably eliminate the federal budget deficit in a few years by taxing the sale of drugs, sex, and gambling. The billions of dollars currently being spent on the "war on drugs" and other moral prohibitions could be reallocated to preventing and treating those who abuse drugs, sex, and gambling.

DIVERSION OF LAW ENFORCEMENT RESOURCES FROM PROTECTING CITIZENS FROM REAL CRIMINALS

By chasing illicit drug users our police are diverted from protecting us from violent criminals such as robbers, muggers, rapists, and murderers. When will the police utilize more of their limited resources for removing impaired drivers from our roads instead of seeking out people who smoke pot in the privacy of their homes or charge money for sex? When will our police stop wasting time and resources setting traps for adults engaging in consensual acts or experiencing pleasure in their chosen ways? Shouldn't the police and criminal-justice system focus on crime that harms and infringes on the rights and physical space of others? Crimes where there are victims?

CORRUPTION

Unreasonable and unenforceable MCP prohibition laws (e.g. drug prohibition) equals corruption. In addition to selective law enforcement and prosecution, the tremendous amounts of drug prohibition generated illicit drug money available today has corrupted many police, prosecutors, judges, attorneys, jurors, corrections officials, fishermen, bank officials, accountants, foreign governments, and has literally impacted all aspects of life.

There are many MCP advocates who have been caught taking bribes to look the other way. Besides suffering expulsion from the MCP and criminal penalties, many of these people "on the take" who get caught eventually fade into the general populace. Some even become more empathetic to the frailties of being human and become Democrats! Some MCP members who get caught taking bribes claim that in a moment of weakness the devil temporarily gained the upper hand and made them take the money. These apprehended criminals do some jail time, become "saved," see the light, renew their allegiance to God and the MCP, repent, and are often forgiven and taken back into the MCP fold.

DISRESPECT FOR THE LAW AND POLICE

Perhaps what is even more disconcerting about having unenforceable legislated morality is how it engenders disrespect for the law and police. Because there are so many unreasonable, inappropriate, and unenforceable MCP-inspired laws (i.e. victimless crimes), people are left to decide for themselves which laws they will abide by and which they will break. I doubt if there is anybody over 18 years of age who has not broken a law. For example, how many people do you know who have turned in to the police a 20-year-old college student possessing or buying alcohol? How many underage tobacco smokers have you turned in to the police? In states with sodomy laws, how many people have turned in gay and lesbian lovers who have "unnatural" sex? Thus, we have created laws that many people may agree with as moral or health guidelines but not to the point of stigmatizing family, coworkers, friends, and fellow citizens with a criminal record.

People tend to support those laws thought to be reasonable and actually helpful in preventing or dealing with crime. Crime where there is an actual victim. Policing the country's morality where there are no victims, but only consenting adults, is a questionable use of tax dollars.

Unenforceable laws also create many societal problems such as disrespect for the law and the criminal justice process and corruption as Ramsy Clark (1971), former Attorney General of the United States points out:

> Laws that cannot be enforced corrupt. Partial enforcement of laws against known violators is inherently unequal except in the most sensitive and skillful hands, and usually even then. We become a government of men rather than of laws, where men choose who will be arrested and who will remain free for the same infraction. Those arrested are bitter, while those permitted to continue unlawful activity corrupt others and themselves. The watching public is cynical. (p. 26)

The bottom line is that our society's moral prohibition laws have never worked. The "war" on drugs, prostitution, and gambling has never effectively controlled these behaviors. The enforcement of morality laws are sometimes successful at moving the illicit activity underground or to a different location. Just as alcohol prohibition failed and was repealed, we need to repeal our moral prohibition laws (i.e. victimless crimes) and allow people to trigger their brains' pleasure centers as they see fit as long as they don't infringe on other people's physical space.

How the Moral Control Patrol Maintains it Control

Since the harm from moral prohibition laws results in more harm to individuals, families, and society than any benefit, how does the MCP retain its influence and power? The MCP maintains it control by threatening to vote uncooperative politicians out of office (e.g. calling for a discussion of the possible alternative to the current dismal failure on our "war on drugs"), boycotting businesses (e.g. TV and movies and adult stores), pressuring employers to fire people (e.g. convicted of a drug crime), social ostracism (e.g. blackball the family involved with a different religion), public humiliation (e.g. President Clinton's sex scandal), and many other overt and covert strategies.

Many moral and health promotion guidelines (e.g. licit and illicit drug use and sexual behavior) are better left to school systems, health care systems, and parents who are responsible for their underage children. Yet, the moral control patrol are not satisfied with advocating for their version of what is moral and acceptable in the form of moral guidelines. Nor are they satisfied with sending their children to MCP sponsored private schools. The MCP want nothing less than complete moral *control* of all people through legislation.

By legislating morality the MCP has marshaled the resources of our government to enforce their moral edicts. MCP legislators and other insecure and easily intimidated legislators, afraid of being labeled by the MCP as being pro-sin, pro-drug, or soft on crime, go along with the never ending MCP morality show of "seeking-and-destroying sin and evil" wherever and whenever it surfaces. Politicians and citizens who disagree with the MCP and their MCP-inspired legislation keep quiet and go along with the MCP out of fear of retribution, intimidation, being voted out of office, and spending the next ten years defending yourself, your family, and your livelihood in society, and possibly in the courts.

I have considered eliminating this chapter from *The Button Therapy Book* because of concerns about the MCP coming after me and my family (i.e. my "safety and security" motivational state) for helping to expose them through this chapter. The MCP can be a very vindictive and potentially destructive group, sometimes never relenting until they have totally annihilated their opposition. However, the goal of illustrating the potential destructiveness to society of some of our Buttons (e.g. morality Buttons of the MCP) and explaining the Button Therapy model (i.e. "control and power," "pleasure," and "spirituality" motivational states) temporarily outweighed my basic safety and survival needs. Of course I say this only after I have achieved full professor and tenure status (i.e. "safety and security" motivational state) in a nationally ranked (15th) and very popular rehabilitation, substance abuse, and clinical counselor education program at a fairly large university.

THE TIMES THEY ARE A CHANGIN'

People are increasingly waking from the "big sleep" (i.e. cultural trance engineered by professional illusionists coming from a "control and power" motivational state) and becoming aware of the harm created by sex, gambling, drug prohibition, and related morality laws. People are beginning to demand that the criminal-justice system focus on real criminals (i.e. those people who harm others and where there is a victim). People are increasingly complaining about spending their tax dollars on unenforceable "victimless crimes."

What's amazing to me is how seemingly mature adults could allow the MCP to dictate what they can and can't do in the privacy of their own homes. How can people let other people dictate to them how they can tickle the pleasure centers of their own brains? Why is it anybody else's business as long as people don't infringe on other people's physical space or commit any crimes violating the rights of other people? Why have grown adults abrogated their personal freedom, self-responsibility, and basic human rights to self-medicate, self-recreate, and self-explore to other adults who have a strong need to control and power-trip their morality on them? How much longer will the citizens of this country allow the tyranny and intimidation tactics of the MCP to continue? How much longer will we allow the MCP to continue their reign of terror? How much longer will adult citizens of this "free" and democratic society allow the MCP to prohibit them from self-medicating, self-exploring, self-recreating, and experiencing their pleasure in their chosen manner? Fortunately, there are some signs of hope.

LIBERTARIAN BACKLASH

To live and let live, without clamor for distinction of recognition; to wait on divine Love; to write truth first on the Tablet of one's own heart—this is the sanity and perfection of living, and my human ideal.
Mary Baker Eddy
MESSAGE TO THE MOTHER CHURCH

There appears to be an increasing awareness of the harm from many of the MCP's moral prohibition policies. In addition, increasing numbers of individuals are willing to risk intimidation, public personal attacks, and their jobs to publicly question the MCP's drug, sex, and other moral prohibition policies. There appears to be a growing rebellion among the populace as individuals increasingly become outraged at the arrogance and intrusion of narrow-minded self-appointed guardians of morality (i.e. the MCP) who pass laws restricting what others put into their mouths or how they use their bodies, minds, and spirits.

There appears to be a growing opposition to the MCP. Also, there appears to be an increase in the number of individuals who believe in a "live and let live" philosophy. These individuals believe that they have the right to develop and follow their own morals and beliefs, which may or may not be in sync with those of the MCP. Increasing numbers of individuals are assuming responsibility for their own health maintenance, self-healing, and self-medication as evidenced by the rapid growth of the alternative and complementary holistic health care movement. People are increasingly taking charge of their bodies, minds, and spirits. Many responsible adults believe that as long as they don't physically invade other peoples' space they have the following rights:

- To self-medicate and self-recreate with any drug they choose
- To have sex in any way with any consenting adult they choose (including for money if they choose)
- To gamble in any way they choose

- To watch any movie or video they choose
- To listen to any type of music they choose
- To trigger their brain's pleasure centers in any way they choose
- To engage in any form of religious or spiritual path they choose with equal tax and other breaks as the government currently provides governmentally approved organized religions (or, eliminate tax breaks for all religions).

I believe the individuals in the "live and let live" group are growing in numbers as a result of increasing awareness, consciousness, and willingness of adults to assume personal responsibility for their own morality, beliefs, and behaviors. I believe most "grown-up" and mature adults want to assume more responsibility for running their own lives, and resent other people and the government trying to control their personal lives.

Recent evidence for this rebellion for personal independence and freedom from governmental and MCP control is seen in the liberalization of marijuana laws by California and Arizona for therapeutic medical purposes in 1996. The MCP-backed courts and administrators in the White House have blocked the full implementation of these laws and the will of the majority of voters in both states. In 1998, voters in Washington, Alaska, Nevada, and Oregon joined California and Arizona and passed initiatives to allow therapeutic marijuana smoking for serious illnesses such as glaucoma and nausea from cancer chemotherapy. Immediately following the election results Barry McCaffrey, the White House drug czar, stated that the election results won't alter marijuana's illegal statues under federal law. General McCaffrey's statement implies that the federal government will block the implementation of these newly passed laws in these additional states as well. "Exit polls in Colorado and Washington, D.C., showed overwhelming support for similar ballot questions that had been voided by legal challenges [from the MCP] before the election" (O'Driscoll, 1998, p. 1A).

Other signs of rebellion against the MCP include: the signature of 500 prominent international leaders and influential individuals calling for a dramatic change in our drug prohibition laws (many of whom are already on record as supporting the elimination of drug prohibition laws); the legalization of prostitution in selected counties in Nevada; the proliferation and legalization of gambling in many states by calling it the state run lottery (and collecting large sums of money for the state budget); the growth of survivalist and militia type anti-government groups; and the growth of the Libertarian and related political parties. I do not support all of these trends but these are signs of taking back autonomy and self-responsibility from a parental-like controlling government infringing on personal freedom.

Another major reason for the recent growth of the "live and let live" group is a direct result of the moral control patrol's direct assault on them or their family members. Every time the MCP tries to impose its beliefs, standards of behavior, and lifestyle on other people through the force of law, courts, and prisons it forces more people to the "live and let live" side. Every time the police dress up like gestapo storm troopers and bust down peoples' doors to their homes trying to catch them smoking marijuana, or having sex for money, the moral control patrol helps convert additional individuals and their families and friends to the "live and let live" side. Every time a student is suspended from school by a righteous MCP school principal and resource officer, forced into drug rehab (with no drug problem), and referred to the juvenile justice system because of his or her non-approved use (vs. drug abuse) of a drug (e.g. underage alcohol use, marijuana use, and tobacco use), instead of letting the student's parents and health care professionals deal with their children's drug use, the morality "control freaks" and "power-trippers" will potentially push some more young people and their families to the "live and let live" group. Every time a student is suspended from school for sharing an aspirin with a friend with a headache, sharing an asthma inhaler with a friend having an asthma attack on a school bus, possessing a novelty pen with legal "sterile marijuana seeds" (i.e. bird seed) encased in a plastic see-through top purchased legally at a tourist shop, there are more converts. Most parents do not like their children treated like criminals because of their adolescent curiosity, immature decision-making, helping fellow students in need, and partaking in adolescent rites of passage.

As is often the case, there will probably be increased initiatives to repeal morality laws and victimless crimes when a sufficient number of family members of legislators, judges, police, clergy, and other influential people become victims of the moral control patrol's sponsored hypocritical policies and laws.

REASONABLE AND ENFORCEABLE MORALITY LAWS. We need codified morals and laws to help prevent unscrupulous and evil people from forcing their will and physical space on others. We need morality laws protecting minors. We need laws to help protect us from criminals deriving their pleasure by forcing their will and physical space on the rest of us through such aberrant activities as child molestation, rape, stealing, murder, and driving while impaired. We also need police and the courts to enforce these laws. However, more importantly, we need laws that most all citizens can support and help enforce. We also need to minimize biased and selective law enforcement and prosecution and develop more widespread respect and support for enforceable laws.

We need correctional facilities to protect us from those who would physically harm us. We need rehabilitation and mental health professionals to help rehabilitate and change these offenders' beliefs and behaviors so they don't do it again. However, we need to repeal many of the MCP- sponsored morality laws involving two or more consenting adults and laws where there are no victims. Our government has no business legislating morality and beliefs (i.e.

victimless crimes) for adults, especially beliefs and behaviors related to drugs, sex, movies, videos, music, gambling, and religion. How we tickle the pleasure centers in our brains is nobody's business but our own.

MORAL REHABILITATION

If an adult triggers the pleasure centers in his or her brain in a non-MCP approved manner, gets caught, and has to suffer the indignities and personal and financial consequences of the police and criminal justice system, all is not lost. There is a five-step moral rehabilitation process that may allow the moral offender to return to his or her premorbid personal, professional, and societal standing, even in the eyes of the MCP!

THE FIVE-STEP MORAL REHABILITATION PROCESS

Once "outed" or caught for a MCP moral offense that does not infringe upon the rights of others, all is not lost. The MCP offender, no matter how distasteful the offense is to the MCP or the criminal justice system (e.g. possession of therapeutic marijuana for nausea from your cancer chemotherapy treatments), can still be rehabilitated and returned as a productive member of society.

If you ever become a victim of the MCP after committing a victimless crime (e.g. possessing a marijuana joint), you might try the following five-step moral rehabilitation procedure. The moral rehabilitation process proceeds in five steps and goes something like this:

> **1. CONFESS** (i.e. Acknowledge your "wrong" or "sin"). You will be better off admitting your mistake and that it was "wrong" without offering any excuses. The MCP tends to believe in absolutes and that everything is either "right or wrong" or "black or white." The MCP has a hard time with shades of gray. However, moral offenders, when confronted by the MCP inevitably try to minimize their "wrong" by explaining it away as a "temporary lapse in judgment" or by offering extenuating circumstances. For example, common excuses offered by the moral offender to the MCP include, "I was drunk." "I was under a lot of stress at work." "I didn't think you cared if I...borrowed your money...borrowed your CD's...etc." "Honey, it was only physical sex at a weak moment. I was temporarily vulnerable. You are the only one I love. It'll never happen again. You don't want to divorce me." "I'm only human." These excuses sometimes work, especially if you are seeking forgiveness

from somebody that wants to maintain a relationship with you regardless of what you've done. Perhaps they are an economically dependent spouse or employer. Excuses, no matter how creative and illogical, allow the offended to save face and forgive you. This "explanation" may prevent them from divorcing or firing you or otherwise breaking off a relationship with you. Acknowledge that what you did was wrong. That it was morally, and possibly legally, wrong.

"I HAVE SINNED." If the moral offense is perceived by the MCP as really bad, you may want to bring in the religious ace card at this point. Sometimes, saying, "I'm sorry," even with feeling and conviction, isn't "enough. In these special instances, it may be necessary to acknowledge the moral offense (e.g. extra-marital affair) as a "sin." You may find yourself saying something direct and unequivocal like, " I have sinned. I had extra-marital sex. "

In extreme cases you may have to play the ultimate religious trump card and blame it on the devil. This card has to be played with sensitivity, good timing, a certain amount of drama, and finesse. You can't just say, "The devil made me do it." This statement may trigger a memory of comedian Flip Wilson dressed in an all red devil's costume claiming that the devil made him do every little thing the MCP didn't approve of. The MCP may think you are not serious and goofing on them with such direct, questionable, and unambiguous claims. You're better off saying something like, "I don't understand why I did it (i.e. the moral offense). Sometimes I am so overcome by impulses to do such horrible things (e.g. have extra-marital sex) that I wonder if I'm not possessed by the devil himself. I don't know what's happening to me. I feel like I am at a loss to fight off these deviant impulses any longer. Can you help me?" At this point the MCP is in its glory and at its best as they are called to action much like a preacher is called to wrestle the devil from a parishioner who has gone astray (i.e. got caught doing a non-MCP approved "immoral" act). This request for help is interpreted as a call to morally rehabilitate you, or better yet, to habilitate you to their religious path as a card-carrying member. You have finally admitted that you have done a moral "wrong" and are too weak to resist the temptations of the flesh, and possibly the call of the devil himself. The MCP's treatment and rehabilitation strategy is now clear. You have put yourself in the MCP's ballpark. The MCP has now been called to take over your life for you in your time of moral and spiritual need.

2. Demonstrate Remorse (Contrition). After you have admitted that you have done something "wrong," you need to say that you are sorry and then demonstrate remorse. Demonstrate your contrition (i.e. you are broken down with sorrow for sinning). Contrition is a two-parter. Your remorse and contrition will be more convincing if you demonstrate your sorrow, remorse, guilt, and emotional suffering for both yourself and the person(s) you offended. Let the offended persons know that you are sorry for any emotional harm or embarrassment that you have caused them. In addition, it helps to express how much emotional pain and embarrassment that you yourself are suffering. Here is where you must be believable.

3. Ask for Forgiveness. This step involves asking forgiveness from the offended. And, if you have gone the, "I have sinned" route, ask forgiveness from your higher power (i.e. God). Clergy from organized religions are essential players in this drama for this form of atonement to be effective. It is important to ask forgiveness of the representatives of the MCP (e.g. clergy, friend) working for your salvation. Remember, you are demonstrating remorse and asking forgiveness from three sources: 1. The Offended 2. Your Higher Power (e.g. God), and 3. The MCP (e.g. clergy, friends, and the public). When asking forgiveness be sure and work into your groveling drama a few key points.

- Point out that *God forgives sinners.* In Paul's second letter to the Corinthians, he writes that "Godly sorrow brings repentance that leads to salvation and leaves no regret, but worldly sorrow brings death." As Cal Thomas (1998), syndicated columnist, points out, "Worldly sorrow is being sorry that you got caught. Godly sorrow acknowledges how short one falls from God's standard and brings with it a turning away from old patterns of behavior to new and better ones" (p. A8).
- *Proclaim that you will go forth and never do the nasty deed again* (i.e. sin no more).
- *God is the only source of judgment and forgiveness for moral sins.*
- *People who live in glass houses shouldn't throw stones.*
- *Let those of you who have not sinned cast the first stone.*

4. Repent. It's time to do penance (i.e. unpleasant grunge work to right a "wrong"). Some common ways of demonstrating this stage of your moral rehabilitation to the MCP include the following:

- *Promise to do good deeds to atone for the moral "wrong."* For example, renew your pledge to help the poor… mow the lawn without having to be asked… give some flowers, with an appropriate message asking for forgiveness, to the offended.
- *Attend a church, synagogue, or temple for a sufficient length of time to achieve atonement and become "saved" or "born again,"* How long you attend depends upon the offense. Some MCP offenses (e.g. a husband having an extra-marital affair with another man) take longer to pay off than others.

You may want to implement the preemptive "repenting" strategy if you have reason to believe the MCP is on to your non-MCP approved "offense." You may want to take some of the thunder out of their confrontation by admitting your "mistake" or "moral lapse of judgment" before they confront you. Remember that the credibility of repentance diminishes the closer one gets to being "outed" (i.e. found out).

5. Become Rehabilitated and "Saved." You need to demonstrate that you are truly a saved and rehabilitated sinner. Your best bet to become "saved" in the eyes of the MCP is through religion. It has to be a mainstream organized religion. The more conservative the religion the better. However, if you want to increase your probability of being forgiven and "saved," you are better off aligning yourself with liberal members of the clergy who are more amenable to recognizing the fallibility of being human. You newagers who are no longer involved in any organized mainstream religion and have developed your own direct personal relationship to God, or your own version of a higher power, are out of luck. The MCP will only further blame your moral "failure" (e.g. smoking marijuana) on your involvement with some non-MCP approved religion or spiritual path. The only way out for new agers is to keep quiet about your personal spiritual path and become a reborn Christian…Jew…Hindu…etc. who is committed to follow the religious values of the MCP-approved organized religion. Liberal members of the clergy are best for this stage of MCP-approved moral rehabilitation. We can turn to former President Clinton and learn from his top legal advisors and political game-players how to handle a sticky situation (sorry about that) such as his sex scandal with the White House intern. For example, President Clinton called upon a trinity of highly visible and well known clergy to facilitate his forgiveness and salvation from his extra-marital sexual affairs (i.e. sin). According to Cal Thomas (1998) former President Nixon held Sunday "morning-worship" services in the White House attended by carefully screened theologically and politically conservative clergy. As a reporter, Mr. Thomas attended these morning services which were, "...strangely sterile events, which were devoid of hellfire and brimstone and any criticism of Nixon's Vietnam or domestic policies. That's because like last Friday's liberal conclave [President Clinton's meeting with three politically and theologically liberal clergy as part of his moral rehabilitation process for his Monica Lewinsky sex scandal], the guests were carefully screened" (p. A8).

Some ways of demonstrating that you have become "saved" include:

- *Announcing that you have "seen the light."* You have seen the error of your ways and will never go down that well trod road of sinners again.
- *Announcing that you have been "saved."* Divulge that you have asked God for forgiveness and that He has forgiven you.
- *Giving up your hang-dog body posture and facial expression for an upright posture and start looking people straight in the eyes.*
- *Giving up the guilty sinner look and adopt a beatific all-knowing righteous smile.* Remember God himself, and hopefully a few well placed mainstream organized religious clergy, has forgiven you and you are now one of the forgiven and blessed ones, much like the MCP members.
- *Sharing that you now feel "cleansed" and "free."*
- *Proclaiming that you are now "stronger" as a result of this unfortunate episode of your life.* For example, President Clinton, in his first interview since acknowledging he "misled" the nation about his relationship with Monica Lewinsky said he has emerged stronger from the ordeal and that it "gives me a chance to make my marriage whole" according to the Associated Press (1998b). President Clinton further explains, "I think any time a person has to go through a searing personal experience and come to terms with truth and genuinely atone, and genuinely make the effort to change, that's an immensely

liberating experience...It makes you stronger. It makes you straighter" (A2).

- *Pointing out that although it was a heck of an ordeal you went through and that you will probably continue to "suffer" for some time to come – life must go on!* Again in the words of President Clinton, "To a person who has a conscience, that's the biggest price you pay." But he said, "Instead of wallowing in regret, I am working at repairing my life and my marriage. My wife is a remarkable woman, and her strength and support are a constant inspiration to me during this painful time" (Associated Press, 1998b, p. A2).
- Acknowledge the strength and wisdom of the offended loved ones who have agreed to let you remain in their lives (e.g. "My wife is a living Saint to stay with me throughout this terrible ordeal").

Semantics is very important when using this five-step moral rehabilitation plan. Be sure and try to work in key words such as wrong, sin, sorry, guilt, regret, remorse, forgive, saved, cleansed, free, rehabilitated, recovered, and reborn into your groveling for forgiveness. The MCP needs to hear some key words in your contrition and atonement in order for them to believe you. If you're going to play the moral rehabilitation game you might as well know how the game is played and play the scene out with drama, flair, gusto, and sincerity.

MORAL REHABILITATION IN THE CRIMINAL JUSTICE SYSTEM

When the moral offense is also illegal (e.g. triggering your brain's pleasure centers with a non-MCP approved psychoactive drug like marijuana) you can use the same five-step moral rehabilitation procedure outlined above. Of course, if you don't care about MCP disapproval you can skip the self-deprecating and demeaning religious part of the moral rehabilitation procedure, unless of course you really want to go this route. However, remember that the MCP can make or break you in our society. You can lose your job, family, and finances trying to protect yourself in court when caught triggering your brain's pleasure center in non-MCP approved ways. However, you may decide to simply use the five-step moral rehabilitation procedure on the police, judge, and parole board without the religion angle. It has worked for countless offenders for centuries. One little piece of advice for anyone doing time in prison. Make friends with the prison chaplain. Become a "born again" religious devotee. Preferably, of the Christian faith. The MCP seems not to question Christian rebirths as much as rebirths into other religions. Too many minorities in those other religions. Then attend every church service. Help the prison chaplain set up his or her church service and other functions. Sing in the choir. It is the prison chaplain who becomes your main advocate for early release or parole from prison. Who better to attest to your moral rehabilitation and readiness to rejoin the human race than a professional moral rehabilitator! The prison chaplain is a leader of the MCP and his or her word goes a long way with the parole board.

This tongue-in-cheek description of the five-step moral rehabilitation procedure is not always as manipulative as it appears. Some people actually do change their self-harmful ways and adopt more life-enhancing moral beliefs and behaviors and become rehabilitated or "saved." Even some hardened criminals and psychopaths actually do change for the better and become upstanding productive citizens. Also, some rehabilitated and "saved" moral degenerates have become active leaders of the MCP and have adopted positive goals such as prison ministry. Some former unethical and immoral offenders go forth after their rehabilitation and salvation with a missionary zeal in order to rehabilitate and save the non-religious heathens still behind bars. However, having worked as a mental health professional with criminals, substance abusers, psychopaths, and just plain evil people, I guess I've become a bit cynical over the years.

THE SHADOW

Violent antipathies are always suspicious, and betray a secret affinity.
William Hazlitt
ON CRITICISM

Dr. Carl G. Jung described the "shadow" as the psychodynamic which is the part of us we suppress, do not acknowledge, and try to hide. The "shadow" part of us, especially that part of us that wants to experience pleasure through sex or drugs, can emerge at the most inopportune and unexpected times resulting in some very unhealthy and embarrassing situations.

There is nothing sadder than watching leaders of the moral control patrol such as the "Rev." Jimmy Swaggart and the PTL's "Rev." Jim Bakker, and numerous other religious, political, national, and community leaders succumb to their own need for tapping into their brains' pleasure centers through illicit means. Unfortunately, individuals with a high need to control the beliefs and morality of others are often so out of touch with their own needs for pleasure that they often make newspaper headlines with their unhealthy, immoral, or illegal expression of their pleasure and sensation-seeking motivational state.

A recent example of the "Shadow" emerging at a most inopportune time relates to Democratic President Bill Clinton's extra-marital sexual escapades and the inevitable lying about it scandal. According to The Associated Press (1998) one Republican legislator called President Clinton a "scumbag" and doesn't believe Clinton is a "man of integrity." Shortly thereafter, this same legislator admitted that he had fathered a child in an extra-marital affair while he was a legislator. The legislator apparently believes he has done the morally right thing under the circumstances in that he said his wife was aware of the relationship, and that he has paid child support through the years. "However, [the legislator] has never officially acknowledged the child as his son. His campaign literature only mentions the three children [the legislator] has with his wife" (p. A2). Another recent example of the Shadow (New York Times, 1998) surrounding the Clinton scandal involves a vocal Clinton critic admitting she had a long-term affair with a married man. "After criticizing President Clinton for the 'sordid spectacle' of an extramarital affair and airing a campaign advertisement in which she says that 'personal conduct and integrity does matter,' [the Republican legislator] admitted Thursday that she herself had once engaged in a long-term affair with a married man" (p. A4). In addition, another Republican legislator, who also happens to be the Chair of the House Judiciary Committee investigating President Clinton and conducting impeachment hearings, has recently been "outed" in *Salon*, a liberal Internet magazine, for having an extra-marital affair from 1965 to 1969 with a beautician. "At the time, she was married to a Chicago furniture salesman and had three children. He was a married father of four and was elected to the Illinois House in 1966" (Lee, 1998, p.9A). This Rep. acknowledged the extra-marital affair and claimed it hit the press because of politics. According to journalist DeWayne Wickham (1998) about 21percent of men and 11percent of women have cheated on their spouses. "While most people think such behavior is wrong, poll after poll show few believe Clinton should lose his job because he had an affair. Starr [special prosecutor] and his supporters argue it is not Clinton's sexual escapades, but the things he allegedly did to hide his infidelity that justify impeachment. It remains to be seen how many Americans will want Congress to treat the lie more harshly than the act. 'If this is going to be the standard' for removing politicians, said John Conyers, ranking Democrat on the House Judiciary Committee, 'we may not have a quorum when it comes time to vote.'" (15A).

It's unfortunate for President Clinton and these three legislators that they are forced to hide and lie (called "perjury" if one has to lie under oath in a legal arena) about their sexual activity because of the MCP's absolutist moral policies and subsequent severe personal and work-related consequences. Humans, including people in the public eye, are fallible and sometimes make mistakes, poor decisions, and get caught by the MCP (or the *National Enquirer!*). Should they be ostracized and expelled from their jobs and the human family for choosing to trigger their brains' pleasure centers in non-MCP approved ways?

Sex between consenting adults is personal and usually a private matter, and should not be the concern of anyone else. And, in the examples of extra-marital affairs cited above, aren't these personal matters better left to the individuals involved, including their families? Why should the MCP decide which drug, type of sex, form of gambling, or videos are okay to stimulate our brains' pleasure centers?

Some people have Buttons related to avoiding pleasure. Most organized religions have adopted restrictions on how one is to experience pleasure, and if pleasure is allowed at all. There are individuals who have much of their self-identity tied up in abstaining from sex, alcohol, and other psychoactive drugs. Some celibates believe this teetotaler stance, and the avoidance of other sensation-seeking behavior, makes them morally strong and spiritual. To each his own (i.e. if you are a Libertarian)! If you are a MCP member you will probably decide what is morally and legally acceptable between consenting adults not only for yourself, but also force your beliefs on everyone else!

Repressing the shadow and banishing our unflattering qualities to the recesses of our unconscious minds is not healthy. It is healthier to become aware of all aspects of ourselves, including the good and the bad, in order to progress on our journey of personal growth. Often times we can transmute the energy associated with our darker tendencies as we become aware of them. Sometimes we can change a behavior even after we have initiated action of a harmful impulse by simply becoming aware of our intention and behavior. In referring to negative prayer when someone wishes harm to someone, Larry Dossey, M.D. (1997) points out that, "Light and shadow are always irrevocably linked. Or, as Friedrich Nietzsche reassured us in Thus Spoke Zarathustra, 'The supreme evil is part of the supreme good'…[and] as Jung said, a whole person is one who has both walked with God and wrestled with the Devil" (pp. 76, 79).

Beware of individuals who become fanatic in their opposition to the *healthy* expression of pleasure in all its varied forms. They may become tomorrow's newspaper headlines as the shadow strikes again!

CHAPTER FIFTEEN

BUTTON REMOVAL AND COGNITIVE RESTRUCTURING

MAKING CONSCIOUS CHOICES ON WHETHER TO KEEP, MODIFY, OR ELIMINATE YOUR BUTTONS

With the relinquishing of all thought and egotism,
the enlightened one is liberated through not clinging.
Buddha
MAJJHIMA NIKAYA

UTILIZING THE SIX-STEP BUTTON THERAPY METHOD: after you become *aware* that you are experiencing stress (step one); identified the activated *Buttons* (step two), *emotions* (step 3) and *motivational states* (step 4) associated with the Button; your next step (five) is to modify or eliminate the Buttons causing your emotional distress. And, if you choose to work on your Buttons, you need to decide whether you want to eliminate the cognitions you are attached to, or keep the cognition and modify the models of how you want things to be to *preferences* versus demands. Once a decision is made concerning whether to modify or eliminate Buttons, you need to decide which cognitive intervention(s) will help you achieve your goals.

MAKING A CONSCIOUS CHOICE TO KEEP, MODIFY OR ELIMINATE YOUR BUTTONS

One would think that after becoming aware of how they are creating their emotional suffering that they would choose to end the suffering. This sounds like a "no-brainer" decision, but not so, says the professional counselor within me with 33 years of counseling and psychotherapy experience.

CHOOSING TO KEEP YOUR BUTTONS

Some people choose to keep their Buttons, knowing that they create their own emotional distress when their Buttons get pushed. There are a variety of reasons for keeping Buttons once we become aware of them. For example, some of our Buttons don't get pushed enough to worry about them or to put energy into changing them. Also, some people are "stress junkies" and thrive on constant levels of high stress, enjoying the feelings and energy rushes experienced by activating the stress or "fight-or-flight" response.

STRESS JUNKIES

Stress junkies enjoy experiencing the periodic adrenaline rushes when encountering a deeply rooted Button (e.g. personal survival). Stress junkies like the novelty and excitement of unpredictability and the thrill of having certain Buttons pushed. Some of these thrill-seeking individuals thrive on danger, excitement, and chaos. And the constant activation of their stress response through the pushing of their Buttons can help them achieve their desired home-ostatic state of high-level chronic stress. Thus not everybody is going to choose to work on their Buttons in order to lower their stress levels and frequency of adrenaline rushes.

Adolescents experience high-risk activities such as surfing, skateboard-ing, horseback riding, wild rides at theme parks, and driving while impaired which routinely trigger the stress response. Engaging in a certain amount of high-risk activities can help adolescents develop their identity and self-esteem and are part of this developmental life stage. Some of these behaviors are plain dangerous to self and others. Not all adolescents will continue this level of risk-taking into adult years and become "stress junkies."

SMILING SUFFERERS

These are people who receive certain rewards and benefits from suffer-ing. Some people use their anger and rage associated with activated Buttons to manipulate others into doing what they want. Some people use their physical and mental illnesses to elicit sympathy and attention. Some individuals display their feelings of outrage associated with certain Buttons to attract an audience for their views. Some individuals use the doom and gloom associated with cer-tain Buttons to help facilitate and structure their social interactions. Playing the "ain't-it-awful game" where individuals swap stories about how bad things are is a favorite pastime for many people. Some people identify themselves by their psychological wounds and receive payoffs to keep this identity from mutual-help groups.

LOW SELF-ESTEEM

Some people have such low self-esteem that they expect their actions will result in personal feelings of inferiority, incompetence, and social exclusion. Individuals with low self-esteem are accustomed to this type of inner experi-ence. To give up their Buttons which reinforce these known "I'm not ok" life positions and inner experiences, for an inner experience that is more positive, yet unfamiliar and unknown, is very scary and they may not want to risk the change. When settling for the status quo, at least they know what to expect and that there is some comfort with the predictability of their current life experience. They've been able to make it through life, with its ups and downs, up to now. So far they haven't lost their jobs, families, friends, or had to check themselves into the local mental hospital. If they make changes in their cognitions, behaviors, emotions, and relationships they are sometimes fearful that their lives will become worse.

Magical Thinkers

People afraid of making needed changes in their lives sometimes believe that the quality of their lives will somehow magically change someday. Their self-talk goes something like…"I'll quit smoking when I graduate from school. My life is too stressful right now." "Things will get better when I pay off this debt." "I'll be more relaxed after I graduate from my master's degree program in two years." "My marriage will improve after the kids enter school… enter college…leave home to start their own families…etc." "When the people and situations in my life change I will be happier." This magical thinking that life will change for the better someday, without any conscious effort, is a common belief and often reflects an external locus of control.

For a variety of reasons, some people will choose not to work on their Buttons. Utilizing the Button Therapy model, people can gain an increased awareness of how they create their own feelings and inner experience and can make a more conscious choice concerning their cognitions and Buttons, realizing they will live with the consequences.

As we become more aware of how we create our own inner experience we realize that we do have choice as to how we are going to interpret our experiences. If we are not satisfied with our inner experience we can decide whether or not to change our cognitions which influence our emotional state and the quality of our inner experience. We do have choice. We can make changes in our lives. If we are not happy, we can take some risks and change our cast of characters in our life drama, change the scenery, and change our cognitions, which determine how we interpret life's events.

Most real change of any significance is going to entail some degree of risk and result in some stress. However, this just may be what the doctor ordered. Working on our personal growth can be both exciting and scary. We become excited and energized with each new insight as to how it all works. However, each major advance in our personal growth may result in some stress as we move out of our comfort zones and habitual patterns of living, and move forward toward self-actualization.

"I HAVE SO MANY BUTTONS - I'M HOPELESS!"

A journey of a thousand miles must begin with a single step.
Lao-Tzu
TAO TE CHING

As we trek along the path of self-actualization and become more aware of where we are on the personal growth continuum we realize how many Buttons we have to work on. With this realization we sometimes become overwhelmed with it all and want to throw up our hands in frustration and exclaim ..."It's hopeless, I'm hopeless. I'll never get free from my attachments to all these programs, scripts, expectations, beliefs, desires and other cognitions in my biocomputer. I'm destined to remain in my unfulfilled, unhappy inner experience for the rest of my life. My fate is to remain an unconscious reactive robot who dances anytime someone pushes my Buttons."

The abandonment of efforts to continue inner and interpersonal work is a common experience for individuals consciously working on their personal growth. However, you can never be "unaware" once you have gained an insight or awareness of some truth. And contrary to some peoples' wish, "ignorance is not bliss." So hang in there and know that you are not alone on this one! Know that working on your personal growth is not easy, but it is also potentially the most rewarding and personally self-fulfilling experience in your life. You can become the master of your own fate and navigator of your life path. Working on your Buttons that cause emotional distress and pull you from the path of becoming more aware, conscious, loving, and compassionate is certainly a challenging task but it's also the most interesting and rewarding game in town. Working on our personal and spiritual growth is what Robert S. De Ropp (1968) calls *The Master Game*.

.

GAMES PEOPLE PLAY

According to Dr. Thomas Szasz (1961), a prominent psychiatrist, what people really need and demand from life is not wealth, comfort, or esteem but *games worth playing*. If we cannot find a game worth playing we become vulnerable to boredom, disenchantment, paralysis of the will, failure of desire, and mental illness.

As Robert De Ropp (1968) adds, "Seek, above all, for a game worth playing. Such is the advice of the oracle to modern man. Having found the game, play it with intensity - play as if your life and sanity depended on it. (They do depend on it.)" (p. 11). If life does not seem to offer a game worth playing, then invent one (Sartre, 1957). De Ropp (1968) divided some of the games we play into two major groups, "object games" (Hog in Trough; Cock on Dunghill; and Moloch Game) and "meta-games" (Art Game; Science Game; Religion Game; and Master Game):

OBJECT GAMES

HOG IN TROUGH. The aim is to get one's nose in the trough as deeply as possible, guzzle as much as possible, and elbow the other hogs aside as forcefully as possible.

COCK ON DUNGHILL. This game is played for fame. It is designed primarily to inflate the false ego and to keep it inflated. Players of Cock on Dunghill are hungry to be known and talked about. They want to be celebrities.

THE MOLOCH GAME. A deadly game played for "glory" or for "victory" by professional killers trained to regard such killing as creditable provided those they kill favor a different religion or political system and can thus be collectively referred to as "the enemy."

These three object games are all more or less pathological activities. The players who "win" win nothing that they can truly call their own. The super rich person may discover that money does not necessarily bring happiness and find him or herself embittered, empty and unhappy, and at a loss to know what to do with the wealth he or she has amassed. The celebrity may discover that his or her fame is a mere shadow and a source of inconvenience. The players of The Moloch Game may wade in blood up to their ears only to find that the victory or glory for which they sacrificed a million lives are empty words, like richly bedizened whores who lure men to their destruction. There is a criminal element in all these games because, in every instance, they do harm both to the player and to the society of which he forms a part. So warped, however, are the standards by which men measure criminality that players of these games are more apt to be regarded as 'pillars of society' than dangerous lunatics who should be exiled to remote islands where they can do no harm to themselves or others" (De Ropp, 1968, pp. 15-16).

A NEUTRAL GAME

THE HOUSEHOLDER GAME. The aim of this game is simply to raise a family and provide it with the necessities of life.

NONPLAYERS

There are "...a certain number of nonplayers, people who, due to some constitutional defect, are unable to find any game worth playing, who are, as a result, chronic outsiders, who feel alienated from society and generally become mentally deranged, tend to become antisocial and criminal" (p. 16).

META-GAMES

THE ART GAME. Ideally, the Art Game is directed toward the expression of an inner awareness of beauty. "The whole Art Game, as played today, is heavily tainted with commercialism, the greed of the collector pervades it like a bad smell. It is further complicated by the tendency to show off that afflicts almost all contemporary artists..." (p. 16).

THE SCIENCE GAME. Much of the Science Game is "...mere jugglery, a tiresome ringing of changes on a few basic themes by investigators who are little more than technicians with higher degrees...Anything truly original tends to be excluded by that formidable array of committees that stands between the scientist and the money he needs for research. He must either tailor his research plans to fit the preconceived ideas of the committee or find himself without funds...The game is played not so much for knowledge as to bolster the scientist's ego." (pp. 16-17).

THE RELIGION GAME. A meta-game with a goal of salvation. In the early developmental period of the Religion Game clergy developed a blissful heaven and a terrible hell. "To stay out of hell and get into the heaven, the player of the Religion Game had to pay the priests, or his relatives had to pay them after his death...A particularly hideous aspect of the Religion Game resulted from the insistence by certain priests that their brand of god was the only god, that their form of the game was the only permissible form. So eager were these priests to keep the game entirely in their own hands that they did not hesitate to persecute, torture or kill any who happened to wish to play the game by other rules" (p. 18). Saints and mystics who obviously did not play the game for material gain have played the Religion Game for nobler aims. These players were attempting the most difficult game of all, the Master Game, the attainment of which is the attainment of full consciousness or real awakening.

> To emerge from this narrow shell, to regain union with the universal consciousness, to pass from the darkness of the ego-centered illusion into the light of the non-ego, this was the real aim of the Religion Game as defined by the great teachers, Jesus, Gautama, Krishna, Hahavira, Lao-tze and the Platonic Socrates...To all these players, it was obvious that the Religion Game as played by the paid priests, with its shabby confidence tricks, promises, threats, persecutions and killings, was merely a hideous travesty of the real game, a terrible confirmation of the truth of the statement: 'These people praise me with their lips but their hearts are far from me...

They have eyes but see not, ears and hear not, neither do they understand. (DeRopp, 1968, p. 19).

THE MASTER GAME. The aim of the game is true awakening, full consciousness, and the full development of the power latent in people.

Object games are played primarily for the attainment of material things, primarily money, and the objects which money can buy. Meta-games are played primarily for intangibles such as knowledge, awakening, consciousness, or the salvation of the soul. "In our culture object games predominate. In earlier cultures meta-games predominated. To the players of meta-games, object games have always seemed shallow and futile, an attitude summarized in the Gospel saying: 'What shall it profit a man if he gain the whole world and lose his own soul?' To the players of object games, meta-games seem fuzzy and ill defined, involving nebulous concepts like beauty, truth or salvation. The whole human population of the earth can be divided roughly into two groups, meta-game players and object-game players...The two have never understood one another and it is safe to predict that they never will" (De Ropp, 1968, p. 12-13).

Dr. Eric Berne (1964) the founder of a type of counseling, psychotherapy, and self-help called Transactional Analysis, devoted an entire book to *Games People Play.* Dr. Berne described "Life Games" such as Alcoholic, Debtor, Kick Me, Now I've Got You-You Son of a Bitch, See What You Made Me Do. "Marital Games" such as corner, courtroom, frigid woman, Harried, If It Weren't for You, Look How Hard I've Tried, and Sweetheart. "Party Games" such as Ain't It Awful, Blemish, Schlemiel, and Why Don't You-Yes But. "Sexual Games" such as Lets You and Him Fight, Perversion, Rape, The Stocking Game, and Uproar. "Underworld Games" such as Cops and Robbers, How Do You Get Out of Here, and Let's Pull a Fast One on Joey. "Consulting Room Games" such as Greenhouse, I'm Only Trying to Help You, Indigence, Peasant, Psychiatry, Stupid, and Wooden Leg. "Good Games" such as Busman's Holiday, Cavalier, Happy to Help, Homely Sage, and They'll Be Glad They Knew Me. Each of these "games" provides an emotional payoff for the players.

DECIDING WHETHER TO ELIMINATE THE BUTTON OR MODIFY IT TO A PREFERENCE

This part of the fifth step is determining how you want to deal with your Button(s). Perhaps you would like to free yourself from all of your Buttons (e.g. attachments and demands), including the current Button you are working on, in order to become less stressed and more conscious, accepting, and loving. Or, perhaps you have decided that freeing yourself from all of your Buttons is a bit too ambitious and unrealistic at this stage of your personal growth. Perhaps you have decided to set a more achievable goal of simply spending less time in a typical day reacting like a robot and becoming upset whenever you have your Buttons pushed. Instead of spending one-third of your waking hours with an inner experience of stress, distress, or being out of harmony, maybe your goal is to cut back the time spent upset and out of harmony to ten percent of your waking hours. Perhaps you are simply fed up with allowing your inner experience and emotions to be controlled by the Button-Pushers in your life. Maybe you're ready to take more responsibility for determining which messages, beliefs, wants, scripts, and other cognitions you allow in to your biocomputer. Whatever your goals, you do have choices. *You* are primarily responsible for creating your inner experience, good or bad. If you are not satisfied with the quality of your inner experience, level of stress, and your relationships, it is up to you to change it!

CHAPTER SIXTEEN

COGNITIVE INTERVENTIONS

*He who recognizes the existence of suffering, its cause, its remedy,
and its cessation, has fathomed the four noble truths.
He will walk in the right path.*

Buddha
ANGUTTARA-NIKAYA

THERE ARE MANY COGNITIVE INTERVENTIONS helpful in
rooting out unwanted Buttons that cause emotional distress. Although the cognitive interventions described in this chapter can be utilized independently,
these techniques are best utilized after implementing all of the preceding four
steps of the Button Therapy model. It is important that you learn, with sufficient practice, early recognition of your subtle physical, mental, and spiritual
cues of stress when a Button becomes activated (step 1); to identify the specific
Buttons responsible for your psychological distress (step 2); and identify the
triggered emotions (step 3) and motivational states (step 4) associated with the
Buttons. Without processing your Buttons through the first four steps of the
Button Therapy model, the following cognitive interventions may simply provide temporary relief from the emotional consequences (i.e. symptoms) of the
activated Button through thought suppression, distraction, and catharsis techniques and not adequately deal with the cause (i.e. Button) of your psychological distress. With a short period of practice all six steps of the Button Therapy
method can be utilized to work on a Button in less than one minute.

The following cognitive techniques can alleviate the emotional distress
associated with a Button and help eliminate Buttons. These cognitive techniques can also help prevent us from saying and doing things that may harm
others or ourselves when our Buttons are pushed. These cognitive interventions
can eliminate Buttons over time with repeated use. These cognitive interventions are effective when used independently or in combination with the other
five steps of the Six-step Button Therapy Method. However, I believe they are
more effective when used in combination with the Six-Step Button Therapy
Method.

The next three chapters are descriptions of cognitive interventions that
can be used in the fifth step of the Six-Step Button Therapy Method. The cognitive interventions have been grouped into three categories. Chapter 17
includes portable self-help cognitive interventions that can be used at the time

a Button becomes activated. Chapter 18 includes cognitive interventions best used during scheduled times in the privacy of your home. Chapter 19 includes cognitive interventions that are best used in conjunction with a mental health professional. Table 18 can be utilized by individuals and professional counselors as a quick review of available cognitive techniques when applying step 5 (i.e. a cognitive intervention) of the Six-Step Button Therapy Method.

TABLE 18

COGNITIVE INTERVENTIONS

PORTABLE SELF-HELP COGNITIVE INTERVENTIONS

1. CHANGING DEMANDS TO PREFERENCES. If the cognition (e.g. thought) associated with the Button (i.e. demand) is still valued, keep the cognition and eliminate the associated psychological distress by changing your demand for the cognition to a preference.

2. SELF-TALK. Utilizing the "self-talk" technique you can modify, or eliminate your thoughts, irrational beliefs, parent messages, programs, scripts, expectations, and other models of how things should be that are triggering emotional distress by changing the way you talk to yourself.

3. DISPUTING TROUBLESOME COGNITIONS. Cognitive disputation makes use of self-talk, persuasion, direct questions and logical reasoning to help dispute irrational beliefs and other troublesome cognitions.

4. COGNITIVE THOUGHT-STOPPING. When a Button that you have targeted for elimination enters your conscious awareness simply shout, "STOP" either out loud or to yourself and chase the thought away. It also accentuates the "shout it out" power if you wear a rubber band around your wrist and snap it as you yell "STOP"!

5. FLOODING. A technique where you can intentionally and fully experience the emotions associated with an activated Button with no attempt to suppress the thought causing your distress. By staying with the distressing thought as long and as intensely as you can you will eventually exhaust the emotional energy associated with the Button making the cognition more amenable to modification or elimination.

6. COUNTING TO 10. When you have a Button pushed and experience intense emotions that are overriding any attempt at rational analysis, sometimes the best thing to do is back off and count to ten before you do or say anything that you may regret. Counting to ten allows some of the emotional intensity associated with your activated Button to dissipate before you act versus react.

7. HERE-AND-NOW. When you become aware of a troublesome thought or Button that you want to eliminate, including "pasting" and "futuring" thinking, first use the "cognitive thought-stopping" technique followed by the "here-and-now" technique to focus on the reality of your now moment.

8. MAD DIRECTOR FANTASY TECHNIQUE. This technique is especially useful for working on Buttons associated with the power and control motivational states. This technique utilizes a combination of fantasy, visualization, and exaggeration techniques.

9. EMPATHY DOUBLER. The EDT is a cognitive intervention whereby you can quickly free yourself from the grips of a Button by simply realizing that at some time in your life you have probably done the same thing that you are getting uptight at someone else for doing.

SCHEDULED COGNITIVE INTERVENTIONS

10. EMPTY-CHAIR. The empty-chair technique can be used to work on troublesome cognitions (TCs) or Buttons by placing the Button or TC (i.e. belief, "should message," injunction, or expectation) in an empty-chair facing you. Create a dialogue between the Button and the more rational healthy nonattached you and switch chairs as you speak for each part of the conflict. Continue the dialogue until there is closure.

11. THE WORRY PLACE. Another thought suppression technique to restrict the amount of time that you experience distress (e.g. anxiety and worrying) from a Button by restricting your worry time to a certain location, such as a certain chair (e.g. the "Worry Chair"). You can worry as much as you want but only in your "Worry Chair" and not in any other place or time.

12. THE SCHEDULED PITY POT. This is another thought suppression technique to restrict the time you spend distressing yourself. With this time allotment technique you can worry, obsess, dwell on unpleasant thoughts or images, and wallow on your "Pity Pot" during a particular designated time each day, but *only* during this time period.

13. MIND CLEANSING. A technique to "clean" out negative thoughts from your mind at the end of each day by either reversing or transmuting the negative thought into a neutral or happy thought.

14. MEDITATION. Meditation helps quiet the undisciplined and scattered mind in order to experience a healthier state of relaxation, inner calm, centeredness, focused awareness, connection with God or the universal life force, and eliminating Buttons (e.g. attachments).

Cognitive Interventions that are Best Used in Conjunction with a Mental Health Professional

15. INJUNCTIONS AND REDECISION WORK. In redecision therapy you learn about your specific injunctions that you acquired as a child, examine their effects on your life, and make new decisions as to whether you want to modify or eliminate them.

16. INNER CHILD AND REPARENTING WORK. Inner child work involves contacting, reclaiming, and nurturing your inner child. Reclaiming and nurturing your inner child may involve going back through your developmental stages and finishing your unfinished business.

17. REFRAMING. Through cognitive reframing you can view the situation that triggered distress from an alternate viewpoint. Reframing is adopting a viewpoint that can alleviate emotional distress or trigger positive feelings.

18. PARADOXICAL INTENTION. These techniques are similar to the popular conception of "reverse psychology" where you ask or advocate for the opposite of what you really want.

19. SELF-HYPNOSIS. Through self-hypnosis you can achieve a state of relaxation and focused attention in order to modify troublesome cognitions and eliminate Buttons.

20. GROUP BUTTON THERAPY EMPTY-CHAIR TECHNIQUE. A combined empty-chair and cognitive group counseling technique that includes group members giving a voice to unverbalized or unintegrated aspects of the inner or interpersonal conflict. This technique is a way of bringing group members into an individual's empty-chair cognitive work and provides multiple viewpoints of an issue.

21. GROUP BUTTON-PULL. This technique can be utilized by professional counselors in group counseling to help individuals working on their Buttons by having the other group members give voices and dramatize the various aspects of the individual's Button.

The Button Therapy Book: How to Work on Your Buttons and the Button-Pushers in Your Life by Lloyd R. Goodwin, Jr. © 2002. Published by Trafford Publishing. www.trafford.com

CHAPTER SEVENTEEN

PORTABLE SELF-HELP
COGNITIVE INTERVENTIONS

...there are stages at which you feel pulled in to inner work and all you seek is a quiet place to meditate and to get on with it. Then there are times when you turn outward and seek to be involved in the market place. Both of these parts of the cycle are a part of one's sadhana [spiritual journey]. For what happens to you in the market place helps in your meditation and what happens to you in meditation helps you to participate in the market place with out attachment.

Baba Ram Dass
BE HERE NOW

THE BEST TIME TO WORK on a Button is when you have one pushed by a friend, love interest, or boss in the marketplace of life. This existential moment, while experiencing the emotional suffering from an activated Button, is an opportune time to eliminate a Button. When you are experiencing the emotional, psychological, behavioral, spiritual, and interpersonal effects and consequences of an activated Button is when you can best channel some of the emotional energy into eliminating the Button. For individuals doing energy work you can channel the fire of the intense emotional energy into dissipating the energy grid of the troublesome belief or model associated with the attachment (i.e. Button) on the etheric plane.

Some activated Buttons trigger such intense and overwhelming emotional reactions that we can not consciously and rationally work the energy when the Button is activated. We may need to utilize a portable self-help cooling off cognitive intervention such as "counting to ten" to keep from doing something irrational, homicidal, or something we may regret later. After we cool off we may want to use one of the other cognitive interventions either alone or with a mental health professional to identify harmful Buttons and eliminate them.

The following are portable self-help cognitive interventions that can be used when a Button becomes activated:

• Changing demands to preferences
• Self-talk

- Disputing troublesome cognitions
- Cognitive thought-stopping
- Flooding
- Counting to 10
- Here-and-now
- Mad director fantasy
- Empathy doubler

CHANGING DEMANDS TO PREFERENCES

He who, having cast off human attachment, has left behind the attraction of the gods, he who is free from all attachment, he, I declare, is a brahmin.
Buddha
UDANAVARGA

If the thought (i.e. cognition) associated with the Button is still valued and you want to keep it, then you can modify the cognition to make it more reasonable, rational, feasible, achievable, positive, and life-enhancing. Or, you may want to keep your cognition (i.e. your model of how things should be) just the way it is with no modifications. The only aspect of this specific cognition (e.g. model of how you want things to be) that you may want to change is the emotional pain and suffering associated with it because you are attached (i.e. addicted, demanding) to this cognition. This can be done simply by changing your *demand* (i.e. Button) for a cognition to a *preference*.

By changing your demands to preferences you keep the goals, wants, desires, and models of what is fair and just that you still value. All you give up is the emotional pain and suffering associated with these cognitions, not the cognitions or wants. As you become more aware of your troublesome and self-defeating cognitions and Buttons you may realize that some of your cognitions have no redeeming value at this stage of your life. You may choose to eliminate not only the Button (i.e. the attachment) to a cognition but also the cognition itself. Many of our unwanted Buttons were acquired early in life and may have served a useful purpose at age seven years old but are no longer appropriate nor helpful at age thirty.

SELF-TALK

We are constantly talking to ourselves. We are usually not aware of the continuous, automatic self-talk in our heads, let alone, how our self-talk affects our feelings and inner experience. Utilizing the "self-talk" technique we can modify, or eliminate our thoughts, irrational beliefs, parent messages, programs, scripts, expectations, and other models of how things should be that are triggering emotional distress by changing the way we talk to ourselves.

When modifying a demand or attachment (i.e. Button) associated with a cognition to a preference, we can simply tell ourselves very succinctly and firmly exactly how we want to modify our cognitions (e.g. models of how things should be). For example, if I have a Button related to everybody understanding and agreeing with The Six-Step Button Therapy Method as a way to work on their stress and personal growth, I may choose to keep the cognition (i.e. the desire that people see worth and value in the Six-Step BT Method) by changing the *demand* for this cognition to a *preference*. Or I may decide, after I identify the Button, that the cognition I am demanding is not something I want to keep in my biocomputer. I may tell myself that expecting *everybody* to understand and agree with the Six-Step Button Therapy Method is ridiculous and that desire (i.e. cognition) needs to go. A more realistic model is that, "I hope some people can benefit from the Six-Step BT Method in their personal growth work."

DISPUTING TROUBLESOME COGNITIONS

Argue for your limitations, and sure enough, they're yours.
Richard Bach
ILLUSSIONS

Some of our cognitions are clearly related to beliefs that we hold about ourselves, others, and the world in general. Some of our beliefs are clearly irrational. According to Dr. Albert Ellis, an early pioneer in cognitive therapy and founder of Rational Emotive Therapy (RET; currently called Rational Emotive Behavioral Therapy) and some of his colleagues (Ellis, McInerney, DiGiuseppe & Yeager, 1988) "irrational beliefs have several overlapping ingredients. They include: a) demandingness, b) awfulizing c) low tolerance for frustration d) rating of self and/or others, and e) overgeneralizing the future. According to RET theory, the first irrational belief, grandiose musts and demandingness, tends to lead to the other four" (p. 7).

COGNITIVE DISPUTING TECHNIQUE. Cognitive disputation is a method that can be helpful when the irrationality of the belief causing your emotional distress becomes immediately obvious. When we become aware of Buttons and troublesome cognitions associated with irrational beliefs we can dispute them by utilizing the cognitive "self-talk" approach described earlier. "Cognitive disputation makes use of persuasion, direct questions and logical reasoning to help clients dispute their irrational beliefs" (Cormier & Hackney, 1987, p.142). Although "RET does *not* consist of cognitive restructuring nor of *disputation*...this is one of its *main* methods" (Ellis, McInerney, DiGiuseppe & Yeager, 1988, p.72). Some examples of questions suggested for cognitive disputation from the RET model include:

- Is that true? Why not?
- Can you prove it?
- How do you know?
- Why is that an overgeneralization?
- Why is that a bad term to use?
- How would you talk a friend out of such an idea?
- What would happen if ____?
- If that's true, what's the worst that can happen?
- So what if that happens?
- How would that be so terrible?
- Where's the evidence?
- How is a disadvantage awful?
- Ask yourself, can I still find happiness?
- What *good* things can happen if X occurs?
- Can you be happy even if you don't get what you want?
- What might happen?
- How terrible would that be?
- Why would that do you in?
- What is the probability of a bad consequence?
- How will you be destroyed if X happens?
- As long as you believe that, how will you feel?
- Whatever I want, I must get." Where will that get you?
- Is it worth it? (Walen, DiGiuseppe & Wessler 1980, pp. 97-99).

I have found it helpful to sometimes utilize self-talk and ask myself some of the suggested questions listed above in order to dispute an irrational belief that is the source of a particular Button. However, unless the irrationality of the belief that I'm attached to is immediately obvious, I rarely utilize this cognitive disputation method. In my personal and clinical counseling experience I have found that individuals with average and above average intellects tend to have well developed rational minds when it comes to utilizing defense mechanisms. And, when asked to question the validity of one of their irrational beliefs these individuals will generate a hundred different reasons why their belief is "rational," "right," "just," or "fair." For example, "You mean I'm being *irrational* to get emotionally distressed when my teacher falsely accuses me of having marijuana seeds at school? No way! Who wouldn't get upset if this happened to them? The principal and resource officer are out to get me ever since I started letting my hair grow long. Both the principal and resource officer don't like male students with long hair!" As Cormier and Hackney (1987) point out, "When the counselor describes the client's thoughts or beliefs as 'irrational,' 'mistaken,' or 'illogical,' clients are sometimes likely to perceive that they themselves, as well as their ideas, are being attacked. A client may say, 'Who me - crazy? I'm not crazy.' This may be especially true for some types of clients (rebellious teenagers or rigid adults, for example). Clients are also likely to have negative reactions if the counselor's labels are given in the context of a highly directive, active, and confrontational therapeutic style that is seemingly devoid of understanding and warmth" (p. 166).

In counseling sessions I avoid spending time examining the "irrational belief" Button as being either right or wrong - or rational or irrational, unless, as I stated earlier, the irrationality of a belief is blatant and jumps out at me immediately. Unfortunately, as described in the BT third step dealing with emotions, when some intense emotions resulting from activated Buttons are triggered, especially those emotions related to perceived threat to ego, core beliefs, or survival, all the rational disputation in the world may not make a dent in someone's belief system. At such times it doesn't matter whether the beliefs are rational or irrational.

By exploring the Button from the context of *attachment* or *demanding* versus *preferring*, there is less need for someone to call out the rational mind troops (e.g. defense mechanisms) to distort reality, protect one's ego and deal with anxiety and stress. I have found it more helpful when confronted with an irrational belief Button to simply recognize that I am *demanding* something (i.e. a belief) to happen a certain way instead of *preferring* it to happen a certain way, and that is what is causing my emotional distress. Now, do I want to modify this Button (e.g. change my demand for the thought, expectation, or model to a preference) or eliminate it. Oftentimes, I have found that the conscious intent underlying my "irrational beliefs" and other troublesome cognitions are fine and I choose to keep them. At other times I realize a belief is clearly irrational. When one of my beliefs becomes "irrational", it is often because I have fallen victim to one or more of the distorted styles of thinking described in an earlier chapter. So, upon reflecting on a belief, I often decide to keep the essence of the belief, clarify the intent, clean up the belief so it is rational, reasonable, and realistic, and change my attachment to it (i.e. Button) to preferential programming. Whatever method(s) you choose to use, it is helpful to recognize and modify or eliminate irrational beliefs, and other troublesome cognitions, to facilitate your journey of personal growth.

In summary, instead of questioning whether or not a cognition or belief is rational or irrational, I choose to simply recognize that I am demanding versus preferring something to be other than it is. I realize that this is the basic psychodynamic of self-generated psychological distress. However, what works for me may not be the same strategies that you find yourself drawn to. So you may want to give this cognitive disputation method a try next time you get a Button pushed when the Button is an attachment to an irrational belief.

COGNITIVE THOUGHT-STOPPING

The cognitive thought-stopping technique can be an effective cognitive intervention after you have already worked on a specific Button utilizing the Six-Step Button Therapy Method and understand the motivational state(s) and emotion(s) associated with the Button. The cognitive thought-stopping technique can be used whenever troublesome cognitions or Buttons, especially cognitions related to core beliefs, should messages, parental injunctions, and addictive obsessive repetitive thoughts, enter your consciousness.

When a Button that you have targeted for elimination enters your conscious awareness simply shout, "STOP" either out loud or to yourself, and chase the thought away. You can amplify the power of the "shout it out" technique if you wear a rubber band around your wrist and snap it as you yell "STOP"! The snapping of the rubber band will trigger the stress response and add some adrenaline and energy to your "STOP" command. If you have an aversion to the mild pain from snapping the rubber band, you can clap your hands loudly and break the hold of the thought on your consciousness. After shouting, snapping, or clapping away the troublesome cognition or Button, fan away the fragmented energy left after the energy is broken free from the Button with your hands. This helps disperse the energy associated with the Button away from your vicinity. The only problem with the clapping the hands part of this technique is that it looks really weird when you do it in public. You may get some strange looks from other people with this one. You may want to save the hand clapping and disposing of broken-up negative energy associated with your Button for those times when you are alone.

This combination of shouting "STOP" and snapping the rubber band, or clapping the hands, can usually temporarily dislodge the most intractable and persistent Button. Over time, by not allowing its expression, nor experiencing the emotional distress when the Button is allowed to surface, the Button will not receive much attention or reinforcement. Hopefully, in time the troublesome thought or Button may stop surfacing and finally cease to exist (i.e. extinguish). Cognitive thought-stopping is a thought suppression technique which will help you change your Button, or troublesome cognition, without processing it through all six of the steps in the BT model.

I say the cognitive thought-stopping technique *may* facilitate the extinction of a Button because even though this technique short-circuits the full expression of an activated cognition or Button, we are still giving it attention by shouting "STOP" at our first awareness of it. This act may possibly reinforce it. It is possible that we can never truly become free of certain cognitions or Buttons by consciously suppressing their expression as they are still with us and have simply gone underground into our subconscious only to surface again when activated.

Ideally, when we have one of our Buttons activated we can face them and begin uprooting them instead of simply suppressing of dissipating the emotional energy associated with Buttons. Ideally we can apply all of the six-steps in the Button Therapy Method, allowing the expression of the activated Buttons and draining them of their emotional energy by connecting the emotions to the Buttons. Then replace the troublesome cognitions and Buttons with positive life-enhancing messages.

If you do utilize the thought-stopping technique after the Button has already triggered emotional distress, remember to channel the emotional energy to the guilty Button and not to the Button-Pusher. Each time you direct the activated emotional energy to the Button that triggered the distress you will continue to uproot the Button as well as divest the Button of its emotional energy. See step three of the Six-Step Button Therapy Method for details of how to use the emotional energy generated when a Button is pushed to modify or uproot a Button.

FLOODING

Flooding is a technique where you can intentionally and fully experience the emotions associated with an activated Button with no attempt to suppress the thought causing the distress. By staying with the distressing thought as long and as intensely as you can you will eventually exhaust the emotional energy associated with the Button. You will eventually feel neutral or bored and the thought or image that you are attached to (i.e. Button) will temporarily lose its power over you. After the emotional energy associated with the Button is depleted the Button is more amenable to modification or elimination. You may have heard of this flooding technique being used when a parent catches his or her underage child smoking cigarettes. The parent may tell the child to go ahead and smoke the whole pack non-stop one after another. This "flooding" technique will generally make the child sick with nicotine poisoning. Hopefully, the child associates smoking cigarettes with nausea and anxiety and gives up smoking. This is a potentially dangerous technique and I do not recommend it for quitting smoking or any other psychoactive substance. Any time you force a psychoactive drug on somebody, especially a child, there is a risk of harmful life threatening adverse physiological reactions. Excessive tobacco intake can result in acute nicotine poisoning with a possibility of cardiac arrhythmia or other adverse cardiovascular consequences. Although "flooding" can be potentially harmful with psychoactive substances, flooding can be a helpful technique with other selected troublesome cognitions and Buttons that don't involve harm to self or others.

COUNTING TO TEN

When you have a Button pushed and experience intense emotions that are overriding any attempt at rational behavior or analysis, sometimes the best thing to do is back off and count to ten before you do or say anything that you may later regret. Counting to ten allows some of the emotional intensity associated with your activated Button to dissipate before you react. Expressing reactive and unconscious emotional energy from an activated Button can result in harm to other peoples' energy fields, psyches, and physical health. Counting to ten when in the grips of overwhelming negative emotions can help prevent your overt expression of distressful emotions from spewing more negative toxins in the air. Counting to ten can also help you gain self-control before you say or do something that you may regret when you become more conscious and proactive (vs. reactive).

By counting to ten before reacting you can switch the focus of your awareness from the activated Button to something else (i.e. counting to ten). There is nothing magical about the number 10 in this refocusing technique. You may feel a need to count to 20, 30, or higher with some activated Buttons before you can dissipate enough negative emotional energy in order to act and not react. This is a useful technique to "time yourself out" in order to gain some self-control and not lay into someone - or yourself.

HERE-AND-NOW

Yesterday is but a dream, tomorrow is but a vision.
But today well lived makes every yesterday a dream of happiness, and every
tomorrow a vision of hope.
Look well, therefore, to this day.

Sanskrit proverb

The here-and-now technique helps you focus your thinking on the existential present moment and stop ruminating about the past or worrying about the future. The "here-and-now" technique is a good technique to use in combination with the cognitive thought-stopping technique (CTST). When you become aware of a troublesome thought or Button that you want to eliminate, including "pasting" and "futuring" type of thinking, first use the CTST followed by the "here-and-now" technique.

One way to get into your here and now is to start describing everything that you become aware of in the present moment. Start off each of your thoughts with the stem "Now I am aware of..." For example, "Now I am aware of music playing on my stereo...incense burning...the computer screen...the light on my desk...my thought to change the comma in this sentence to..." By describing your internal and external environment, as you become aware of it, you can change your focus from ruminating about the past or worrying about the future to attending to the here-and-now present moment. If there is something you can do to finish some unfinished past business or plan for the future, then do it now. If you have done all that you can do to deal with a past situation such as making amends for something you've done or you've done everything you can to prepare for some future event then let it go. Utilize the cognitive thought-stopping and here-and-now techniques to focus on the reality of your now moment.

MAD DIRECTOR FANTASY TECHNIQUE

The Mad Director Fantasy Technique (MDFT) utilizes a combination of fantasy, visualization, and exaggeration techniques. The MDFT is a fantasy exercise that can be utilized once a Button has been activated and identified. The MDFT is especially useful for working on Buttons associated with the power and control motivational states.

To illustrate the MDFT, let's suppose I have a Button related to *everybody* agreeing with me that the Button Therapy (BT) model and Six-Step Button Therapy Method of working on Buttons is the best cognitive therapy model. Suppose I am presenting this BT model to a group of counselors-in training (which I do frequently) and a few of the counseling students let me know they don't agree with some aspect of the BT model. If I am addictively demanding (i.e. have a Button) that, "*all* my counseling students agree that the BT model is the best cognitive therapy model," I will get myself uptight if just one counseling student says something like, "I think the ABCD mnemonic acronym in Rational-Emotive Behavioral Therapy model is much easier to remember than ABE's MBA mnemonic acronym (explained in chapter 24) in the BT model." Utilizing the MDFT, after this Button becomes pushed I imagine:

> ... myself dressed as a movie director with a black beret and khaki knickers. I'm holding a megaphone, and sitting in a director's chair with "Director" stenciled on the back. I imagine a counselor education classroom scene with myself as the professor and my counseling students sitting in the classroom. When a student questions some aspect of the BT model in a disbelieving manner I become a very mad movie director and jump out of my director's chair and yell through the megaphone "STOP this scene! CUT! This scene is all wrong! The scene is supposed to go like this: The professor explains the BT model and *all* the counseling students are impressed with the brilliance and simplicity of all aspects of the BT model and immediately and enthusiastically want to learn how to utilize

the BT model in their counseling and psychotherapy sessions with clients. After all, the ABE's MBA acronym is only a stupid mnemonic device for people who can't remember six steps! Now that everybody understands how the scene is supposed to go let's retake the scene. And this time, let's get it right (i.e. My Way)!

The MDFT is most effective for me with Buttons associated with the control and power motivational state. When you imagine yourself as the movie director, really ham it up and exaggerate your model of how things should be going to the max! It is through the exaggeration that you will see the ridiculousness of trying to force other people into your scripts of how life's dramas should be played out. When I use this technique I quickly break free from my attachment (i.e. Button) to having all of life's dramas go according to the way that Lloyd Goodwin has written the scripts. I become aware of my egotistical, narcissistic, and power-tripping self. I often end this exercise with a good laugh at myself for over identifying with life's dramas and the realization that I still have many control and power Buttons to work on.

EMPATHY DOUBLER TECHNIQUE

The empathy doubler technique (EDT) is a cognitive intervention whereby you can quickly free yourself from the grips of a Button by simply realizing that at some time in your life you have probably done the same thing that you are getting uptight at someone else for doing. The EDT is a technique, originally called the "instant consciousness doubler" by Ken Keyes, Jr. in his Living Love system of personal growth (1975).

To utilize the EDT simply ask yourself if you have ever done the same, or similar, thing that you are angry with someone else for doing. For example, suppose that you do not want cars switching lanes in front of you so closely that you have to jam on your brakes to avoid hitting them. A good want. However, because you are addictively demanding it and get yourself uptight when it happens, you, by definition, have a Button related to this driving scenario. Utilizing the EDT, when this Button gets pushed (i.e. a car pulls in front of me too closely nearly causing an accident) and I realize my blood pressure just shot up, my adrenaline is racing through my body, and I am emotionally distressed (i.e. anxious, scared, and angry), I immediately pinpoint the Button and then ask myself, "Have I ever inadvertently pulled in front of someone with my car too closely and almost caused an accident?" The answer for me is yes. With this realization I am more likely to realize that the other driver most likely was momentarily careless and not intentionally trying to run me off the road or involve me in an accident. That is why they are called "accidents." Accidents are unintentional.

Also, I realize that I've been in more than one accident in my 43 years of driving motorcycles and automobiles. Sometimes when I use the EDT this is all I have to do to let go of my demand (i.e. Button) that, "automobile drivers never cut me off on the road." It's not a Button that I encounter frequently enough to want to eliminate or modify. Besides, this particular automobile driver Button is one that triggers a dramatic stress response (i.e. fight or flight response) that helps me generate a beneficial quick evasive action (i.e. "flight" response) to avoid a collision. I am usually able to dissipate the emotional energy associated with having this specific Button activated and return to a relatively homeostatic, centered, and healthier state relatively soon after the incident occurred and I am out of danger – and, after I've questioned the offending driver's parentage and cursed the crackerjack box that provided the driver with a license.

CHAPTER EIGHTEEN

SCHEDULED COGNITIVE INTERVENTIONS

*God, grant me the serenity to accept the things I cannot change, the courage
to change the things I can, and wisdom to distinguish the one from the other.*
Attributed to Reinhold Niebuhr and
adopted by Alcoholics Anonymous

THE COGNITIVE INTERVENTIONS described in this chapter
are not as portable and immediately available to us in the marketplace of life
when a Button becomes activated as the techniques just described in the previous chapter. These cognitive interventions are best used in the privacy of your
home when you can schedule their use:

- Empty-chair
- The worry place
- The scheduled pity pot
- Mind-Cleansing
- Meditation

EMPTY-CHAIR

Derived from Gestalt Therapy, the empty-chair technique is a useful
cognitive intervention to work on troublesome cognitions (TC's) or Buttons. To
utilize the empty-chair technique to work on a Button or a TC, place two chairs
facing each other. Place the rational healthy nonattached you (RHNY) in one
chair. Place the Button or TC (i.e. attachment, addiction, belief, "should message," injunction, or expectation) in the other chair. Create a dialogue between
the Button and the RHNY.

Start by sitting in the Button chair. Become the Button and describe
yourself as the Button. Then talk to the RHNY in the opposite chair and explain
how you (Button) affect the total you, especially the RHNY. After you have
described yourself as the Button and explained how the Button affects the total
you, switch chairs and become the part of you that is more rational, nonattached, and mentally healthy (i.e. RHNY) and respond to the Button in the

other chair. Explain to the Button why you want to eliminate it. Tell the Button exactly what you think and feel about it. Also, let the Button know what you have decided to do about it in a firm no nonsense manner. Now, switch chairs and become the Button again. How does the Button respond? What does the Button have to say about the RHNY's plans for its modification or demise?

Keep switching chairs as you keep the dialogue between the RHNY and the Button going until you have achieved closure or, at least, an understanding about how things are going to be around your total self from now on.

ILLUSTRATION OF EMPTY-CHAIR WORK

To illustrate this empty-chair technique let's say you are a 20-year-old female and have a Button related to a parental injunction that says "don't be sexy." Because of this parental injunction, you dress conservatively, in drab colors, and become anxious about even looking at the section of the clothing store that displays sexy outfits. You become embarrassed even casting a glance over at the skirts with high hemlines and low cut blouses that show a lot of cleavage. You blush even walking past the Victoria's Secret clothing store in the mall. The thought of purchasing such sexy clothing items is totally out of the question.

Now, let's suppose you are getting bored with your clothes and make-up, and are ready for a complete makeover. However, you can't muster the courage to make the change in your appearance. Thoughts like, "What would people think if I wore clothes like that?" keep surfacing every time you contemplate such a change. You subsequently become aware from reading *The Button Therapy Book* that one reason you are unable to make a change is because you have the parental injunction "don't be sexy" in your biocomputer. You realize that the parental injunction is more than a troublesome cognition. It is now a fully formed Button because you get yourself uptight just thinking about sexy clothes, let alone looking at them, or wearing them.

You decide to utilize the *empty-chair* technique to eliminate the "don't be sexy" Button. You put the "don't be sexy" Button in one chair and the RHNY in the other chair. Here's how the dialogue may go:

DON'T BE SEXY (DBS) BUTTON: I am your DBS Button. I've been around since you were five years old. I was put in your mind when your mother caught you playing with her makeup and wearing one of her black evening dresses and high heels. She became very angry and grabbed the red lipstick out of your little hand and said, "take off those clothes and makeup and don't ever use my makeup or clothes again. It's not nice for little girls to wear makeup or dress sexy." This wasn't the only time you were caught playing grown-up as a child by your parents. Your mother and father caught you two more times playing with your mother's makeup and clothes over the next two years. Each time they caught you they reinforced my (i.e. "don't be sexy" Button) with intense negative emotional energy. I am so ingrained in your mind – you will never get rid of me!

RHNY: Thanks for sharing. It's nice to know why I get so anxious and uptight every time I consider changing my appearance. I would also like you to know that I'm now 20 years old and I'm in charge here now and you can take a hike. I want to change my look and become more attractive, outgoing, and sexy. I want to wear a red sexy dress. I want a little more excitement in my life. And I've decided you need to go.

DBS BUTTON: I'm not going anywhere. I like it here. I have quite a bit of influence and control here in my little area of your life domain. So give it up. Stop even looking at sexy clothes and makeup. I will make you so anxious and uptight whenever you do that you might as well not even think about fooling with me. You can't get rid of me. I've been here since you were 5 years old and am not going away.

RHNY: You have made my life miserable for years and I feel very restricted, programmed, and nonspontaneous. I'm ready to make some changes. I am hereby banishing you to the trash bin of purged Buttons, where you will be burned. Your energy will be transmuted by the etheric flames and merged into the universal life source. Your identity as a "don't be sexy" Button will be gone forever!

DBS BUTTON: Not so fast old great Button-Hunter. I don't give up that easily. You forget that I have been with you since a very early age and have been reinforced with psychic cement many times over the years. I'm here to stay. Besides, do you want people to think you are a tramp? Wearing a sexy outfit like that is going to attract a lot of male attention and they will be thinking of only one thing - sex! Everybody, male and female, will be thinking that you are nothing but a tramp!"

RHNY: Because I spice up my wardrobe and makeup to make me more attractive and add a little excitement to my life does not make me a "tramp." You have been able to operate because I was not conscious of your existence. I am now aware of you and the "black and white" and "catastrophic thinking" styles that you trick me with — and now you have to go! You are restricting my life and causing me a lot of distress. I decide which messages and beliefs in my biocomputer stay and which ones go - And you have to go! Goodbye, I can't say it's been nice knowing you.

Keep the dialogue going until you have achieved closure and eliminated the Button or modified the troublesome cognition. You will know when you have successfully modified or eliminated your Button when you speak from your RHNY side with a firm conviction and a sense of certainty and hope. You may not completely eliminate a Button and it may rear its ugly head sometime in the future, but here-and-now you can be relatively sure you have deflated the energy associated with it and diminished it's power. If the Button regains some power over time you can work on it in the future whenever it becomes activated.

Empty-chair work is an excellent technique for not only exploring and eliminating Buttons and troublesome cognitions, but also for getting in touch with the emotions and consequences associated with the Buttons. Exaggerate both the Button and the RHNY side when doing empty-chair work. Really ham it up. Make outrageous exaggerated statements from both the Button and the RHNY chairs. Explore the extreme polarities of any continuum related to a Button. In the example of the "don't be sexy" Button empty-chair work above, on one end of the appearance continuum you could exaggerate yourself as a conservatively dressed, no makeup prude and on the polar opposite of the continuum you could exaggerate yourself as a heavily made-up sexily dressed tramp. By becoming both polar extremes of the continuum and creating a dialogue between both polarities we can more clearly see the injunctions or "should" messages operating in our minds. Through playing and exaggerating both polar extremes we can arrive at more realistic cognitions or models of how we want things to be in our minds. Also, by exploring both aspects of the self (e.g. the don't be sexy Button and the RHNY) you can better appreciate how much havoc and distress your Buttons have caused in your life.

THE WORRY PLACE

The "Worry Place" is a thought suppression technique to restrict the amount of time that you experience distress (e.g. anxiety and worrying) from a Button by restricting your worry time to a certain location, such as a certain chair (e.g. the "Worry Chair"). You can worry as much as you want but only in your "Worry Chair" and not in any other place.

Just as we can accumulate negative energy in a "Worry Place," we can develop positive energy in a special place that we associate with spirituality, peace, and joy such as a meditation room or church. Places can hold certain meaning and energy for us. Many college students have certain chairs they sit in for each classroom. Some individuals develop a mild Button (i.e. attachment) to "their" chair. If they enter the class late and someone else is sitting in "their" chair there is a brief twinge of discomfort until they can refocus their attention on other matters (hopefully their professor's lecture) and dissipate the emotional energy associated with the "That's My Chair" Button. Sometimes I play with this phenomenon in my group counseling training sessions with counseling students by occasionally sitting in a different chair.

THE SCHEDULED PITY-POT TECHNIQUE

This is another thought suppression technique to restrict the time you spend distressed. With this time allotment technique you can worry, obsess, dwell on unpleasant thoughts or images, and wallow on your "Pity-Pot" during a particular designated time each day, but only during this predetermined time period. Set a timer (e.g. kitchen timer) for a designated period, such as ten or fifteen minutes. During this time, you can dwell on the unpleasant thoughts, images, or feelings all you want. Worry as much as you want about things that have happened to you in the past or about the catastrophic things that may happen to you in the future. However, as soon as the timer rings, you must get off the "Pity-Pot" and go on to another activity or task. You can allot a limited predetermined time frame all at one time or at specified times during the day to think about negative or worrisome thoughts. For example, you can sit on your Pity-Pot and indulge your negative thoughts, images, or feelings for the first five minutes of each hour and at no other time.

The "Worry Chair" and "Scheduled Pity-Pot Technique" are both thought suppression techniques that help restrict the *place* and *time* for indulging your activated Buttons and troublesome cognitions and help you gain self-control. You will often find yourself being able to suppress a distressing thought with the knowledge that you can totally indulge your Button at night when you get home from school or work and sit on your "Pity Pot" or "Worry Chair." Chances are that later on when you arrive home from a hard day at work or school you will no longer feel distressed from the Button which was pushed earlier in the day and feel no need to sit on the "Pity Pot" or "Worry Chair." You then get into the flow of home and family activities with the distress triggered earlier in the day a distant memory.

MIND-CLEANSING

Mind-Cleansing is an exercise to "clean" out negative thoughts from your mind. Mind-Cleansing is a technique developed as part of the DME (Drugless Mind Expansion) Yoga program (Ware & Goodwin, 1968), a prevention and treatment program for substance abusers based on the drugless alternative concept. "Negative thoughts will occur in daily life. When they do occur the individual is trained to either reverse of transmute the negative into a neutral or happy thought. 'Transmutation is flowing with it until it blends out and enters into a happy thought. Reversal is simply thinking its opposite. Daily

Mind-Cleansing helps break up negative thought patterns which may have become habitual" (Ware & Goodwin, 1968, p. 15).

Mind-Cleansing can also be practiced at the end of each day as you lie in bed before going to sleep. Before passing into slumberland review your daily activities and identify any situations that triggered your Buttons. As you recall a Button-activating situation try to relive it as if it was happening all over again. However, this time imagine yourself handling the situation from a centered, loving, and proactive space instead of a reactive negative space. For example, you may have had negative thoughts about somebody during the day. Even though you didn't act on them, the person clearly triggered one of your Buttons and you didn't like the way you reacted to this individual. As you relive the Button-pushing situation imagine yourself staying centered, loving, and aware. You may gain some increased awareness concerning the event. Perhaps the Button-Pusher was having a bad day or really didn't mean anything by his or her comment. Perhaps the Button-Pusher was reacting to the situation because of one of his or her own Buttons. As a result of hindsight and some distance from the actual Button-pushing event you are more likely to respond in the way you would prefer in your imagination. Sometimes you may have to stay with reliving the situation in your mind awhile until you can transmute the negative energy into either neutral or positive thoughts and feelings. Mind-Cleansing helps prevent the accumulation of negative thoughts and feelings, which carry into the next day and throughout your life. Mind-Cleansing also helps break up negative thought patterns that may have become habitual because of long standing troublesome cognitions and Buttons.

We can also utilize the Mind-Cleansing cognitive technique review past events in our lives going back a day, weeks, months, or to our earliest memories. This can be done at the end of the day just before going to bed as described above or during a relaxed meditative state during the day.

I recommend that you practice Mind-Cleansing every evening before going to sleep. Some couples practice a variation of the Mind-Cleansing technique by agreeing to work out any problems they may have had during the day before they go to bed at night.

MEDITATION

Meditation is an umbrella word, which includes a variety of mental and spiritual techniques to achieve a variety of goals. Our minds tend to be hyperactive and scattered, jumping from one thought to another. This is much like a monkey's mind with scattered and hyperactive thoughts and impulsive actions. The activity of the undisciplined and scattered mind has been referred to as "monkeymind" by some experienced meditators. Throughout the day we tend to be thinking or worrying about things that have happened in the past, things that we need to do now, or things that may or may not happen in the future. One minute we are fully engrossed in an activity, the next minute we are wondering what time it is or answering the phone. After tending to the caller's needs and hanging up the phone we wonder what we were doing before the phone interruption. "Hmm, maybe I'll get some coffee or tea and try to get back to whatever I was doing before the phone interruption." Very often our days tend to go from one interruption or crises to another with little planning or goal direction. We sometimes feel like automatons going through the motions of living each day. At the end of the day we may ask ourselves, "What did I accomplish today," and have trouble answering. And we can become more discouraged and disappointed when we ask ourselves, "What did I do today that was meaningful and worthwhile? Did I make any progress toward my major life goals? Did I become more conscious, aware, loving, compassionate, and self-actualized today? Did I complete any major projects?" When asking ourselves such questions we often discover that our personal, interpersonal, and work lives have become shallow, hollow, and devoid of any real meaning. And, if we do have depth to our lives and valued meaning in our relationships, work, and personal lives we often have untamed "monkeyminds" that create regular stress and distress distracting us from enjoying our activities and our ability to be totally present in the moment. Meditation can help us become human *beings* as well as human *doers*. Meditation helps quiet the undisciplined and scattered mind in order to experience a healthier state of relaxation, inner calm, centeredness, and focused awareness.

How Does Meditation Differ from Prayer?

Prayer is talking to God, and, usually involves asking God for something. Meditation is listening to God. Or, after quieting your scattered hyperactive monkeymind you listen to your inner, more conscious, aware, and "higher" self. Although meditation is often a technique used by many religions and spiritual paths, meditation itself is not a religion.

Goals of Meditation

The method that the Buddha discovered is meditation. He discovered that struggling to find answers did not work. It was only when there were gaps in his struggle that insights came to him. He began to realize that there was a sane, awake quality within him which manifested itself only in the absence of struggle. So the practice of meditation involves "letting be."

Chogyam Trungpa
CUTTING THROUGH SPIRITUAL MATERIALISM

There are three major goals of meditation. One goal of meditation is to connect with God or the universal life source. A second goal of meditation is to become more aware, conscious, and enlightened. A third major goal for some meditators is more practical in nature and oriented toward achieving specific personal growth goals such as reducing stress, eliminating Buttons (e.g. attachments), and increasing powers of concentration.

How to Meditate

There are many types of meditation such as sitting meditation and meditation through movement (e.g. tai chi). The following are guidelines for the sitting type of meditation to work on attachments or "Buttons."

1. QUIET ENVIRONMENT. Find a quiet place to meditate. This may be outside in nature or indoors. If you plan on meditating in a room in your home select a place where you will not be disturbed. Take the phone off the hook and turn off the television.

CREATE A SACRED PLACE. Create an atmosphere conducive to meditating. Select a room that has a lot of natural sunlight and some plants. Try lighting some incense. Dim the lights if you are meditating at night. Some people use a meditation cushion. Some people play soothing instrumental music such as Steven Halpern's new age music, or soft classical music, on their stereo. You can build up good energy that can facilitate your meditations if you meditate in the same place(s). This is partly due to a conditioned attitude, mood, and spiritual focus that becomes associated with that particular place because of the repeated experiencing of the pleasant and quiet meditative state occurring in that place. It is also possible that we invest that space with positive life-enhancing spiritual energy that builds up and remains over time.

2. SITTING POSTURE. Sit cross-legged on the floor or on a small cushion with your spine erect. If you have a physical disability that prevents you from sitting on the floor then sit erect in your wheelchair or in a comfortable chair. Keep your back and spine erect and your head looking straight ahead. Allow your breathing to occur naturally and fully. This erect sitting posture allows energy to flow freely up and down your spine.

HAND POSITIONS. There are a number of ways to position your hands. One common position is to rest both hands in your lap. Place one hand in the other hand, both palms facing up, with thumbs touching. Another basic position is to rest your left hand on your left knee and your right hand on your right knee. Touch your left thumb and forefinger and your right thumb and forefinger together to create circles and allow your remaining three fingers to extend naturally on each hand.

3. BECOME RELAXED AND CENTERED. Close your eyes fully or partially. To help find your "center" gently start swaying forward and backward then from one side to the other until you feel balanced and "centered." Take a minimum of three deep breaths and allow any stress and tension to leave with each exhalation. Imagine yourself inhaling positive, loving energy and exhaling negative energy. Allow the stress to leave with each exhalation, as you become calm, relaxed, and centered. If necessary, take more than three deep breaths to become relaxed and centered.

4. FOCUS ON AN OBJECT. Focus on any object you are comfortable with. You can focus on the repetition of a sound or word such as "one", "OM", or "AUM." You may focus on a visual object such as a burning candle, mandala, or symbol. For this example, focus on your breathing. Breathe naturally and continue to let any remaining tension dissipate on your exhalation. Focus your attention on your breathing. As thoughts enter your consciousness simply note them, let them go, and bring your attention gently back to your breathing. Do this for about 3 to 5 minutes.

5. PASSIVE AWARENESS. Gently let go of focusing on your object (e.g. breathing). With a passive awareness become aware of whatever thoughts, feelings, and imagery enter your mind. As thoughts enter your mind become aware of them without clinging to them. Simply become aware of them and let them go. As interesting, pleasant, stressful, or anxiety provoking thoughts enter your consciousness don't reject them nor cling to them. Simply watch them enter and then leave the screen of your mind's eye. Become a "witness" to the movie screen of your mind's drama. Do this for approximately 5 to 10 minutes with an attitude of passive awareness.

6. ATTACHMENTS AND BUTTONS. Now that you are in a meditative state of passive awareness you can work on troublesome cognitions (TC's) and Buttons. There are at least two basic ways to work on TC's and Buttons. One way is to identify the TC's and Buttons as they enter your mind. As you become aware of a TC or a Button watch it from a passive awareness state of consciousness. Don't reject it. Don't react to it. Don't try to change it. Just watch it as the thought, image, feeling, or belief surfaces and then drifts away. Much like a fish jumping in a still pond. Watch the fish as it breaks the stillness of the water and then drifts back under water. Watch the ripples spread from the site and eventually lose their energy and form and merge with the stillness of the water. Don't reject it. Don't react to it. Don't try to change it. Just accept it as part of the beauty and synergy of life. As you become passively aware of the emerging, peaking, drifting away, and letting go of your troublesome cognitions and attachments (i.e. Button) you may gain a deeper level of awareness and understanding of the Button. By not clinging to, or reacting to a troublesome cognition or Button as it enters your conscious awareness it looses it power over you.

A second basic approach to working on your attachments (i.e. TC's and Buttons) with meditation is to actively bring into your consciousness a TC or

Button that you want to modify or eliminate. While in the passive awareness state of meditation recall a Button that you want to work on. As the TC or Button enters your awareness and begins to trigger distress catch it immediately and apply the Six-Step Button Therapy Method.

With practice, this meditative approach can eventually help you free yourself from your attachments (i.e. Buttons). Your attachments will eventually lose their power and fade away. Remember that it all starts with awareness. Meditation is probably the most effective strategy to become aware and gain insight into our TC's and Buttons. Meditation combined with the Six-Step Button Therapy method is a powerful combination of cognitive therapeutic strategies to work on TC's and Buttons.

WHEN TO MEDITATE

Meditation is most effective when practiced regularly, preferably daily. Some people find meditation most effective when practiced the same time of the day. For many meditators the best time to work meditation into their daily schedule is in the morning after showering, brushing teeth, and other hygienic rituals and before breakfast. Some meditators occasionally skip their morning meditation and meditate in the early evening between dinner and bedtime. It is best not to meditate immediately after eating or when sleepy. However, it is more important to meditate whenever you can find the time rather than avoid it because the conditions are not ideal.

CHAPTER NINETEEN

COGNITIVE INTERVENTIONS THAT ARE BEST USED IN CONJUNCTION WITH A MENTAL HEALTH PROFESSIONAL

You teach best what you most need to learn.
Richard Bach
ILLUSIONS

ALTHOUGH MOST of the cognitive interventions in this chapter can be utilized as self-help tools, they are best used in conjunction with a mental health professional. Working with cognitions, especially troublesome cognitions and Buttons, can be a very slippery and elusive endeavor. As pointed out earlier in the book, our troublesome cognitions and Buttons can be minimized, projected on to others, or simply denied by our psychological defense mechanisms and altered perceptions. Often times we need the unbiased and objective feedback from a qualified mental health professional to help us identify, own, set therapeutic goals, and utilize appropriate cognitive interventions. Also, cognitive counseling should be only one component of a holistic counseling approach that takes into account the whole person, including the physical, psychological, behavioral, spiritual, interpersonal, and environmental aspects of our lives. In addition, two of the cognitive interventions described in this chapter are to be used primarily by mental health professionals in group counseling or therapy settings.

The following are cognitive interventions best utilized with a trained mental health profession:

- Injunctions and redecision work
- Inner child and reparenting work
- Reframing
- Paradoxical intention
- Self-hypnosis
- Group Button Therapy empty-chair technique
- Group Button-Pull

INJUNCTIONS AND REDECISION WORK

Redecision work is a cognitive strategy from the "Transactional Analysis (TA)" model. An *injunction* is a parental-like message, usually given with strong emotion from a parent's own pain, disappointment, anger, and secret desires to their children. If the child believes a pathological message (i.e. injunction), especially from a parent, it may result in chronic life-long problems. Injunctions are similar to the distorted styles of thinking described in chapter six, especially the "should messages." Some common injunctions adapted from Goulding and Goulding (1979) include:

- *Don't.* This is an injunction given out of fear by a parent to their child. Out of their fear, they do not allow the child to do many normal things and can be heard saying such things as, "Don't go near the steps (to toddlers); Don't climb trees; Don't roller skate," etc. The child grows up believing that nothing he does is right or safe, doesn't know what to do and not do, and looks around for someone to tell him what to do. Such a child will have great difficulty making decisions later in life.
- *Don't be.* This is one of the most lethal messages. It may be given in subtle ways, "If it weren't for you children, I'd divorce your father." The parental message that says "If you hadn't been born, our lives would be better."
- *Don't be close.* Lack of physical touching, hugging, and lack of positive stroking lead to such an interpretation by the child. Also, if a child loses a parent through divorce or death, the child may give himself or herself this injunction by self-talk such as, "What's the use of getting close, they just die anyway" and decide never to be close again.
- *Don't be important.* For example, if a child is prevented from talking at the dinner table and told "Children are to be seen, not heard," or is discounted in some other way (e.g. at school), the child may hear, "Don't be important."
- *Don't be a child.* This message is given by parents who ask the older child to play surrogate parent and take care of the younger child. It is also given by parents who try to bowel train early, make "little men" or "little women" out of their toddlers, and stroke them for being polite before they learn what politeness means.
- *Don't grow.* A mother often gives this injunction to her youngest child. The parent may not want the child to leave home (i.e. leave her). Another example is the father who stops physically touching and hugging his daughter as soon as she begins to mature, and she interprets this as, "Don't grow up or I won't love you."
- *Don't succeed.* If a father stops playing tennis with his son after the son starts to beat him, this may be interpreted by the son as, "Don't win or I won't

like you," which gets converted into, "Don't succeed."

- *Don't be you.* This is most frequently given to the child who is the "wrong" sex. For example, a father may give up trying for a boy after four girls and teach the fourth to do "boy" and "man" things, such as playing football.

- *Don't be well and Don't be sane.* If parents give children strokes or attention for being sick and give none when the children are well, this can be interpreted as, "Don't be well." If crazy behavior is rewarded, or if crazy behavior is modeled and not corrected, the child may interpret this as, "Don't be sane."

- *Don't belong.* If parents constantly act like they should be somewhere else, such as another country or another part of the country, the child may receive the message that she too, doesn't belong, even though he or she was born there. For example, some individuals, originally from Cuba, living in the United States for over 20 years are still waiting for the demise of Castro and communism so they can return to their native land.

- *Don't feel.* For example, when children experience anger or other unpleasant emotions their parents may say, "Don't you talk to me in that tone." This may be interpreted by the child as, "Don't feel," or "Don't feel that... (specific emotion).

These are some of the more common injunctions. There are many more injunctions such as, *"Don't think"* or *"Don't be sexy."* In redecision therapy you learn about your specific injunctions that you acquired as a child, examine their effects on your life, and make new decisions as to whether you want to modify or eliminate them. It is important to get in touch with the emotions associated with these troublesome cognitions (i.e. step three of the Six-Step Button Therapy Method) to maximize their modification or elimination.

INNER CHILD AND REPARENTING WORK

The concept of the "inner child" has been around for a long time and has its roots in ancient mythology and fairy tales. The inner child has many aspects and has been explained in many different ways. Carl Gustav Jung, an early pioneer in psychology, referred to one variant of the inner child as the "divine child" archetype. Many religions include stories of the divine child who is unusual from his conception or birth, becomes abandoned, orphaned, or has its life threatened, and proceeds to its destiny of becoming a savior, hero, or leader (e.g. Jesus, Moses, Oedipus, Krishna, Romulus and Remus).

A psychological rebirth and a renewed sense of hope and possibilities, often follow the process of letting go of certain views of ourselves, and life in general (Metzner, 1990).

Jung (1990) believed one of the essential features of the child motif is its futurity. The occurrence of the child motif in the psychology of an individual represents an anticipation of future developments. This is probably why so many of the mythological saviors are child gods. The "child" image represents a link to the past, to our childhood, and to the potential next step in the evolution of our consciousness in our future. The archetype of the child expresses our wholeness. "The 'child' is all that is abandoned and exposed and at the same time divinely powerful; the insignificant, dubious beginning, and the triumphal end. The 'eternal child' in man is an indescribable experience, an incongruity, a handicap, and a divine prerogative; and imponderable that determines the ultimate worth or worthlessness of a personality" (p. 30).

The child with its naive view of life is usually curious and interested in many things. It is fully and intensely alive unless totally de-spirited by pathological parenting. This is why adults sometimes yearn to recapture the innocent intense vitality of yesteryear. The inner child represents a possibility of rebirth, renewal, aliveness, and wholeness. However, we must go beyond just finding our inner child. As John Bradshaw (1990a) states, "To find our Inner Child is the first leap over the abyss of grief that threatens us all. But finding the Inner Child is just the beginning. Because of his isolation, neglect and neediness, this child is egocentric, weak and frightened. He must be disciplined in order to release his tremendous spiritual power" (p. 233).

COSMIC CONSCIOUSNESS ILLUMINATION

The inner child represents a possibility of spiritual rebirth and wholeness. Richard Maurice Bucke, M.D. described the transformative aspect of the rebirth experience around the turn of the century. Dr. Bucke (1969) studied individuals throughout history who he believed had experienced "cosmic consciousness illumination." Dr. Bucke reviewed their written works and contemporaries' accounts of their lives. Bucke himself experienced a cosmic consciousness illumination at the age of 35. The results of this remarkable study was originally published in 1898 as *Cosmic Consciousness*. This book is a classic investigation of the development of man's mystic relationship to the infinite. Bucke described cosmic consciousness as a consciousness of the cosmos, that is, of the life and order of the universe. "Along with the consciousness of the cosmos there occurs an intellectual enlightenment or illumination which alone would place the individual on a new plane of existence - would make him almost a member of a new species. To this is added a state of moral exaltation, an indescribable feeling of elevation, elation, and joyousness, and a quickening of the moral sense, which is fully as striking and more important both to the individual and to the race than is the enhanced intellectual power. With these come, what may be called a sense of immortality, a consciousness of eternal life, not a conviction that he shall have this, but the consciousness that he has it already" (p. 3).

This spiritual-mystical experience which Bucke calls "cosmic consciousness illumination" is increasingly being achieved as our human species evolves. This transcendental spiritual experience has been referred to by many names. Buddhists call it "Nirvana" because of the "extinction" of certain lower mental faculties such as the sense of sin, fear of death, and desire of wealth. This subjugation of the old personality along with the birth of the new is, in fact, almost equivalent to the annihilation of the old and the creation of a new self. The word Nirvana is defined as the state to which the Buddhist saint is to aspire as the highest aim and highest good. Jesus called the new condition "the Kingdom of God" or the Kingdom of Heaven." Paul called it "Christ." Paul speaks of himself as "a man of Christ," and "them that are in Christ." Paul also calls it "the Spirit" and "the Spirit of God." Mohammed called the cosmic sense "Gabriel." Dante called it "Beatrice" ("Making Happy"), a name similar to "Kingdom of Heaven" (Bucke, 1969).

The inner child motif and the transformative nature of the rebirth experience in mythology and Jungian psychology is enlightening. And in more contemporary times, the Transactional Analysis counseling model has provided an excellent description of our inner world, including the inner child, utilizing such concepts as the Parent, Child, and Adult ego states. The Parent part of us incorporates the should messages and injunctions and provides us with our rules for living. The Child self reacts to the Parent messages, injunctions, and rules with feelings. The Adult self thinks rationally, makes decisions, and solves problems without contamination from Parental "should messages" or the reactive feelings from the Child ego state. Inner child work has been adapted and applied by numerous counselors, therapists, and authors such as Charles Whitfield, M.D. (1987), John Bradshaw (1990), and Lucia Capacchione, Ph.D. (1991).

In recent years, the metaphor "Inner Child" has been used to refer to the activities of the unconscious old brain with its associated feelings of fear, grief, jealousy, anger, irritation, rage, hurt, resentment, and boredom as well as the more enjoyable feelings of love, playfulness, exhilaration, and peaceful relaxation (Keyes, 1995). Our Inner Child resides at the core of our being and is a powerful presence. Our child starts off with certain characteristics such as curiosity, enthusiasm, instincts, trust, playfulness, creativeness, and a sense of aliveness, adventure, and spontaneity but as it grows and encounters the harsh realities of life it becomes altered. According to Drs. McKay and Fanning (1991), "The inner child is more than an interesting metaphor. It explains why people act 'childishly,' or 'immaturely.' It's because some stressful event reminds them of a childhood trauma and awakens a younger version of themselves. They react as if they were still two or five or ten years old" (p. 122). As Capacchione (1991) explains:

As time goes on the child runs head-on into the demands of the adult world. The voice of grown-ups, with their own needs and wants, begins to drown out the inner voice of feelings and instincts. In effect, parents and teachers say, "Don't trust yourself, don't feel your feelings. Don't say this, don't express that. Do as we say, we know best...

With time those very qualities that gave the child its aliveness - curiosity, spontaneity, ability to feel - are forced into hiding...The inner child is constantly trying to get our attention, but many of us have forgotten how to listen. When we ignore our true feelings and gut instincts, we are ignoring the Inner Child. When we fail to nurture our body and soul, we neglect the Child Within. When we talk ourselves out of childlike needs with the excuse that they are not rational or practical - not the adult thing to do - we abandon the Inner Child...When our Inner Child is blocked, we are robbed of our natural spontaneity and zest for life. Over time this may lead to low energy, chronic or serious illness...and separate ourselves from others. (pp. 16-17)

THE WOUNDED INNER CHILD

If our normal developmental needs are not adequately met we can become adults with a wounded inner child. "When a child's development is arrested, when feelings are repressed, especially the feelings of anger and hurt, a person grows up to be an adult with an angry, hurt child inside of him. This child will spontaneously contaminate the person's adult behavior" (Bradshaw, 1990, p.7). Wounded inner child behaviors include throwing temper tantrums, being overly polite and obedient, speaking in a childlike voice, manipulating, and pouting. John Bradshaw (1990) describes some of the ways the wounded inner child contaminates our lives using the word and acronym *contaminate*. Each letter stands for a significant way in which the wounded inner child sabotages adult life.

* **C**o-Dependence
* **O**ffender Behaviors
* **N**arcissistic Disorders
* **T**rust Issues
* **A**cting Out/Acting In Behaviors
* **M**agical Beliefs
* **I**ntimacy Dysfunctions
* **N**ondisciplined Behaviors
* **A**ddictive/Compulsive Behaviors
* **T**hought Distortions
* **E**mptiness (Apathy, Depression)

Our unconscious mind doesn't relate to time in the same manner as our conscious mind. To our unconscious mind, things that happened when we were six months old can be just as important and immediate as things that happened recently (McKay & Fanning, 1991).

Inner Child and Reparenting

In recent years, techniques have been developed to "reparent our inner child" and help heal our wounded inner child. The wounded inner child is the source of much suffering in our adult lives. Inner child work involves contacting, reclaiming, and nurturing our inner child. "Your inner child will experience things the way you first experienced them in childhood, but this time your adult self will be there to protect and support your child as he completes important unfinished business" (Bradshaw, 1990, pp. xiv-xv). The basic reparenting process entails:

> ... you imagine that you, a wise, experienced adult, are visiting yourself as a child during a particularly hard time - a specific scene that you have already identified as contributing to one of your negative beliefs about yourself. You impart to your younger self the wisdom you have acquired and the skills you later developed to deal with hard times. Specifically, you counter the negative belief that is being formed with a more positive, more accurate version. You actually become, in your imagination, the perfect parent and friend that you needed at the time but didn't have. (p. 122)

"Reclaiming your inner child involves going back through your developmental stages and finishing your unfinished business" (Bradshaw, 1990, p. 56). Like the concept of time, your unconscious mind deals with reality differently than your conscious mind. The unconscious mind doesn't distinguish between actual experience and dreams or fantasies. The good advice and support that you give your inner child in your imagination, years after the event, can be processed and stored and used by your unconscious just as if it had really happened. Also, it doesn't matter to your unconscious mind that you have two contradictory versions of the same memory because it doesn't insist that things make logical sense (McKay & Fanning, 1991).

According to Drs. McKay & Fanning (1991), "Visiting your inner child is a two-way street. You go back in time to bring your child the experience, wisdom, and strength that you lacked at the time to understand the world and protect yourself. And your inner child comes forward in time to return to you the spontaneity, creativity, and pure joy of living that you had to suppress in order to survive as an adult" (p. 123). "Reclaiming your wounded inner child is a Zenlike experience. Children are natural Zen masters; their world is brand-new in each and every moment. For the unwounded child, wonder is natural. Life is a mystery to be lived. Homecoming is the restoration of the natural. Such a restoration is not grandiose or dramatic; it is simply the way life ought to be" (Bradshaw, 1990, p. 56). To help you heal your wounded inner child, professional counselors and therapists such as John Bradshaw (1990), Lucia Capacchione (1991), Rokelle Lerner (1990), and Cathryn Taylor (1991) have developed numerous techniques to facilitate inner child and reparenting work. Some of these resources are described in the recommended reading section at the end of this book.

REFRAMING

Everything has its beauty but not everyone sees it.
Confucius

Reframing is an approach whereby we give a new interpretation to events in our lives, especially those events that create emotional distress. When we have a Button pushed and emotionally react we tend to see only selected parts of a situation, only the distress producing parts. We don't see the total event or situation accurately. In the midst of emotional distress triggered by a Button, we tend to filter the information coming into our biocomputers through our currently dominant motivational state(s), defense mechanisms, expectations, and other cognitive distortions. Through cognitive reframing we can view the situation that triggered distress from an alternate viewpoint. A viewpoint that can alleviate emotional distress and trigger positive feelings. For example, after three days of overcast drizzly rain we can say to ourselves, "What a bummer. Three rainy days in a row. I'm missing out on three days of tennis." Or, we can cognitively reframe this event and say to ourselves, "I'm glad mother earth and the farmers are getting some much needed rain. This also gives me a break from tennis for a few days and catch up on some reading I've been trying to do." Cognitive reframing is finding the silver lining in the rain clouds.

PARADOXICAL INTENTION

Paradoxical techniques are similar to the concept of "reverse psychology." When people say they used "reverse psychology" they usually mean that they tricked or manipulated someone into doing or believing something by asking or advocating for the opposite of what they really wanted. Paradoxical techniques can be used to work on our cognitions and Buttons in a variety of ways.

ADVOCATE FOR THE OPPOSITE OF WHAT YOU WANT

One type of paradoxical approach is to *exaggerate the opposite of something that you want*. For example, if I'm trying to loose weight and avoid high caloric and high fat foods. The next time I'm at a restaurant and I desire the hot fudge sundae on the menu I tell myself, " The hot fudge sundae on the menu looks so good, I should order two of them!" Hopefully, as a result of going with the desire for a hot fudge sundae in an exaggerated way, and not providing any resistance, I can allow the thought of ordering a hot fudge sundae to run its course before the waitress arrives to take my order with minimal psychological distress - and avoid the behaviour of ordering it when the server arrives. The idea is to offer no resistance to a desired thought and even exaggerate it in order to allow it to run its course and dissipate the energy associated with it before it gets acted out behaviorally. We give power to that which we resist. In the martial arts discipline of Judo an individual uses the energy flow of his or her opponent to defeat the opponent, not by overpowering or resisting the other individual, but by redirecting the opponent's energy flow.

SCHEDULING THE TARGET BEHAVIOR YOU WANT TO CHANGE

Another paradoxical strategy is to schedule the target behavior, thought, or feeling that you want to modify or eliminate. With the hot fudge sundae example, you might say to yourself, "I'm going to eat a hot fudge sundae after every dinner this week. I will start on Monday." The idea of offering no resistance to the desire of eating a hot fudge sundae is the same as in the first example with the exception that now you are forcing the desire. Very often this activation of a desire or viewpoint toward one end of a continuum will activate and empower a more rational and realistic viewpoint toward the opposite end of the continuum to assert itself. Another example relates to insomnia. When you have difficulty falling asleep at night tell yourself, "I am going to lay in my bed and stay up as late as I can and count 300 sheep jumping over a fence before I fall asleep." You will most likely fall asleep way before you reach 300.

Most thoughts, behaviors, and feelings can be viewed on a continuum. By prescribing, exaggerating, or scheduling a target behavior that we want to modify or eliminate we are calling to action a part of ourselves that wants to achieve a goal more toward the opposite side of the continuum.

There are other types of paradoxical strategies, but they require a qualified mental health professional to safely implement. I do not recommend that you utilize paradoxical strategies targeting self-destructive and, under no circumstances, homicidal intentions. Because paradoxical strategies are tricky to use, and potentially harmful, I recommend that you seek the services of a qualified mental health professional to assist you in the utilization of these techniques.

SELF-HYPNOSIS

Hypnosis is a state of relaxed focused attention. Hypnotized individuals are more open to suggestions and instructions from self or the hypnotist. Hypnosis does not take away a person's will. The hypnotic state allows individuals to suspend the tendency to challenge, evaluate, judge, or critically analyze an offered suggestion. According to Karen Olness, M.D. (1993), a medical school professor at Case Western Reserve University, "...research indicates that many brain wave changes associated with hypnosis can also be triggered by other methods of deep concentration, such as the relaxation response. It seems that a hypnotic state can also occur spontaneously while reading a book, watching television, driving a car, listening to music, dancing, or doing t'ai chi. During most of these activities, people often recognize that they are in a different, but pleasant, state of focused awareness" (p. 279).

DIFFERENCE BETWEEN THE HYPNOTIC AND RELAXATION STATE. During the induction phase of hypnosis the person is in a deep state of relaxation. The major difference between the relaxation state and the hypnotic state is that in hypnosis you or a hypnotist introduces specific messages into your mind while in the relaxed state. "Hypnosis allows your body and mind to respond to your thoughts as though they were real. With self-hypnosis you are always fully in control. You choose what you want to think about, imagine, feel, and do" (Sobel & Ornstein, 1996, p. 100).

Mental health professionals have used hypnotherapy in the treatment of various mental and physical problems including anxiety, phobias, insomnia, psychological trauma, irritable bowel syndrome, psychoactive drug abuse, habits, pain, warts, erectile dysfunction, and the management of chronic illnesses such as reducing bleeding in hemophiliacs, stabilizing blood sugar in diabetics, alleviating symptoms of autoimmune disease, lessening the side effects of chemotherapy, and reducing the severity of asthma attacks. Hypnotherapy has also been used as a form of analgesia or sedation for medical and dental procedures (Hales & Hales, 1995; Olness, 1993; Weil, 1999). Individuals should consult a health care professional before attempting to self-treat a medical condition.

Self-hypnosis is a state of self-induced relaxation and focused attention that allows you to place messages into your mind. In this state of relaxed hypersuggestibility you can offer yourself suggestions to modify or eliminate troublesome cognitions and Buttons. For example, to eliminate a nicotine addiction (i.e. tobacco Button):

1. **Set aside 20 to 30 minutes of uninterrupted time.** Take the phone off the hook, go to a quiet room, put a "do not disturb sign on the door," dim the lights, lay on the couch or floor or sit in a reclining chair, put on some soft music if you like, and get as comfortable as you can.

2. **Get into your focused relaxation state.** You can utilize any of the many relaxation routines that trigger the relaxation response such as progressive relaxation (i.e. the systematic contracting and relaxing of the body's major muscle groups interspersed with deep breathing) or simply take several slow, deep breaths imagining the release of any mental or body tension with each exhalation. You can consult most any stress management book such as *Stress Management: A Comprehensive Guide to Wellness* by Charlesworth and Nathan (1984) for methods to trigger the relaxation response.

3. **Deepen your relaxed state with hypnotic trance induction techniques.** Once you are relaxed and focused:

   * Close your eyes and focus your attention on your breathing.
   * Take several deep breaths imagining yourself going into a deeper state of relaxation with each exhalation.
   * Breathe normally and count backwards from 10 to 1. Tell yourself that as you count backwards from 10 to 1 you will become more and more deeply relaxed with each number. Begin counting backwards from 10 to 1 and tell yourself the following after each number:

   10. "I am becoming more and more relaxed, peaceful, and serene."
   9. "I am letting go and becoming even more deeply relaxed and calm.
   8. "I am very comfortable, peaceful, and relaxed."
   7. "With each number I feel more and more relaxed. I feel my total body letting go and becoming deeply relaxed."
   6. "My arms and legs are becoming very heavy. Very, very heavy. My total body is becoming very very heavy."
   5. "I am drifting deeper and deeper into total relaxation and calm."
   4. "I am very drowsy and sleepy. I am so relaxed I could go to sleep."
   3. "I am so relaxed and limp I feel like a rag doll. I feel at total peace and calm."
   2. "I am drifting deeper and deeper into relaxation and sleep. I feel heavier and heavier and more and more limp."
   1. "I am totally relaxed, calm, and open to suggestions for freeing myself from my smoking addiction."

   * You may want to repeat this counting procedure to deepen your state

of focused relaxation. Each repetition will help you achieve a more relaxed, focused, and receptive state.

4. **Give yourself specific messages to modify or eliminate your trouble-some cognition or Button.** Utilize this state of deep relaxation and focused awareness to place specific and positive messages into your bio-computer that will help improve your physical or mental health. You can utilize a tape recorder or self-talk to place your messages into your mind. Keep your messages short and the language positive. This is not the time to critically evaluate or judge the messages you choose to give to yourself. Plan ahead of time and decide what positive health promoting messages you want to place in your mind to help you on your journey of self-actual-ization and personal growth. Repeat each specific message at least three or four times. The following example is for eliminating a cigarette smoking addiction (Button):

> *Specify the negative part of the Button.* "Smoking cigarettes is a filthy and unhealthy addiction. My breath smells nasty after I smoke and peo-ple don't want to be around my smelly self. I don't like the sight and smell of nicotine stained ashtrays filled with cigarette butts. I am no longer going to damage my heart, lungs, and every body tissue involved with breathing of cigarette smoke and metabolizing the byproducts out of my body. I can stop smoking. I can't stand the taste and smell of cigarettes."
>
> *Give yourself specific suggestions for dealing with the Button when it's activated.* "When I have the urge to smoke I will remember this state of relaxation and gently watch the wave of desire to smoke as it rises, peaks, and fades away. Whenever I have the urge to smoke this is my signal to take three deep breaths imagining the desire to smoke fading with each exhalation. I will not become upset when I have an urge to smoke. I know the urge only lasts a short time, maybe 15 seconds, and I will simply watch the urge rise, peak, and go away from a relaxed state while I take a few deep breaths and become even more relaxed and calm. I know the urges to smoke will become less frequent and less intense with time. I will deal with one passing urge or desire at a time until they are gone forever."
>
> *Visualize yourself free from the Button.* Visualize yourself going through a typical day without smoking. Imagine yourself successfully handling some typical high-risk situations that usually trigger your smoking behavior. Say to yourself, "I am a healthy nonsmoker. I picture myself enjoying good health and full of vital energy as I interact with people at work and during my free time. My family, friends, and

coworkers appreciate my nonsmoking and admire my choice for health and life over self-destruction. I am glad I am exercising my will power and have taken back my power to make healthy choices in my life. I am more powerful than any addiction and feel my freedom and energy grow now that I am free from my unconscious smoking addiction. Some of my coworkers and friends smoke and I see myself interacting with them with no desire to join them in their smoking behavior. I picture myself finishing a meal and reaching for a beverage as I converse with friends. I can see myself enjoying my coffee, tea, or other beverage without smoking. I feel my creative juices flow as I write, paint, draw, or play music without relying on a jump-start from the stimulant nicotine. I can handle the stressors in my life with healthy activities such as focused breathing exercises, yoga, meditation, jogging, swimming, tennis, playing a musical instrument, or simply taking a brief walk. I feel full of energy and my body thanks me for not smoking."

5.   **Awakening from your hypnotic trance.** No one has ever failed to awaken from a hypnotic trance. The worst case scenario is you may fall asleep during the trance induction phase and awaken after your nap, usually after 5 to 30 minutes. When you have finished putting your messages into your biocomputer start counting from 1 to 10. As you begin counting combine the numbers with positive suggestions for well-being and alertness. Say to yourself, " Now I am going to wake up. When I hear the number 10 I will feel alert, refreshed, and feel good." Begin counting from 1 to 10, pausing after each number to repeat phrases such as, "I am ready to wake up now. I am feeling just fine. I am feeling alert, refreshed, happy, confident, and wide awake. I am confident that I can enjoy a healthy life as a nonsmoker. I will gently and consciously watch the wave of desire to smoke as it occurs and watch it peak and fade away. Ten. I am fully awake and alert now. I am feeling very refreshed and looking forward to enjoying the rest of the day."

You may want to write out a script using the above guidelines and make an audio tape. Once you have achieved a relaxed state you can play your audio tape to place your self-help messages into your mind. Remember that many of your Buttons have years of programming behind them and will take practice and repetition to modify or eliminate. There are also commercially produced self-hypnosis tapes for many problem areas such as smoking, weight control, pain control, and for healing most of the common health disorders.

You may want to consult with a mental health professional who is knowledgeable about hypnosis and altered states of awareness. A professional can help you achieve a deep state of focused relaxation and help you develop a script for working on certain problem behaviors or developing health enhancing life skills. A mental health professional can also assess whether or not hypnosis is appropriate for what you are attempting to treat. A typical course of hypnotherapy may require from one to five sessions lasting approximately 45 minutes to one hour each. With medical conditions, a consultation with a health care professional is needed before attempting to self-diagnose and self-treat with self-hypnosis. Your health insurance may pay for hypnotherapy if performed by a qualified physician or mental health professional.

GROUP BUTTON THERAPY EMPTY-CHAIR TECHNIQUE

This counseling technique can be used by professional counselors during group therapy.

This counseling technique is a combined empty-chair and cognitive group counseling technique that includes other group members. This technique is a way of bringing in other group members into an individual's cognitive work during empty-chair work.

Here is how this counseling technique works. While an individual is doing empty-chair work, as described in the previous chapter, the group counselor puts his or her hand on the chair and gives a voice to some unverbalized or disowned aspect of the part of the inner conflict or other person in that chair. After the group counselor models how to approach the chair and give a voice to some aspect of that part of the conflict in that chair, the other group members are encouraged to do the same if they have something helpful to offer. By giving voice to some part of the conflict that is not being said by the individual doing the empty-chair work it forces the individual to deal with it now that it's out in the open.

This technique helps individuals doing the empty-chair work to:

- Face parts of the conflict, issue, problem, or person that they are avoiding.
- Helps them break through impasses (i.e. blocks that prevent them from movement toward closure or finishing unfinished business).
- Provides multiple viewpoints of a problem area from group members and not just the counselor.
- Provides a therapeutic climate of empathy and feelings of care and concern from the group members and counselor.
- Participating group members experience the therapeutic effect of helping another group member.

The timing of this technique is important. It is most helpful after an individual has spent sufficient time doing empty-chair work and the individual is at an impasse. With group support individuals doing empty-chair work can face the most distressing aspects of their troublesome cognitions and Buttons. Sometimes, when an individual has imagined another individual (e.g. parent, spouse, boss, etc.) in the empty-chair, group members can help the individual confront and verbalize suppressed thoughts, feelings, and fears about the other person. In utilizing this group counseling technique group members sometimes become confidence boosters and provide courage and an instant support network for individuals facing troublesome cognitions, other people, and their Buttons.

GROUP BUTTON-PULL

The "Group Button-Pull" is a group counseling technique that combines Button Therapy and group therapy. Professional counselors can utilize this technique by asking group members to simultaneously give a voice and dramatize the various aspects of a group member's Button.

Before utilizing the "group Button-Pull" technique the counselor should first ask a group member who has identified a problem if he or she would like to try an experiment that will involve physical touching by the other group members. The individual is told that the exercise should help the individual gain a better understanding of the problem and hopefully, facilitate therapeutic closure on the issue. If there is sufficient trust developed in the group for the counselor and other group members the individual usually agrees to try the exercise. If the group member agrees to experience the Group Button-Pull technique, the counselor then asks the individual to stand in the center of the group and asks the other group members to form a circle around the individual. The group members are then instructed to physically hold parts of the individual's clothes and arms. The group members are then directed to each verbalize a specific thought, feeling, or some other aspect of the Button. Verbalizations may be something that the individual has already stated earlier in the group session or a thought or feeling the group member thinks the individual might be experiencing related to the identified problem or issue. As group members periodically give voice to the individual's thoughts or feelings they are instructed to simultaneously gently pulling the individual toward them by the individual's arm or clothing with enough strength to move them slightly off balance. The verbalizations can be exaggerated to give the individual the full experience of hearing someone else say out loud what he or she has been thinking about a particular issue, conflict, person, or Button.

Hearing these cognitions and feelings verbalized out loud, exaggerated, and dramatized by group members gives the individual a unique opportunity to gain an increased awareness of, and more fully experience, different aspects of troublesome cognitions and Buttons. This technique can provide a powerful experience for an individual working on Buttons and can result in the individual experiencing more fully the strength and pulling power of certain Buttons.

An example of how a dialogue might progress utilizing this technique with a group member contemplating a divorce from his wife might go something like the following:

COUNSELOR: John as you stand in the middle of the group and allow the other group members to hold your arms and clothing (e.g. shirt, belt, pants) do not respond when they verbalize what they think you are thinking or feeling about possibly divorcing your wife. Just hear it, let it in, and fully experience the message. You will have time after the exercise to process the messages and your experience of this exercise. The group members begin verbalizing what they think John is thinking or feeling about the possibility of divorcing his wife while simultaneously gently pulling on his clothes or arms.

GROUP MEMBER (GM) 1: Gently pulls on John's right arm as she verbalizes, "John you know that you don't want to leave your wife. You are just going through a temporary period of discontent with your wife and your marriage. It'll blow over and you'll feel better about the relationship. You've been through this scenario thousands of times."

GM 2: Gently pulls on John's left arm and verbalizes, "You know you have been unhappy in this marriage for years and need to separate from your wife. You've tried talking things out and you have even tried professional marriage counseling and nothing has changed. You need a divorce!"

GM 3: Gently pulls on the front of John's shirt and verbalizes, "You've been unhappy in this marriage for years and yet you keep putting off making a decision about a separation. You have no guts. You are a coward. You are afraid to confront this issue and do what you know you have to do!"

GM 4: Gently pulls on the front of John's belt and verbalizes, "If you divorce your wife you won't be able to find another woman to meet your love and intimacy needs. You are middle-aged, overweight, balding, and no female would want to be with you. You'll be alone and lonely with no one for you to love or to love you. You better stay in the marriage and put up with the crap and resign yourself to your unhappiness."

GM 5: Gently pulls on the back of John's shirt and verbalizes, "What about the kids? They are only in grade school. They will be devastated and emotionally scarred for life. They will think I am a monster for abandoning their mother and them. My wife will get primary custody. I'll only be able to visit them on every other weekend and for a month in the summer. My wife will turn them against me and, for all practical purposes, I will lose my kids."

GM 5: Gently pulls on the back of John's shirt and verbalizes, "You don't have to live the rest of your life unhappy in an unsatisfying marriage. You know what you need to do. The kids will still love you. You will always be their father who will always love and care for them. They may be upset for awhile but they'll adjust. Plus, they probably will be better off in the long run living around happier parents and less fighting. Also, as far as finding someone else, there are other fish in the sea. And who says I need to marry again anyway? Maybe I'll meet someone else or maybe I won't. I can develop my own support system to satisfy my friendship, intimacy, sex, and love needs without another marriage. All I know for sure is what is going on with me now. I'm not happy and I have to make some changes. Who knows what the future will bring?"

The group members would continue with this behavior for as long as it takes to verbalize everything that is relevant and meaningful to John related to his marital separation issue. After the group members have a chance to verbalize at least one of John's thoughts or feelings while giving him a tug, the counselor moves on to the processing phase of the exercise.

The counselor asks John and the other group members to remain standing in their places and begins by asking John to verbalize what he experienced during the exercise. John may share that he has a clearer sense of his feelings and thoughts surrounding this issue he is struggling with. Then the group members are asked to share their experiences of playing the different parts of this divorce issue. By sharing how it felt to verbalize certain aspects of the Button it often triggers additional sharing by the individual who is working on an issue.

I have found it helpful to begin the processing phase while remaining standing and then after 5 or 10 minutes continue the processing as everyone informally takes a seat.

It is important to allow time after any structured group exercise, including the Group Button-Pull, for the individual and other group members to process their experiences. Processing provides an opportunity for more thorough integration of the experience, closure by the individual and other group members, and more counseling, if necessary.

CHAPTER TWENTY

SOME COMMONLY ASKED QUESTIONS
ABOUT COGNITIVE INTERVENTIONS

Truly I tell you, if you have faith the size of a mustard seed,
you will say to this mountain,
"Move from here to there," and it will move;
and nothing will be impossible for you.

Jesus
HOLY BIBLE

A monk who is skilled in concentration can cut the Himalayas in two.
Buddha

SINCE I BEGAN developing and integrating cognitive counseling approaches into my personal growth work and professional clinical counseling work in 1972 I have noticed some commonly asked questions by my clients.

CAN I USE ANY OF THE COGNITIVE INTERVENTIONS DESCRIBED IN THIS BOOK?

Yes. You can use all of the cognitive interventions. The two cognitive interventions for group counseling are primarily to be used by mental health professionals. However, even in group counseling/therapy, members should feel free to initiate any therapeutic intervention that they think will be helpful to them during a therapeutic group counseling session. Group counseling members can initiate either of the two group cognitive interventions, described in the last chapter, during a group session. The interventions will probably be more successful if a group member asks permission from the group leader and briefly explains the technique and purpose to the group leader and members (if it's during a group session) prior to initiating the intervention. Many professional counselors will gladly accommodate any reasonable request from a group member that is potentially therapeutic. Requesting a specific therapeutic technique during a counseling session indicates a strong motivation to work on oneself, and will most likely be appreciated by a counselor or therapist.

The cognitive interventions described in the last chapter can be used as self-help cognitive interventions and can be found in numerous self-help books. However, as pointed out in an earlier chapter many of these cognitive interventions especially the ones described in the last chapter, will probably be more meaningful and effective if used in conjunction with a mental health professional. You may want to go to a mental health professional to learn the cognitive interventions that you are interested in to make sure you are doing them correctly and then proceed to practice them on your own. For example, you may not be using appropriate self-programming phrases with the self-hypnosis intervention. Also, with self-hypnosis you may be trying to eliminate a symptom of a medical disorder that needs to be addressed medically. By trying to make the symptom disappear you could be endangering your health, if the underlying medical disorder is left unattended.

CAN I COMBINE COGNITIVE INTERVENTIONS?

Yes. You may want to combine more than one cognitive intervention. An example was given earlier in this chapter when the "redecision therapy" from TA was combined with the "empty-chair" work from Gestalt Therapy. Another example described earlier was combining the "thought stopping" and "here-and-now" techniques. Many other combinations can be utilized. However, you may want to gain some experience with a single cognitive intervention before combining them. A mental health professional skilled in cognitive counseling will be able to choose the best cognitive intervention, or combination of interventions, depending on the particular type of Button.

DO I HAVE TO USE ALL SIX STEPS OF THE SIX-STEP BT METHOD EVERY TIME I WORK ON A BUTTON?

No. When working on modifying or eliminating deeply rooted Buttons you may only need to utilize the six steps of the Button Therapy method the first time or two that the Button gets pushed. After you can immediately identify the Button, the emotions and motivations associated with the Button, and choose the cognitive intervention(s) to best work on this particular Button, the next time you encounter that same Button you may find yourself going right to a favorite cognitive intervention without needing to consciously process the Button through any of the other six steps.

HOW DO I GET RID OF DEEPLY ROOTED BUTTONS THAT DON'T WANT TO BE UPROOTED?

It is harder to crack a prejudice than an atom.
Attributed to Albert Einstein

Some of our Buttons are easy to change once we become aware of them. However, many of our programmed expectations, needs, or scripts have the force of many years of conditioning behind them and are more difficult to modify or eliminate.

The more difficult Buttons to change are usually the ones that early in life were put into the limbic system, a portion of our "old brain" (phylogenetically) which is concerned with drive systems in addition to emotional and motivational behavior (Gevarter, 1975).

> In the early years, the child builds in the old brain a basic value system and a basic way of looking at the world. New Brain (cerebral cortex) powers are relatively undeveloped so that dogma, rules, models and ideology enter the old brain relatively uncritical. If this programming has strong emotional content associated with it, then in later years it becomes especially intractable. As the old brain is the ultimate decision maker, this programming is particularly important. The control that one has over oneself is dependent upon self-awareness, intracerebral mechanisms, and environment. Awareness is a new brain function. Though awareness may develop unaided in a favorable environment, it can be suppressed or destroyed by an unfavorable one. Ideally, it is nurtured and brought to full fruition by a humanistic education. Even given awareness, however, one is not free to act on new brain programs alone. The old brain is the ultimate decision maker, particularly when the stimuli elicit a strong emotional response from the old brain programming. (Gevarter, 1975, p. 88)

Gaining awareness of our old and new brain programming (cognitions) is one of the first essential steps for self-directed change. Once aware, we can use our rational minds to modify or eliminate those cognitions that we are attached to (i.e. Buttons) in our new brain relatively easy. Deep-seated old brain Buttons, especially those programs put into our biocomputer early in life and fused into place with an intense emotional experience, are extremely difficult to defuse, modify, or eliminate, and require intense and persistent work if any substantial lasting changes are to be expected (Goodwin, 1981).

DOES GIVING UP MY BUTTONS MEAN I HAVE TO GIVE UP MY WANTS, DESIRES, AND GOALS AND LET PEOPLE RUN OVER ME?

Man is presently caught in a plane of consciousness which is nourished by the workings of his rational mind. That is, the plane of consciousness which is nourished by the workings of his rational mind. That is, the plane of polarities...of good and evil....and left and right...of old and young...of us and

them...and of man and woman.
To be "not caught" means to unattached. To be unattached does not mean to
be uninvolved, it means to be involved "without attachment."
Baba Ram Dass
BE HERE NOW

No. This is one of the most common misunderstandings of Button Therapy and cognitive therapy models in general. Freeing ourselves from our Buttons does not mean that we become passive recipients of life's fate with no active striving to actualize our own wants or preferences. Nor does it mean you stop trying to correct the injustices of the world. It does mean that we can choose to free ourselves from our Buttons that when pushed result in unconscious robot-like emotional reactions. When we are free to assert our wants and preferences in a non-reactive, centered, free, conscious state, we will increase our probability of actualizing our goals, and reduce our stress when we encounter delays or barriers to implementing our goals.

We do not need to give up our wants, desires, goals, values, scripts, or models of how we want things to be in our lives. What we give up is the distress and uptightness triggered when our attachments, demands, or addictions to our models of how things should be are not currently being met. We can choose to keep our goals and desires, and at the same time stop demanding them and start preferring them.

By working on our Buttons we do not become doormats for the more aggressive, greedy, and insensitive people in our lives. Also, as we encounter people with questionable ethics and values we can better deal with these types of people, and all other Button-Pushers, from a proactive, centered, and conscious place versus a reactive, off-centered, and unconscious place. It is to our advantage to be as aware as possible when problem-solving and making life decisions, especially when dealing with sociopaths and the Button-Pushers in our lives.

The second step of the Six-Step Button Therapy Method is the essence of the Button Therapy model in that we connect most of our psychological suffering to *our* Buttons. Once we gain this awareness we need to then realize that we are primarily responsible for creating and maintaining the quality of our inner experience as we respond to the internal and external events in our lives.

After we realize that we are in charge of our emotions and inner experience we do not have to remain the reactive effect of people and situations around us. We can, with conscious effort, break the reactive patterns of thought, emotion, and behavior triggered by other people and situations and, with increasing confidence, become free to choose how we want to interpret and experience life. The focus of responsibility shifts from others, including our counselors, teachers, clergy, and gurus, to self. This fifth step provides numerous cognitive interventions we can use to modify or eliminate our troublesome cognitions and Buttons.

The sixth and last step involves cultivating our mind's garden. This entails consciously placing life-enhancing affirmations and new cognitions into our minds that will facilitate our journey of personal growth.

CHAPTER TWENTY-ONE

AFFIRMATIONS AND CULTIVATING YOUR MIND'S GARDEN

A morning prayer:

Dear Lord,
You awaken me
and I am born
into a new day.
Make me speak
soft, sweet words,
and behave calmly
and compassionately towards all.
May I do good deeds
which bring happiness to all.
May I be an ideal example
as Jesus was.
May I serve You well this day.

Sai Baba
AN EASTERN VIEW OF JESUS CHRIST:
DIVINE DISCOURSES OF SATHYA SAI BABA

THE SIXTH AND LAST STEP in the Six-Step Button Therapy Method is cultivating our minds by consciously placing and reinforcing those messages and affirmations that we choose to place in our minds in order to help us along on our journey of personal growth.

Working on identifying and weeding out Buttons is essential to improving the quality of our inner experience. However, we don't want to go through life just modifying or eliminating our distress-producing Buttons. This chapter provides some suggested positive affirmations and guidelines for "seeding your mind's garden."

CULTIVATING YOUR MIND'S GARDEN

James Allen (1968) writing in the period around the turn of the century, summed up the essence of this sixth step with a poetic analogy.

A man's mind is like a garden, which may be intelligently cultivated or allowed to run wild. But whether cultivated or neglected, it must and will, bring forth. If no useful seeds are put into it, then an abundance of useless weed seeds will fall into it, and will continue to produce their useless kind. Just as a gardener cultivates his plot, keeping it free from weeds, and grows the flowers and fruits which he needs, so may a man tend the garden of his mind weeding out all the wrong, useless, and impure thoughts, and cultivating all the right, useful and pure thoughts. By this process, a man sooner or later discovers that he is the master gardener of his soul, the director of his life. (p. 21)

REPROGRAMMING YOUR BIOCOMPUTER

The sixth step in the Button Therapy model is reprogramming our biocomputers, using the computer analogy. John Lilly, M.D. (1974) states that, "All human beings, all persons who reach adulthood in the world today are programmed biocomputers. No one of us can escape our own nature as programmed entities. Literally, each of us may be our programs, nothing more, nothing less" (p. viii).

Most of our programming is necessary. It helps us handle the continuous incoming stimuli without having to consciously decipher each input and our responses to it. Also, our lives would be very confusing if we had to continuously learn and re-learn each of our present habitual behaviors like driving a car, walking, or writing.

...you and I, as users of our magnificent biocomputers, should realize that our consciousness can only be aware of perhaps one-millionth of the incoming information each second of the day... this tremendous mass of data going into our biocomputer second by second would be absolutely overwhelming if it were not for the underlying systems of organization that automatically abstract, classify, suppress, or distribute this huge flood of incoming sensory information. Our consciousness operates on preprocessed filtered abstractions of abstractions received from various parts of our biocomputer. (Keyes, 1975, pp. 158-159)

CULTIVATING NEW COGNITIONS THAT FACILITATE YOUR BECOMING HAPPIER, AND MORE AWARE, CONSCIOUS, AND LOVING. We are currently operating on the basis of our present programming, conditioning, and learning, often on an unconscious level. Thus as we become aware of cognitions that are no longer working for us, we need to remove or alter them, as well as add new models, beliefs, and programs that will allow us to live our lives more effectively. Once we become aware of our inner programming, we have to make a choice. We can choose to do nothing and continue to operate on our current programming which will allow our biocomputers to continue to be both unconsciously and consciously programmed. Or, we can choose to take responsibility for what goes into and stays in our biocomputers. Ken Keyes, Jr. (1975) adds, "to use our great biocomputer optimally, it is necessary for us to repeatedly and definitely give instructions to ourselves to eliminate the old programming and to replace it with non-addictive preferential programming" (p. 167).

As to the limits of how far we can develop the potential within our minds, Dr. John Lilly (1974) states that, "In the province of the mind, what one believes to be true is true or becomes true, within certain limits to be found experientially and experimentally. These limits are further beliefs to be transcended. In the mind, there are no limits" (p. xii).

By now you have probably realized that most of us carry around a lot of baggage and legacies. As you become aware of your self-defeating cognitions, you may decide to work on uprooting these weeds through the first five steps of the Six-Step Button Therapy Method and plant new seeds in the garden of your mind (i.e. sixth step).

SUGGESTIONS FOR THE CULTIVATION OF YOUR MIND

You are the creator of the reality that you experience. Every event that occurs around you takes on meaning when you put your attention on it. During your lifetime you have been exposed to a lot of conditioning, but you have selected what seemed valid to you and made it part of your programming. If reality is getting you down, examine the programming that is in the biocomputer you call your mind. That programming can be changed at any time because you are your own programmer.

Camden Benares
ZEN WITHOUT ZEN MASTERS

Our expectations, models, and scripts that we carry around in our minds did not magically appear. The acquisition of our mental programming usually followed an understandable course of development. Also, our cognitions are heavily influenced by our culture. Those models, beliefs, and scripts that are fundamental to the culture in which we were raised are more difficult to change. In order to intentionally change any of our programming, we first need to become aware of our cognitions and Buttons that we want to change. And, as our Buttons get pushed we need to more closely examine our cognitions (e.g.

beliefs, values, and attitudes) that we are attached to and work on modifying or eliminating the troublesome or self-defeating ones. Then we can place new positive, life-enhancing messages into our biocomputers. Out with the old self-defeating cognitions and Buttons and in with new life-enhancing beliefs, scripts, programs, and models.

Author and physician Deepok Chopra, M.D. (1998b) shares his thoughts on change and "renewal":

> The fact is that life is a constant interplay of creation, maintenance, and renewal. This is happening all the time. Think about it: Your stomach cells are re-created every five days; your skin cells are replaced once a month; your DNA is re-created every six weeks; and so on throughout your physical body. The major insight from this is that transformation and change are the only constants. When I see you, your physical body is constantly transforming, your emotions are constantly transforming. In fact, you are actually the Spirit that is expressing itself in this endless transformation.
>
> All too often, though, we get into habitual patterns that interfere with the spontaneity of this endless transformation. We are lured into holding on to the past, clinging to our ideas and memories of the way things were instead of living in the present moment with the way things are. We get attached to something that is an illusion: we get attached to non-change. When we get attached to this illusion, we disrupt the process of renewal. (pp. 1-2)

PLANTING NEW SEEDS

> *Growth is a rare phenomenon. It is natural, yet rare. When the seed has found its right soil, it grows. It is very natural; growth is natural but to find the right soil—that is the very crux of the matter.*
>
> Osho
> DISCOURSES

When we begin to consciously plant positive life-enhancing seeds into the gardens of our minds we are taking control of our lives and deciding what type of inner experience we want, what we value, what we want to become, and what direction we want our lives to go. And, like seeds in a garden, we must give our life-enhancing guidelines, messages, and affirmations time, energy, and nourishment if we want to actualize the seeds' potential.

AFFIRMATIONS

> *Go placidly amid the noise and haste and remember what peace there may be in silence.*

As far as possible without surrender be on good terms with all persons.
Speak your truth quietly and clearly and listen to others, even the dull and
ignorant; they too have their story.
Avoid loud and aggressive persons, they are vexations to the spirit.
If you compare yourself with others, you may become vain and bitter for
always there will be greater and lesser persons than yourself. Enjoy
your achievements as well as your plans.
Keep interested in your own career, however humble; it is a real possession in
the changing fortunes of time.
Exercise caution in your business affairs; for the world is full of trickery.
But let this not blind you to what virtue there is; many persons strive for
high ideals; and everywhere life is full of heroism.
Be careful.
Strive to be happy.

Anonymous
DESIDERATA

Affirmations are positive statements of beliefs, wants, and models of the way we want things to be in our lives. Positive affirmations are life-enhancing guidelines for living and are used to reprogram your biocomputer or replace negative self-statements in your mind. We can be put affirmations into our minds consciously through the cognitive self-talk approach, visualization techniques, and self-hypnosis techniques.

GUIDELINES FOR USING AFFIRMATIONS. The following are some basic guidelines for using cognitive self-talk to place affirmations into your mind:

- *Positive.* Keep your affirmation or message positive. Do not use negative words. For example, say, "I accept and love myself" instead of, "I will not say negative things about myself."
- *Keep the affirmation brief.* This is primarily a right brain procedure. Don't get intellectual by including explanations, reasons, or justifications for your affirmation. Just state it as simply and briefly as possible in a positive manner with active declarative language.
- *Present tense.* Make your statement in the present tense as if it has already occurred. When using affirmations, or utilizing visualization techniques, it is helpful to imagine what you want as already having been actualized. By first imagining and visualizing your want as already actualized in your mind's eye it can then materialize on the physical plane.
- *Make it rhyme.* We tend to more easily remember aphorisms that rhyme (e.g. "fake it 'till you make it").

RESOURCES FOR AFFIRMATIONS. There are many potential sources of life-enhancing guidelines for living. For some these guidelines come from religion. Others are more eclectic and draw their affirmations and guidelines from a variety of religious, spiritual, poetry, musical, and self-help sources. Many find their primary guidelines from professional counseling. All of these sources can be inspiring and helpful. There are a number of recommended readings at the end of this book that provide sources for life-enhancing affirmations, especially those described in the spiritual and personal growth section.

The important point to remember in this sixth step is that *YOU* pick those guidelines, messages, and affirmations for *YOUR* mind that helps you become what *YOU* want to become. It is easy to fall back on what your religion, parents, spouse, and other significant others want for you. This sixth step is about taking responsibility for cultivating your own mental garden. This means removing outdated and self-defeating weeds, maintaining the plants, flowers, and herbs that you enjoy, and planting those new seeds needed to complete and fully actualize the most beautiful and enjoyable garden you can imagine.

There are so many positive life-enhancing guidelines for living that I am hesitant to offer any specific suggestions. However, there are some resources and guidelines that I have found particularly helpful in my journey of personal and spiritual growth that you may find helpful in your journey. Some of these recommended resources are briefly described in the last chapter. The following are thirty "seeds" (affirmations) that I have distilled from a variety of sources and personal life experiences. You may want to plant and nourish some of them in your mind's garden. These thirty guidelines can also be used as part of your cognitive restructuring when you work on a Button. As you modify or eliminate the Button that created your psychological distress pick one or more of these thirty positive guidelines for living. Think of the affirmation as, "If I were following this guideline for living I wouldn't have gotten myself all bent out of shape right now."

30 "SEEDS"
FOR YOUR MIND'S GARDEN

COGNITIVE GUIDELINES

1. **Responsibility:** I take full responsibility for my cognitions (inner programming, scripts, and models) that create my inner experience, including my feelings of distress and joy.

2. **Be-Here-Now:** I am focusing my awareness in my here-and-now and spending less time regretting the past and worrying about the future.

3. **Love:** I come from the "acceptance and love" motivational state, especially when I interact with other people, animals, and plants.

4. **Honest and Upfront:** I am honest and upfront with myself and other people.

5. **Inner Work:** I work on my Buttons whenever I have them pushed and avoid spreading negative toxins in the environment or acting out my negative stuff with others.

6. **Humor:** I maintain a sense of humor, especially when I begin to take myself too seriously.

7. **Keep an Open Mind:** I keep an open mind concerning possible alternative realities outside of the third dimension such as multi-dimensional realities, UFOs, chakras, energy fields around all life forms, auras, psychic activities, angels, spirit guides, channeling, mind-body healing, and the possibility of healing through working on peoples' energy fields. I also keep an open mind concerning the intentions of other people no matter how bad they appear to be.

8. **Continuum Thinking (The Wisdom of Insecurity):** Everything is on a continuum versus being absolute (e.g. "Black and White" thinking). My feelings of insecurity are reminders of the illusion of permanence and of my desire for absolutes, certainty, and predictability in my life.

9. **Remember the Purpose and Goals of My Life:** I am focused on the goals of becoming more aware, conscious, compassionate, and loving.

10. **Cultivation of My Mind:** I am consciously cultivating new cognitive models (e.g. thoughts) which facilitate my becoming more aware, conscious, compassionate, and loving.

RELATIONSHIP GUIDELINES

11. **Role and Game Playing:** I continue to play the roles (e.g. professor, counselor, author, lover, father, and friend) and games in my life drama with intensity, enthusiasm, and loving energy - all the while remembering that I am not these roles nor attached to the outcome of the roles and games that I play. I realize that the "master game" is to become fully conscious, aware, compassionate, and loving.

12. **Button-Pushers are my Teachers:** I appreciate my Button-Pushers (i.e. the messages provided by life experiences) for getting me in touch with my Buttons that I need to modify or eliminate in order to become more conscious, loving, compassionate, and self-actualized.

13. **See Things Clearly:** I perceive people and situations clearly, especially peoples' intentions, without filtering information through distorted and biased lens (cognitions). I am continually cleaning my perceptual lens.

14. **Positive Thoughts toward Others:** I think positive thoughts about other people. I imagine that people can hear everything I think about them.

15. **Golden Rule:** I treat other people like I want to be treated.

16. **Compassion:** I have compassion for people who create emotional distress within themselves and the people around them whenever they have their Buttons pushed.

17. **Forgiveness:** I forgive people when they have their Buttons pushed and act-out their emotional distress or self-defeating thoughts, feelings, and behaviors toward me.

18. **Support Network:** I maintain a support network of proactive, loving, and nourishing people who mutually support each other's journeys of personal growth and self-actualization.

WELLNESS PRACTICES

19. **Stress Management:** I practice my relaxation routines (e.g. yoga, meditation, and exercise) daily to help me maintain my physical and mental health and improve the quality of my life.

20. **Nutrition:** I eat healthy meals, and keep my weight down. If ill, I use vitamins, minerals, and herbs instead of pharmaceuticals, and other natural healing practices whenever possible, to facilitate my healing.

21. **Exercise:** I exercise regularly.

22. **Balance Work, Family, and Play:** I maintain a balance of work, family, friends, play, and personal time.

23. **Psychoactive Drugs:** I avoid certain psychoactive drugs such as nicotine, cocaine, narcotics, and depressants. I use selective psychoactive drugs such

as caffeine and alcohol responsibly and sparingly. I use drugless alternatives to trigger highs, pleasure, and alter moods. I realize that psychoactive drugs reinforce the illusion that the effects they trigger are in the psychoactive drugs instead of in me.

SPIRITUAL PRACTICES

24. **Donate My Time and Service:** I give a portion of my time and energy in the service of helping others.
25. **Meditation:** I meditate regularly to quiet my rational mind and become more centered, relaxed, harmonious, aware, conscious, loving, compassionate, and in touch with God.
26. **Universal Life Force Connection:** I experience and stay connected to the universal life energy that flows through all living things and the universe.
27. **Intuition:** I listen carefully to my inner voice and higher self. I trust my intuitive knowledge.
28. **God:** I appreciate the many and varied faces of God. I strive to actualize the God-like aspect within me.
29. **Believe In Miracles:** I believe in the power of manifesting my destiny. I can create and manifest on the material plane almost anything I can imagine in my mind's eye.
30. **Nonattachment:** I am fully involved with life without becoming attached (i.e. have a Button) to the outcome or any Guru, teacher, positive affirmation or personal growth method, including the Six-Step Button Therapy Method.

More Resources for Affirmations. There are many potential sources for positive affirmations and life-enhancing guidelines for living. The bookstores and websites are full of books, videos, and audio tapes offering life-enhancing guidelines for living. Many of these resources are full of wisdom and helpful life-enhancing strategies including daily meditations and affirmations to help us on our journey of self-actualization. Some of my favorite sources are described in the recommended reading list at the end of the book.

The Button Therapy Book: How to Work on Your Buttons and the Button Pushers in Your Life by Lloyd R. Goodwin, Jr. © 2002.Published by Trafford Publishing. www.trafford.com

DAILY CULTIVATION OF THE MIND

People are choosing all the time, but they don't want to admit it.
You are free when you accept the responsibility for your choices.
                                    Mildred Newman and Bernard Berkowitz
                                    HOW TO BE YOUR OWN BEST FRIEND

REMINDERS AND REPETITION. The new positive life-enhancing messages, affirmations, and models that help us grow into what we want to become must be reinforced with much repetition. You may want to place copies of the *30 Seeds for Your Mind's Garden* and other short positive affirmations that relate to freeing yourself from specific Buttons in prominent places around the house. You might put a copy on the refrigerator door at home and on the file cabinet or on the wall next to your desk in your office. Highlight the ones you are drawn to and focusing on implementing into your life now. These 30 "seeds" for your mind's garden can act as constant reminders of what you are consciously choosing to place into your mind. Repeating your affirmations throughout the day keeps your conscious and unconscious mind focused on the changes you want to make.

Desired changes usually take time and proceed in spurts forward, slips backward, and plateaus or stagnation periods with no observable progress. Be patient. Like developing any new knowledge or skill, personal growth takes time, the accumulation of many life experiences, and concentrated repetition. Your mind is constantly accumulating new learning daily through life experiences so why not consciously decide what you want that new learning to be? It is up to you to consciously decide what you want to place in your mind's garden. It is up to you to decide what you want growing in your mind's garden and what you want your mind's garden to look like. It is up to you to decide what type of existence and inner experience you want to create for yourself. If you are not satisfied with your current life and inner experience, including career, friends, leisure time activities, appearance, and health then you can take charge of your life and make changes. Once you become aware of how to operate your bio-computer you do have a choice as to what you want to make of your limited lifetime on earth this time around.

The visualization of that which you wish to become, or the process of cultivating the mind is the sixth and final step toward the facilitation of growth into higher levels of functioning, consciousness, and being.

CHAPTER TWENTY-TWO

THE SPIRITUAL DIMENSION

*Everyone who is seriously involved in the pursuit of science
becomes convinced that a spirit is manifest
in the laws of the universe.*
                                    Albert Einstein

*There are not countless religions.
There is only one religion -
the religion of Divine Love.
There is only one race -
the race of mankind.
There is only one language -
the language of Divine Love in your heart.
There is only one God.
He is present everywhere.*
                                    Sai Baba
                                    An Eastern View of Jesus
                                    Christ: Divine Discourses of
                                    Sathya Sai Baba

THE BUTTON THERAPY MODEL is primarily a holistic cognitive counseling approach that includes emotional, behavioral, interpersonal, systems, and spiritual components. By eliminating Buttons that are responsible for our psychological distress we can choose to spend more time centered and in harmony with others, our environment, and ourselves. We can spend more time coming from the love and spiritual motivational states. The spiritual dimension of the Button Therapy model is a recommended, but optional component of the sixth step described in the previous chapter. Steps one through five of the Six-Step Button Therapy Method provide a model from which to recognize when we get ourselves emotionally upset and offers five steps to modify or eliminate our Buttons causing our emotional distress. The sixth step encourages us to place new proactive life-enhancing affirmations and messages into our minds which facilitate our becoming happier, satisfied, higher functioning, and, if we so choose, more spiritual individuals.

Each of us can decide what sort of inner experience and life existence we would like to actualize. I have shared with the reader throughout this book my primary life goals, which I am working on actualizing for myself. To summarize, I have chosen to put seeds (i.e. affirmations and messages) in my mind's garden that facilitate my becoming more centered, happy, aware, conscious, loving, and compassionate. I also strive to periodically experience transcendental states of consciousness and become one with God or the universal life force energy. To me, these are primarily spiritual goals. Spirituality is expressed in many different ways and can be achieved through many different pathways. What is spiritual to me may be viewed by others as simply aspects of personal growth or self-actualization, and not necessarily spiritual. Spirituality related themes include meaning to life; ability to forgive, love and have compassion; will to live; sense of connectedness or unity with others and a higher power; peaceful, centered, and harmonious living; happiness; prioritization of values and life activities; and reverence and respect for all life forms.

DISTINCTION BETWEEN RELIGION AND SPIRITUALITY

Whether a man remains deluded or gains Illumination
depends upon himself, not upon differences or similarity of doctrine.
Hui Hai
THE ZEN TEACHINGS OF HUI HAI

❧

The Buddha spoke gently, "once a person is caught by belief in a doctrine, he
loses all his freedom. When one becomes dogmatic, he believes his doctrine is
the only truth and that all other doctrines are heresy. Disputes and conflicts
all arise from narrow views. They can extend endlessly, wasting precious
time and sometimes even leading to war. Attachment to views is the greatest
impediment to the spiritual path. Bound to narrow views, one becomes so
entangled that it is no longer possible to let the door of truth open."
Thich Nhat Hanh
OLD PATH WHITE CLOUDS:
THE LIFE STORY OF THE BUDDHA

❧

I am for religion, against religions.
Victor Hugo
LES MISERABLES

There is an important distinction between the concepts of *religion* and *spirituality*. The concept of religion is usually associated with an organized religion including that religion's beliefs, rituals, and dogma (e.g. Baptist, Roman Catholic, Lutheran, Methodist, Judaism, etc.). Organized religions include a spiritual dimension. However, the concept of spirituality is broader than religion and can also include a direct transcendental experience and communion with God or the source without going through intermediaries such as the clergy or the structure of an organized religion.

Have you ever felt at a loss to fill out forms that ask about your involvement in religion? You may consider yourself spiritual but you are not a member of a church or involved in any organized religion and there is no box to check for "personal spiritual path." A recent national opinion poll of adult Americans was commissioned by the *Spirituality & Health* magazine (Scott, 2001) to find out what people mean when they say, "I'm spiritual, but I'm not religious." Results indicate that: 59 percent of Americans describe themselves as both religious and spiritual; 65 percent have positive associations with the word "religion" and 15 percent have a negative association; 74 percent find the word "spirituality" positive and 6 percent disagree; 20 percent see themselves as solely spiritual, and among this group, 47 percent view religion negatively; 8 percent say they are only religious; 23 percent view spirituality as the broader concept that embraces religion; 7 percent say religion is broader; 19 percent consider the two identical; 13 percent see them as entirely different; 80 percent of those who define themselves as spiritual say that their spirituality influences every aspect of their lives; 42 percent said that religion plays a central role in their lives (for another 36 percent it plays some role); and for nearly all of them this role is the same as, or greater than, it used to be. Another Gallup poll (Joseph & Pompa, 2001) indicates that the majority of American adults (55 percent) believe religion is losing influence on American life; 39 percent believe that religion is gaining influence; 3 percent believe there's no change; and 3 percent have no opinion.

WHAT'S A SPIRITUAL ACT? As part of the *Spirituality & Health* poll people were asked what activities, if any, they found spiritual. Ninety-one percent saw praying as a spiritual activity followed by attending worship services (81 percent), parenting (80 percent), walking in the woods (67 percent), making love (52 percent), and cleanliness (29 percent).

HOW DO PEOPLE UNDERSTAND GOD? The *Spirituality & Health* (Scott, 2001) poll found: 71 percent described God as "loving" when given a list of characteristics and asked to pick the one that best describes God; 14 percent chose "creating"; 5 percent find God primarily "remote"; 2 percent chose "judging"; 2 percent chose "controlling"; and 84 percent view God as being "everywhere and in everything" rather then "someone somewhere." The concept of God as the stern judgmental white bearded old man with long white flowing robes sitting on a throne is finally gone, except maybe for children under 18 years old who were not included in this poll.

I personally do not belong to any organized religion. However, I consider myself a spiritual being. I have integrated spiritual concepts and rituals from many different religions, philosophies, and more conscious individuals further along the spiritual path than I, into a personally meaningful spiritual belief system and spiritual path. My personal spiritual journey is not fixed and is constantly changing to accommodate new insights and learning as I become more aware and conscious. I attempt to live by the spiritual beliefs that are meaningful to me. Also, I attempt to model spiritual characteristics by living a moral, ethical, centered, aware, conscious, loving, and compassionate existence for my children, coworkers, friends, and all people that I encounter. I try to respect all living things.

It really doesn't matter how anybody else defines your personal spiritual path. The sixth step of the Button Therapy Method encourages you to consciously choose those affirmations and messages that allow *you* to become what *you* want to become. It's totally your choice. You don't need anybody else's definitions of spirituality or religion or need permission from others to place your life-enhancing guidelines for living into your biocomputer. It's your mind and your life!

WHY INCLUDE A SPIRITUAL DIMENSION IN A COGNITIVE COUNSELING AND PSYCHOLOGICAL SELF-HELP MODEL?

Current cognitive-behavioral therapy models do not include a significant spiritual component. Does the spiritual dimension have a place in cognitive therapy models? Should the spiritual dimension be included in *any* of the professional counseling and psychological self-help models and approaches. I firmly believe the answer to both of these questions is *yes*. The spiritual dimension is included in the Button Therapy model for three main reasons:

1. The Button Therapy model is a holistic cognitive therapy model which includes the whole person, including the body, mind, and spiritual dimensions.

2. Spirituality is an integral part of most people's lives.

3. Spirituality related cognitions can be either a positive or negative factor in health, healing, and rehabilitation.

THE BUTTON THERAPY MODEL IS A HOLISTIC COGNITIVE THERAPY MODEL

If we adopt a holistic perspective when helping others and ourselves then this means taking into account the whole person, including body, mind, and spirit. It is essential for health and mental health professionals to work with the whole person and not just the presenting physical or mental health disorder, or problem (Goodwin, 1986, 1997a, 1997b, 1999). "The reciprocal interactions among cognitive, behavioral, spiritual, environmental, physiological, and genetic factors must be given consideration in a holistic perspective to the etiology of disease and disability as well as to healing and rehabilitation" (Goodwin, 1986, p. 31). People are whole people, with some parts functioning more effectively than others. The parts that aren't functioning in a healthy harmonious manner can adversely affect the entire person. Effective physical, mental, and spiritual healing involves assessing and providing interventions from a holistic perspective with the whole person, including the family, school, work, and other systems of which they are a part.

Research supports the inclusion of the spiritual dimension in cognitive therapy. Controlled studies (Propst, 1980; Propst, Ostrom, Watkins, Dean & Mashburn, 1992) found that the effectiveness of cognitive-behavioral therapy for depression with religiously oriented clients was substantially increased when their spiritual perspectives were incorporated into the treatment. This effect occurred whether or not the clinicians were themselves religiously oriented. Herbert Benson's (1996) research found religious clients were more apt to stay with the relaxation method if they used short prayers from their religious orientations as the focus of their meditation rather than using a meaningless or neutral phrase such as "one." Benson believes that the faith factor is important to health and healing.

It is our Buttons that, when activated, pull us off center and out of our love and spiritual motivational states. The more Buttons we eliminate, the more choice we have as to which motivational states we come from at any given moment. The spiritual component is an integral part of most people's lives and is a key piece of the physical and psychological health and healing picture.

SPIRITUALITY IS AN INTEGRAL PART OF MOST PEOPLE'S LIVES

Since the beginning of recorded history people have conceived of reality in a way that is not limited to the material domain that we know through our senses. Most cultures have included a transcendental spiritual aspect to their existence that is beyond the material world. According to a national poll (Gallup, 2001) of American adults, 95 percent say they believe in God; 92 percent state a religious preference; 68 percent are members of a church; 44 percent attended church in last 7 days; 59 percent say religion is very important in their lives; 65 percent believe religion answers problems; 56 percent have high confidence in organized religion; and 60 percent give a high rating to ethical standards of clergy. For most people, religious and spiritual beliefs are a vital part of their lives. According to another poll (Pew Research Center, 1997) 71 percent of respondents say that they never doubt the existence of God. The poll also found that 61 percent of Americans believe miracles come from the power of God. And 53 percent said prayer is important to daily life. As these polls indicate spirituality is an integral part of most people's lives.

VARIETY OF RELIGIOUS GROUPS.

There are approximately 2,100 religious groups listed in the latest edition of the *Encyclopedia of American Religions*, a figure that has almost doubled in 20 years. They range from Judaism and Christianity to UFO cults. The influx of Asian religions is reflected in the rapid rise of Islam with about 3.5 million adherents. Buddhism is said to be the fastest-growing faith with 750,000 believers, including 100,000 American converts. The statistics indicate that we live in a very religious country. The United States is considered to be the most religious country in the Western industrial world (Creedon, 1998). Ninety-six percent of Americans believe in God, compared with 70 percent of Britons according to a special issue on religion in *Life* magazine (McCourt, 1998).

The religious preference of Americans is a varied smorgasbord. Sixty-two percent are Protestant, 20 percent are Roman Catholic, 7 percent claim no religion, 4 percent are non-Christian, and 3 percent are Jewish (Woodward, 1999). America's God has many faces. We are one multicultural nation under many Gods. America is unlike more monocultural nations such as Iran or Italy who share one view of God. Though 95 percent of adults believe that God exists, there's growing disagreement about how to describe God. God has been described as a universal life force, cosmic energy, pure awareness and consciousness, Goddess, and as an old white-bearded white man.

Although approximately 80 percent of American adults consider themselves Christians, most are hazy about the basic tenets of their faith. According to George Barna in *The Index of Leading Spiritual Indicators* America is transitioning from a Christian nation to a spiritually diverse society (Creedon, 1998). A new perception of religion and spirituality is developing. One that is more individualized and allows for a direct communication with God without the necessity of professional clergy intermediaries. Some individuals become involved in multiple religions, utilizing the beliefs, rituals, and teachings that they are attracted to from many spiritual paths. As Sri Swami Satchidananda (1998), founder of Integral Yoga Institutes Worldwide says,

> Each religion may offer different prayers and practices, but all are designed to help us to commune with God or a Higher Power. Even though my motto has always been "Truth is one, paths are many," I don't recommend trying to walk on all the different paths at once because you will never reach your goal that way. Instead, you may draw from the practices of various paths and faith, but integrate them into one unified and harmonious path. Then follow that spiritual path with your goal in mind and stay with it consistently. Delve deep into your practices with consistency and earnestness and you will certainly reap all the spiritual benefits. (p. 48)

New Age Spirituality

Belief in "new age" phenomena has grown sharply since the 1970s. Approximately 20 percent of American adults are New Agers according to George Barna (Creedon, 1998). According to a survey by Yankelovich and associates cited in *USA Today* (Carey & Visgaitis, 1998) 52 percent of adults believe in spiritualism, 45 percent in faith healing, 37 percent in astrology, 30 percent in UFO's, 25 percent in reincarnation, and 14 percent in fortune telling. Children hold many of the same "new age" beliefs as adults.

A survey conducted in 1997 in Great Britain by Childwise, an independent research company specializing in children's issues, gathered data through surveys and discussion groups on 700 children aged 10-15 years. This research was reported in *Spirituality and Health* (Scott, 1998). Seventy-five percent agreed with the statement, "Science can't explain everything." The children said, "Science can't explain things like God, ghosts, what's going to happen after you die. Science can't explain human feelings." In the realm of the supernatural and paranormal, a large majority (80 percent) believe that events you dream while sleeping sometimes come true in real life. Seventy-three percent find it likely that some houses have ghosts in them. Fifty-nine percent believe that some people can read minds. Fifty-seven percent believe that animals understand how humans feel. Eleven percent expect their pets to be reincarnated. Fifty-four percent believe in astrology. Fifty-three percent believe in an afterlife and that, "there is a heaven." And, immediately following the afterlife is the belief that there is life on other planets.

Prayer

National surveys have found that most people pray as part of their spiritual practices and many use prayer frequently for coping with life's problems. In a Yankelovich Partners survey for the Lutheran Brotherhood (Hall & Lynn,

1998) 90 percent of adults say they pray. The things they pray for most include: their families (98 percent), world's children (81 percent), world peace (77 percent), co-workers (69 percent), enemies (61 percent), and the U.S. president (48 percent). Studies reviewed by McCullough and Larson (1999) indicate that people use prayer as a coping resource more frequently when their problems are more severe, intractable, or unresponsive to conventional interventions and their needs are greatest. According to a Gallup poll (Ehmann, 1999) membership in a church or synagogue, attendance, and intensity of belief all increase with age. Also, 70 percent of 18 to 29 year-olds say that religion is losing its influence in American life, compared to only 46 percent of those 75 and older who share this view.

In a related survey by Yankelovich Partners for Lutheran Brotherhood (Hall & Laird, 1999) participating adults indicated that if they could ask and receive a direct and immediate answer from a god or supreme being they would ask for the following: What's my purpose here? (34 percent); will I have life after death? (19 percent); why do bad things happen? (16 percent); is there intelligent life elsewhere? (7 percent); how long will I live? (6 percent); other (6 percent); and not sure (12 percent).

Afterlife

Eighty percent of Americans believe in an afterlife; 72 percent believe in heaven and 56 percent in hell (McCourt, 1998). Sixty-six percent of adults polled by *Newsweek* in November 1995 believe in the devil, and more than one-third say he has tempted them. Among evangelical or "born again" Protestants, 85 percent say they believe in Satan; 59 percent blame the devil for crime; and 43 percent blame him for the gay-rights movement (*USA Today*, 1995). With these beliefs about heaven, hell, and a devil it is no wonder so many fear death. These beliefs also present a challenge to mental health professionals counseling the dying and the grieving survivors.

Two recent surveys cited in the *New Age Journal* (1998) suggest that belief in an afterlife is soaring. The first survey by the University of Chicago's National Opinion Research Center found that 81 percent of Americans believe in life after death, more than at any time in the past 25 years. The second survey by *U.S. News and World Report* concludes that up to 15 million Americans may have had vivid near-death experiences that reinforced their belief of an afterlife.

However, although there is a strong spiritual dimension to most peoples' lives, few would turn to clergy for help if they were dying. Many want spiritual comfort in their final days but only about one-third think clergy would be very helpful in providing it, according to a Gallup poll. In a phone survey of 1,200 adults, many individuals anticipate their last days as "a time of serious spiritual and emotional work." Thirty-six percent say clergy would be comforting in many ways, compared with 81 percent who cite family and 61 percent friends. Clergy are seen as ministers of religion and boxed in by creeds and dogmas. Most people don't want religion, they want spirituality, according to theological historian Robert Webber of Wheaton College (Elias, 1997).

SPIRITUALITY AND CHILDREN

Many parents help prepare their children for life by exposing their kids to religious beliefs. In a Yankelovitch Partners poll of 1,000 adults, 85 percent said they taught their children to pray, and 59 percent said they required them to attend church, synagogue or another religious service (Cox New Service, 1998). A Gallop poll of 404 parents with children under age 12 conducted for *Parenting* magazine (December/January issue) indicates that 95 percent believe in God, 64 percent say grace at meals and bedtime prayers with their children, 78 percent say it's all right if their children choose to practice a different faith, and 40 percent say religion has become more important since they had children (Manning & Hellmich, 1995).

Many of today's teenagers are interested in more than sex, drugs, and rock and roll. According to a recent Gallup poll of teens aged 13 to 17, many are eager to learn about many of the world religions. The survey found that 54 percent of the teenagers were interested in learning more about Roman Catholicism, 52 percent about Protestantism, 44 percent about Native American spirituality, 29 percent about Islam, 27 percent about Buddhism, 27 percent about Judaism, 22 percent about Hinduism, 16 percent about Paganism, and 15 percent about Mormonism (*New Age Journal*, 1999).

BENEFITS OF THE SPIRITUAL DIMENSION

Religious and spiritual beliefs can provide numerous benefits including: A sense of meaning and purpose.

- A framework to set priorities and place life's stresses in perspective.
- Comfort in the face of illness and crises.
- Support for a healthy lifestyle and avoidance of cigarettes, drugs, and alcohol.
- Opportunities for social contact and to develop supportive relationships.
- Reasons to be of service and help to others.
- Sense of being part of something larger and feeling connected to something outside of oneself. (Mental Medicine Update, 1996)

SPIRITUALITY AND HEALTH

Spirituality and healing have been intertwined from the beginning of both the medical and religious professional disciplines. The founders of the world's great religions were healers. Buddha, Jesus, and Muhammad were all gifted healers. "The earliest Christians were primarily a healing community, and centuries before Jesus the Hebrew prophets, Elijah, Elisha, and Isaiah were acknowledged healers. Moses is said to have healed many Israelites from serpent bites. Medicine men and healing shamans throughout Africa, Asia, and the Americas held some of the most esteemed positions in their tribes" (Targ & Katra, 2001, p. 146). All the great religions include healing in one form or another. "From the earliest human times, perhaps 100,000 years ago, when trepanning (the boring of holes into the skull) was performed to let out the evil spirits, healing and religion have been intertwined" (Shealy, 1999, p. 9).

> The New Testament contains numerous accounts of Jesus as physician. In ancient times, faith and medicine went hand-in-hand. Priests in black robes were called upon to treat the body as well as the spirit. 'With the scientific revolution, there was more and more separation,' said Dr. Dana King, an associate professor in the Department of Family Medicine at the East Carolina University School of Medicine. Healers hung up their black robes, and with that, many suspended their ideas of mixing religion with medicine. 'Just in the last few years, I think there's been a recognition of the importance of spirituality in people's lives,' King said. 'Patients are whole people. We need to treat them as whole people.' (Grizzard, 1998, p. E1)

Religious and spiritual practices have been used since ancient times to influence health. With the current emphasis on holistic health the spiritual aspect of healing is receiving increased attention by health care practitioners. Health care practitioners who want to help heal their patients, instead of just treating symptoms of illness, realize they must treat the whole person including body, mind, and spirit.

Evidence of the influence of spirituality in health maintenance, healing, and health promotion has been accumulating in recent times. As Larry Dossey, M.D. (1999a) points out,

> A review in 1987 uncovered more than 200 studies containing religious terminology published in the medical literature during the previous 100 years (Levin & Schiller, 1987). Systematic reviews (Larson, Pattison, Blazer, Omran & Kaplan, 1986) and meta-analyses (Witter, Stock, Okun & Haring, 1985) have quantitatively shown that religious involvement is an epidemiologically protective factor (Levin, Larson & Puchalski, 1997). Reviews have examined cause-specific morbidity and mortality rates (Jarvis & Northcutt, 1987), such as those for cancer (Troyer, 1988) and hypertension (Levin & Vanderpool, 1989), in samples of Catholics, Protestants, Jews, Hindus, Buddhists,

Parsis, and Muslims. Statistically significant associations between religious groups have appeared in studies of several diseases, including heart disease, hypertension, stroke, cancer, and gastrointestinal disease, as well as of health status indicators (eg, self-reported health, symptomatology, disability, and longevity) (Levin, Larson & Puchalski, 1997). These findings are so consistent and robust they have led to a new field of research called the "epidemiology of religion" (Troyer, 1988). (Dossey, 1999a, p. 16)

Many people want their health care providers to include the spiritual dimension in their health care through prayer. For example, in a survey of 203 family practice hospitalized adult patients King and Bushwick (1994) found that 48 percent wanted their physicians to pray with them. Many people want the spiritual dimension addressed in their mental health care as well. "In a 1992 Gallup Poll, 66 percent of the people surveyed said they would prefer to see a professional counselor with spiritual values and beliefs, and 81 percent said they would want to have their own values and beliefs integrated into the counseling process" (Bart, 1998, p. 1). According to Mary Bart (1998), "One of the fears about discussing spiritual issues with clients is a counselor's own lack of religious knowledge...Not to worry. It is a respectful sensitivity to religious values and a willingness to learn that's important for counselors, not encyclopedia-like knowledge of all the world's religions" (p. 6).

Herbert Benson, M.D., associate professor of Medicine at Harvard Medical School and the Deaconess Hospital, president and founder of their Mind/Body Medical Institute, author of *The Relaxation Response, Timeless Healing,* and other books on behavioral medicine, has researched and currently utilizes the "faith factor" in his clinical work. In teaching people how to elicit the relaxation response utilizing a meditation approach, Dr. Benson reports that most of his patients, when given the choice between secular or spiritually oriented phrases to focus on, chose the words or phrases that are religious or spiritual in nature. Eighty percent of Benson's patients picked prayers as the focus of their elicitation, be they Jewish, Christian, Buddhist, or Hindu and about 25 percent of his patients reported feeling "more spiritual" as a result of eliciting the relaxation response, whether they chose a religious or a secular focus. Benson adds that his 25 percent rate may be conservative considering a 1994 *Newsweek* poll which revealed that 45 percent of people polled had "sensed the sacred" during meditation. Not only did Benson and his colleagues' research reveal that 25 percent of people feel more spiritual as the result of the elicitation of the relaxation response, but their research showed that those same people have fewer medical symptoms than do those who reported no increase in spirituality from the elicitation of the relaxation response (Benson, 1996). A 1995 survey of more than 1,000 Americans conducted by Dr. Herbert Benson found that many Americans believe religion was a factor in their healing.

BEING-VALUES AND METANEEDS

We may actually "need" to nurture the spiritual aspect of our lives to become and remain healthy. Dr. Abraham Maslow's study of self-actualization and the development of his "hierarchy of needs" theory convinced Dr. Maslow that healthy mental and physical functioning includes the spiritual dimension. Maslow referred to the spiritual dimension as "being-values" and "metaneeds" (see chapter 12 for a description of Dr. Maslow's hierarchy of needs). Dr. Maslow (1972) observed that,

> Self-actualizing people are, without one single exception, involved in a cause outside their own skin, in something outside of themselves. They are devoted, working at something, something which is very precious to them - some calling or vocation in the old sense, the priestly sense...All, one way or another, devote their lives to the search for what I have called the "being values" ("B for short), the ultimate values which are intrinsic, which cannot be reduced to anything more ultimate. There are about fourteen of the B-Values, including truth and beauty and goodness of the ancients and perfection, simplicity, comprehensiveness, and several more...These B-Values behave like needs. I have called them *metaneeds*. Their deprivation breeds certain kinds of pathologies which have not yet been adequately described but which I call *metapathologies* - the sickness of the soul which come, for example, from living among liars all the time and not trusting anyone. Just as we need counselors to help people with the simpler problems of unmet needs, so we may need *metacounselors* to help with the soul-sicknesses that grow from the unfulfilled metaneeds. In fact, I would go so far as to claim that these B-Values are the meaning of life for most people, but many people don't even recognize that they have these metaneeds. Part of the counselors' job may be to make them aware of these needs in themselves, just as the classical psychoanalyst made his patients aware of their instinctoid basic needs. Ultimately, perhaps, some professionals shall come to think of themselves as philosophical or religious counselors. (pp. 43-44)

THE SPIRITUAL INFLUENCE IN HEALING PRACTICES CAN BE HELPFUL

Physician and author Larry Dossey, M.D. has broken with the traditional scientific medical model and has become one of the main proponents for returning spirit to the art of healing. Dr. Dossey describes his beliefs and research about the spiritual dimension in health care in such books as *Meaning & Medicine* (Dossey, 1992), *Healing Words* (Dossey, 1993), *Prayer is Good Medicine* (1996), and *Reinventing Medicine: Beyond Mind-Body to a New Era of Healing*

(1999b) and has utilized prayer in his medical practice for many years. Dr. Dossey found over 100 experiments exhibiting the criteria of "good science," many conducted under stringent laboratory conditions, over half of which showed that prayer brings about significant changes in a variety of living beings. Dr. Dossey (1993) believes that, "The most practical reason to examine prayer in healing is simply that, at least some of the time, it *works*. The evidence is simply overwhelming that prayer functions at a distance to change physical processes in a variety of organisms, from bacteria to humans. These data ... are so impressive that I have come to regard them as among the best-kept secrets in medical science" (p. 2).

DISTANCE HEALING

More than 30 years of research clearly demonstrate that a person's focused intentions can directly influence the physiological processes of someone far away. There is evidence that the distance between the person receiving a healing prayer and the person(s) doing the praying doesn't matter. The healing prayer is just as effective accompanied by a healing touch in the same room as from halfway around the world. As Larry Dossey, M.D. (1993), who has researched and written numerous books on the theme of prayer in medicine points out, "... numerous controlled studies have validated the nonlocal nature of prayer. Much of this evidence, moreover, suggests that praying individuals – or people involved in compassionate imagery or mental intent, whether or not it is called prayer – can purposefully affect the physiology of distant people without the 'receiver's' awareness" (p. 45).

MEDICAL DIAGNOSIS AT A DISTANCE. Two of the best known people able to provide a medical diagnosis of people at a long-distance are Edgar Cayce and Caroline Myss, neither of whom had any formal medical training.

EDGAR CAYCE (1877-1945) known as the "sleeping prophet" did not get beyond the seventh grade in school and was working in a bookstore by the age of 16. Cayce practiced medical diagnosis by clairvoyance for forty-three years. Cayce could go into a self-induced trance and give the health status, medical diagnoses, and recommend treatment for people many of whom he never met. He did health or life "readings" for people located in different states or countries. As his reputation spread physicians would refer some of their patients that they had trouble diagnosing to Cayce. His health diagnoses were usually accurate and often verified by the person's physician. According to his biographer, Thomas Sugrue (1994), he left stenographic reports of 30,000 or these diagnoses along with hundreds of complete case reports, containing affidavits by the patients and reports by physicians. Today there are health care practitioners around the world who provide health care based on his past "readings" for individuals with specific illnesses. Edgar Cayce never made any public demonstrations of his powers and was never on the stage. He never sought any publicity nor did he seek wealth. His economic situation was often quite precarious. "He did not use his ability except to prescribe for the sick and to give spiritual advice and vocational guidance when these were specifically requested" (p. 6). From health "readings" Cayce went on to "life readings" which included such themes as philosophy, metaphysics, paranormal phenomenon, reincarnation, accounts of past lives, astrology, and other mysteries of the universe such as the pyramids, Atlantis, and soul development.

The *Association for Research and Enlightenment (ARE)* houses all of Cayce's "readings" related to health issues as well as other more esoteric subjects. The *ARE* and the *Heritage* store, another repository of Cayce recommended materials, are both located in Virginia Beach, Virginia and provide many of the Cayce books and resources, including nutritional, and homeopathic remedies that he recommended for various illnesses and health maintenance.

CAROLINE MYSS, a theologian, author (Myss, 1996, 1997), and publisher is a modern day intuitive medical diagnostician. A study to determine the accuracy of Myss's intuitive medical diagnoses was conducted by C. Norman Shealy, M.D., a Harvard-trained neurosurgeon and researcher who co-founded the American Holistic Medical Association. The results of this study are described in *The Creation of Health: The Emotional, Psychological, and Spiritual Responses that Promote Health and Healing* (Shealy & Myss, 1993). According to Dr. Shealy's research, Myss achieved a fantastic 93 percent accuracy rate in long-distance diagnoses of peoples' medical illnesses! In the study Dr. Shealy and Caroline were located in different states. Caroline was given only the patient's name and birth date. Dr. Shealy would usually have the patient in his office while he talked with Caroline on the phone. Caroline would then start telling Dr. Shealy the health condition and medical diagnoses of the patient. Given that physicians are generally about 80 percent accurate in their diagnoses, a 93 percent accuracy rate from a distance and never having met the patients, is quite remarkable (Shealy & Myss, 1993).

THE DUKE UNIVERSITY MANTRA STUDY. Cardiologist Mitchell W. Krucoff and nurse practitioner Suzanne Crater, two Duke University researchers are investigating the effects of prayer and other nonmedical practices on patients' recovery after angioplasty. The MANTRA study (Monitor and Actualization of Noetic TRAinings) at the Durham, North Carolina, Veterans Affairs Medical Center consisted of a group of patients who had prayers said for them, three other groups were exposed to touch, guided visualization, or stress relaxation. A fifth group served as a control group and did not receive any prayers or treatments. The study found that angioplasty patients with acute coronary syndromes who were prayed for did 50 to 100 percent better (in terms of heart rate, blood pressure, and EKG results) than did patients in the control group. Patients who received guided imagery, touch, or stress relaxation assistance also benefited, showing a 30 to 50 percent trend toward improved outcomes.

Several different religious groups from around the country and world offered prayers. Each religious group received the same information on the patient - the name of a male patient who was undergoing a catheter procedure. The prayers were sent from Buddhist monasteries in Nepal and France, from Moravians in North Carolina, and from Carmelite nuns in Baltimore who prayed during evening vespers. In Jerusalem, a Jewish group inserted prayers in the city's Western Wall. Fundamentalist Christians, Baptists, and Unitarians prayed as well.

The prayers proved effective even though the MANTRA patients didn't know they were being prayed for. A larger study of 1,500 patients is now under way at hospitals in North Carolina, San Diego, Washington, D.C., and Oklahoma City (Sokoloff, 1999).

THE TARG STUDY ON AIDS. Another recent example of distant healing is from a study of patients with AIDS conducted by Elisabeth Targ, M.D. at the California Pacific Medical Center in San Francisco. This controlled study indicates that after six months of prayers from a distance the patients needed fewer doctor visits, they spent less time in the hospital, and they felt better than before the study began. Dr. Targ selected 40 healers from around the country. All of the healers donated their time. The healers had an average of 17 years of professional experience. About half of the healers specialized in energy healing, another quarter practiced contemplative healing or visualizations, and the last quarter were religious healers who used intercessionary prayer. The healers were comprised of a Native American healer, a Chi Kung master, a Jewish kabbalist, Christian healers, Buddhist healers, and secular healers from all around the country. Researchers gave the healers nothing more than a picture, a name, a T-cell count, and a list of symptoms to work with in this study. From their homes many miles away, the healers focused their attention on the patients, and slowly but surely, the group began to feel better. Compared to the control group that only received standard medical care and not the distant healing, the group that did had measurably improved health, as judged by physical and psychological tests. As Dr. Targ wrote in the December 1998 issue of the *Western Journal of Medicine*, the treatment clearly had "a positive therapeutic effect." Dr. Targ refers to this technique as distant healing (Barret, 1999).

THE MOST FAMOUS PRAYER STUDY. In 1988 Randolph Byrd, M.D., a cardiologist, randomized 393 patients in the coronary care unit at San Francisco General Hospital to either a group receiving intercessory prayer (192 patients) or to a control group (201 patients). While hospitalized the first group were prayed-for by participating Christians praying outside the hospital; the control group did not receive prayers from those participating in this study. In this prospective randomized double-blind study, in which neither the patients, physicians, nor nurses knew who was receiving prayer the prayed-for patients did better on several measures. In the prayed-for group there were fewer deaths (though not statistically significant); fewer patients required endotracheal intubation and ventilator support; they required fewer potent drugs including diuretics and antibiotics; they experienced a lower incidence of pulmonary edema; and they required cardiopulmonary resuscitation less often (Byrd, 1988). This study suggests that sending healing prayers to ill people has a beneficial therapeutic effect. However, critics have pointed out that controlled studies of prayer are impossible, because there is no way to control for the prayer of people in the control group by loved ones. As Dossey points out, "If both groups are prayed for, the experiment becomes not a test of prayer versus no prayer, but a test of the degree or the amount of prayer" (p. 14). These research problems can be overcome by using other life forms besides nonhumans as research subjects.

Nonhuman Studies

Studies of human intention on nonhuman life forms such as plants, animals, bacteria and yeast using spiritual energy provides additional evidence for distance healing. One way to minimize the effect of self-fulfilling prophecy and expectations is to conduct research on nonhuman living organisms. There have been a number of studies that provide evidence of the power of a nonmaterial form of energy that can affect living organisms. These studies suggest that spiritual healing effects can operate independent of the awareness or desire of the recipient and that the effects of spiritual healing are not solely the result of suggestion or a placebo response.

Daniel J. Benor, M.D., an American psychiatrist working in England, surveyed the research of experimental evidence for "spiritual healing" published prior to 1990. He defined "spiritual healing" as "the intentional influence of one or more people upon another living system without utilizing known physical means of intervention." He found 131 studies, most of them in nonhumans. In fifty-six of these studies, there was less than one chance in a hundred (i.e. .01 probability level of statistical significance) that the positive results were due to chance. In an additional twenty-one studies, the possibility of a chance explanation was between two and five chances in a hundred (i.e. .02 and .05 probability levels) (Dossey, 1993). In Healing Research (1992) Dr. Benor examined more than 150 controlled studies from around the world. "He reviewed psychic, mental, and spiritual healing experiments done on a variety of living organisms, including enzymes, cell cultures, bacteria, yeasts, plants, animals, and humans. More than half of the studies demonstrated significant healing" (Targ & Katra, 2001, p. 146). The review of these studies can be found in Benor (1990, 1992). Because of the many confounding variables such as the placebo, or expectancy effect, associated with research on humans, in some ways research on the "spiritual" effects on nonhumans is even more remarkable. Some of the results of the studies on "spiritual" effects on nonhuman life forms have interesting implications for humans.

IMPLICATIONS OF
NONHUMAN SPIRITUAL HEALING STUDIES

These experiments on nonhuman subjects have interesting implications for healing, health, and illness in humans. Larry Dossey, M.D. (1993) describes seven of these implications:

1. The ability to inhibit or increase the growth of bacterial or yeast populations could be a valuable health resource. There may be times when it would be helpful to inhibit the growth of pathogenic microorganisms, such as in the case of infections or to increase certain good microorganisms after treatment with antibiotics, which kill "good" bacteria in addition to pathogenic ones.
2. If genetic mutations can be influenced by the conscious efforts of others, then abnormal genes can mutate to normal ones. This "reverse mutation" has been discovered to occur in myotonic dystrophy, a disease causing severe muscle weakness. Scientists don't know what causes "good" mutations. Could the mind possibly be involved?
3. These studies suggest that spiritual healing can occur whether or not the recipient of the healing actively wants it. We can assume that the microorganisms did not know they were subjects in an experiment. The observed effects do not depend on what the subject thinks.
4. These studies support the claim of healers that spiritual healing operates as powerfully at a distance as it does nearby.
5. It seems that ordinary people have the ability to bring about biological changes in other living organisms. This suggests that everyone may posses some degree of innate healing ability.
6. Negative effects (inhibition of growth) as well as positive effects (promotion of growth) were observed in some of the studies. This raises the possibility of a dark side to spiritual healing. Does this mean that people can use prayer or thought to harm people?
7. Skeptics often criticize spiritual healing as being simply the result of suggestion or a placebo response. These nonhuman studies suggest that the effects of spiritual healing can be completely independent of the "psychology" of the subject unless skeptics wish to attribute a high degree of consciousness to bacteria and yeast.

Religious commitment is consistently associated with better health. Many religions actively promote healthy lifestyles and behaviors. For example, Mormons and Seventh-Day Adventists dissuade their members from smoking, drinking, or having extramarital sex (which is associated with a greater risk of sexually transmitted diseases) and encourage healthful diets and exercise. "Religious people consistently report greater life satisfaction, marital satisfaction, well-being, altruism, and self-esteem than do nonreligious people" (Benson, 1996, p. 176). "Many people turn to religion for solace in the face of situations over which they have little control. Their religious beliefs and involvement may counteract feelings of helplessness, provide meaning and order to challenging life situations, and restore a sense of control" (Mental Medicine Update, 1996, p. 7).

DO THE MEDICAL AND HEALTH INSURANCE ESTABLISHMENTS SUPPORT THE INCLUSION OF SPIRITUALITY IN HEALTH CARE?

A 1997 poll by The American Academy of Family Physicians cited in *Alternative Medicine* (1998) reported 99 percent of family physicians agreed that spiritual beliefs could aid medical treatment, cut down on hospital stays, and improve life quality for patients. Fifty-five percent of those polled said they currently use relaxation or meditative techniques as part of their conventional medical treatment.

MANAGED CARE. Health care in the United States is increasingly coming under the control of managed care companies. According to the *Alternative Medicine* magazine/journal (July,1999) seventy-five percent of insured working Americans are covered by managed health care. Also, there is a growing trend to include complementary and alternative medical treatments by health maintenance organizations (HMOs). A recent survey of HMOs in 13 states conducted by Landmark Healthcare in 1996 (cited in *Alternative Therapies*, 1997) found that 58 percent of HMOs responding to the survey were planning to offer their members alternative medicine treatment options within the next 1 to 2 years. Additionally, 70 percent of HMOs offering managed care plans have reported an increase in the requests by members for coverage of alternative therapies. Seven alternative therapies were used in the survey: acupuncture (identified by 56 percent of respondents as a therapy that members have expressed interest in), chiropractic (45 percent), massage therapy (25 percent), as well as acupressure, biofeedback, hypnotherapy, and reflexology.

Along with the complementary and alternative medicine approaches included in the Landmark study are healing modalities more directly related to spirituality. One survey of 300 HMO executives by the John Templeton

Foundation showed that 94 percent believe that personal prayer, meditation, or other spiritual practices can assist a medical treatment and speed up the healing process. However, the HMO executives said they would need "direct evidence of clinical effectiveness" (76 percent), cost savings (65 percent), and patient satisfaction (62 percent) before they incorporated spirituality practices into their policies. In addition, 89 percent of the HMO executives said the policies of their organization's health plans do not yet take into account the research regarding spirituality and health (*Alternative Medicine*, 1998).

The public is increasingly demanding that their health insurance plans include complementary and alternative healing modalities. Two recent polls, one of Americans by Landmark released in 1998, one of Canadians by Angus Reid Group conducted in 1997, show that use and acceptance of, and overall interest in, alternative therapies continues to grow. The poll of Americans showed that 42 percent had used some type of alternative therapy in the past year. In addition 45 percent of those polled would be willing to pay more each month to have access to alternative care, and 67 percent said the availability of an alternative healthcare component was an important consideration in choosing a health plan. Of those reporting alternative medicine use, 74 percent integrate it with conventional healthcare and 61 percent say their conventional primary care practitioner is aware of their use of such therapies (*Alternative Therapies*, 1998).

Most of the expense of complementary and alternative healthcare modalities are currently paid for by the consumer, not their health insurance plan. However, as consumers increasingly utilize alternative healthcare practitioners they will put increasing pressure on health insurance companies to include them in their healthcare plans.

CAN DISTANCE OR NONLOCAL HEALING HELP HEAL A WHOLE CITY?

THE MAHARISHI EFFECT. The theory behind the "Maharishi Effect" is that, "...if a large enough group of people – and they [Transcendental Meditation practitioners] had a formula for estimating the number [a minimum of 1% of a population] – were all drawing on the calm, coherence, and wisdom deep within the silent human mind, then those qualities would prevail in the environment and the right changes, whatever they were, would come about" (Aron & Aron, 1986, p. 2). A number of studies by professional researchers have provided convincing evidence for a strong association between the percentage of people practicing transcendental meditation and improvements in social indicators. *The Maharishi Effect* by Elaine and Arthur Aron (1986) reports on many of the studies measuring the social effects of group meditation. The Aron's summarize these findings with some potential implications for society:

If large groups of people continue to meet together to experience pure consciousness, and especially if these groups are permanent and number at least 7,000, we can infer from the research results reviewed in this book [*The Maharishi Effect*] that crime, divorce, suicide, and accident rates should continue to drop, international tensions lessen, world war should continue to be unknown, arms agreements should be signed, military spending should lessen, the world's economy should improve, more international cooperation should be evidenced, poor countries should develop faster while maintaining their traditions better, environmental problems should be solved faster, alternative energies explored and applied at a greater rate – and you personally should notice more success in achieving your life's goals. Among other things. (p. 156)

If the research evidence correlating the relationship between a large group of meditators and declines in crime, accidents, suicides, unemployment, beer and cigarette sales, and environmental pollution is so "convincing" why haven't more social scientists and national leaders embraced the theory? One reason for not accepting the research is because many people are skeptical of researchers who can "prove" almost anything with a certain research design, methodology, and use of statistics. One problem with correlational research is that this type of research only measures the degree of relationship between two variables. If there is a high correlation then a change in one variable should result in a change in the other variable. However, it is next to impossible to declare with absolute certainty that the introduction or change in one variable (e.g. 1 percent of a city's population meditating) causes the change in another variable (e.g. declines in crime, accidents, and other measures of social problems). In reviewing some of the TM studies on the Maharishi Effect the Arons (1986) cite professor David Orme-Johnson who calculated that, "...the probability of the association between TM percentage and subsequent crime rate decline being a coincidence was now less than one in five billion!" (p. 50). However, skeptics can always claim that other variables could have been responsible for the results of correlation research.

In addition to the problem of utilizing correlation research designs to attribute causation of one variable affecting another variable, the belief that a sufficiently large group of meditators improving the attitudes and behaviors of other people in the surrounding environment is not part of our general cultural belief system. Thus, the research will have to be extremely overwhelming before social scientists and the general public will accept the theory of the Maharishi Effect.

Pessimism and skepticism aside, there is a growing belief that the human species is evolving into a more aware and conscious state of being. As Elaine and Arthur Aron (1986) state, "We are developing a new style of consciousness, a sort of global nervous system, a coherent and highly integrated collective consciousness. Just as multicellular life began with a few independent cells learning to cooperate and communicate as a whole, so we independent humans may soon recognize that we are part of a larger organism. The optimism comes from the thought that with this broader awareness of our oneness, we will treat each other and take care of our spaceship earth as we would our own self and body" (pp. 155-156).

HEALTH BENEFITS OF SPIRITUALITY IN HEALING

Dr. Dale A. Matthews, Dr. David B. Larson and Ms. Constance P. Barry in a review of the scientific literature on the medical effects of spiritual experiences found evidence that religious factors have a widespread and profound influence on health. Matthews, Larson, and Barry (1994) found that religious factors were involved with:

- Increased survival.
- Reduced alcohol, cigarette, and drug abuse.
- Reduced anxiety, depression, and anger.
- Reduced blood pressure.
- Improved quality of life for patients with cancer and heart disease.

Research summarized in Mental Medicine Update (1996) suggests that religious and spiritual beliefs may help improve health:

- In a study of hospitalized male patients, one in five reported that religion is "the most important thing that keeps me going." Nearly half rated religion as very helpful in coping with their illness. And religious coping helped these men be significantly less depressed.
- In a seven year study of seniors, religious involvement was associated with less physical disability and less depression. One interesting finding was that death rates were lower than expected before important religious holidays suggesting that faith may even postpone death.
- Church-attenders have nearly one-half risk of heart attack and lower blood pressure, even after controlling for the effects of smoking and socioeconomic status.
- Patients undergoing open-heart surgery who received strength and comfort from religion were three times more likely to survive than those who had no comfort from religious faith.
- A variety of studies find that religious belief and practice is associated with less risk of self-destructive behaviors (suicide, smoking, drug and alcohol abuse), less perceived stress, and greater overall life satisfaction.
- In a study of 300 terminally ill and nonterminally ill hospitalized adults

those with the greatest spirituality showed resilient emotional health. Spirituality was significantly related to low death fear, low discomfort, decreased loneliness, emotional adjustment, and positive death perspectives among terminal cancer and other seriously ill patients. (Reed, 1987).

- In a study of 100 geriatric patients at a clinic, researchers found that those who had little religious activity had much higher rates of cancer, chronic anxiety, depression, cigarette smoking, and alcohol use. Patients with high levels of religious activity enjoyed better overall physical and mental health (Koenig, Moberg & Kvale, 1988).
- Longer lifespan. Regular worshipers live 10 percent longer than those who never attend services according to a national study to be published in the May issue of *Demography*, a professional journal (Willing, 1999).
- Receiving healing energy, which many healers consider spiritual energy, can facilitate healing of any physical or mental disorder, sometimes quite dramatically (e.g. miracles) (see distance healing studies cited earlier in chapter).

While skeptics contend that religion's only positive effect on health is its discouragement of risky behavior, new research is showing that faith alone, rather than a virtuous lifestyle, can be important in preventing illness, according to David Larson, M.D., president of the National Institute of Healthcare Research in Rockville, MD, a nonprofit group that studies the health benefits of religion (Cool, 1997).

In an eastern North Carolina study, about 90 percent of patients surveyed said they believed in medical miracles. More than half said they could point to a medical miracle in their own lives or in the lives of people they know (Grizzard, 1998). Spiritual beliefs and practices are clearly part of the healing experience for many people.

DYSFUNCTIONAL SPIRITUALITY

Just as cognitions such as health-enhancing beliefs about etiology of illness and healing can potentially help our recovery and rehabilitation, other health-related cognitions can have a negative influence on our health and help create illness and hinder healing. Assessment of the spiritual dimension as part of patients' health care is now required by the U.S. Joint Commission for Accreditation of Healthcare Organizations (JCAHO) in order for health care facilities to become accredited. The fourth edition of the *Diagnostic and Statistical Manual of Mental Disorders (DSM-IV*; American Psychiatric Association, 1994) categorizes and describes mental disorders and is the primary reference for mental health professionals. The *DSM-IV* has included a category for religious or spiritual problems. "This category can be used when the focus of clinical attention is a religious or spiritual problem. Examples include distressing experiences that involve loss or questioning of faith, problems associated with conversion to a new faith, or questioning of spiritual values that may not necessarily be related to an organized church or religious institution" (p. 685). It is important for health maintenance, healing, and achieving high-level wellness to examine our beliefs and other cognitions related to illness, health, and healing.

BELIEFS AFFECT HEALTH. In the author's study of cognitions, Buttons, and motivational states described in Appendix C, it was found that people hold some interesting beliefs about illness and disability. These beliefs may play an important part in health, healing, and rehabilitation. For example, 20 percent of the individuals surveyed agreed with the statement, "If people have enough faith in God and his healing powers He will cure them of their disability." And 16 percent agreed with the statement, "If people have enough faith in God or a higher spiritual power they can heal themselves from any illness." In a Gallup survey 41 percent of Americans say their faith has healed them of physical or mental ailments. In a 1996 poll conducted for *USA Today*, 88 percent of American women and 73 percent of men believe faith can help people recover from illness or injury, and 60 percent of women say belief has actually aided their healing (cited in Cool, 1997). While faith can be be an asset in healing, what happens when the person doesn't get better? Some people believe the reason they don't get better is because they don't have enough faith. When healing fails, some individuals redouble their spiritual or religious efforts and still don't get better. These failed efforts can result in some people becoming angry and forsaking God or their religion. Sometimes people turn their blame inwards and condemn themselves as weak and ineffectual people who lack sufficient faith. Separation from one's faith, hope, and support network plus harboring anger and disappointment are not healthy attitudes and behaviors and may fuel a disease process already in progress.

In addition, 1 percent of the individuals surveyed in the author's cognitions study (described in Appendix C) believe, "People have illnesses or disabilities because God is punishing them," 3 percent believe, "People have illnesses or disabilities because it is part of their Karma (past deeds in either this life or a past life)," and 52 percent believe, "There are no coincidences in life – everything happens for a reason." The healing influence of hope, optimism, and faith may be lacking in people who hold these beliefs. In addition the motivation to seek professional or self-help health care may be lacking in these individuals as they resign themselves to the inevitable with such beliefs as, "It's my karma" or "It's God's will, I've done wrong."

Another belief that directly affects our health relates to how we deal with problems in our lives. Fourteen percent of those surveyed in the author's study agreed with the statement, "If I don't pay any attention to my problems they will go away." This is not a healthy belief for dealing effectively with mental health problems such as depression nor potential physical problems such as a lump in a woman's breast. In addition, 10 percent of those surveyed either "frequently" or "very frequently" used the defense mechanism of denial (i.e. "A conscious attempt to suppress unpleasant reality"). Denial may help fuel a disease progression or prevent healing. For example, denial is a common defense mechanism utilized by individuals who abuse alcohol and other psychoactive drugs, enabling this biopsychosocial disorder to continue without awareness or acknowledgment. If health and mental health professionals are counseling individuals with these and similar beliefs it is important to become aware of them. Mental health professionals can help people modify those beliefs and other cognitions that hinder awareness and the healing process. Our beliefs about health, illness, and healing can either hinder or facilitate the healing and rehabilitation process.

SPIRITUALITY WITHOUT PRACTICE. Having beliefs related to spirituality, but not practicing them, may not be enough to provide a health benefit. Recent research cited in *Spirituality & Health* (1999) indicates that viewing oneself as spiritual and not following through with spiritual practice or behaviors may not provide health benefits and may actually be harmful. As part of a bereavement study in San Francisco researchers interviewed gay men who were caring for partners with AIDS and heterosexual men and women caring for family members dying from cancer. "Participants fell into three groups: "spiritual" people who regularly attended organized religious services; "spiritual" people who didn't attend services; and people who didn't consider themselves spiritual. All three groups were given standard tests to measure distress (particularly depression). Least depressed were the spiritual people who attended services. Next were those who were not at all spiritual. The most depressed were those who described themselves as spiritual but did nothing about it" (p. 17). It appears that health benefits come from practicing our spirituality and not just viewing ourselves as "spiritual" beings.

THE SPIRITUAL DIMENSION IN MEDICAL SCHOOL AND COUNSELOR EDUCATION CURRICULA

The increasing recognition of the holistic perspective, including the spiritual dimension, in health care by health care professions is bringing about a change in the way physicians, nurses, and mental health professionals are being trained. Neglecting information on the spiritual dimension which is such an integral part of peoples' physical and mental health means an incomplete professional preparation and is bad science as well. According to the *Chronicle of Higher Education* (cited in the *New Age Journal*, 1997) nearly one-third of America's 126 medical schools now include the impact of spirituality in medicine in their curricula. In addition, the Templeton study of 300 HMO executives referred to earlier reports that 89 percent strongly support the view that relaxation and meditation techniques should become a standard feature in medical school training.

The holistic perspective, including the spiritual dimension, has been included within the curricula of some university based mental health professional preparation programs for years. For example, a humanistic psychology course and individualized personal growth program, which included the spiritual dimension, (Goodwin, 1980) was developed for graduate students in a counselor education program at the State University of New York at Buffalo by the author in 1978. The spiritual dimension has been integrated into the rehabilitation counseling and substance abuse and clinical counseling programs at East Carolina University where the author has taught for the past 12 years and is increasingly being included within the curricula of many other counselor education programs around the country as they adopt a more holistic perspective to counseling and rehabilitation services.

SUMMARY

The cultivation of spiritual health can dramatically influence our physical, mental, and emotional health. People with religious and spiritual faith seem to weather crises better, possibly because they can find purpose and meaning in life despite the illness or health crises. With some people their illness provided the impetus to look more closely at their lives including their beliefs, lifestyle, relationships, and life goals in order to enhance the quality of the remainder of their lives. Spirituality can help people interpret a health crisis as a wake-up call as well as an opportunity for personal and spiritual growth.

It is ideal, but not always possible, to have a health care provider who has nourishing positive therapeutic energy as well as technical health care expertise. Unfortunately, many health care providers, including mental health care professionals, have received the necessary training, credentials, and licenses to provide the technical aspect of health care services but can not provide the nourishing therapeutic healing energy that many people also desire. Surgical and pharmaceutical interventions, along with faith in the health care provider, are so potent that the qualitative dimensions of the health care provider often doesn't make too much of a difference in recovery from illness. Some people recover from illness in spite of neutral, or sometimes toxic, health care providers, thanks to powerful therapeutic drugs, surgical interventions, and faith in their healing and health care porviders.

If your belief systems are open to the therapeutic effect of healing energy whether its through hands-on touch or distance healing (e.g. healing prayer groups) then don't be afraid to ask for it from your healing support network of friends, clergy, church members, health care providers, and healers. On the other hand, if your beliefs and other cognitions are making you ill and hindering your physical, mental, and spiritual healing then take an inventory of your cognitions and eliminate or modify those cognitions that are barriers to high-level wellness. Taking the *Cognitive Self-Assessment Inventory* (CSAI) in Appendix A is a good place to begin identifying possible troublesome cognitions and Buttons that may be harmful to your physical, mental, and spiritual health. You may need the unbiased assistance of friends or a mental health professional to assist you in this self assessment process.

CHAPTER TWENTY-THREE

BUTTON PUSHERS

Love your enemies, do good to those who hate you,
bless those who curse you,
pray for those who abuse you.

Jesus
HOLY BIBLE

Hatreds do not ever cease in this world by hating, but by love;
this is an eternal truth...
Overcome anger by love, overcome evil by good.
Overcome the miser by giving, overcome the liar by truth.

Buddha
DHAMMAPADA

BUTTON-PUSHERS are the people and situations in our lives that push our Buttons. Contrary to popular belief our Button-Pushers are not sent by the devil himself on a direct mission from Hell. Nor are Button-Pushers S.O.B.s whose sole mission in life is to make our lives miserable. Some people are simply rotten, lousy, evil, and very toxic to be around. Not even the Button Therapy model can change this reality.

BLAMING THE BUTTON-PUSHERS. Our natural tendency when we get a Button pushed is to blame the Button-Pusher, *"You* made me angry!" By viewing our Button-Pushers as the cause of our feelings we are giving them power over us. We are allowing them to push our Buttons and giving them the pleasure of watching us go through our predictable reactive dance. We go through our unconscious robot-like reactions every time they push one of our Buttons. We become like puppets on a string and our Button-Pushers are the puppeteers.

OUR PRIMARY BUTTON-PUSHERS KNOW US BEST. Our primary Button-Pushers tend to be the ones closest to us. Our spouses, children, relatives, coworkers, and friends. If you have raised a teenager you can probably stop reading at this point as you undoubtedly know all there is to know about Button-Pushers. It's like Button-Pushers have an uncanny ability to hone in on our most deeply rooted Buttons. Button-Pushers push our Buttons and watch us dance as they stand by with an innocent expression that says, "Was it something I said or did?" Deep down we know they pushed our Buttons on purpose but we can't accuse them of intentionally pushing our Buttons because we don't want to give them the satisfaction of acknowledging that we are upset or that we even have a Button. Also, we don't want to let them know that they have the power to turn us into a raving lunatic simply by pushing one of our juicier Monster Buttons.

KILL THE MESSENGER. We react to Button-Pushers in various ways. However, if it weren't for the thin veil of acculturation and social correctness, and the possibility of spending the rest of our lives behind prison bars, many of us would lunge at some of our favorite Button-Pushers, throttle them by the neck, and rid the earth of a toxic blight. As you can probably tell, I still have some Buttons to work on. I also lean toward the Mad Director Fantasy Technique a lot (described in Chapter 17), where I can allow my imagination free reign while working on many of my deeper seated Buttons.

WHEREVER YOU GO YOU TAKE YOUR BUTTONS WITH YOU. It amuses me to hear people speak of their plans of moving to a different city or state because they are not happy in the city they are currently living in. They don't like the city, culture, geography, weather, etc. They believe that if they could just move to a different city or state they would be happy instead of miserable all the time. Sometimes, moving to a different city or state may actually improve someone's mood. There are valid reasons to move such as preferring a better climate, better job, getting away from a tyrannical supervisor or employer, larger or smaller city, etc. But there is a big difference between whether one moving because of trying to escape the consequences of one's Buttons or because one is preferring a better life as a result of a proactive conscious decision. Before long, in all probability, the people who are moving because of their Buttons will have similar complaints about the job, people, and city in the new location because people take their Buttons with them wherever they go. Life will continue to offer us the messages (i.e. Button-Pushers) in the form of new faces, settings, and situations that we need until we get the message - That we still have Buttons (e.g. attachments) in these areas of our lives that we need to work on to progress on our journey of self-actualization and become more loving, compassionate, aware, and conscious human beings.

When working on our Buttons related to a Button-Pusher, it is helpful to utilize the cognitive *reframing* technique described in Chapter 9.

REFRAMING OUR BUTTON-PUSHERS AS OUR TEACHERS

Every person, all the events of your life, are there because you have drawn them there. What you choose to do with them is up to you.
Richard Bach
ILLUSIONS

When our Buttons get pushed, it is useful to view the uncomfortable feelings of separateness from self or others as opportunities for personal growth. In the Button Therapy model any person or event capable of triggering our Buttons becomes our teacher. Button-Pushers are life teachers to help us become aware of our Buttons that when activated trigger emotional distress, disharmony, and separates us from our sense of connectedness with each other and the unified universal life force. As Ken Keyes, Jr. (1975) describes it:

> Everyone and everything around you is your teacher. If your washing machine won't work, you are being checked out on your ability to peacefully accept the unacceptable. If you are addicted to your appliances always working, you will suffer. If you prefer them to operate well, you will not compound your problem by superimposing your uncomfortable emotions on the here and now realities of repairing them. (p. 24)

As long as you continue to blame the Button-Pusher (i.e. life's messenger) for your emotional distress you avoid eliminating your Buttons which are the actual cause of your emotional distress. And, you remain stuck in the illusion that other people and events are responsible for your feelings and inner experience. The bottom line is that you are giving the control of your emotions and inner experience over to the Button-Pushers as long as you keep blaming the Button-Pushers for your emotional distress. If you are tired of allowing your spouse, children, boss, coworkers, and friends control your emotions and inner experience, and want to gain more self-control and responsibility for your own life, then the Six-Step Button Therapy Method is just what this doctor orders. Some alternatives are to keep your Buttons and try to hide them from your Button-Pushers and lead a less spontaneous and more repressed and restricted life. Or, you can put energy into pretending that you aren't upset when your Buttons get pushed. In addition, you can always pay the medical bills later when the suppressed and withheld negative emotions and distress manifest in your body as stress-related physical and mental health disorders.

"DOES THIS MEAN
I SHOULD STAY WITH THE BUTTON-PUSHERS
IN MY LIFE?"

Life is a continuing process of change. Resistance to change and personal growth is one of the most difficult ways to attempt to live because it requires a denial of the process. One of the hazards of refusing to accept change in yourself is getting locked into the habit of trying to change others so you can have the illusion of remaining the same. That way of living will take all your energy and yield no personal returns. Why waste your energy on

changing others? You can use it to flow with the changes that are happening to you and enjoy the unfolding of your own life.
Camden Benares
ZEN WITHOUT ZEN MASTERS

No. There are some Button-Pushers that are so toxic or dangerous (e.g. spouse batterers, child molesters, and psychopaths) that you need to use your common sense and leave them immediately. Also, we go through psychosocial and spiritual developmental stages as we mature and progress toward self-actu-alization. At certain stages of our personal development we may encounter intense energy in the form of people or situations (i.e. Button-Pushers) that is simply too much to transmute. For example, when a female teenager is con-fronted with her first opportunity for sexual intercourse, and she is clearly not mature enough (e.g. 13 years old) to handle this intense emotional situation, the teenager is probably better off removing herself from the Button-Pusher or the situation, that allows that particular sex Button to be pushed. At this young age and level of psychosocial development the fire is just too intense to work with. Think back to periods or situations in your life and you can probably recall times when you were clearly playing with fire that was too hot to handle. You were probably able to recognize when the high-risk situation occurred that you were playing with intense, dangerous, and sometimes exciting energies. Depending on how much of a thrill-seeking personality type you are, you either experienced and played with this energy, titillating your sensation and pleasure center, played it cool and skirted around the flame, or you ran like hell. And those of you in your mellow forties, fifties, sixties, and beyond can probably recall the exact age, cast of players, emotions, and sensations surrounding each of these events in your past. As we age we tend to avoid taking such risks in our lives as they may endanger our nice, and sometimes boring, secure relationships, health, families, or jobs.

However, when a Button-Pusher enters your life stage you have been given a message to work on some of your Button(s) and you can learn from the teaching. You don't need to hang out with the Button-Pushers or seek them out, but when you encounter one, hear the message and learn from the teaching. You may want to remove yourself from the Button-Pusher before you have gotten free from your Button because the fire is simply too hot to handle and you become completely irrational and overwhelmed when certain Buttons gets pushed. Or you have learned the teaching from your Button-Pusher and are now aware of your Buttons that a particular Button-Pusher can easily push, but you decide that the Button-Pusher is a lower life form incapable of learning the most rudimentary rules of interpersonal interaction and you decide to leave the Button-Pusher (e.g. a toxic and wayward spouse perhaps?) for your mental health and because you choose to hang out with more nourishing and loving people. You take your Buttons with you but maybe they are not as likely to be pushed in a different type of relationship with a more nourishing, loving, and considerate individual. In any event, be assured that life will continue to offer you the teachers and messages you need for your personal and spiritual growth.

DON'T MAKE MAJOR LIFE DECISIONS WHILE UNDER THE INFLUENCE OF AN ACTIVATED BUTTON. As you encounter your Buttons don't automatically run from the Button-Pusher. Try to learn about your Buttons that are being pushed, work on them, and then decide from a more aware conscious place whether to conduct major surgery on the scenery or cast of characters in your life drama or simply make some minor modifications. These decisions are best made from a centered, aware, and conscious place instead of from a reactive, unconscious, and emotional place while in the emotional grips of an activated Monster Button. In marriage counseling I advise couples to wait at least two weeks before they tell a loved one they want a separation or divorce instead of demanding a divorce while under of the emotional distress of an activated Button. Wait until your rational mind can kick in after a Button has been pushed and you can process the situation more clearly from a less emotional and more conscious and proactive place. If, after two weeks, you still want to separate then tell your partner, talk it over, and process your desires with your spouse and possibly a professional counselor. But it's not healthy for you, your partner, or your children to demand a separation or divorce while your judgment is impaired under the influence of an activated Button. Just like it is not appropriate to make this type of decision while under the influence of psychoactive drugs (e.g. drunk on alcohol), it is not appropriate to make any major life decision while under the emotional influence of an activated Button. Your judgment can be just as impaired while under the influence of both psychoactive drugs or internally produced (i.e. endogenous) psychoactive drugs (e.g. stress hormones and neurotransmitters). Wait at least two weeks before you make major life decisions, except when confronted with life-threatening people or situations.

CHAPTER TWENTY-FOUR

THE SIX-STEP BUTTON THERAPY METHOD:
AN OVERVIEW

Loving more and demanding less are not only the nicest things you can do for yourself. They're also the most caring things you can do for the whole world!
Ken Keyes, Jr.
PRESCRIPTIONS FOR HAPPINESS

BUTTON THERAPY is a psychological self-help model and a cognitive counseling model from a holistic perspective. The Six-Step Button Therapy Method is a self-help tool that can be taught to clients by mental health professionals. Also, the Button Therapy model and Six-Step Method is described in this book so that relatively mentally healthy individuals with at least average intelligence and no limiting cognitive impairments can learn and utilize this six-step psychological self-help method without the assistance of a mental health professional. Table 19 provides a summary outline of the Six-Step Button Therapy Method.

ABE's MBA: A MNEMONIC DEVICE
FOR REMEMBERING THE SIX STEPS

I might repeat to myself, slowly and soothingly,
A list of quotations beautiful from minds profound;
if I can remember any of the damn things.
Dorothy Parker
THE LITTLE HOURS

You may wonder, "How do I remember the six steps of the Button Therapy Method, especially when I've just had a Button pushed and am in the midst of emotional distress and acting like a raving maniac?" Sometimes we experience such intense emotional pain from having certain deeply rooted and highly emotionally charged Buttons pushed that no cognitive method will work to immediately alleviate the emotional pain. All we can do in such emotionally overwhelming and painful situations is hold on for the roller coaster ride knowing that the emotional intensity will let up in time. At such times, many people find temporary emotional relief talking to a trusted friend or mental health professional. As soon as the emotional intensity diminishes to the point that you no longer feel engulfed and drowning in a sea of emotional energy and can come up for air, you can then begin using some cognitive techniques. When you come up for air and are able to utilize your conscious rational mind you can apply the six-steps of the Button Therapy Method. *ABE's MBA* is an acronym and mnemonic device to help remember the six steps of the Button Therapy Method.

- **A**wareness of Stress and Distress
- **B**utton Identification
- **E**motions activated
- **M**otivational states
- **B**utton Removal (Cognitive Restructuring)
- **A**ffirmations (Cultivating and planting the life enhancing seeds in the Garden of Your Mind)

ILLUSTRATION OF APPLYING THE SIX-STEP BUTTON THERAPY METHOD TO A PERFECTIONIST THINKING BUTTON

The following is an illustration of my working on a current perfectionist Button resulting in procrastination behaviors and feelings of frustration and anxiety that I have experienced on numerous occasions while writing this book. Utilizing the *ABE's MBA* acronym to help remember the six-steps of the Button Therapy Method I process my need to do things perfectly, preferably the first time around, as follows:

STEP 1. AWARENESS OF STRESS AND DISTRESS

I am aware that procrastination has reared its ugly head repeatedly as I write this book. Each time I procrastinate I am aware of this behavior and the emotional distress that is triggered. When I procrastinate writing this book I am aware of feeling anxious, frustrated, and sometimes angry with myself. My anxiety, frustration, and other unpleasant feelings are my main cues that a Button has been activated. Also, I suspect that my hypertension may be related to my perfectionistic Button which can trigger feelings of anxiety, frustration, and anger as well as procrastination behavior. I am aware that my perfection Button has many emotional and health consequences.

Step 2. Button Identification: Pinpointing Your Buttons

The script I am demanding is that *I sit down at my computer and work on this book every time I have some free time.* When I don't sit down and write this book when I have some free time I get myself uptight. What I sometimes do is find all kinds of distracting behaviors to keep me from sitting at the computer and working on this book. I have caught myself in procrastination behaviors such as excessively watching television including the soap *Days of Our Lives* and *The Jerry Springer Show,* reading *The National Enquirer,* and even cleaning the kitchen floor a day after it was thoroughly washed. This reminds me of an old late night TV soap opera back in the 1960s called *Mary Hartman, Mary Hartman.* Mary Hartman used to periodically stay up till the wee hours in the morning wondering if there was a yellow dirty buildup on the linoleum in her kitchen. I sometimes think I will find almost anything that needs doing rather than sit at the computer and produce a completed manuscript. I am attached to the script that says, " when I have some free time, I should sit down at my computer and work on *The Button Therapy Book.*" The reality of the situation is that I don't always work on my writing projects when I have "free time" and this creates a cognitive conflict or dissonance. Cognitive dissonance creates stress and sometimes suffering.

Step 3. Emotions: Identifying, experiencing, releasing, and channeling the emotional energy associated with my Button(s).

I fully experience the *frustration, anxiety,* and *anger* at myself for procrastinating writing this book. I take full responsibility for my attachment (i.e. Button) to the script, "I work on The Button Therapy Book every time I have some free time," which creates some of my procrastination, stress, and the emotions of frustration, anxiety, and anger.

Step 4. Motivations. Determining the Motivational States Associated With Your Buttons.

I ask myself, "why am I motivated to write *The Button Therapy Book* and why do I think I have to use all of my free time to work on this project?" If I could write this book it would make me feel good about myself (*Love & Self-Acceptance Motivational State*). I would have accomplished something out of the ordinary. Not everybody has written a book! Also, if it gets published and enough people read *The Button Therapy Book* it would provide a more holistic model for cognitive-behavioral therapy in the marketplace of ideas. Button Therapy would be a new cognitive therapy model that includes the spiritual dimension. If mental health professionals and the public click with this counseling and psychological self-help model I would have positively influenced many people and helped them on their journeys of personal and spiritual growth *(Control & Power Motivational State)*. My perfection models are responsible for much of my procrastination. I sometimes demand that I write things perfectly, preferably the first time around. So if I don't have sufficient time to sit down at the computer and give it my best shot and compose the perfect holistic cognitive counseling and psychological self-help book then I better wait until I have sufficient time for this challenging task *(Control & Power Motivational State)*. The publication of a book would bring me more recognition and job security at work. After all, university professors are supposed to publish. On the other hand, what if nobody purchases my book. Or, after reading it, what if people thought it sucked *(Safety and Security/Insecurity Motivational State)*. Publishing a book would also bring me pleasure *(Pleasure & Sensation-seeking Motivational State)*. Researching and clarifying concepts that I have been using clinically and writing about since 1968 is also a continued learning and personal growth experience for myself *(Personal Growth & Self-Actualization Motivational State)*. The part of this Button that has to do with using all my free time to write this book is associated with my control motivational state. I've told myself that I should have enough willpower and self-discipline (i.e. control) to focus on completing the task of writing this book within a short period of time. The reality is that it is taking much longer than I expected to complete this task.

Each time I have the perfectionistic Button pushed and experience procrastination I have gotten in touch with one or more of these motivational states associated with this Button. I am obviously not experiencing this Button at this moment because I am currently sitting at my computer writing this book. The goal of Step two is to get in touch with the motivational state(s) associated with the activated Button when it gets pushed. Let me take the high road and say that I am aware of the desire to sit down at the computer and write this book because, "I believe this Six-Step BT Method will help people in their self-actualization." Thus, people will progress, in part, because of a model that I developed. I will have contributed to their personal growth *(Control & Power Motivational State)*.

STEP 5. BUTTON REMOVAL (COGNITIVE RESTRUCTURING): MAKING A CONSCIOUS EFFORT TO KEEP, MODIFY, OR ELIMINATE YOUR BUTTONS.

I decide to modify the script that, "I need to sit down at the computer and write this book every time I have some free time." I go to the summary of cognitive interventions (Table 18) in chapter 16 of *The Button Therapy Book* and look over the list of possible cognitive interventions. I decide to use a combination of several cognitive techniques. I start with the cognitive *self-talk technique* and ask myself, "Do I have to write this manuscript perfectly on the first draft?

Is that a realistic expectation? Is that a rational belief? *(Disputing a Troublesome Cognition technique* described in chapter 17)." I decide that writing a manuscript perfectly on the first draft is unrealistic (see the cognitive distortion of *perfectionist thinking* described in chapter 6). I need to modify this expectation. I decide to adopt a more realistic script of how my writing this manuscript should be actualized. A more realistic expectation is to sit down at the computer, write the manuscript, and not worry about making mistakes or revisions, especially on the first draft. Mistakes are natural and part of being human. And, creating drafts and making revisions is a natural part of the creative writing process. Creativity is creating something that previously didn't exist. The creativity process involves a lot of trial and error. Creating part of the whole, then another part, and eventually trying to splice all the parts together into a meaningful whole. Integrating the parts into a meaningful whole is not an easy feat with a challenging task such as writing a book. I decide my perfection model sucks and has to go. It's creating too much stress in my life and my physical health is starting to suffer (e.g. hypertension). It's also triggering too many delays in this and my other writing projects. I have a number of other writing projects in the works and planned, and my perfection models are a major source of my procrastination, which is slowing me down too much.

I also decide to modify the part of the script that I am attached to that has to do with "whenever I have some free time." I ask myself, "Is this a realistic expectation? *(Disputing a Troublesome Cognition)*" It clearly is not realistic nor rational. I am involved with many other responsibilities and activities. For example, I have a nineteen-year-old daughter, and a seventeen-year-old son who I love very much. I want to be available to them when they want to interact with me and I with them. In addition to my family role and responsibilities I have numerous professional responsibilities. I have so many professional responsibilities as a university professor, program director, and interim department chair that I could not even begin to list them. I also play United States Tennis Association (USTA) competitive team tennis. Tennis takes up a healthy chunk of time for play and exercise.

So when I have "free time" is it really free? I suppose that I could put my family, work, recreational, and exercise activities on hold while I complete my writing projects. However, this would put my life on hold forever, because I have enough writing projects planned to last at least five lifetimes. So I decide that working on my book every time I have some "free time" is totally unrealistic and that this expectation I'm carrying around in my biocomputer needs to be modified. I decide to place another more realistic script related to my writing projects into my biocomputer: "I still value the writing that I do, especially on *The Button Therapy Book.* However, I also value my family, work, tennis, and other leisure-time activities like eating out at restaurants, reading, and playing the guitar, and visiting with friends. I choose to live a more balanced life and make sure I spend time with all the people and activities that I value and enjoy. I still *prefer* to work on my book and have as few revisions and mistakes as possible but I will not *demand* that I work on it during all my "free time" nor that I write it perfectly the first time with no mistakes or revisions (The *Changing Demands to Preferences* is a cognitive intervention described in chapter 17). Also, I will lead a more balanced life between family, work, personal growth activities, and play and stop allowing my workaholism to encroach on these other areas of my life."

Since I have had this perfectionistic Button that results in procrastination behavior for quite awhile, I decide to use another cognitive intervention in addition to the techniques of *cognitive self-talk, disputing troublesome cognitions, changing demands to preferences,* and setting more realistic expectations related to my writing behavior. I decide to also use the *paradoxical intention* technique (described in chapter 19). I decide to prescribe the symptom (i.e. procrastination). I tell myself that I should not attempt to work on this book more than two hours a week. I tell myself that I should not push myself so hard. That the book will get done in due time. It's not worth getting myself all distressed over and missing out on family, personal growth activities, recreational, and exercise activities. By telling myself that I can only spend two hours a week on writing this book it takes the pressure off me to sit down and write "every time I have some free time." I have now freed myself up to write whenever I can find time without concern for the procrastination behavior, as well as maintain a more balanced lifestyle.

STEP 6. AFFIRMATIONS (CULTIVATING THE GARDEN OF YOUR MIND): CONSCIOUSLY CULTIVATING NEW COGNITIVE MODELS THAT FACILITATE YOUR BECOMING MORE AWARE, CONSCIOUS, AND LOVING.

I look over the list of "30 seeds for your mind's garden" in chapter 21 and find a couple of life-enhancing guidelines that relate to the perfectionist type of "thinking distortion." The first "seed" in the list having to do with taking "responsibility" jumps out at me and I apply it to my perfectionist thinking: *"I take full responsibility for my perfectionist thinking distortion to which I am attached (i.e. Button) and subsequent emotional distress that is part of my perfectionist Button."* As I continue down the list of 30 guidelines for healthy living I feel drawn to number nine which definitely applies to my procrastination behavior: *"I am constantly reminding myself of the purpose and goals of my life.* One of my goals is to live a balanced life between family, work, exercise, personal growth, spiritual practices, and play." All work and no play makes Lloyd a very poor father, friend, and unhealthy person.

As I continue down the list of life-enhancing guidelines, number eighteen captures my attention. This guideline reminds me of the value of *having a group of positive nourishing friends to help sustain me through my life journey.* I can best work on my Buttons and self-actualization with the loving support and confrontation of valued friends. It is also therapeutic for me to help others in their process of self-actualization. I am fortunate to have a job where I can help others through my teaching, clinical counseling, and writings on a regular basis. Returning to the list of 30 guidelines, numbers nineteen through twenty-two which deal with the need to *practice stress management and relaxation routines, eat better nutritionally, exercise* more regularly, and *"balance work, family, and play"* jump out at me. I definitely need to spend more time in these life-enhancing and wellness activities. The last guideline to jump out at me in relation to my perfectionist Button is number twenty-nine. *"I believe in miracles.* I believe that I can continue my work on this book until it is manifested on the material plane and hopefully remain *nonattached to the outcome* (seed number thirty)."

I hope that my working on one of my Buttons has been helpful to your understanding the Six-Step Button Therapy Method. I think I will now take a break from writing this manuscript for a couple of weeks and catch up with the soaps on television. I wonder what's happening to Bo and Hope on *Days of Our Lives?* Have they finally gotten back together? And what about Stephano and Victor? You couldn't ask for more interesting and devious psychopaths! Have Abe and Roman arrested those dastardly psychopaths yet? And what about catching up on all those back issues of *The National Enquirer?* I feel totally out of the mainstream loop. Has Liz Taylor had any more life threatening illnesses and surgeries? Is Opra Winfry's weight going up or down? Has the government finally admitted they covered up the UFO incident at Roswell? And what about the secret underground joint government and UFO base in Area 51 in New Mexico? Any more major UFO sightings? The world can wait another couple of weeks for *The Button Therapy Book* while I take a mental health break and jump back into the mainstream of life (i.e. the culturally conditioned "Big Sleep").

SHORT-CUTS
FOR THE SIX-STEP BUTTON THERAPY METHOD

It is not necessary to process every Button that gets pushed through all six of the steps. After learning the six steps of the Button Therapy Method you may choose to utilize only those steps that seem appropriate for a particular Button. After I have processed a Button through the six steps so that I understand the Button, including why I am demanding it, the emotions associated with it, and have chosen a cognitive technique to modify or eliminate the Button, the next time I get that particular Button pushed I may choose to simply remind myself that I still have the Button and use one of the cognitive interventions (i.e. 5th step) described in chapters 16, 17, and 18 to free myself from my Button.

After you gain some experience applying the six steps to an activated Button, what initially took 5 minutes to process may take only 5 seconds. I seldom utilize all six of the steps when I have the same Button pushed more than once. I use parts of the six steps depending on the Button and how psychologically distressing it is. For example, with the perfectionist Button described earlier, whenever I get this Button pushed I usually just; become aware that it's been pushed (1st step), become aware that it's the perfection Button rearing its ugly head again (2nd step), and own the feelings associated with this activated Button (3rd step). Usually, my process of simply becoming aware of this activated Button is enough for me to let go of my perfection models and regain my inner harmony and consciousness. In other words, I take a short cut and simply *ABE* it, instead of applying the entire six steps (i.e. *ABE's MBA*).

After you have gained proficiency utilizing all six steps of the Button Therapy Method you will find yourself using a variety of short-cuts, depending on the Button and the circumstances. I usually use the short cuts and process most of my Buttons that get pushed in approximately five seconds (e.g. I usually *ABE* it!). When I have a deeply rooted emotionally charged Button activated I need more time and apply more of the cognitive tools from other steps. Sometimes I have to hold on for the emotional roller coaster ride until I no longer feel like I'm drowning and can poke my nose above the water for a breath of calmer air. As I calm down I apply whichever steps are appropriate to free myself from the emotional distress and work on modifying a cognition or eliminating the Button.

SPIRIT WARRIORS

Spirit Warriors are motivated toward self-actualization and the liberation of their souls. They have consciously made a decision to take on the culturally programmed unconscious "Big Sleep" that is our default setting. You may be wondering, "What would a relatively Button-free and conscious individual look like? How would he or she behave?" A Spirit Warrior:

- Fearlessly confronts his or her Buttons no matter how painful.
- Is a thorn in the side of the grand illusionists such as politicians, and other web spinners of the "Big Sleep."
- Is an enigma to those who sleepwalk through life.
- Is a nonentity to government, politicians, bureaucracies, corporate America, and others who seek to survey, control, and financially enslave their consumers.

- Triggers insecurity and anxiety in the soldiers of the status quo because of their unpredictability and desire for truth, ethical behavior, and simply "doing the right thing."
- Is not intimidated by the Moral Control Patrol and their Grand Inquisitors.
- Approaches life with optimism, joy, and positive nourishing energy.
- Listens to the subtle voice of his or her own intuition, gut, and heart.
- Shows compassion to those who are unconsciously caught up in their life dramas and Buttons.
- Patiently continues on the roller coaster journey of personal growth, appreciating the periodic company of fellow travelers.
- Seeks a healthy, centered, aware, loving, and compassionate life.
- Does not allow past psychological or physical wounds to drain their life force and healing energy.
- Seeks to fully engage life in the here-and-now without developing attachments (i.e. Buttons) to the dead past or imagined future.
- Seeks to become aware of the intricacies of connections, interdependencies, and the subtle web of life.
- Is a natural healer and conduit of healing creative energy from the universal life force.
- Is able to "see" and experience the whole including the God-like energy in the "empty" spaces between objects, people, and events.
- Is open and accepting of the cornucopia of individual differences and the many diverse faces of God.

Go Forth and Slay the Button Dragons

You now have the psychological self-help tools to free yourself from your Buttons that create emotional distress, inner turmoil, and hinder your inner work and personal growth. You also have the cognitive tools to start cultivating your mind's garden with the life-enhancing seeds of happiness, awareness, love, and compassion. Thoughts and other cognitions are already in your biocomputer and more will continue to be added as you go through life. Now that you have a better understanding of how your biocomputer (i.e. mind) works you can make more conscious choices as to which seeds become planted and cultivated in your mind's garden. Happy gardening!

TABLE 19

SIX-STEP BUTTON THERAPY METHOD
FOR
PSYCHOLOGICAL SELF-HELP

1. **AWARENESS OF STRESS AND DISTRESS:** Recognizing the stress when your Buttons get pushed by tuning in to your:
- Body
- Feelings
- Acceptance-rejection of self or others

2. **BUTTON IDENTIFICATION:** Pinpointing your Buttons.

3. **EMOTIONS:** Identifying, experiencing, releasing, and channeling the emotional energy triggered by your Buttons *to your Buttons.*

4. **MOTIVATIONS:** Determining the motivational states associated with your Buttons.
- Safety & Security
- Pleasure & Sensation-seeking
- Control & Power
- Love & Acceptance
- Personal Growth & Self-Actualization
- Spiritual & Transcendental

5. **BUTTON REMOVAL AND COGNITIVE RESTRUCTURING:** Choosing to keep, modify, or eliminate your Buttons by utilizing cognitive interventions.

6. **AFFIRMATIONS AND CULTIVATING THE GARDEN OF YOUR MIND:** Cultivating new cognitions that facilitate your becoming happier, more conscious, and loving.

The Button Therapy Book: How to Work on Your Buttons and the Button-Pushers in Your Life by Lloyd R. Goodwin, Jr.
© 2002.Published by Trafford Publishing. www.trafford.com

CHAPTER TWENTY-FIVE

RECOMMENDED READINGS

COGNITIVE THERAPY

A New Guide to Rational Living by Albert Ellis, Ph.D. and Robert A. Harper, Ph.D. North Hollywood, CA: Wilshire Book Co., 1975. Originally published as *A Guide to Rational Living in 1961*, this book is one of the first self-help books. Dr. Albert Ellis is the originator of Rational Emotive Behavior Therapy and founder of the Institute for Rational Emotive Behavior Therapy. He is the author of more than fifty books.

Gathering Power Through Insight and Love by Ken Keyes, Jr., Penny Keyes, and Staff. Coos Bay, OR: Living Love Publications, 1987. A practical handbook that gives detailed instructions on how to develop the love inside you.

Handbook to Higher Consciousness (5th ed.) by Ken keyes, Jr. Berkeley, CA: Living Love Center, 1975. The Handbook to Higher Consciousness has sold over a million copies and has changed the lives of many people who have implemented the Living Love System of personal growth and spirituality. One of the features of this book is that it provides workable methods to help people achieve the goals of personal growth. This book is my personal favorite for personal growth.

Homecoming: Reclaiming and Championing Your Inner Child by John Bradshaw. NY: Bantam Books, 1990. John Bradshaw has worked as a counselor, theologian, management consultant, public speaker and is a prominent figure in the addictions and family counseling fields. Bradshaw has touched millions through his nationally televised PBS series and his best-selling books, *Bradshaw On: The Family, Healing the Shame That Binds You*, and *Homecoming*. This book is about "inner child" work. "Reclaiming your inner child involves going back through your developmental stages and finishing your unfinished business." The book provides questionnaires to help pinpoint the key years of childhood, from infancy to adolescence, when the natural, healthy course of development was interrupted. You can see what you needed and didn't get and learn to reconnect with the frozen feelings of the past. Bradshaw offers a number of practical techniques such as giving your child permission to break destructive family rules and roles; teaching new rules that allow pleasure and honest self-expression; learning to deal with anger and difficult relationships, paying attention to your innermost purpose and desires. An excellent self-help resource as well as a book for mental health care practitioners.

How to Enjoy Your Life in Spite of it All by Ken Keyes, Jr. St. Mary, KY: Living Love Publications, 1980. This book focuses on Keyes' twelve pathways to higher consciousness, which are condensed wisdom of the ages.

Prisoners of Belief: Exposing & Changing Beliefs that Control Your Life by Matthew McKay, Ph.D. and Patrick Fanning. Oakland, CA: New Harbinger Publications, Inc., 1991. Belief is ultimately the key to happiness. Your core beliefs determine your feelings of worth, competence, belonging, loveability, security, trust, and self-reliance. This book shows you how to uncover your core beliefs, shift your more negative convictions, and escape from the prison of belief to a freer, more satisfying life.

Pulling Your Own Strings by Wayne W. Dyer, Ph.D. NY: Avon Books, 1979. Each chapter is organized around a major principle for not being victimized, with tactics for dealing from a position of strength with co-workers, clerks, bureaucrats, relatives, lovers, and yourself.

Thoughts & Feelings: The Art of Cognitive Stress Intervention by Matthew McKay, Ph.D., Martha Davis, Ph.D. and Patrick Fanning. 1981. An excellent resource presented in workbook format and can be utilized as a self-help resource as well as a cognitive therapy resource for mental health practitioners.

Your Erroneous Zones by Wayne W. Dyer, Ph.D. NY: Avon Books, 1977. A popular classic cognitive self-help book that has sold more than 6 million copies. Offers positive and practical advice and strategies for breaking free from negative thinking.

Your Life is a Gift: So Make the Most of It! by Ken Keyes, Jr. with Penny Keyes. Coos Bay, OR: Love Line Books, 1987. Full of illustrations, this short book provides the basic cognitive self-help principles and can be read in about an hour. In the past, I have given copies of this book to individuals in my private counseling and psychotherapy practice whenever I utilized a cognitive therapy intervention. Now I give copies of *The Six-Step Button Therapy Method*.

EMOTIONAL HEALING

Achieving Emotional Literacy: A personal Program to Increase Your Emotional Intelligence by Claude Steiner and Paul Perry. NY: Avon Books, 1997. Describes how to reverse self-destructive emotional patterns that can rule a person's life. And how to open your heart and mind to honest and effective communication, how to survey the emotional landscape, and how to take responsibility for your emotions.

Emotional Intelligence by Daniel Goleman. NY: Bantam Books, 1995. This best selling book explains the many facets of emotion and is full of practical insights for parents, teachers, and counselors. "What factors are at play, for example, when people of high IQ flounder and those of modest IQ do surprisingly well? I would argue that the difference quite often lies in the abilities called here *emotional intelligence*, which include self-control, zeal and persistence, and the ability to motivate oneself."

Feeling Good: The New Mood Therapy by David Burns, M.D. NY: Signet, 1980. This book introduces the principles of cognitive therapy and applies it to the treatment of depression. This psychiatrist outlines a systematic program for controlling thought distortions that lead to pessimism, lethargy, procrastination, low self-esteem, and other "black holes" of depression. Includes sections on ten types of distorted thinking, ways to boost self-esteem, ways to avoid being a love addict, ways to handle criticism and hostility, ways of defeating guilt, and overcoming approval addiction.

The Feeling Good Handbook by David Burns, M.D. NY: Plume, 1990. This book is a sequel to Feeling Good: The New Mood Therapy and provides cognitive self-help information and strategies that help you cope with the full range of everyday problems including fears, phobias, panic attacks, obsessive-compulsive disorder, self-defeating attitudes, poor communication skills, marital conflict, and procrastination. An excellent self-help book and resource for professional counselors.

Molecules of Emotion by Candace Pert, Ph.D. NY: Touchstone, 1999. This book helps to provide the science behind mind-body medicine. Dr. Pert explains the biochemical links between consciousness, mind, and body and helps explain why we feel the way we do.

ENERGY HEALING

Anatomy of the Spirit: The Seven Stages of Power and Healing by Carolyn Myss, Ph.D. NY: Harmony Books, 1996. Dr. Myss is a "medical intuitive" and researcher in energy medicine. In this book she presents a unique program for promoting spontaneous physical, emotional, and spiritual healing. *Anatomy of the Spirit* shows the links between emotional and spiritual stresses and specific illnesses in the context of the anatomy of the human energy system. For example, fears regarding financial matters affect the health of the lower back. Also, a strong need to control others or your environment influences the health of the sexual areas of the body. Anatomy of the Spirit also presents Dr. Myss's model of the body's seven centers of spiritual and physical power, in which she synthesizes the ancient wisdom of three spiritual traditions - the Hindu chakras, the Christian sacraments, and Kabbalah's Tree of Life. With this model she shows you how to develop your own latent powers of intuition as you simultaneously develop your personal power and spiritual maturity. As you begin to understand the anatomy of your spirit, you will discover the spiritual causes of illness, as well as how to sense and correct an energy imbalance before it expresses itself as physical illness, and how to recover emotionally and physically from an illness you may already have.

The Book of Chakra Healing by Liz Simpson. NY: Sterling Publishing Co., Inc., 1999. A beautifully illustrated guide to work on your chakras and shows how to unblock and rebalance your energy.

Energy Tapping by Fred Gallo, Ph.D. and Harry Vincenzi, Ed.D. Oakland, CA: New Harbinger Publications, Inc., 2000. The authors are two psychologists and describe mind/body treatments that take less than a minute to complete that can help balance your body's energy system leading to overcoming fears, painful memories, and help you reach peak performance at work, in sports, and in your personal life.

Finding the Energy to Heal: How EMDR, Hypnosis, TFT, Imagery, and Body-Focused Therapy Can Help Restore Mindbody Health by Maggie Phillips, Ph.D. NY: W.W. Norton & Co., 2000. The author is a psychologist in private practice in California. This book is a useful guide for describing the various forms of energy medicine and psychology.

Hands of Light: A Guide to Healing Through the Human Energy Field by Barbara Ann Brennan. NY: Bantam Books, 1988. A classic on the human energy field. With the clarity of a physicist and the compassion of a healer the author presents the first in-depth study of the human energy field. Our energy body, long known to healers and mystics, is the starting point of all illness. This book offers a new paradigm for the human in health, relationships, disease, and healing. This book includes beautiful illustrations and guidelines for healing the self and others.

Instant Emotional Healing: Acupressure for the Emotions by Peter Lambrou, Ph.D. and George Pratt, Ph.D. NY: Broadway Books, 2000. The authors are both clinical and consulting psychologists on the faculty of the University of California at San Diego and on staff at Scripps Memorial Hospital in La Jolla, California. This book explores the science behind Thought Field Therapy, and presents easy-to-follow exercises that will enable you to master the breathing techniques, focused-thought exercises, and tapping methods that can restore complete emotional balance, relaxation, and well-being in a matter of minutes. Thought Field Therapy is a blend of Western Psychotherapy and Chinese medicine that uses the body's meridian energy systems to treat emotional issues that can take years to unravel through traditional, talk-based therapy. A combination of breathing and relaxation exercises, affirmations, and tapping specific pressure points on the body, Though Field Therapy can instantly eliminate problems such as a fear of flying, public speaking, addictive urges, or painful emotions.

Light Emerging: The Journey of Personal Healing by Barbara Ann Brennan. NY: Bantam Books, 1993. Another classic and must read for energy workers. *Hands of Light* established the author as the leading expert in energy work. In this illustrated book she describes how each of us can tap our innate power to heal ourselves and others. She provides information about energy interactions in relationships and how to break through negative patterns to new, positive contracts with those closest to us. She also explains the connection between healing, creativity, and transcendence.

The Sevenfold Journey: Reclaiming Mind, Body & Spirit Through the Chakras by Anodea Judith, M.A. & Selene Vega, M.A. Freedom, CA: The Crossing Press, 1993. If you want to learn about the chakras from your own experience through journaling, movement, and creative exercises, this is the book for you. Well organized and easy to read.

Tapping the Healer Within: Using Though Field Therapy to Instantly Conquer Your Fears, Anxieties, and Emotional Distress by Roger J. Callahan, Ph.D. Lincolnwood, IL: Contemporary Books, 2001. Dr. Callahan is a former psychology professor at Eastern Michigan University and is currently in private practice in California. Dr. Callhan is the founder and top authority on Thought Field Therapy (TFT) which he has been developing for the past 20 years. TFT is based on contemporary principles from Western psychology and Chinese medicine which theorizes that energy flows along meridians in the body. When energy is blocked, a person becomes ill. TFT is a method of tapping into that energy and clearing up blockages.

The Truth About Chakras by Anodea Judith, St. Paul, MN: Llewellyn Publications, 1994. A great little book (51pages) which describes the seven major chakras which are "...spinning vortices of energy that can effect incredible life transformation and healing!"

Vibrational Medicine: New Choices for Healing Ourselves by Richard Gerber, M.D. Santa Fe, NM: Bear & Company, 1996. Dr. Gerber practices internal medicine in Michigan. This book is one of the primary textbooks for energetic medicine and alternative healing approaches. Dr. Gerber presents an encyclopedic treatment of subtle-energy fields, acupuncture, Bach flower remedies, crystals, radionics, chakras, meditation, and homeopathy.

Wheels of Life: A User's Guide to the Chakra System by Anodea Judith, Ph.D. St. Paul, MN: Llewellyn Publications, 2000. Dr. Judith is a somatic therapist, counselor, and yoga teacher. This book takes you on a journey through the transcendent levels of consciousness. The author views this ancient metaphysical system using metaphors such as bodywork and quantum physics. She helps the reader explore the chakras using poetic meditations, physical expression, and visionary art.

Wheels of Light: Chakras, Auras, and the Healing Energy of the Body by Rosalyn Bruyere. NY: A Fireside Book/Simon & Schuster, 1994. The author is a healer, clairvoyant, and medicine woman. Trained as an engineer, she was instrumental in the research on the human electromagnetic field conducted at UCLA. *Wheels of Light* explores the seven chakras, or energy centers, of the body with particular focus on the first chakra, which has to do with our basic life force, our physical bodies, and our sexuality. Drawing on scientific research, Native American culture, the ancient traditions of the Egyptians and Greeks, the philosophies of the Hindus, and the religions of the East, the author presents a unique perspective on the value and healing potential of the chakra system.

GUIDE TO SELF-HELP BOOKS

The Authoritative Guide to Self-Help Books by John W. Santrock, Ann M. Minnett, and Barbara D. Campbell. NY: The Guilford Press, 1994. Based on a national survey of more than 500 mental health professionals' ratings of 1,000 self-help books. The categories of self-help books include: Abuse and recovery; addiction and recovery; adult development; aging; anger; anxiety; assertiveness; career development; child development and parenting; family; friendship, loneliness, and single adult life; infant development and parenting; love, intimacy, and marriage; men's issues; positive thinking and self-talk; pregnancy; relaxation, meditation, and stress; self-esteem; self-fulfillment and happiness; self-improvement and motivation; sexuality; stepfamilies; teenagers and parenting; women's issues; the 25 best self-help books; and nine strategies for selecting a self-help book.

HOLISTIC HEALTH AND HEALING

Alternative Medicine: Expanding Medical Horizons. A Report to the National Institutes of Health on Alternative Medical Systems and Practices in the United States (#017-040-00537-7). Washington, D.C.: U.S. Government Printing Office, 1992. This document represents the input of more than 200 practitioners and researchers of alternative medicine from throughout the United States.

Alternative Medicine: The Definitive Guide by the Burton Goldberg Group. Puyallup, WA: Future Medicine, 1993. Excellent resource for alternative healing approaches.

High-Speed Healing: The Fastest, Safest and Most Effective Shortcuts to Lasting Relief by the Editors of *Prevention* Magazine Health Books, William LeGro (Ed.). Emmaus, PA: Rodale Press, 1991. Provides hundreds of practical, easy-to-understand helpful hints for a wide variety of health problems.

The Medical Advisor: The Complete Guide to Alternative & Conventional Treatments by The Editors of Time-Life Books. Alexandria, VA: Time-Life Books, 1996. Good resource for combining conventional and alternative healing practices. Includes symptom charts of more than 40 common complaints, a quick reference to more than 3,000 ailments and treatment options, and over 800 drugs and natural medicines.

The Merck Manual of Medical Information. Home Edition by Robert Berkow, M.D., Mark H. Beers, M.D., and Andrew J. Fletcher, M.B., B.Chir., (Eds.). Whitehouse Station, NJ: Merck Research Laboratories, 1997. This is the home reference version of *The Merck Manual*, which has been used by physicians and other health care professionals since it was first introduced in 1899. It contains virtually all of the information in the physicians' version, but is written in easy-to-understand, everyday language with a reader-friendly format. Written by 200 medical experts it covers diseases and disorders, symptoms, diagnoses, and treatment options. Contains sections on anatomy and physiology, pregnancy, infancy, adults, and geriatric care; men's and children's health; psychiatry; legal issues; and care of those who are dying. The definitive health care home reference book.

Natural Health, Natural Medicine: A Comprehensive Manual for Wellness and Self-Care by Andrew Weil, M.D. Boston, MA: Houghton Mifflin Co., 1990. A medical self-care book which incorporates a nutritional guide, the first critical assessment of vitamins and supplements available in health food stores, and one of the first presentations of botanical remedies by a medical doctor. Dr. Weil is one of the leading experts in combining conventional and alternative (i.e. integrative) medicine.

Radical Healing: Integrating the World's Great Therapeutic Traditions to Create a New Transformative Medicine by Rudolph Ballentine, M.D. New York: Harmony Books, 1999. Dr. Ballentine went to medical school at Duke University and is a physician, psychiatrist, herbalist, Ayurvedic practitioner, homeopath, teacher, author and provides a model for the health practitioner of the future. He created and directs the Center for Holistic Medicine in New York City. Drawing on thirty years of studying and practicing varied healing systems, Dr. Ballentine has integrated the wisdom of the great traditional healing systems, especially Ayurveda, homeopathy, Traditional Chinese Medicine, European and Native American herbology, nutrition (he's the author of the classic book *Diet and Nutrition*), psychotherapy, and bodywork. I highly recommend this book by a healer who walks the talk.

Spontaneous Healing: How to Discover and Enhance Your Body's Natural Ability to Maintain and Heal Itself by Andrew Weil, M.D. NY: Fawcett Columbine, 1995.

In this best-selling book which was also the subject of a PBS documentary Dr. Weil explains how mechanisms of self-diagnosis and self-healing are part of biology. He shows how spontaneous healing has worked to resolve life-threatening diseases, severe trauma, and chronic pain. The book also outlines an eight-week program that each of us can use to alter our diet, avoid environmental toxins, and reduce stress in order to enhance our innate healing powers. Highly recommended.

Total Wellness: Improve Your Health by Understanding the Body's Healing Systems by Joseph Pizzorno, N.D. Rocklin, CA: Prima Publishing, 1996. Dr. Pizzorno, a naturopathic physician, explains how seven core systems maintain the body's strength and vitality, and how all illnesses can be traced to weaknesses in one or more of these systems. As imbalances in the overstressed system are gently corrected, the body heals itself. This holistic approach focuses on the source of disease, not the symptoms, and promotes overall good health. Dr. Pizzorno is a teacher and clinician and recommends appropriate herbs, supplements, dietary modifications, and other safe, natural treatments for hundreds of common conditions. Dr. Pizzorno is one of the leading authorities on science-based natural medicine. He is co-author of *A Textbook of Natural Medicine* and *Encyclopedia of Natural Medicine* and founding president of Bastyr University, the first fully accredited, multidisciplinary university of natural medicine in the United States. Health care practitioners and patients alike can benefit from this book.

The Wellness Encyclopedia of Food and Nutrition: How to Buy, Store, and Prepare Every Variety of Fresh Food by Sheldon Margen, M.D., and the Editors of the University of California at Berkeley Wellness Letter. NY: REBUS. 1992. A comprehensive guide to more than 500 fresh and whole foods.

INNER CHILD AND REPARENTING WORK

Reclaiming the Inner Child by Jeremiah Abrams (Ed.). Los Angeles, CA: Jeremy P. Tarcher, Inc. 1990. This an edited book of 37 articles on the inner child by such authors as C.G. Jung, Charles Whitfield, Joseph Campbell, John Bradshaw, Hal Stone, M. Scott Peck, Alice Miller, June Singer, Bruno Bettelheim, Erik Erikson, Jean Houston, Ralph Metzner, Alexander Lowen, Nathaniel Branden, Theodore Reik, and others.

Homecoming: Reclaiming and championing your inner child, 1990.by John Bradshaw. See Cognitive Therapy section for a description.

Recovery of Your Inner Child by Lucia Capacchione, Ph.D. NY: Simon & Schuster. Dr. Capacchione is an art therapist with a Ph.D. in psychology. This book shows you how to have a firsthand experience of your inner child including its emotions and recapturing its sense of wonder by writing and drawing with your non-dominant hand. Dr. Capacchione shares scores of hands-on activities that will help you to embrace your Vulnerable Child and your Angry Child, find the Nurturing Parent within, and finally discover the Creative and Magical Child that can heal your life.

Affirmations for the Inner Child by Rokelle Lerner. Deerfield Beach, FL: Health Communications, Inc., 1990. This book presents a method of reparenting your inner child to experience a healthier life. Lerner provides 352 life-enhancing affirmations specifically targeting common themes such as anger, fear, forgiveness, letting go, limits, perfectionism, positive thoughts, self-esteem, trust, and self-talk. A wealth of positive affirmations.

The Inner Child Workbook: What to Do With Your Past When It Just Won't Go Away by Cathryn L. Taylor, M.A., M.F.C.C. NY: G.P. Putnam's Sons, 1991. Recovery therapist Cathryn Taylor offers a step-by-step guide to reparenting the wounded children within and healing their shame, anger, and feelings of abandonment. Using written and verbal exercises, guided imagery, journalizing, drawing, mirror work, and rituals, you can change your experience of the past today. The author takes the reader through six steps for each of the seven stages of childhood:
1. Identify your pain
2. Research its childhood roots
3. Reexperience the pain
4. Separate from it
5. Grieve the losses of each stage
6. Ritually release the pain
7. Reclaim the joy of each inner child

MIND/BODY HEALING

Altered States of Consciousness by Charles T. Tart, Ph.D. (Ed.). NY: HarperCollins, 1990. The classic anthology on consciousness. A fascinating collection of readings from William James, Stanley Krippner, Milton H. Erickson, Willis Harman, and many others. Combining the best of the humanistic and scientific traditions, this book covers the effects of marijuana and psychedelic, yoga, self-hypnosis, meditation, brain wave feedback, and dream consciousness.

Complementary Therapies in Rehabilitation: Holistic Approaches for Prevention and Wellness by Carol M. Davis, Ed.D. (Ed.), PT.Throfare, NJ: SLACK Inc., 1997. This book is primarily for the student and the health professional and includes the concepts of codependency and recovery; communication; death, dying, and grief; depression; dieting and weight loss; divorce; eating disorders; exercise; the therapeutic presence, holism, energy and mind/body connection and how they can be used to enhance current rehabilitation practice. Individual chapters focus on a total of 20 treatments, including Psychoneuroimmunology, Myofascial

Release, Rosen Method, Rolfing, Hellerwork, Soma, Non-Contact Therapeutic Touch, Biofeedback, Yoga, T'ai Chi, The Alexander Technique, Feldenkrais, Trager, Acupuncture, Polarity, Reflexology, Touch for Health, Jin Shin Do, Qi Gong, and Homeopathy.

Healing and the Mind by Bill Moyers. NY: Doubleday, 1993. Bill Moyers is an author and television journalist. *Healing and the Mind* was also a PBS series on television. The book is a series of interviews with experts and lay people alike looking at Mind/Body healing practices. The book includes very interesting art from around the world.

The Healthy Mind, Healthy Body Handbook by David S. Sobel, M.D. and Robert Ornstein, Ph.D. Los Altos, CA: DRx, 1996. An excellent self-help resource on how to use your mind to relieve stress, boost immunity, stay well, improve mood, and manage illness. This is a book health care and mental health care providers should recommend to their patients.

Mind Body Medicine: How to Use Your Mind for Better Health by Daniel Goleman, Ph.D. and Joel Gurin (Eds.). Yonkers, NY: Consumer Reports Books, 1993. This book discusses the connection between stress and disease; examines such mind/body approaches as biofeedback, hypnosis, meditation, and psychotherapy; explains how psychological and social support can lead to better health; and explores the mind's role in pain, heart disease, cancer, the immune system, diabetes, skin problems, arthritis, asthma, gastrointestinal disease, and infertility. The editors have brought together a "who's who" of top researchers including Herbert Benson, M.D., Kenneth Pelletier, Ph.D., Jon Kabat-Zinn, Ph.D., and 24 other leading authorities from major medical centers including Harvard, Stanford, Johns Hopkins, Case Western, and the Mayo Clinic. This book is a definitive source on the subject and is packed with self-tests and how-to instructions, it is an excellent resource for both the professional counselor as well as a self-help book.

Prevention Magazine's Hands-On Healing: Massage Remedies for Hundreds of Health Problems by the Editors of Prevention Magazine Health Books, John Feltman (Ed.). NY: Wings Books. 1989. A guide to holistic methods of healing put together by the editors of *Prevention* magazine one of the leading health magazines.

Timeless Healing: The Power and Biology of Belief by Herbert Benson, M.D. with Marg Stark. NY: Scribner, 1996. Dr. Benson is on the faculty at Harvard Medical School, on the staff of Deaconess Hospital, and President and founder of their Mind/Body Medical Institute. He is the author of *The Relaxation Response* and many other books about the relationship between the body and mind. Dr. Benson is a cardiologist and a pioneer in the field of Mind/Body medicine. In this book, Dr. Benson explains how he became convinced that humans are genetically encoded with a need for and nourishment from faith. He documents that when people call upon faith, they activate neurologic pathways for self-healing. Detailing the scientific evidence, he shows how anyone, along with a caring physician or healer, can tap into a reservoir of "remembered wellness" to affect and cure up to 90 percent of medical complaints.

You Can Heal Your Life by Louise L. Hay. Carlsbad, CA: Hay House, Inc. 1987. Louise Hay is a metaphysical lecturer and teacher and the author of 20 books including *Heal Your Body*. This book includes a list of health symptoms and their probable association with certain psychological issues. For example, the probable cause of addictions is, "Running from the self. Fear. Not knowing how to love the self." Ms. Hay also suggests a new thought pattern for each symptom. The list of symptoms and probable causes provides interesting material to explore to determine if it holds true for you.

PERSONALITY

The New Personality Self-Portrait: Why You Think, Work, Love, and Act the Way You Do by John M. Oldham, M.D. and Lois B. Morris. NY: Bantam Books, 1995. Dr. Oldham is Professor and Associate Chairman of the Department of Psychiatry at Columbia University College of Physicians and Surgeons, is Director of the New York State Psychiatric Institute and Chief Medical Officer for the New York State Office of Mental Health. This book reflects the latest scientific information in the field of personality development. The book includes: a personality self-test which reveals 14 personality styles; common traits and behaviors for each personality style; tips for living and working with each personality type; exercises to help change character weaknesses into strengths; danger signals that could indicate when a personality style has become a personality disorder.

Toxic People: 10 Ways of Dealing With People Who Make Your Life Miserable by Lillian Glass, Ph.D. NY: Simon & Schuster, 1995. Dr. Glass is a communications specialist. In her book she describes "…thirty types of toxic people who make your life miserable." Using examples from her own practice, she illustrates the problems toxic people cause - physical, emotional, and mental. She also provides skills and strategies for coping with the toxic people in your life.

SPIRITUAL AND PERSONAL GROWTH

HINDUISM

The Bhagavad Gita As It Is with Introduction, Translation and Authorized Purport by Swami A.C. Bhaktivedanta. NY: Collier Books, 1968. One of the great spiritual books. According to Thomas Merton, the word Gita means "Song." The Bhagavad Gita is, for Hinduism, the great song that finds the secret of human life in the surrender to and awareness of Krishna. "The Bhagavad Gita is a battlefield dialogue between Sri Krishna, the Supreme Personality of Godhead, and Arjuna, His friend, devotee, and disciple. The dialogue consists of seven hundred verses, in which the Lord brings Arjuna from the dark bewilderment of material consciousness to the stage of serene and joyful enlightenment regarding everything - literally" (Editor, p. 9).

BUDDHISM

Awakening the Sleeping Buddha by The Twelfth Tai Situpa, edited by Lea Terhune. Boston, MA: Shambhala, 1996. The most basic, clear principles of Tibetan Buddhism are here lucidly presented by a modern teacher and monk. The Twelfth Tai Situpa is abbot of Sherab Ling Monastery in northern India. Tai Situpa illuminates Buddhist teachings in commonsense terms, using down-to-earth examples, making this a good handbook for beginners as well as an excellent companion for long-time students.

Buddhism: A Way of Life and Thought by Nancy Wilson Ross. NY: Vintage Books, 1981. From Joseph Campbell's review of this book: "...an enlightening and fascinating introduction for readers only now discovering this first and greatest of the world religions" (Back cover).

Essential Tibetan Buddhism by Robert A.F. Thurman. NY: HarperCollins, 1996. Surveys the basic varieties and teachings of Tibetan Buddhism. *Essential Tibetan Buddhism* includes all the vital texts, freshly translated. Robert Thurman, is a professor of Indo-Tibetan Studies at Columbia University and an advocate for the liberation of Tibet and the Dalai Lama's cultural liaison to the United States. This book won the Tricycle (a Buddhist Journal) prize for excellence.

Gospel of Buddha: According to Old Records by Paul Carus. Tucson, AZ: Omen Communications, Inc., 1972. This classic collection of translations from Pali Buddhist sources remains one of the finest introductions to the authentic teachings of Buddha. Paul Caras was an American Buddhist.

The Illustrated Encyclopedia of Buddhist Wisdom by Gill Farrer-Halls. Wheaton, IL: Theosophical Publishing House, 2000. My favorite book on Buddhism. The meditation instructions, the beautiful photographs and artwork, and essential Buddhist teachings make this an excellent book. The book includes the life story of Prince Siddhartha, beliefs and philosophies of Buddhism, inspiring quotations from famous teachers, and instructions on how to meditate in the Theraveda, Zen, and Tibetan traditions.

Jesus and Buddha: The Parallel Sayings by Marcus Borg (Ed.). Berkeley, CA: Ulysses Press. Jesus and Buddha's sayings are presented for the first time in a format of facing pages to fully reveal the singular nature of their message. It becomes quickly apparent that both provided the same advice on loving, living a full life, and experiencing the sacred. "One came from the West, the other from the East; and they created two distinctly different religions. But the words they left us on how to keep our lives simple, appreciate the world around us, and open our souls to other people, are the same. At the heart of these amazing parallels lies a mystery that puzzles historians even today. How could Jesus, living five hundred years after Buddha and three thousand miles from India, espouse the same teachings?" The editor, Marcus Borg explores some possible explanations for the single message in their dual teachings in this book.

The Meditation Handbook by Geshe Kelsang Gyatso. London: Tharpa Publications, 1995. A step-by-step manual, providing a clear, practical guide to Buddhist meditation.

CHRISTIANITY

The Holy Bible: Containing the Old and New Testaments. King James Version. A Regency Bible from Nelson Publishers, 1990. This Bible contains the text of the King James Version, originally published in 1611. The *Bible* is the main spiritual book for all the Christian based religions and the source of morality, wisdom, comfort, and Jesus's teachings for millions of Christians around the world.

Jesus and Buddha: The Parallel Sayings by Marcus Borg (Ed.). See description under Buddhism section above.

NEW AGE

The Aquarian Gospel of Jesus the Christ by Levi. Santa Monica, CA: DeVorss & Co., Publishers, 1972. Levi H. Dowling, born in 1844, was a devout Christian and began preaching at the age of sixteen; and at the age of eighteen was pastor of a small church. He was a Chaplain in the United States Army during the Civil War. He was a graduate of two medical colleges and practiced medicine for a number of years. Levi spent 40 years in study and silent meditation and "...then he found himself in that stage of spiritual consciousness that permitted him to enter the domain of these superfine ethers and become familiar with their mysteries. He then learned...that every thought of every living thing is there recorded [Akashic Records] (p.14)." From the Akashic Records: "The story of Jesus, the man from Galilee, and how he attained the Christ consciousness open to all men. A complete record of the 'lost' eighteen years so strangely silent in the New Testament; a period spent traveling and learning from the masters, seers and wisemen in the temples and schools of Tibet, Egypt, India, Persia and Greece." (back cover).

The Complete Ascension Manual: How to Achieve Ascension in This Lifetime by Joshua David Stone, Ph.D. Sedona, AZ: Light Technology Publishing, 1994.

This book one of a four-volume series, and a easy-to-read encyclopedia of the spiritual path. Excellent resource for "new age" spiritual seekers.

TAOISM

Tao Te Ching by Lao Tsu, a new translation by Gia-Fu Feng and Jane English. NY: Vintage Books, 1972. "The essence of Taoism is contained in the eighty-one chapters of the book - roughly 5,000 words - which have for 2,500 years provided one of the major underlying influences in Chinese thought and culture, emerging also in proverbs and folklore. Whereas Confucianism is concerned with day-to-day rules of conduct, Taoism is concerned with a more spiritual level of being" (preface; pages not numbered). The *Tao Te Ching*, written most probably in the sixth century B.C. by Lao Tsu, has been translated more frequently than any work except the Bible. This book includes the Chinese version as well as beautiful illustrations.

GENERAL

Cosmic Consciousness by Richard Maurice Bucke, M.D. NY: E.P. Dutton & Co., 1969. Written in 1901, Dr. Bucke discovered that at intervals certain individuals have appeared who a gifted with the power of transcendent realization, or illumination. The author shows from available records that this transfiguring endowment of illumination is on the increase, and he gives full details of practically all the cases on record up to the time the book was written in 1901. Some of the individuals who Dr. Bucke believes achieved cosmic consciousness illumination include Gautama the Buddha, Jesus the Christ, Paul, Mohammed, Dante, Frances Bacon, William Blake, Walt Whitman, Moses, Socrates, William Wordsworth, Ralph Waldo Emerson, and Henry David Thoreau.

Handbook to Higher Consciousness (5th ed.) by Ken Keyes, Jr. See Cognitive Therapy Recommended Reading section for description of this book.

Healing Yourself with Self-Hypnosis (Rev. ed.) by Frank Caprio, M.D., Joseph R. Berger, and revised by Dr. Caroline Miller, Paramus, NJ: Prentice Hall Press, 1998. A practical guide for using hypnotherapy to improve your physical and emotional health. Specific concerns addressed include: excess weight; substance abuse; pain management; stress and fatigue; marriage and parenting; sports performance; allergies and asthma; smoking; insomnia; sex; anxiety; guilt, anger and depression; childbirth; and personal power.

How to Hypnotize Yourself & Others by Rachel Copelan, NY: Bell Publishing Co., 1981. A well written applied and practical book describing how to use hypnosis to eliminate unhealthy habits and increase healthy behaviors. It also includes a chapter on "unusual and specialized techniques" describing the use of hypnosis for such things as age regression, time regression, automatic writing, time distortion, and uncovering secrets.

Living in Balance: A Dynamic Approach for Creating Harmony & Wholeness in a Chaotic World by Joel Levey, Ph.D. and Michelle Levey, M.A., Berkeley, CA: Conari Press, 1998. This book offers a synthesis of ancient wisdom with new research. The Leveys help the reader explore body, mind, and soul in a very conscious and loving manner. This book is a gem.

Manifest Your Destiny: The Nine Spiritual Principles for Getting Everything You Want by Wayne W. Dyer, Ph.D. NY: Avon Books, 1997. Dr. Dyer teaches the process of meditation as a way to bring what we most desire into out lives.

The Power of Unconditional Love by Ken Keyes, Jr. with Penny Keyes. This book shows you how to bring the enormous power of unconditional love into your marriage or relationship and create deeper levels of intimacy and trust. This book includes seven guidelines for going into a relationship; seven guidelines for creating a successful relationship; and seven guidelines for decreasing your involvement, if necessary.

Prescriptions for Happiness by Ken Keyes, Jr. St. Mary, KY: Living Love Publications, undated. A short book which describes his three prescriptions for happiness:
> 1. Ask for what you want - But don't demand it.
> 2. Accept whatever happens - for now.
> 3. Turn up your love - Even if you don't get what you want.

Real Magic: Creating Miracles in Everyday Life by Wayne W. Dyer, Ph.D. NY: HarperPaperbacks, 1993. According to Dr. Dyer, real magic means creating miracles in everyday life. Quitting smoking or drinking, achieving new job success, or finding a happy relationship are all miracles because they transcend our perceived limitations. Dr. Dyer asks the reader to imagine what would make them happy, then offers specific strategies for attaining those goals. Dr. Dyer offers suggestions on how to achieve higher consciousness through service to others and unconditional love.

The Sky's the Limit by Wayne W. Dyer, Ph.D. NY: Pocket Books, 1981. This book includes sections on learning to live more in the now, transcending authoritarian thinking, learning to tune into and trust your instincts, how to recapture your childlike qualities, respect your higher needs, and cultivating a sense of purpose and meaning.

Staying on the Path by Wayne W. Dyer, Ph.D. Carson, CA: Hay House, Inc., 1995. Dr. Dyer is one of the most widely read authors in the field of self-help. He has written numerous best selling books including *Your Erroneous Zones*, *Real Magic*, and *Pulling Your Own Strings*. Dr. Dyer created this book for those already on the path to spiritual and personal growth, as well as those who are just trying to get there. The book is a collection of inspirational quotes and observations.

Still Here: Embracing Aging, Changing, and Dying by Ram Dass, Ph.D. NY: Riverhead Books, 2000. Ram Dass, is a psychologist and spiritual teacher who left his faculty position at Harvard in the 1960s. He helped shape the awakening consciousness of a generation with his landmark two-million-copy bestseller *Be Here Now.* A co-founder of the Hanuman and Seva foundations, he works with environmental organizations, the socially conscious business community, and the dying. He is an excellent storyteller and writer and lectures around the country and lives in California. Ram Dass has been one of my primary spiritual mentors since the 1960s. In *Still Here,* Ram Dass helps us explore the joy, pain, and opportunities of aging. Writing with his trademark humor and wisdom, sharing stories from his own life, and meditation exercises to integrate the teachings into daily life, Ram Dass offers us a new perspective on the territory that lies ahead. It is a perspective on aging, changing, and dying that will make the process a little easier for all of us.

Words of Wisdom to Live By: An Encyclopedia of Wisdom in Condensed Form compiled and edited by Alfred Armand Montapert. Books of Value, 2458 Chislehurst Dr., Los Angeles, CA 90027, 1986. A great collection of distilled wisdom and quotable quotes.

You'll See It When You Believe It: The Way to Your Personal Transformation by Wayne W. Dyer, Ph.D. NY: Avon Books, 1990. Dr. Dyer shows you how to tap the power within and direct the course of your destiny. Presents information and strategies for personal transformation, visualization, oneness, abundance, detachment, synchronicity, and forgiveness.

Your Road Map to Lifelong Happiness: A Guide to what you want by Ken Keyes, Jr. Coos Bay, OR: Love Line Books, 1995. This was Ken's last book before he died. This is a practical book that simplifies psychological healing, inner child work, relationship problems, and personal growth. It is illustrated and reveals the simplicity and accessibility of your unconscious mind. It shows you how to make a friend of your unconscious and dialogue with it. Learn how your unconscious mind picks the person you romantically fall in love with. Find out how you can learn to use the inevitable power struggle with your partner to heal childhood injuries in both of you. Keyes offers ways to resolve marital conflicts. This book explains how inadequate wiring in your two brains causes poor coordination between your conscious and unconscious minds. You'll discover ways you can expand your happiness by compensating for these inborn, life-damaging quirks.

Your Sacred Self by Dr. Wayne W. Dyer. NY: HarperPaperbacks, 1996. This book presents information on "preparing for the sacred journey," "the four keys to higher awareness," "transcending our ego identities," and "toward an egoless world." Dr. Dyer includes a lot of good information and many bulleted lists that are practical and to the point.

STRESS MANAGEMENT

Comprehensive Stress Management (4th ed.) by Jerrold S. Greenberg. Dubuque, IA: Brown & Benchmark, 1993. There is an abundance of scientific and statistical information in this book, but it also includes many anecdotes, humor, and personal experience. Numerous assessment exercises are provided so that content takes on personal meaning for each reader. One of the most comprehensive and best of the many stress management books on the market. It can be used as a self-help resource and is an excellent text for mental health practitioners.

Controlling Stress & Tension: A Holistic Approach (4th ed.) by Daniel A. Girdano, Ph.D., George S. Everly, Jr., Ph.D. and Dorothy E. Dusek, Ph.D. Englewood Cliffs, NJ: Prentice Hall, 1993. Complete with eleven self-assessment exercises for creating your own personal stress profile, this book helps you target specific areas that promote debilitating tension and stress. An excellent self-help resource, textbook, and resource for mental health practitioners.

Managing Stress: Principles and Strategies for Health and Wellbeing (2nd ed.) by Brian Luke Seaward, Ph.D. Sudbury, MA: Jones and Bartlett Publishers. A comprehensive and contemporary resource on stress management and health psychology. The second edition is web enhanced for tapping into the internet. Presents a holistic approach.

The Relaxation Response by Herbert Benson, M.D. with Miriam Z. Klipper. NY: Avon Books, 1976. This book brings together and synthesizes scientific data with age-old Eastern and Western writings that establish the existence of an innate relaxation response. The book describes a simple meditative technique that can trigger the healing relaxation response.

Stress Management: A Comprehensive Guide to Wellness by Edward A. Charlesworth, Ph.D. and Ronald G. Nathan, Ph.D. NY: Ballantine Books, 1985. The authors have compiled a comprehensive and authoritative guide of proven stress-reducing techniques including progressive relaxation, scanning, countdown, deep muscle relaxation techniques, autogenics, imagery and visualization, and many more special features. This book gives complete scripts for each of the stress reduction techniques that can be read into a tape recorder for personal use. An excellent stress management book for self-help, textbook, or professional counseling purposes. Highly recommended.

TRANSACTIONAL ANALYSIS

Born to Win: Transactional Analysis with Gestalt Experiments by Dr. Muriel James and Dr. Dorothy Jongeward. 1971. Reading, MA: Addison-Wesley. An excellent overview of Transactional Analysis theory and its application to the daily life of the average person. The book includes Gestalt-oriented exercises to help integrate the material.

Changing Lives Through Redecision Therapy by Mary McMlure Goulding, MSW and Robert L. Goulding, M.D. 1979. NY: Brunner/Mazel. The Gouldings present a blend of Transactional Analysis, desensitization, imagery work, and their own techniques to help individuals take responsibility for their feelings and actions, resolve old issues, break through impasses, and *redecide* to change.

Games People Play: The Psychology of Human Relationships by Eric Berne, M.D. 1964. NY: Grove Press. A good description of the types of interpersonal relationships from a Transactional Analysis perspective. Dr. Berne describes 120 of the games which people play including "Frigid Man," "Protective PTA," "Blemish," and "Now I've Got You, You...S.O.B." Ways of breaking through the game-playing and interacting more constructively are provided.

I'm OK-Your OK: A Practical Guide to Transactional Analysis by Thomas Harris. 1969. NY: Harper & Row. Dr. Harris describes four life positions underlying people's behavior. They are: (1) I'm Not Ok-You're Ok (the anxious dependency of the immature); (2) I'm Not Ok-You're Not Ok (the "give-up" or despair position; (3) I'm Ok-You're Not Ok (the criminal position); (4) I'm Ok-You're Ok (the response of the mature adult, at peace with him or herself, and others). Most people still operate unconsciously from the I'm Not Ok-You're Ok position.

Scripts People Live: Transactional Analysis of Life by Claude Steiner, Ph.D. 1974. NY: Grove Press. Scripts come from decisions you made early in your childhood. They're patterns of action that keep you from living a full and free life. Like...*Mother Hubbard* who takes care of everyone but herself. She spends her life feeling that her worth is measured only by how much she gives to others. *Big Daddy* is an exaggerated version of the responsible husband and father. The absolute ruler of his household, he knows everything best. Scripts like these can make you feel powerless over your life course. This book helps you identify the scripts you are living and how to modify or eliminate them in order to lead a more free and fulfilling life.

TA Today by Ian Stewart, Ph.D. and Vann Joines, Ph.D. 1987. Lifespace Publishing Co., 103 Edwards Ridge, Chapel Hill, NC. 27514. (919) 929-1171. An excellent presentation of the current ideas and concepts of Transactional

Analysis as it is practiced today. The book is illustrated and the material is presented in a straightforward way.

The TA Primer: Transactional Analysis in Everyday Life by Adelaide Bry, M.Ed. 1973. NY: Harper & Row/Perennial Library. A fully illustrated brief description of the basics of TA. This book can be read in about one hour and is a good bibliotherapy resource.

YOGA AND CHAKRAS

Lilias, Yoga and Your Life by Lilias M. Folan. NY: Collier Books, 1981. Lilias is the best-known yoga teacher in the United States. Her syndicated television program has been shown on nearly 200 public television stations. Her first book *Lilias, Yoga and You*, has sold over a quarter of a million copies. *Lilias, Yoga and Your Life* presents a series of specialized programs that you can adapt to your needs including backache, sports, office, elderly, preschool children, pregnancy, the performing arts, and disabilities.

The Sivananda Companion to Yoga by Lucy Lidell, Arayani Rabinovitch and Giris Rabinovitch. NY: A Fireside Book, 1983. This book gives you all the information you will need to practice at home. A complete fully illustrated guide to the physical postures, breathing exercises, diet, relaxation, and meditation techniques of yoga.

Yoga and Psychotherapy: The Evolution of Consciousness by Swami Rama, Rudolph Ballentine, M.D., and Swami Ajaya (Allan Weinstock, Ph.D.). Glenview, IL: Himalayan Institute, 1976. This book include sections on the body and Hatha Yoga; breath and energy; the mind (ancient and modern concepts); Buddhi, guide through the unknown; the secrets of sleep; psychosis and mysticism; and an excellent section on the seven centers of consciousness (chakras).

Yoga for Handicapped People by Barbara Brosnan, M.B., Ch.B. Available from Brookline Books, 29 Ware St., Cambridge, MA 02138, 1982. The author, a physician and yoga practitioner, has used yoga in her medical work for many years. She has found that yoga can be of benefit to people with a wide range of disabilities including mental disabilities, spasticity, spina bifida, and paralysis. The benefits are not merely physical, although yoga will help suppleness and improve posture, but are also spiritual, bringing a build-up in confidence, a diversion of energy and decline in tension.

Yoga the Iyengar Way by Silva Mehta, Mira Mehta and Shyam Mehta. NY: Alfred A. Knopf, 1996. This is a fully illustrated guide to the method developed over the last 50 years by B.K.S. Iyengar, a well known exponent of yoga. It includes sections on breathing, meditation, postures, the history and philosophy of yoga, and remedial programs for a range of common problems.

COGNITIVE SELF-ASSESSMENT INVENTORY

Lloyd R. Goodwin, Jr., Ph.D.

The Cognitive Self-Assessment Inventory (CSAI) is designed to help you identify and gain a better understanding of your core beliefs, "should messages," defense mechanisms, personality traits, thought distortions, and Buttons (i.e. attachments or demands). The CSAI is designed to be used in conjunction with **The Button Therapy Book: How to Work on Your Buttons and the Button-Pushers in Your Life** by Lloyd R. Goodwin, Jr. *The Button Therapy Book* more fully explains the cognitions on the *CSAI* as well as the concept of "Buttons" and "Button Therapy". Button Therapy includes a six-step psychological self-help method based on a holistic cognitive therapy model.

Answer the following questions truthfully, as the *CSAI* is primarily an inventory to explore and *self-assess* your thoughts and other cognitions. You are fooling nobody but yourself by not providing honest responses.

Compare Your Responses to a Sample of Adults. When you are finished completing the *CSAI* you may want to compare your responses to a sample of 293 adults who have taken the *CSAI* as part of a norming group. The results from this norming group follow the questions on the *CSAI*. Most subjects (81percent) in this sample were undergraduate or graduate college students ranging in age from 19 to 63 years of age and their responses may not be representative of your cognitions.

Professional Counseling Aid. There are many advantages to bringing your completed *CSAI* to a mental health professional. A professional counselor can help you explore your responses, insights, and questions. Oftentimes, you may not receive accurate unbiased feedback from a spouse or close friend. A counselor can help you explore your cognitive, as well as emotional, behavioral, and interpersonal domains. A counselor can give you unbiased feedback to help you identify and explore thought distortions, self-defeating core beliefs, defense mechanisms, personality traits, and Buttons that may be causing negative feelings and hindering your personal growth and self-actualization.

Your professional counselor may ask you to complete the *CSAI* at home and return it for use in your counseling sessions. Your answers on the *CSAI* are confidential and will be used by your mental health professional as part of your therapeutic counseling.

The *CSAI* takes approximately 60 minutes to complete.

GENERAL INFORMATION

Name_____Date_____

Address:_____

Telephone: Day _____ Night _____ Age_____

Male __ Female __ Highest educational degree (and major): _____

Currently in school? Yes ____ No ____ What grade/level? _____

Attend school at _____

Currently employed? Yes ____ No ____ Full or part time? _____

Where/job titles? _____

Marital/"significant other" status: Single ____ Married ____ Separated ____ Cohabiting ____ Other _____

Describe your living arrangement: _____

Name and ages of your children:_____

Parents: Mother: Age ___ or Year deceased ___   Father: Age ___ or Year deceased _____

List any prescription or over-the-counter medications, herbs or vitamins you take:

_____

Have you ever been hospitalized for psychological or drug problems? Yes ___ No ___

Dates/Reason: _____

_____

_____

Have you ever received professional counseling or psychotherapy services? Yes ___ No ___

Dates/Reason _____

Have any of your family ever had psychological or drug problems? Yes ___ No ___ Unknown _____

Describe _____

Have you ever had an alcohol or drug problem?   Yes ___   No ___   Don't know ___

Describe: _____

_____

Do you have a physical or mental disability or disorder?   Yes ___   No ___   Don't know ___

Describe: _____

I probably have a psychological disorder, but haven't been diagnosed yet (explain): _____

_____

Have you ever attempted suicide?   Yes ___ No ___

Explain: _____

Describe any spiritual or religious path that you follow: _____

_____

THOUGHTS

Circle each of the following that describe you:

Intelligent	or	Stupid	Attractive	or	Ugly
Responsible	or	Irresponsible	Honest	or	Dishonest
Competent	or	Inadequate	Happy	or	Suicidal thoughts
Dependable	or	Undependable	Sense of humor	or	Seldom laugh
Moral	or	Moral degenerate	Naive	or	Jaded
Conservative	or	High risk-taker	Go-getter	or	Lazy
Calm	or	Stressed	Spiritual	or	Agnostic/atheist
Rational	or	Impulsive	Loving	or	Angry
Giving	or	Self-centered	Positive	or	Evil

LIST YOUR FIVE MAIN FEARS

1._____

2._____

3._____

4._____

5._____

12 STYLES OF THINKING

Please circle the number that most accurately reflects your opinion on each of the following items:

Strongly disagree = 1   Disagree = 2   Neutral = 3   Agree = 4   Strongly agree = 5

Black & White Thinking

1. There is a right way and a wrong way of doing things.   1 2 3 4 5

Blaming

2. Other people (e.g. spouse, boss) make me angry, sad, or happy.   1 2 3 4 5

Comparing

3. I compare myself to other people, especially in terms of   1 2 3 4 5
   appearance, money, intellect, or possessions.

4. Other people are happier than I am.   1 2 3 4 5

Catastrophic Thinking

5. I tend to worry excessively about all the possible things   1 2 3 4 5
   that could go wrong in situations, relationships, and work.

Fair and Just Thinking

6. People treat me unfairly.   1 2 3 4 5

7. Everything happens for a reason.   1 2 3 4 5

8. I get very upset when people don't receive the   1 2 3 4 5
   appropriate consequence for their wrongful acts.

Overgeneralizing

   I frequently say things like:

9. "You never admit it when you are wrong."   1 2 3 4 5

10. "You are always belittling me."   1 2 3 4 5

11. "You never do anything to help out around the house."   1 2 3 4 5

Perfectionist Thinking

12. I should not make mistakes.   1 2 3 4 5

Strongly disagree = 1   Disagree = 2   Neutral = 3   Agree = 4   Strongly agree = 5

Mind Reading Form of Communication

13. I know what someone is (e.g. spouse, boy/girlfriend)   1 2 3 4 5
    communicating to me without them verbalizing it.

14. I know what people "really mean," even if they   1 2 3 4 5
    verbalize something else in their communication.

15. My spouse or good friends know the way I like things   1 2 3 4 5
    to be done without me having to tell them.

Negativistic Thinking

16. I tend to focus on the negative aspect of a person   1 2 3 4 5
    or situation, ignoring the strengths or assets.

Pasting

17. I spend a lot of time thinking about things I should have   1 2 3 4 5
    said or done in the past.

18. I focus on distressing events that have recently   1 2 3 4 5
    occurred or poor decisions that I have made.

Futuring

19. I tend to get very concerned and anxious worrying about   1 2 3 4 5
    what may happen in the future.

I'm "Right" and You're "Wrong" Thinking

20. I have a strong need to be "right."   1 2 3 4 5

21. I have a strong need to win arguments.   1 2 3 4 5

22. I want people to admit it when they are wrong and I am right.   1 2 3 4 5

SHOULD MESSAGES

23. I should please my parents.   1 2 3 4 5

24. It is very important to please other people.   1 2 3 4 5

25. I should make other people feel better when they are upset.   1 2 3 4 5

26. I should remain centered, balanced, harmonious, and   1 2 3 4 5
    focused on my personal and spiritual growth at all times.

27. Everyone should like and accept me because I'm basically   1 2 3 4 5
    a good and decent person.

Strongly disagree = 1   Disagree = 2   Neutral = 3   Agree = 4   Strongly agree = 5

28. I should like and accept all people.   1 2 3 4 5

29. I should love, or at least like, both of my parents.   1 2 3 4 5

30. My parents should have been better parents.   1 2 3 4 5

31. I should like all of my children equally (leave blank if appropriate).   1 2 3 4 5

32. Sex is for having children - not for pleasure.   1 2 3 4 5

33. I shouldn't dress, feel, or behave sexy.   1 2 3 4 5

34. I should be independent and self-sufficient and not have to
    rely on other people.   1 2 3 4 5

35. I should keep control of my feelings.   1 2 3 4 5

36. I should not express my love to my
    spouse/boyfriend/girlfriend because I will get hurt emotionally.   1 2 3 4 5

37. I should never get emotionally upset.   1 2 3 4 5

38. I should not share personal information about family or myself.   1 2 3 4 5

39. I should play it safe and not take risks.   1 2 3 4 5

40. I should live life to its fullest.   1 2 3 4 5

41. I should take more risks with men/women, career, and life in general.   1 2 3 4 5

42. I should be making more progress than I am in my
    mental health and personal growth .   1 2 3 4 5

CORE BELIEFS

BELIEFS ABOUT SELF

43. If I don't pay any attention to my problems they will go away.   1 2 3 4 5

44. I am a victim of life's circumstances.   1 2 3 4 5

45. Other people currently control my life.   1 2 3 4 5

46. I don't deserve to be loved.   1 2 3 4 5

47. I don't deserve to be happy.   1 2 3 4 5

48. I'm not attractive.   1 2 3 4 5

Strongly disagree = 1   Disagree = 2   Neutral = 3   Agree = 4   Strongly agree = 5

49. I'm not sexy.   1 2 3 4 5

50. I'm not capable of really loving somebody.   1 2 3 4 5

51. If I allow myself to feel really excited or good about someone or something it will be followed by something equally terrible.   1 2 3 4 5

52. I must please and agree with people to be accepted.   1 2 3 4 5

53. I am not as intelligent or as competent as most of my friends.   1 2 3 4 5

54. If people really knew me they wouldn't like me.   1 2 3 4 5

55. I'm boring and not very interesting to be around.   1 2 3 4 5

56. I'm a loser.   1 2 3 4 5

57. I'm a toxic person and turn people off around me.   1 2 3 4 5

58. I'm a bad person because of some things that I've done.   1 2 3 4 5

59. Most people are better off than I am.   1 2 3 4 5

60. Most people are doing better than I am.   1 2 3 4 5

BELIEFS ABOUT RELATIONSHIPS

61. I resent my spouse (boy/girlfriend) for some things he or she has done to hurt me.   1 2 3 4 5

62. I'm waiting for Mr. or Miss Right to come along.   1 2 3 4 5

63. Divorce is a sign of failure or a sin.   1 2 3 4 5

BELIEFS ABOUT LIFE

64. The world is basically a fearful and unsafe place.   1 2 3 4 5

65. Most people are only out for themselves and will cheat or betray you sooner or later, usually sooner.   1 2 3 4 5

66. I'm entitled to be taken care of - I didn't ask to be brought into this world with all its problems.   1 2 3 4 5

67. The bottom line in life is accumulating money, nice things and power.   1 2 3 4 5

68. There are no coincidences in life - everything happens for a reason.   1 2 3 4 5

BELIEFS ABOUT ILLNESS AND DISABILITY

69. People have illness or disability because God is punishing them.   1 2 3 4 5

Strongly disagree = 1 Disagree = 2 Neutral = 3 Agree = 4 Strongly agree = 5

70. People have illness or disability because it is part of their Karma (past deeds in either this life or a past life). 1 2 3 4 5

71. If people have enough faith in God and his healing powers He will cure them of their disability. 1 2 3 4 5

72. If people have enough faith in God or a higher spiritual power they can heal themselves from any illness. 1 2 3 4 5

BELIEFS ABOUT ALCOHOL AND OTHER DRUGS

73. There is nothing wrong with psychoactive drugs. 1 2 3 4 5

74. All drugs should be legalized. 1 2 3 4 5

75. People have a fundamental human right to self-medicate with any drug. 1 2 3 4 5

76. Life without using alcohol or other drugs is boring. 1 2 3 4 5

77. I don't have any major problems with my alcohol and drug use. 1 2 3 4 5

78. I rely on drugs to help me feel more comfortable in social situations. 1 2 3 4 5

79. Psychoactive drugs help me be more creative and productive. 1 2 3 4 5

80. I can't imagine going through the rest of my life without drugs. 1 2 3 4 5

81. I have no desire to give up alcohol and other drugs (leave blank if appropriate). 1 2 3 4 5

82. I can't function without alcohol or other drugs. 1 2 3 4 5

83. I shouldn't have to feel any unpleasant feelings or pain. 1 2 3 4 5

84. I've already screwed up my life with my drug use and I might as well continue drinking and drugging (leave blank if appropriate). 1 2 3 4 5

85. I don't have enough willpower to stop using alcohol or other drugs. 1 2 3 4 5

86. If I stopped my drug use the withdrawal and drug cravings would be too much to bear. 1 2 3 4 5

87. People who have the disease of alcoholism or drug addiction and will have it the rest of their lives. 1 2 3 4 5

88. Only someone who has experienced alcohol or another drug addiction can help another alcoholic or drug addict. 1 2 3 4 5

89. Alcoholics Anonymous and related 12 step mutual-help groups are the best approaches to help substance abusers. 1 2 3 4 5

Strongly disagree = 1   Disagree = 2   Neutral = 3   Agree = 4   Strongly agree = 5

90. If recovering alcoholics or other drug addicts use alcohol or other mood altering drugs they will relapse and die prematurely. 1 2 3 4 5

91. Problem drinkers and other drug abusers can learn to drink/drug responsibly. 1 2 3 4 5

PERSONALITY TRAITS AND STYLES

Indicate the degree to which each of the following personality traits capture the real you:

92. I enjoy taking risks, thrill-seeking behavior, and living on the edge. 1 2 3 4 5

93. I like competition and challenges. 1 2 3 4 5

94. I get bored quickly with the same old thing. 1 2 3 4 5

95. I thrive on stress and am probably a "stress junkie." 1 2 3 4 5

96. I get into a lot of arguments and fights. 1 2 3 4 5

97. I feel inadequate. 1 2 3 4 5

98. I am very sensitive to negative feedback. 1 2 3 4 5

99. I have unstable relationships. 1 2 3 4 5

100. I have anger outbursts. 1 2 3 4 5

101. I am dependent on my spouse (girl/boyfriend). 1 2 3 4 5

102. I am devoted to my spouse (girl/boyfriend). 1 2 3 4 5

103. I want to be noticed as the center of attention. 1 2 3 4 5

104. I am more competent and capable than the average person. 1 2 3 4 5

105. I am very orderly, perfectionistic, and punctual. 1 2 3 4 5

106. I am distrustful and suspicious. 1 2 3 4 5

107. I am a loner and very uncomfortable in close relationships. 1 2 3 4 5

108. I am even-tempered and am seldom extremely sad or happy. 1 2 3 4 5

109. I am unconventional and nonconformist. 1 2 3 4 5

110. I am very interested in mysticism, paranormal phenomenon, metaphysics, dreams, and "new age" topics. 1 2 3 4 5

111. I am eccentric and considered an "oddball" by some people. 1 2 3 4 5

112. I can be cruel, coldhearted, and intimidating to get what I want. 1 2 3 4 5

Strongly disagree = 1   Disagree = 2   Neutral = 3   Agree = 4   Strongly agree = 5

113. I like to serve others and make sure their needs are met.   1 2 3 4 5

114. I am a natural leader. I feel comfortable taking charge,   1 2 3 4 5
     and assuming responsibility and authority.

115. I am very self-critical, sad, depressed, and can't relax.   1 2 3 4 5

116. I have more of a toxic vs nourisher type of personality.   1 2 3 4 5

117. I am socially inhibited.   1 2 3 4 5

DEFENSE MECHANISMS

Defense mechanisms are periodically used to protect our egos and to help cope with the stresses of life. Which of the following defense mechanisms do you tend to rely on the most?

1 =Not at all   2 = Sometimes   3 = Don't Know   4 = Frequently   5 = Very frequently

118. **Altruism.** Focusing on serving others, partly to fulfill one's   1 2 3 4 5
     own needs.

119. **Attack.** The striking back at a Button-Pusher with physical   1 2 3 4 5
     or verbal aggression when psychological or physical pain is
     experienced.

120. **Compensation.** The protection of self-esteem by masking   1 2 3 4 5
     weaknesses or developing certain positive traits to make up
     for limitations.

121. **Denial.** A conscious attempt to suppress unpleasant reality.   1 2 3 4 5

122. **Displacement.** The redirecting of emotional energy, often   1 2 3 4 5
     angry feelings, triggered from a Button-Pusher to a less
     threatening and safer target (e.g. Get mad at boss and come home
     and take it out on spouse or children).

123. **Fantasy.** The retreat into daydreams and imagination to   1 2 3 4 5
     escape problems or to avoid conflicts.

124. **Humor.** The use of humor to reduce anxiety, stress, or fear.   1 2 3 4 5

1 =Not at all   2 = Sometimes   3 = Don't Know   4 = Frequently   5 = Very frequently

125. **Idealization.** The unwarranted praise of another or oneself
by exaggerating virtues.   1 2 3 4 5

126. **Identification.** Internalizing the characteristics of others
or identifying with a winner in order to overcome fear,   1 2 3 4 5
inadequacy, low self-esteem or to cope with loss or helplessness.

127. **Intellectualization.** An attempt to avoid painful feelings
by escaping one's rational mind.   1 2 3 4 5

128. **Isolation of Affect.** The compartmentalization of painful
emotions from the events associated with them (e.g. rape   1 2 3 4 5
victim who can recount details of the rape without recalling
the feelings associated with the event).

129. **Projection.** Attributing unacceptable thoughts, feelings,
wishes, traits, and impulses to others.   1 2 3 4 5

130. **Rationalization.** Providing a plausible, self-serving
false reason to justify failure or unacceptable emotions or ideas.   1 2 3 4 5

131. **Reaction Formation.** A type of feeling substitution whereby
individuals adopt the exaggerated opposite attitude and   1 2 3 4 5
behavior from the way they really feel and believe.

132. **Regression.** A return to an earlier and less mature coping
style when confronted with overwhelming stress.   1 2 3 4 5

133. **Repression.** The unconscious exclusion of threatening or
painful thoughts, feelings, impulses, and wishes from   1 2 3 4 5
awareness (e.g. forgetting and amnesia).

134. **Sublimation.** The redirection of unacceptable drives,
feelings, and impulses into socially acceptable goals and behaviors   1 2 3 4 5
(e.g. an individual with sadistic desires takes a job in a governmental
bureaucracy in order to frustrate and distress consumers).

135. **Substitution.** The substitution of one unavailable option
for another available option (e.g. A student can't make the swim   1 2 3 4 5
team because of a disability becomes the swim coach's assistant).

1 =Not at all   2 = Sometimes   3 = Don't Know   4 = Frequently   5 = Very frequently

136. **Suppression.** The conscious avoidance of unacceptable   1 2 3 4 5
thoughts, feelings, and behaviors.

137. **Withdrawal.** Withdrawal when the pain of stress, anxiety,   1 2 3 4 5
or frustration is too much to bear (e.g. avoiding stress
and flight into failure).

STOP

SOLICIT A SECOND OPINION

You may want to have your spouse, or a close friend, complete the *CSAI* as he or she perceives you. Comparing your answers with your spouse or significant other can open up many hours of dialogue. As a cautionary note, there is a certain degree of risk to your relationship that goes with sharing your personal viewpoints of each other. An open and honest communication process, especially with your spouse, is like a double-edged sword. It can help you strengthen and improve your relationship. However, it can also help send both of you to divorce court!

Sometimes knowing some of your spouse's thoughts and beliefs about him or herself, you, and life in general can be a bit unsettling. If you are not ready to take this kind of risk in your marital relationship, then simply complete the *CSAI* for yourself. If you have a shaky marital/cohabiting relationship, you and your spouse or significant other, each of you may want to complete the *CSAI* and explore your responses, insights, and questions with a professional counselor. However, the *CSAI* may be used as a self-help, pre-marital, marital, and individual counseling tool with, or without, a professional counselor.

Scoring

There are no right or wrong answers to the *CSAI*. The *CSAI* is simply an inventory to help you identify, organize, and explore your core beliefs, "should messages," defense mechanisms, personality traits, thought distortions, and Buttons (i.e. attachments or demands).

SOME USEFUL WAYS TO UTILIZE THE RESULTS ON YOUR CSAI INCLUDE THE FOLLOWING:

- **How are my cognitions affecting my life?** Review the items that you answered "agree" or "strongly agree," "frequently," "very frequently," and "strongly disagree" and explore the ways your life may be affected by operating from those cognitions (i.e. beliefs, "should messages").
- **How do my cognitions** (e.g. thoughts and beliefs) **compare to other adults?** See how your response on each item compares to the responses from a sample of adults in the norming group. Determine whether your responses on the *CSAI* fall above, below, or the same as the mean (i.e. arithmetic average) response from the sample of adults? You may want to examine more closely those items that have a point difference of more than one from the average response from the norming group.
- **How many and what type of Buttons do I have?** The items marked "Strongly Agree" and "Strongly Disagree" are indications of *potential* Buttons. How many potential Buttons do you have? What types of Buttons do you have?
- **Professional counseling aide.** You can give your *CSAI* to your professional counselor for his or her feedback. Your counselor can help you explore your responses on the *CSAI* during your counseling sessions.

HOW DO YOUR ANSWERS COMPARE TO OTHER PEOPLE'S?

Here is how 293 adults answered the items on the *CSAI*. Seventy-five percent of the subjects in this sample were undergraduate or graduate college students ranging in age from 19 to 63 years of age. The modal or most frequent age was 20 years old. The following are the percentage of people in the norming group who "agreed" or "strongly agreed" with each cognition (i.e. thought or belief).

THOUGHTS

The following are the percent (in italics) of subjects in the norming group responding to each item. Not all subjects answered all items:

Item	Percent	Item	Percent	Item	Percent	Item	Percent
Intelligent	*98*	or Stupid	*1*	Attractive	*88*	or Ugly	*4*
Responsible	*98*	or Irresponsible	*2*	Honest	*97*	or Dishonest	*0*
Competent	*96*	or Inadequate	*1*	Happy	*94*	or Suicidal	*2*
Dependable	*96*	or Undependable	*2*	Sense of humor	*94*	or Seldom laugh	*3*
Moral	*94*	or Moral degenerate	*2*	Naive	*48*	or Jaded	*34*
Conservative	*66*	or High risk-taker	*26*	Go-getter	*74*	or Lazy	*18*
Calm	*45*	or Stressed	*52*	Spiritual	*89*	or Agnostic/atheist	*5*
Rational	*78*	or Impulsive	*21*	Loving	*92*	or Angry	*4*
Giving	*88*	or Self-centered	*9*	Positive	*93*	or Evil	*2*

FIVE MAIN FEARS

Two hundred and seventy-six of the 293 subjects listed fears. Also, some of the 276 subjects responding to this question listed fewer than five fears. The subjects' fears fell into the following categories. The fears are rank-ordered with the most frequently reported fear listed first. Each fear is followed by the percentage of respondents reporting that item as a fear.

Rank	Fear	Percent Responding
1.	**Failure** to achieve goals or not being successful in life (e.g. completing college/ achieving tenure/ passing licensure exam/ spiritual quest)	49
2.	**Death of loved one** (e.g. family member/ child/ parent)	46
3.	**Death and Dying** (includes having a terminal illness/dying before I achieve my life goals/a slow agonizing death/dying alone)	33

4. **Physical illness and diseases** (e.g. unhealthy/cancer/ burns/AIDS=5)   25
5. **Being alone** (e.g. loneliness/ not finding a partner/ not belonging/   20
    and includes growing old alone=2)

COGNITIONS

Here is how 291 adults in the norming group responded on a 5-point scale to the 137 cognitions on the *CSAI*. See the *CSAI* for the items. Following each item number is the percentage (in italics) of the sample that either "agreed" or "strongly agreed" with the item.

STYLES OF THINKING

Item %	Item %	Item %	Item %	Item %	Item %	Item %	Item %
1. *44*	2. *43*	3. *47*	4. *17*	5. *40*	6. *9*	7. *76*	8. *41*
9. *2*	10. *11*	11. *18*	12. *27*	13. *60*	14. *45*	15. *50*	16. *12*
17. *42*	18. *39*	19. *50*	20. *41*	21. *31*	22. *42*		

SHOULD MESSAGES

23. *63*	24. *39*	25. *72*	26. *55*	27. *51*	28. *34*	29. *76*	30. *14*
31. *20*	32. *4*	33. *4*	34. *67*	35. *59*	36. *7*	37. *3*	38. *10*
39. *11*	40. *88*	41. *48*	42. *43*				

CORE BELIEFS

BELIEFS ABOUT SELF

43. *1*	44. *11*	45. *6*	46. *2*	47. *1*	48. *4*	49. *6*	50. *3*
51. *9*	52. *5*	53. *6*	54. *5*	55. *3*	56. *1*	57. *1*	58. *1*
59. *5*	60. *9*						

BELIEFS ABOUT RELATIONSHIPS

Item	%	Item	%	Item	%	Item	%	Item	%	Item	%	Item	%	Item	%
61.	24	62.	32	63.	18										

BELIEFS ABOUT LIFE

64.	11	65.	10	66.	4	67.	7	68.	51						

BELIEFS ABOUT ILLNESS AND DISABILITY

69.	1	70.	3	71.	20	72.	15								

BELIEFS ABOUT ALCOHOL AND OTHER DRUGS

73.	21	74.	17	75.	28	76.	10	77.	79	78.	11	79.	9	80.	7
81.	22	82.	1	83.	13	84.	1	85.	4	86.	2	87.	2	88.	12
89.	29	90.	11	91.	43										

PERSONALITY TRAITS AND STYLES

92.	33	93.	77	94.	59	95.	27	96.	9	97.	9	98.	42	99.	11
100.	25	101.	13	102.	60	103.	16	104.	51	105.	41	106.	9	107.	7
108.	33	109.	28	110.	34	111.	19	112.	16	113.	55	114.	51	115.	17
116.	2	117.	9												

DEFENSE MECHANISMS

118.	35	119.	18	120.	34	121.	10	122.	11	123.	19	124.	68	125.	7
126.	11	127.	16	128.	9	129.	11	130.	20	131.	6	132.	10	133.	8
134.	9	135.	16	136.	17	137.	16									

POTENTIAL TROUBLESOME COGNITIONS

Those items (i.e. cognitions) that you responded to with an "Agree" response indicate potential "troublesome cognitions". Go back over these items and determine if these cognitions are creating problems in your life.

The average (i.e. mean) number of "agree" responses from the norming sample of 291 adults:

CSAI: **22**   My score: _____

POTENTIAL BUTTONS

Those items (i.e. cognitions) that you responded to with a "Strongly Agree" response indicate a potential Button. Go back over these items and determine if you have an attachment, demand, or need for these cognitions that may be creating problems in your life.

The average (i.e. mean) number of "Strongly Agree" responses from the norming sample of 291 adults:

CSAI: **8**   My score: _____

"STRONGLY DISAGREE" RESPONSES (POTENTIAL BUTTONS)

We can be just as "attached" (i.e. have a Button) to being against something as we are for something! Go back over the cognitions you strongly disagree with to determine if you may be protesting too much or overreacting to something that may be true.

The average (i.e. mean) number of "Strongly Disagree" responses from the norming sample of 291 adults:

CSAI: **28**   My score: _____

MOTIVATIONAL STATES INVENTORY

Lloyd R. Goodwin, Jr., Ph.D.

The *Motivational States Inventory* (*MSI*) is a tool to help you become aware of the motivational states that are associated with your troublesome cognitions (TC's) and Buttons. The Centers of Consciousness Scale (CCS) helps you become aware of those motivational states or centers of consciousness you are currently hanging out in.

Name _____

Address _____

City _____ State _____ ZIP _____

Phone _____

BUTTONS

We all have **"Buttons."** Buttons are the demands, attachments, and needs that we develop to certain models we carry around in our minds of how things should be. Whenever we get ourselves upset, it can usually be related to a demand or attachment we have related to other people, our environment, or ourselves. The *feelings* that tend to be associated with activated Buttons in each of the six categories of "motivational states" are provided at the beginning of each category. In addition, some potential areas of concern are listed for each of the six motivational states.

MOTIVATIONAL STATES

Many of our thoughts and behaviors are related to certain common and identifiable intentions or motivations. The following six categories of motivational states are adapted from the seven chakras in yoga, the seven centers of consciousness as described by Ken Keyes, Jr., and the hierarchy of needs as described by Abraham Maslow.

CENTERS OF CONSCIOUSNESS

Motivational states can also be viewed as "centers of consciousness" as in yoga, Ken Keyes Jr., and other models of consciousness. While you are thinking and behaving the motivational state that initiated the thoughts or behaviors can be viewed as a "center of consciousness." The *Motivational States Inventory* includes a "Centers of Consciousness Scale" to help you determine which centers of consciousness (i.e. motivational states) you are spending the most time, regardless of whether or not you are reacting to activated Buttons.

SIX MOTIVATIONAL STATES

DIRECTIONS

In the past few weeks, when you became emotionally upset from having your Buttons pushed - from which of the following "motivational states" did your Buttons tend to be associated?

1 =Not at all   2 = Sometimes   3 = Don't Know   4 = Frequently   5 = Very frequently

1. **"Safety and Security" Motivational State:**
   "Overall, in the past few weeks I have felt insecure in   1 2 3 4 5
   my work, family, and relationships."
   (*Feelings* of insecurity, fear, worry, and anxiety tend to be activated
   when Buttons related to our safety and security wants and needs
   are pushed.)
   "Specifically, I have had a number of my Buttons pushed and
   felt insecure related to my.."
   A. Job concerns   1 2 3 4 5
   B. Relationship concerns   1 2 3 4 5
   C. Money concerns (e.g. bills, debt).   1 2 3 4 5

2. **Pleasure and Sensation-seeking Motivational State:**
   "Overall, in the past few weeks I have been upset related to   1 2 3 4 5
   my pleasure and sensation-seeking efforts."
   (*Feelings* of boredom, disappointment, pleasure, pleasant sensations,
   and jealousy tend to be activated when Buttons related to our pleasure
   and sensation-seeking wants and needs are pushed.)
   "Specifically, I have recently had a number of my Buttons pushed
   and have been frustrated or upset related to my wants and
   needs for ..."
   A. Mood-altering drugs   1 2 3 4 5
   B. Sex   1 2 3 4 5
   C. Exercise   1 2 3 4 5
   D. Food   1 2 3 4 5
   E. Relaxation   1 2 3 4 5

3. Control and Power Motivational State

"Overall, I have recently been upset related to my need to
control other people and situations in my life."   1 2 3 4 5
(*Feelings* of irritation, anger, hostility, impatience,
inferiority, superiority, resentment, and fear of loss tend to be
activated when these Buttons are pushed.)
"Specifically, I have recently had a number of Buttons pushed
and felt angry or upset resulting in ..."

A. My being aggressive   1 2 3 4 5
B. My being critical and judgmental   1 2 3 4 5
C. My being competitive   1 2 3 4 5
D. Thoughts of becoming an administrator at work   1 2 3 4 5
E. Thoughts of running for political office   1 2 3 4 5
F. Relational, marital, or family conflicts   1 2 3 4 5

4. Love and Acceptance Motivational State

"Overall, I have recently been upset related to my wants   1 2 3 4 5
and needs related to my accepting and loving myself and others."
(*Feelings* of being unloved, rejected, empty, and isolated tend
to be activated when these Buttons are pushed.)
"Specifically, I have recently had a number of Buttons pushed
related to my wants and needs related to ..."

A. Intimacy   1 2 3 4 5
B. Compassion   1 2 3 4 5
C. Sense of belonging   1 2 3 4 5
D. Self-acceptance/love   1 2 3 4 5

5. Personal Growth and Self-Actualization Motivational State

"Overall, I have recently been upset related to my wants and   1 2 3 4 5
needs related to my personal growth."
(*Feelings* of frustration, disappointment, stress, and disharmony
tend to be activated when these Buttons are pushed.)
"Specifically, I have recently had a number of Buttons pushed
related to my wants and needs ..."

A. For counseling and personal growth activities and groups   1 2 3 4 5
B. To enjoy life, be playful, and have a sense of humor   1 2 3 4 5
C. To be alive and spontaneous   1 2 3 4 5
D. To be focused in my here-and-now   1 2 3 4 5
E. To be comfortable with shades of Gray vs. Black and White thinking   1 2 3 4 5
F. To be honest, truthful, moral, and have a clear sense of right and wrong   1 2 3 4 5
G. Having a balanced lifestyle between work, family, play, and personal   1 2 3 4 5
and professional growth activities

6. **Spiritual and Transcendental Motivational State**

"Overall, I have recently been upset related to my wants and needs   1 2 3 4 5
to actualize more of my spiritual potential."

(*Feelings* of unconsciousness, ignorance, cynicism, disharmony,
uprootedness, and going crazy tend to be activated when these
Buttons are pushed.)

"Specifically, I have recently had a number of Buttons pushed
related to my wants and needs for ..."

A. Love and compassion   1 2 3 4 5
B. Peace and inner calm   1 2 3 4 5
C. Unity with God   1 2 3 4 5
D. Appreciation of nature, beauty, and kindness   1 2 3 4 5
E. Having a meaning to life   1 2 3 4 5
F. Being centered and in touch with the subtler energies   1 2 3 4 5
   within and around me

CENTERS OF CONSCIOUSNESS RANKING SCALE

DIRECTIONS

At this time in your life how much time are you spending in the following motivational states or "centers of consciousness" (See descriptions of the six motivational states described earlier)?

Rank order each category (i.e. center of consciousness/motivational state) with **1** being the center of consciousness that you currently spend the most time in and **6** being the least:

_____1. **Safety and Security** (i.e. Are you spending your waking hours seeking or being concerned with your job, relationships, money, etc.?)

_____2. **Pleasure and Sensation-seeking** (i.e. Are you spending time seeking or concerned with sex, food, mood altering drugs, music, exercise, etc.?)

_____3. **Love and Acceptance** (i.e. Are you spending time seeking or concerned with gaining and/or giving acceptance, love, and compassion?)

_____4. **Control and Power** (i.e. Are you spending time trying to control other people in your life? Are you spending time being judgmental and critical of others?)

_____5. **Personal Growth and Self-Actualization** (i.e. Are you spending time seeking and/or concerned about your personal growth and self-actualization? Are you spending time enjoying life and feel alive and spontaneous?)

_____6. **Spiritual and Transcendental** (i.e. Are you spending time on your spiritual development and experiencing transcendental states of consciousness? Are you experiencing a lot of love and compassion for others? Are experiencing a sense of connectedness and unity with God and all living things?)

STOP

COMPARE YOUR SCORES TO OTHER ADULTS

Here is how a sample of 105 adults responded to the items on the *Motivational States Inventory*. Eighty-two of the subjects in this sample were undergraduate and graduate college students ranging in age from 19 to 63 years. The *MSI* was part of a larger study on cognitions conducted by the author for *The Button Therapy Book* (Goodwin, 2000):

Mean	**Score**
1. Safety and Security (As a category of "motivational states")	2.87
A. Money concerns (e.g. bills, debt)	3.07
B. Relationship concerns	2.68
C. Job concerns	2.49
2. Pleasure and Sensation-seeking (As a category)	3.05
A. Relaxation	3.00
B. Food	2.78
C. Exercise	2.72
D. Sex	2.64
F. Mood-altering drugs	1.75
3. Control and Power (As a category)	2.82
A. Competitive	2.65
B. Critical and judgmental	2.49
C. Family conflicts	2.22
D. Aggressive	2.14
E. Thoughts of becoming an administrator at work	2.07
F. Thoughts of running for political office	1.53
4. Love and Acceptance (As a category)	3.16
A. Compassion	3.00
B. Self-acceptance	2.96
C. Sense of belonging	2.93
D. Intimacy	2.82
5. Personal Growth and Self-Actualization (As a category)	3.09
A. Honest, truthful, moral, and clear sense of right and wrong values	3.45
B. Enjoys life, playful, and sense of humor	3.38

C. Alive and spontaneous	3.17
D. Comfortable with shades of Gray vs. Black and White thinking	3.14
E. Here and now focus	3.00
F. Balanced lifestyle between work, family, play, and personal and professional growth activities	2.98
G. Counseling and personal growth activities and groups	2.17

6. Spiritual and Transcendental (As a category)	2.85
A. Have meaning to life	3.27
B. Appreciate nature, beauty, and kindness	3.21
C. Love and compassion	3.05
D. Centered and in touch with subtler energies within and around you	2.98
E. Unity with God	2.96
F. Peace and inner calm	2.88

RANKED CATEGORIES OF MOTIVATIONAL STATES

The norming group of 105 adults who responded to the section on motivational states in the study of cognitions indicated that most of their Buttons are associated with the "Love and Acceptance" motivational state followed by the "Personal Growth and Self-Actualization," "Pleasure and Sensation-seeking," "Safety and Security," "Spiritual and Transcendental," and "Control and Power."

Rank	Mean Score
1. Love and Acceptance	3.16
2. Personal Growth and Self-Actualization	3.09
3. Pleasure and Sensation-seeking	3.05
4. Safety and Security	2.87
5. Spiritual and Transcendental	2.85
6. Control and Power	2.82

RANKED CENTERS OF CONSCIOUSNESS

The Centers of Consciousness Rating Scale (CCRS) from *The Motivational States Inventory* (*MSI*) was administered along with the *Cognitive Self-Assessment Inventory* in this study. Eighty-nine adults (N=89) responded to this section of the study and rank-ordered how much time they are spending in the six "motivational states" or "centers of consciousness" on the CCRS. A rank order of 1 indicates that this sample of subjects as a whole are spending most of their time in the "Control and Power" motivational state or "center of consciousness" followed by the "Spiritual and Transcendental," etc.

RANK

1. **Control and Power:** Spending time judging, criticizing, or trying to control other people in your life.
2. **Spiritual and Transcendental:** Spending time experiencing love, compassion, transcendental states, and a sense of connectedness and unity with God and all living things. Spending time on spiritual development.
3. **Pleasure and Sensation-seeking:** Spending time seeking or concerned with sex, food, mood altering drugs, music, and exercise.
4. **Safety and Security:** Spending time seeking or being concerned with such things as job, relationships, and money.
5. **Love and Acceptance:** Spending time seeking or concerned with gaining and/or giving acceptance, love, and compassion.
6. **Personal Growth and Self-Actualization:** Spending time enjoying or concerned with life, feeling alive, acting spontaneously and seeking personal growth and self-actualization.

STUDY OF COGNITIONS, BUTTONS, AND MOTIVATIONAL STATES UTILIZING THE COGNITIVE SELF-ASSESSMENT INVENTORY AND MOTIVATIONAL STATES INVENTORY

Lloyd R. Goodwin Jr., Ph.D.

East Carolina University

In 1998 through 1999 Dr. Lloyd R. Goodwin Jr. conducted a study of cognitions, Buttons, and motivational states utilizing the *Cognitive Self-Assessment Inventory* (*CSAI*) and the *Motivational States Inventory* (*MSI*) in Greenville, North Carolina.

METHOD

INSTRUMENTS

The *Cognitive Self-Assessment Inventory* (*CSAI*) and *The Motivational States Inventory* (*MSI*), including the "Centers of Consciousness" Rating Scale (CCRS), were developed and pretested on a sample of 10 college students and faculty in the Department of Rehabilitation Studies at East Carolina University. Both instruments were revised as a result of the feedback from the pretest group. For this study the *CSAI* was combined with the *MSI* on the first 106 subjects of the total sample of 293 subjects. The *CSAI* is designed to assess cognitions, potential troublesome cognitions, and Buttons. The *MSI* was developed to assess six motivational states. The CCRS part of the *MSI* provides a listing of six "centers of consciousness" (also referred to as "motivational states"). Subjects were asked to rank how much time they are spending in each "center of consciousness" or "motivational states." See Appendix A for the *CSAI* and Appendix B for the *MSI*, which includes the CCRS.

SUBJECTS

The *CSAI* and *MSI* were given primarily to students taking classes in the Department of Rehabilitation Studies, School of Allied Health Sciences, East Carolina University (ECU) in Greenville, NC. Some of these students were undergraduate majors in rehabilitation services and graduate students in rehabilitation counseling. However most of the subjects in this study were undergraduate students taking an undergraduate course titled "Introduction to Alcohol and Drug Abuse" offered within the department of Rehabilitation Studies. Most of these students taking this course were from all over campus and majoring in a variety of areas from business to nursing. Many of these students had not yet declared a major. A few other subjects completed the *CSAI* and *MSI* whom were medical students in the Medical School at ECU, practicing mental health professionals, or other adults willing to complete the inventory. There were 293 useable inventories returned. The following is a summary profile of the 293 subjects. Not all subjects completed all items so the responses do not always total 293.

RESULTS

Age: Ages ranged from 19 years old to 63 years old. Modal age was 20 years old. The number not responding to this item was 144.

Gender: Males = 81 Females = 211 Not Responding = 1

Highest Educational Degree Attained: High School = 161, Community College = 5 Bachelor's Degree = 73, Master's Degree = 21, Ph.D. or Ed.D. = 20, M.D. = 2, Not Responding = 12

Currently in School: Yes = 237 No = 56 Not Responding = 0

Current Grade Level: University Freshman = 3, Sophomore = 49, Junior = 65, Senior = 44, Graduate Student = 58, Non-degree Graduate Student = 1, Not Responding = 73

Currently Employed: Yes = 187 No = 93 Not Responding = 13. All employed subjects were working in the human services field.

Marital/Significant Other Status: Single = 189, Married = 72, Separated = 2, Cohabiting = 12, Other = 11, Not Responding = 7

Living Arrangements: With Family (this includes with parents and/or with spouse and children) = 89, Alone = 51, Roommate = 108, Dormitory = 24, Not Responding = 22

Number Who Have Children: Yes = 66 No = 216 Not Responding = 11

Have Been Hospitalized for Psychological or Drug Problems:
Yes = 14 No = 273 Not Responding = 6

Have Received Professional Counseling or Psychotherapy Services:
Yes = 99   No = 194   Not Responding = 0
Family Members With Psychological or Drug Problems:
Yes = 111   No = 165   Not Responding = 17
Had a Drug Problem: Yes = 39   No = 247   Not Responding = 7
Have a Physical or Mental Disability or Disorder: Yes = 32   No = 255   Not Responding = 6
Attempted Suicide: Yes = 11   No = 279   Not Responding = 3
Follow any Spiritual or Religious Path: Yes = 182   No = 28   Agnostic = 2
Not Responding =81

FIVE MAIN FEARS

Subjects were asked to list their five main fears. Two hundred and seventy-six of the 293 subjects listed fears. Seventeen subjects did not list any fears. Also, some of the 276 subjects responding to this question listed fewer than five fears. The subjects' fears fell into the following categories. The fears are rank-ordered with the most frequently reported fear listed first. Each fear is followed by the percentage of respondents reporting that item as a fear. Those fears only listed by one person are included in the last category:

Rank Fear	Percent Responding
1. **Failure** to achieve goals or not being successful in life (e.g. completing college/ achieving tenure/ passing licensure exam/ spiritual quest)	49
2. **Death of loved one** (e.g. family member/ child/ parent)	46
3. **Death and Dying** (includes having a terminal illness/dying before I achieve my life goals/a slow agonizing death/dying alone)	33
4. **Physical illness and diseases** (e.g. unhealthy/cancer/ burns/AIDS=5)	25
5. **Being alone** (e.g. loneliness/ not finding a partner/ not belonging/ and includes growing old alone=2)	20
6. **Financial problems and being poor** (includes being poor when old=2)	18
7. **Uncertainty of future** (e.g. career choice/ getting a job/ boring job/unknown)	13
8. **Becoming disabled** (e.g. head injury/ dementia/alzheimer's)	11
9. **Relationship problems** (e.g. people not liking me/betrayed by a loved one)	10
10. **Lack of intimacy** (e.g. not being loved/not getting married)	8
11. **Snakes**	7
12. **Poor health and mental health of loved one (e.g. injury to loved one)**	6
12. **Spiders**	6
12. **Heights**	6

15. Growing old   5

15. State of world affairs (e.g. crime victim/ violence)   5

15. Unhappiness   5

18. Accidents (e.g. car)   4

18. Drowning   4

18. Let my family or other people down   4

18. Loss of job   4

18. Physical or emotional dependence on others   4

18. Public speaking   4

18. Getting fat   4

25. Being emotionally or physically hurt (e.g. being shamed)   3

25. Closed in spaces   3

25. Family (e.g. family members/not being close with family/
    having my child taken from me/ welfare of family members)   3

25. Going to hell   3

25. Not having a baby/family   3

30. Being Raped   2

30. Flying   2

30. Success (includes receiving too much attention)   2

30. Abandonment   2

30. Competency as a professional after graduation (e.g. counselor/ physician)   2

30. God and God's rejection   2

30. Marriage (e.g. having a bad marriage)   2

30. Personal or professional embarrassment   2

30. Poor mental health   2

30. Pain   2

40. Discrimination and racism   1

40. Catastrophic natural disasters   1

40. Competence as a parent   1

40. Losing control   1

40. Offending or hurting someone   1

40. Not finding and marrying the one I truly love   1

40. Not fulfilling my dreams   1

40. The dark   1

40. Becoming a selfish person   1

40. Inadequacy (e.g. not being good enough)   1

40. Not experiencing the world and life   1

40. Pregnancy   1

40. Relapse to drug abuse

41. **All of the following had less than 1percent response each**: adulthood (e.g. growing up)/ alcohol and other drug addiction/ animals (other than domestic pets)/ becoming a workaholic/ becoming conservative/ becoming bitter/ becoming noncompetitive/ being assertive around

authority figures/ being unattractive/ big bodies of water/ being a poor loser/ being snuck up on and scared/ being late/ believing others/ being physically restrained/ big trucks/ choosing the wrong major/ commitment/ birds/ cease growing/ childbirth labor/ clowns/ cops/ conformity/ corporate power and selfishness/ crowded spaces/ crazy people/ country music/ destruction of world by politics/ dishonest people/ dog attack/ drinking after someone/ driving alone late at night/ end of world/ ending up like my mother/ environmental pollution and destruction/ evil people/ ex-girlfriend/ falsely accused of fathering a child/ feeling that my ideas are less important than others/ fire/ getting a ticket or arrested/ getting lost while traveling/ getting shot/ ghosts/ guns/ how I am perceived by others/ going to prison/ having a child before I'm stable or ready/ having regrets/ homelessness/ hospitals and doctors/ inability to impact events/ lack of sense of community and polarization/ legal problems/ lightning/ losing contact with friends/ living a passive life/ losing faith/ loss of self-esteem/ love/ making others unhappy/ making wrong decisions/ mankind/ men that I don't know/ mice/ mother-in-law or mother moving in for awhile/ needles/ never getting over losing a past boyfriend/ New York on New Years eve 2000/ not being seen as a good person or appreciated after death/ not doing what's best for me/ loss of property/ not going to heaven/ panic attacks/ patriotic people/ politicians and government/ postal workers/ religious people/ relying on prescription drugs forever/ responsibility/ return of anything resembling Nazism (e.g. loss of freedom)/ roller coasters/ security (e.g. loss of home/someone breaking in my home) / sharks/ stock market crash/ stress/ suffocating/ telling a lie/ tests/ that I might forget my place in this world/ unconsciously not following God's will for my life/ wars/ work/ you might find out how afraid I am/ losing irreplaceable photos and momentos/

THOUGHTS

The following are the percent of subjects in the norming group responding to each item (not all subjects answered all items):

Item	Percent	Item	Percent	Item	Percent	Item	Percent
Intelligent	98	or Stupid	1	Attractive	88	or Ugly	4
Responsible	98	or Irresponsible	2	Honest	97	or Dishonest	0
Competent	96	or Inadequate	1	Happy	94	or Suicidal	2
Dependable	96	or Undependable	2	Sense of humor	94	or Seldom laugh	3
Moral	94	or Moral degenerate	2	Naive	48	or Jaded	34

Item	Percent	Item	Percent	Item	Percent	Item	Percent
Conservative	66	or High risk-taker	26	Go-getter	74	or Lazy	18
Calm	45	or Stressed	52	Spiritual	89	or Agnostic/atheist	5
Rational	78	or Impulsive	21	Loving	92	or Angry	4
Giving	88	or Self-centered	9	Positive	93	or Evil	2

COGNITIONS

Here is how 293 adults in the norming group responded on a 5-point scale to the 137 cognitions on the *CSAI*. See the *CSAI* for the items. Following each item number is the percentage of the sample that either "agreed" or "strongly agreed" with the item.

STYLES OF THINKING

1. 44	2. 43	3. 47	4. 17	5. 40	6. 9	7. 76	8. 41
9. 2	10. 11	11. 18	12. 27	13. 60	14. 45	15. 50	16. 12
17. 42	18. 39	19. 50	20. 41	21. 31	22. 42		

TOP TEN STYLES OF THINKING

Rank	Percent Agreeing or Strongly Agreeing
1. Everything happens for a reason **(Fair & Just Thinking)**.	77
2. I know what someone (e.g. spouse, boy/girlfriend) is communicating to me without them verbalizing it **(Mind Reading)**.	60

Rank

**Percent Agreeing or
Strongly Agreeing**

3. I tend to get very concerned and anxious worrying
about what may happen in the future (**Futuring**).   50

3. My spouse or good friends know the way I like things
to be done without me having to tell them (**Mind Reading**).   50

5. I compare myself to other people, especially in terms of
appearance, money, intellect, or possessions (**Comparing**).   47

6. I know what people "really mean," even if they verbalize
something else in their communication (**Mind Reading**).   45

7. There is a right way and a wrong way of doing things
(**Black & White Thinking**).   44

7. Other people (e.g. spouse, boss) make me angry, sad, or happy
(**Blaming**).   44

9. I want people to admit it when they are wrong and I am right
(**I'm "right" and you're "wrong" thinking**).   43

10. I spend a lot of time thinking about things I should have
said or done in the past (**Pasting**).   42

SHOULD MESSAGES

Item %	Item %	Item %	Item %	Item %	Item %	Item %	Item %
23. 63	24. 39	25. 72	26. 55	27. 51	28. 34	29. 76	30. 14
31. 20	32. 4	33. 4	34. 67	35. 59	36. 7	37. 3	38. 10
39. 11	40. 88	41. 48	42. 43				

TOP 10 SHOULD MESSAGES

Rank		Percent Agreeing or Stongly Agreeing
1.	I should live life to its fullest.	89
2.	I should love, or at least like, both of my parents.	77
3.	I should make other people feel better when they are upset.	73
4.	I should be independent and self-sufficient and not have to rely on other people.	68
5.	I should please my parents.	64
6.	I should keep control of my feelings.	60
7.	I should remain centered, balanced, harmonious, and focused on my personal and spiritual growth at all times.	56
8.	Everyone should like and accept me because I'm basically a good and decent person.	52
9.	I should like all of my children equally.	51
10.	I should take more risks with men/women, career, and life in general.	49

CORE BELIEFS

BELIEFS ABOUT SELF

Item	%	Item	%	Item	%	Item	%	Item	%	Item	%	Item	%	Item	%
43.	1	44.	11	45.	6	46.	2	47.	1	48.	4	49.	6	50.	3
51.	9	52.	5	53.	6	54.	5	55.	3	56.	1	57.	1	58.	1
59.	5	60.	9												

TOP 10 CORE BELIEFS ABOUT SELF

Rank	Percent Agreeing or Stongly Agreeing
1. If I don't pay any attention to my problems they will go away.	14
2. I am a victim of life's circumstances.	11
3. If I allow myself to feel really excited or good about someone or something it will be followed by something equally terrible.	10
4. Most people are doing better than I am.	9
5. Other people currently control my life.	7
6. I'm not sexy.	6
6. I am not as intelligent or as competent as most of my friends.	6
8. I must please and agree with people to be accepted.	5
8. Most people are better off than I am.	5
8. If people really knew me they wouldn't like me.	5

BELIEFS ABOUT RELATIONSHIPS

Item	%	Item	%	Item	%					
61.	24	62.	32	63.	18					

TOP 3 CORE BELIEFS ABOUT RELATIONSHIPS

1. I'm waiting for Mr. or Miss Right to come along.	33
2. I resent my spouse (boy/girlfriend) for some things he or she has done to hurt me.	25
3. Divorce is a sign of failure or a sin.	19

BELIEFS ABOUT LIFE

Item	%	Item	%	Item	%	Item	%	Item	%							
64.	11	65.	10	66.	4	67.	7	68.	51							

TOP 5 CORE BELIEFS ABOUT LIFE

1. There are no coincidences in life – everything happens for a reason.   52

2. The world is basically a fearful and unsafe place.   11

3. Most people are only out for themselves and will cheat or betray you sooner or later, usually sooner.   10

4. The bottom line in life is accumulating money, nice things and power.   7

5. I'm entitled to be taken care of – I didn't ask to be brought into this world with all its problems.   4

BELIEFS ABOUT ILLNESS AND DISABILITY

69.	1	70.	3	71.	20	72.	15	68.	51							

THE TOP 4 CORE BELIEFS ABOUT ILLNESS AND DISABILITY

1. If people have enough faith in God and His healing powers He will cure them of their disabilities.   20

2. If people have enough faith in God or a higher spiritual power they can heal themselves from any illness.   16

3. People have illness or disability because it is part of their Karma (past deeds in either this life or a past life).   3

4. People have illness or disability because God is punishing them.   1

BELIEFS ABOUT ALCOHOL AND OTHER DRUGS

Item	%	Item	%	Item	%	Item	%	Item	%	Item	%	Item	%	Item	%
73.	21	74.	17	75.	28	76.	10	77.	79	78.	11	79.	9	80.	7
81.	22	82.	1	83.	13	84.	1	85.	4	86.	2	87.	2	88.	12
89.	29	90.	11	91.	43										

TOP 10 CORE BELIEFS
ABOUT ALCOHOL AND OTHER DRUGS

Rank

**Percent Agreeing or
Stongly Agreeing**

1. I don't have any major problems with my alcohol and drug use.   82

2. Problem drinkers and other drug abusers can learn to drink/drug   43
   responsibly.

3. I have no desire to give up alcohol and other drugs (leave blank   35
   if appropriate.

4. People who have the disease of alcoholism or drug addiction   34
   will have it the rest of their lives.

5. People have a fundamental human right to self-medicate with any drug.   30

6. Alcoholics Anonymous and related 12 step mutual-help groups   29
   are the best approaches to help substance abusers.

7. There is nothing wrong with psychoactive drugs.   22

8. All drugs should be legalized.   18

9. I shouldn't have to feel any unpleasant feelings or pain.   13

10. Only someone who has experienced alcohol or another   12
    drug addiction can help another alcoholic or drug addict.

PERSONALITY TRAITS AND STYLES

Item %	Item %	Item %	Item %	Item %	Item %	Item %	Item %
92. 33	93. 77	94. 59	95. 27	96. 9	97. 9	98. 42	99. 11
100. 25	101. 13	102. 60	103. 16	104. 51	105. 41	106. 9	107. 7
108. 33	109. 28	110. 34	111. 19	112. 16	113. 55	114. 51	115. 17
116. 2	117. 9						

TOP 10 PERSONALITY TRAITS

Rank	Percent Agreeing or Stongly Agreeing
1. I like competition and challenges.	78
2. I am devoted to my spouse (girl/boyfriend).	62
3. I get bored quickly with the same old thing.	59
4. I like to serve others and make sure their needs are met.	56
5. I am more competent and capable than the average person.	52
5. I am a natural leader. I feel comfortable taking charge and assuming responsibility and authority.	52
7. I am very sensitive to negative feedback.	43
8. I am very orderly, perfectionistic, and punctual.	42
9. I am very interested in mysticism, paranormal phenomenon, metaphysics, dreams, and "new age" topics.	35
10. I enjoy taking risks, thrill-seeking behavior, and living on the edge.	33
10. I am even-tempered and am seldom extremely sad or happy.	33

DEFENSE MECHANISMS

Item	%	Item	%	Item	%	Item	%	Item	%	Item	%	Item	%	Item	%
118.	35	119.	18	120.	34	121.	10	122.	11	123.	19	124.	68	125.	7
126.	11	127.	16	128.	9	129.	11	130.	20	131.	6	132.	10	133.	8
134.	9	135.	16	136.	17	137.	16								

RANK-ORDERED DEFENSE MECHANISMS

The most frequently used defense mechanisms by the norming group in the study of cognitions described in Appendix C are rank-ordered based on the mean scores of each defense mechanism. The percent indicating their use of a defense mechanism "frequently" or "very frequently" is also provided. The norming group as a total sample tend to rely on "humor" the most frequently followed by "altruism," etc.

Rank		Mean Score	Percent	Rank		Mean Score	Percent
1.	Humor	3.83	70	11.	Displacement	2.21	11
2.	Altruism	2.92	35	12.	Isolation of Affect	2.19	9
3.	Compensation	2.81	34	13.	Withdrawal	2.18	16
4.	Rationalization	2.46	21	14.	Identification	2.11	11
5.	Intellectualization	2.41	16	15.	Reaction Formation	2.07	6
6.	Fantasy	2.38	20	16.	Denial	2.03	10
7.	Attack	2.31	18	17.	Repression	1.99	8
8.	Substitution	2.28	16	18.	Projection	1.97	11
9.	Suppression	2.23	18	19.	Regression	1.92	11
10.	Idealization	2.22	8	20.	Sublimation	1.79	9

POTENTIAL TROUBLESOME COGNITIONS

Those items (i.e. cognitions) that you responded to with an "Agree" response indicate potential "troublesome cognitions." Go back over these items and determine if these cognitions are creating problems in your life.

The average (i.e. mean) number of "agree" responses from the norming sample of 293 adults:

CSAI: 22   My score: _____

POTENTIAL BUTTONS

Those items (i.e. cognitions) that you responded to with a "Strongly Agree" response indicate a potential Button. Go back over these items and determine if you have an attachment, demand, or need for these cognitions that may be creating problems in your life.

The average (i.e. mean) number of "Strongly Agree" responses from the norming sample of 293 adults:

CSAI: 8   My score: _____

"STRONGLY DISAGREE" RESPONSES (POTENTIAL BUTTONS)

We can be just as "attached" (i.e. have a Button) to being against something as we are for something! Go back over the cognitions you strongly disagree with to determine if you may be protesting too much or overreacting to something that may be true.

The average (i.e. mean) number of "Strongly Disagree" responses from the norming sample of 293 adults:

CSAI: 28   My score: _____

TOP 10 BUTTONS

The rank-ordered top ten combined "agree" and "strongly agree" cognitions from the first 117 items on the *Cognitive Self-Assessment Inventory (CSAI)*. These are the potential top 10 Buttons (i.e. attachments) from the sample of 293 adults in the norming group for the *CSAI*.

Rank	Percent Agreeing or Stongly Agreeing
1. I should live life to its fullest.	89
2. I don't have any major problems with my alcohol and drug use.	82
3. I like competition and challenges.	78
4. I should love, or at least like both of my parents.	77
4. Everything happens for a reason.	77
6. I should make other people feel better when they are upset.	73
7. I should be independent and self-sufficient and not have to rely on other people.	68
8. I should please my parents.	64
9. I am devoted to my spouse.	62
10. I know what someone (e.g. spouse, boy/friend) is communicating to me without them verbalizing it.	60
10. I should keep control of my feelings.	60

TOP 10 DEFENSE MECHANISMS

The most "frequently" and "very frequently" used defense mechanisms by the norming group in this study.

Rank	Percentage who use "frequently" or "very frequently"
1. Humor	70
2. Altruism	35
3. Compensation	34
4. Rationalization	21
5. Fantasy	20
6. Attack	18
6. Suppression	18
8. Intellectualization	16
8. Substitution	16
10. Withdrawal	16

MOTIVATIONAL STATES

The " *Motivational States Inventory*" (*MSI*), including the Centers of Consciousness Rating Scale (CCRS), was administered along with the *Cognitive Self-Assessment Inventory* (*CSAI*) in this study. A number of subjects in the first group of in the total sample of 293 adults were not clear about what was meant by "motivational states" and "centers of consciousness." The norming group for the *MSI* is composed of the first 106 of the 293 total subjects to complete the *MSI* in the norming group. See Appendix B for the *MSI*.

Subjects were asked to indicate which motivational states their current Buttons were associated with. After a brief definition of Buttons, motivational states, and centers of consciousness the directions to the subjects in this study were: "In the past few weeks, whenever you became emotionally upset from having your Buttons pushed - from which of the following 'motivational states' did your Buttons tend to be related?" The subjects were asked to rate each item from one to five:

1 =Not at all   2 = Sometimes   3 = Don't Know   4 = Frequently   5 = Very frequently

The following is how the norming group of 106 subjects answered the *MSI*:

	Mean Score
1. Safety and Security (As a category of "motivational states")	2.87
A. Money concerns (e.g. bills, debt)	3.07
B. Relationship concerns	2.68
C. Job concerns	2.49
2. Pleasure and Sensation-seeking (As a category)	3.05
A. Relaxation	3.00
B. Food	2.78
C. Exercise	2.72
D. Sex	2.64
F. Mood-altering drugs	1.75
3. Control and Power (As a category)	2.82
A. Competitive	2.65
B. Critical and judgmental	2.49
C. Family conflicts	2.22
D. Aggressive	2.14
E. Thoughts of becoming an administrator at work	2.07
F. Thoughts of running for political office	1.53
4. Love and Acceptance (As a category)	3.16
A. Compassion	3.00
B. Self-acceptance	2.96
C. Sense of belonging	2.93
D. Intimacy	2.82
5. Personal Growth and Self-Actualization (As a category)	3.09
A. Honest, truthful, moral, and clear sense of right and wrong values	3.45
B. Enjoys life, playful, and sense of humor	3.38
C. Alive and spontaneous	3.17
D. Comfortable with shades of Gray vs. Black and White thinking	3.14
E. Here and now focus	3.00
F. Balanced lifestyle between work, family, play, and personal and professional growth activities	2.98
G. Counseling and personal growth activities and groups	2.17
6. Spiritual and Transcendental (As a category)	2.85
A. Have meaning to life	3.27

B. Appreciate nature, beauty, and kindness	3.21
C. Love and compassion	3.05
D. Centered and in touch with subtler energies within and around you	2.98
E. Unity with God	2.96
F. Peace and inner calm	2.88

BUTTONS ASSOCIATED
WITH MOTIVATIONAL STATES CATEGORIES

The 106 subjects who were a subset of the total 293 subjects in this study indicated on the *Motivational States Inventory (MSI)* that most of their Buttons are associated with the "Love and Acceptance" motivational state followed by the "Pleasure and Sensation-seeking," "Personal Growth and Self-Actualization," "Safety and Security," "Spiritual and Transcendental," and "Control and Power."

Rank	Percent indicating "frequently or "very frequently"
1. Love and Acceptance	45
2. Pleasure and Sensation-seeking	41
3. Personal Growth and Self-Actualization	38
4. Safety and Security	32
5. Spiritual and Transcendental	30
6. Control and Power	29

TOP 10 BUTTONS
WITHIN THE SIX MOTIVATIONAL STATES

How 106 adults, most (82 percent) of whom were college students, rated some of their Buttons within each of the six motivational states on the *Motivational States Inventory (MSI)*. See Appendix B for the *MSI* and Appendix C for a more detailed description of the study. After a brief definition of Buttons, the directions to the subjects in this study were: "In the past few weeks, whenever you became emotionally upset from having your Buttons pushed -

from which of the following 'motivational states' [and items within each motivational state] did your Buttons tend to be related?" The subjects were asked to rate each item from one to five:

1 =Not at all 2 = Sometimes 3 = Don't Know   4 = Frequently 5 = Very frequently

Rank   **Percent Indicating "Frequently"**
                                                                      or "Very Frequently"

1. Honest, truthful, moral, and clear sense of right and wrong values.   64
   (Personal Growth and Self-Actualization Motivational State)

2. Enjoys life, playful, and sense of humor.   63
   (Personal Growth and Self-Actualization Motivational State)

3. Having meaning to life.   56
   (Spiritual and Self-Transcendental Motivational State)

4. Appreciate nature, beauty, and kindness.   55
   (Spiritual and Self-Transcendental Motivational State)

5. Money concerns.   53
   (Safety and Security Motivational State)

6. Alive and spontaneous.   52
   (Personal Growth and Self-Actualization Motivational State)

7. Comfortable with shades of gray vs. black and white thinking.   48
   (Personal Growth and Self-Actualization Motivational State)

7. Love and compassion.   48
   (Spiritual and Self-Transcendental Motivational State)

9. Relaxation.   46
   (Pleasure and Sensation-Seeking Motivational State)

9. Compassion.   46
   (Love and Acceptance Motivational State)

CENTERS OF CONSCIOUSNESS

The Centers of Consciousness Rating Scale (CCRS) from *The Motivational States Inventory (MSI)* was completed by 89 of the 293 subjects in this study. A rank order of 1 indicates that the subjects completing this section of the *MSI* are spending most of their time in the "Control and Power" motivational state or "center of consciousness" followed by the "Spiritual and Transcendental," etc.

RANK

1. **Control and Power:** Spending time judging, criticizing, or trying to control other people in your life.
2. **Spiritual and Transcendental:** Spending time experiencing love, compassion, transcendental states, and a sense of connectedness and unity with God and all living things. Spending time on spiritual development.
3. **Pleasure and Sensation-seeking:** Spending time seeking or concerned with sex, food, mood altering drugs, music, and exercise.
4. **Safety and Security:** Spending time seeking or being concerned with such things as job, relationships, and money.
5. **Love and Acceptance:** Spending time seeking or concerned with gaining and/or giving acceptance, love, and compassion.
6. **Personal Growth and Self-Actualization:** Spending time enjoying or concerned with life, feeling alive, acting spontaneously and seeking personal growth and self-actualization.

DISCUSSION

The primary purpose of this study of cognitions, troublesome cognitions (TCs), and Buttons was to develop normative scores for the *Cognitive Self-Assessment Inventory (CSAI)* and *Motivational States Inventory (MSI)*. Thus mental health professionals and people who take the *CSAI* and *MSI* can compare their scores with a normative group of 293 adults. The CSAI is a tool to assess cognitions. Utilizing the CSAI a person's cognitions can be mapped out into the categories of general self-descriptors; fears; styles of thinking; should messages; core beliefs about self, relationships, life, illness and disability, and psychoactive drug use; personality traits; and defense mechanisms. The *MSI* is a tool to help people become aware of the motivational states that are associated with their troublesome cognitions and Buttons. The Centers of Consciousness Scale part of the *MSI* helps people become aware of those motivational states or "centers of consciousness" they are currently spending the most time in. The MSI was not given to all the subjects in this study. Some of the subjects in the first group of subjects to complete the *CSAI* and *MSI* were confused about the questions on the *MSI*. In addition the CSAI and the MSI taken together took approximately 60 minutes. Thus future subjects were only given the *CSAI* and the *MSI* was no longer given to subjects. Information from the first 106 subjects to complete the *MSI* are included for norming purposes.

The primary caution in interpreting the results of this study is that the majority of adults included as the normative group for the *CSAI* and *MSI* in this study were primarily undergraduate and graduate college students. Seventy-five percent of the adults in the normative group for the *CSAI* were college students. Eighty-two percent of the adults in the normative group for the *MSI* were college students. Thus both normative groups are not representative of the total adult population in the United States. However, since the subjects included undergraduate and graduate students from a public university in a wide cross section of majors, from business to the human services; racial and ethnic groups; educational levels, from freshmen to Ph.D.'s; and age ranges from 19 to 63 year olds the normative groups do provide a broad cross-section of adults in our society. The normative group can provide a comparison base for many similar adults taking the *CSAI* and *MSI*.

A possible area of future studies can be to develop normative data for the *CSAI* and *MSI* on more representative samples of adults as well as other groups such as adolescents, various cultural groups, individuals with disabilities, and psychoactive substance abusers.

REFERENCES

Administrative Office of the U.S. Courts. (1967). **Federal offenders in the United States District Courts.** Washington, D.C.: Government Printing Office.

Allen, J. (1968). **As a man thinketh.** Kansas City, MO: Hallmark Cards.

Alternative medicine: Expanding medical horizons. A report to the National Institutes of Health on alternative medical systems and practices in the United States. (1994). (#017-040-00537-7). Washington, D.C.: U.S. Government Printing Office.

Alternative Medicine. (July, 1999). Politics of medicine: The struggle for freedom of medical choice. Author. 86-88.

Alternative Therapies. (1997). 58 % of HMOs to offer alternative therapy coverage, survey shows. Author, 3 (3), 29-30.

Alternative Therapies. (1998). Popularity of alternative medicine still growing in US, Canada, polls find. Author. 4 (2), 29.

American Psychiatric Association. (1987). **Diagnostic and statistical manual of mental disorders** (3rd ed.-Revised). Washington, DC: Author.

American Psychiatric Association. (1994). **Diagnostic and statistical manual of mental disorders** (4th ed.). Washington, DC: Author.

Arnkoff, D.B. & Glass, C.R. (1992). Cognitive therapy and psychotherapy integration. In D.K. Freedheim (Ed.), **History of psychotherapy: A century of change** (pp.657-694). Washington, D.C.: American Psychological Association.

Aron, E. & Aron, A. (1986). **The Maharishi effect: A revolution through meditation.** Walpole, NH: Stillpoint Publishing.

The Associated Press, (Sept. 5, 1998a). Lawmaker says he fathered child in extra-marital affair. **Daily Reflector,** A2.

The Associated Press, (September 28, 1998b). Clinton: 'Wallowing in regret is a cop out'. **Daily Reflector,** A2.

Barrett, J. (July, 1999). Going the distance. **Intuition,** 26-31, 53-57.

Bart, M. (December, 1998). Spirituality in counseling finding believers. **Counseling Today,** 1,6.

Beck, A.T. (1967). **Depression: Clinical, experimental and theoretical aspects.** NY: Harper & Row.

Beck, A.T. (1979). **Cognitive therapy and emotional disorders.** NY: New American Library.

Beck, A.T., Wright, F.D., Newman, C.F. & Liese, B.S. (1993). **Cognitive therapy of substance abuse.** NY: The Guilford Press.

Beck, J.S. (1995). **Cognitive therapy: Basics and beyond**. NY: Guilford.

Benedetto, R. (September 29, 1998a). Primary turnout at new low. **USA Today,** 5A.

Benor, D.J. (1990). Survey of spiritual healing research. **Complementary Medical Research, 4,** 9-33.

Benor, D.J. (1992). **Healing Research. Vol. 1.** Munich, Germany: Helix Verlag.

Benson, H. & Stark, M. (1996). **Timeless healing: The power and biology of belief.** NY: Scribner.

Berne, E. (1964). **Games people play: The psychology of human relationships.** NY: Grove Press.

Borg, M. (Ed.). (1997). **Jesus and Buddha: The parallel sayings.** Berkeley, CA: Ulysses Press.

Bradshaw, J. (1990). **Homecoming: Reclaiming and championing your inner child.** NY: Bantam.

Bradshaw, J. (1990a). Liberating your lost inner child. In J. Abrams (Ed.) **Reclaiming the inner child.** Los Angeles, CA: Jeremy P. Tarcher, Inc. pp. 224-233.

Brennan, B.A. (1988). **Hands of light: A guide to healing through the human energy field.** NY: Bantam Books.

Bucke, R. M. (1969). **Cosmic Consciousness: A study in the evolution of the human mind.** NY: E.P. Dutton & Co.

Buckley, W.F., Jr. (February 12, 1996). The war on drugs is lost. **National Review,** 34-48.

Burns, D. (1989). **The feeling good handbook.** NY: Plume

Byrd, R.C. (1988). Positive therapeutic effects of intercessory prayer in a coronary care unit population. **Southern Medical Journal, 81** (7), 826-829.

Campbell, E. & Brennan, J.H. (1994). **Body Mind & Spirit: A dictionary of new age ideas, people, places, and terms**. Rutland, VT: Charles E. Tuttle Co.

Capacchione, L. (1991). **Recovery of your inner child.** NY: Simon & Schuster.

Carey, A.R. & Visgaitis, G. (April 20, 1998). Belief in the Beyond. **USA Today,** 1A.

Carus, P. (1972). **The gospel of Buddha: According to old records.** Tucson, AZ: Omen Communications.

Charlesworth, E.A. & Nathan, R.G. (1984). **Stress management: A comprehensive guide to wellness**. NY: Ballentine Books.

Chopra, D. (January,1998a). Mastering your life: Ten essential keys. **Infinite Possibilities for Body, Mind & Soul,** 2 (4), 1,8.

Chopra, D. (January, 1998b). From Deepak. **Infinite Possibilities for Body, Mind & Soul, 2**(4), 1-2.

Clark, R. (1971). **Crime in America**. NY: Pocket Book.

Collingwood, R.G. (1945). **The idea of nature.** London: Oxford University Press.

Cool, L.C. (November, 1997). Faith & Healing. **American Health,** 48-52.

Corey, G. & Corey, M.S. (1997). **I never knew I had a choice** (6th ed.). Pacific Grove, CA: Brooks/Cole Publishing Co.

Cormier, L.S. & Hackney, H. (1987). **The professional counselor: A process guide**

to helping. Englewood Cliffs, NJ: Prentice-Hall.

Cox News Service. (June 7, 1998). Poll shows parents think teaching their young children about God is important. **Daily Reflector,** E2.

Creedon, J. (July-August, 1998). God with a million faces. **Utne Reader,** 42-48.

De Ropp, R.S. (1968). **The master game.** NY: Delacorte Press.

Dobson, K.S. (1988). **Handbook of cognitive-behavioral therapies.** NY: Guilford.

Doskoch, P. (September/October, 1995). The safest sex. **Psychology Today,** 46-49.

Doskoch, P. (March/April, 1998). Food for thought. **Psychology Today,** p.5.

Dossey, L. (1992). **Meaning & medicine.** NY: Bantam.

Dossey, L. (1993). **Healing words: The power of prayer and the practice of medicine.** NY: HarperCollins.

Dossey, L. (1996). **Prayer is good medicine.** NY: HarperSanFrancisco.

Dossey, L. (1997). The return of prayer. **Alternative Therapies, 3** (6), 10-17, 113-120.

Dossey, L. (March/April, 1997). Can prayer harm? **Psychology Today,** 49-52, 75-76,79.

Dossey, L. (1999a). Do religion and spirituality matter in health? A response to the recent article in *The Lancet.* **Alternative Therapies, 5** (3), 16-18.

Dossey, L. (1999b). **Reinventing medicine: Beyond mind-body to a new era of healing.** NY: HarperSanFrancisco.

Dyer, W.W. (1976). **Your erroneous zones.** NY: Avon Books.

Dyer, W.W. (1979). **Pulling your own strings.** NY: Avon Books.

Dyer, W.W. (1981). **The sky's the limit.** NY: Pocket Books.

Ehmann, C. (July 14, 1999). **The age factor in religious attitudes and behavior.** The Princeton, NJ: Gallup Organization. www.gallup.com/poll/releases/pr990714b.asp.

Elias, M. (December, 9, 1997). Few would turn to clergy for help if they were dying. **USA Today,** 1A.

Ellis, A. (1975). **How to live with a neurotic.** (Rev. ed.). NY: Crown.

Ellis, A., McInerney, J.F., Digiuseppe, R. & Yeager, R.J. (1988). **Rational-emotive therapy with alcoholics and substance abusers.** NY: Pergamon Press.

Fox, V. (1985). **Introduction to Corrections.** (3rd ed.). Englewood Cliffs, NJ: Prentice Hall.

Freud, S. (1959). **Collected papers.** Volume 4. NY: Basic Books.

Friend, T. (February 18, 1993). Human genes can mutate to correct defects. **USA Today.**

Gallup, G., Jr. (March 29,2001). **Americans more religious now than ten years ago, but less so than in 1950s and 1960s.** Princeton: The Gallup Organization. www.gallup.com/poll/releases/pr010329.asp.

Gershon, M.D. (1999). **The second brain.** NY: HarperPerennial.

Gervarter, W.B. (1975). Humans: Their brain and their freedom. **Journal of Humanistic Psychology, 15** (4), 79-90.

Glass, L. (1995). **Toxic people: 10 ways of dealing with people who make your life miserable.** NY: Simon & Schuster.

Goble, F. (1971). **The third force.** NY: Pocket Books.

Goldman, C. (May/June, 1998). Molecules of emotion: A conversation with Candace Pert. **Intuition**, pp.21-25, 49-55.

Goleman, D. (1995). **Emotional intelligence**. NY: Bantam Books.

Goleman, D. (Ed.) (1997). **Healing emotions: Conversations with the Dalai Lama on mindfulness, emotions, and health**. Boston: Shambhala.

Goodwin, L.R., Jr. (1981). Psychological self-help: A five-step model. **Journal of Humanistic Psychology, 21**(1), 13-27.

Goodwin, L.R., Jr. (1986). A holistic perspective for the provision of rehabilitation counseling services. **Journal of Applied Rehabilitation Counseling, 17**(2), 29-36.

Goodwin, L.R., Jr. (1997a). **The rehabilitation counseling profession**. (booklet). Counseling Resources, 102 Breezewood Dr., Unit E, Greenville, NC 27858.

Goodwin, L.R., Jr. (1997b). **Rehabilitation counseling: A profession with a future**. (pamphlet). Counseling Resources, 102 Breezewood Dr., Unit E, Greenville, NC 27858.

Goodwin, L.R., Jr. (1999). **Licensed professional counselors** (pamphlet). Counseling Resources, 102 Breezewood Dr., Unit E, Greenville, NC 27858.

Goodwin, L.R., Jr. (2002). **The six-step button therapy method**. British Columbia, Canada: Trafford Publishing.

Goodwin, L.R., Jr. (2002), **Cognitive self-assessment inventory**. British Columbia, Canada: Trafford Publishing.

Goulding, M.M. & Goulding, R.L. (1979). **Changing lives through redecision therapy**. NY: Brunner/Mazel.

Grizzard, K. (March 8, 1998). Faith & medicine. **The Daily Reflector**. Greenville, NC. E1.

Hales, D. & Hales, R.E. (1995). **Caring for the mind: A comprehensive guide to mental health**. NY: Bantam Books.

Hall, C. & Jerding, G. (January 28, 1998). A nation of cynics? **USA Today**, 1A.

Hall, C. & Laird, B. (May 28,1999). Going to a higher authority. **USA Today**, 1A.

Hall, C. & Lynn, G. (April 10, 1998). In need of prayer. **USA Today**, 1A.

Halpern, J. (1977). Projection: A test of the psychoanalytic hypothesis. **Journal of Abnormal Psychology, 86,** 536-42.

Hoehn-Saric, R. (1978). Emotional arousal, attitude change, and psychotherapy. In J.D. Frank, R. Hoehn-Saric, S.D., Imber, B.L. Liberman & A.R. Stone. **Effective ingredients of successful psychotherapy** (pp.73-106). NY: Brunner/Mazel.

Holden, E.M. (1975). What happens to the brain and body during a Primal? In A. Janov & E.M. Holden. **Primal man: The new consciousness**. NY: Thomas Y. Crowell.

Hubbard, L.R. (1950). **Dianetics: The modern science of mental health**. Los Angeles, CA: The Church of Scientology of California Publications Organization.

Jackson, D. (February, 1996). Sex on the brain. **New Woman**, 46.

Jarvis, G.K. & Northcutt, H.C. (1987). Religious differences in morbidity and mortality. **Social Science Medicine, 25,** 813-824.

Johnson, J. (September, 1997). Americans' views on crime and law enforcement. **National Institute of Justice Journal**, 9-14.

Joseph, L. & Pompa, F. (May 29, 2001). Religion as a force. **USA Today**, 1A.

Judith, A. (1994). **The truth about chakras**. St. Paul, MN: Llewellyn Publications.

Jung, C.G. (1990). The psychology of the child archetype. In J. Abrams (Ed.) **Reclaiming the inner child**. Los Angeles, CA: Jeremy P. Tarcher, Inc., pp.24-30.

Kelly, G.A. (1955). **The psychology of personal constructs** (2 vols.). NY: Norton.

Keyes, K., Jr., (1972). **Handbook to higher consciousness**. Berkeley, CA: Living Love Center

Keyes, K., Jr., (1975). **Handbook to higher consciousness** (5th ed.). Coos Bay, OR: Love Line Books.

Keyes, K., Jr. (1995). **Your road map to lifelong happiness: A guide to the life you want**. Coos Bay, OR: Love Line Books.

King, D.E. & Bushwick, B. (1994). Beliefs and attitudes of hospital patients about faith healing and prayer. **Journal of Family Medicine, 39**, 349-352.

Koenig, H.G., Moberg, D.O. & Kvale, J.N. (1988). Religious activity and attitudes of older adults in a geriatric assessment clinic. **Journal of the American Geriatric Society, 36**(4), 362-374.

Krieger, D. (1993). **Accepting your power to heal: The personal practice of therapeutic touch**. Santa Fe, NM: Bear & Co.

Larson, D.B., Pattison, E.M., Blazer, D.G., Omran, A.R. & Kaplan, B.H. (1986). Systematic analysis research on religious variables in four major psychiatric journals, 1978-1982. **American Journal of Psychiatry, 143**, 329-334.

Leahy, R.L. (1996). **Cognitive therapy: Basic principles and applications**. Northvale, NJ: Jason Aronson, Inc.

Lee, J. (September 17, 1998). Hyde acknowledges affair, says revelation won't hinder any proceedings against Clinton. **USA Today**, 9A.

Lerner, R. (1990). **Affirmations for the inner child**. Deerfield Beach, FL: Health Communications.

Levin, J.S. & Schiller, P.L. (1987). Is there a religious factor in health? **Journal of Religious Health, 26**, 9-36.

Levin, J.S. (1997). Religious research in gerontology, 1980-1994: A systematic review. **Journal of Religious Gerontology, 10** (3), 3-31.

Levin, J.S., Larson, D.B. & Puchalski, C.M. (1997). Religion and spirituality in medicine: Research and education. **Journal of the American Medical Association, 278** (9), 792-793.

Levin, J.S. & Vanderpool, H.Y. (1989). Is religion therapeutically significant for hypertension? **Social Science Medicine, 29**, 69-78.

Liberman, B.L. (1978). The role mastery in psychotherapy: Maintenance of improvement and prescriptive change. In J.D. Frank, R. Hoen-Saric, S.D. Imber, B.L. Liberman & A.R. Stone (Eds.), **Effective ingredients of successful psychotherapy** (pp.35-72). NY: Bruner/Mazel.

Lilly, J.C. (1974). **Programming and metaprogramming in the human biocomputer.** NY: Bantam Books.

Mahoney, M.J. & Arnkoff, D.B. (1978). Cognitive and self-control therapies. In S.L. Garfield & A.E. Bergin (Eds.), **Handbook of psychotherapy and behavior change** (2nd ed.). NY: Wiley.

Maltz, M. (1967). **Psycho-Cybernetics.** NY: Essandess Special Editions.

Manning, A. & Hellmich, N. (December 12, 1995). Parents and kids share faith at home, survey says. Associated Press. **USA Today,** 5D.

Marano, H.E. (March/April, 1999). Depression: Beyond serotonin. **Psychology Today,** 30-36, 72-74, 76.

Maslow, A.H. (1954). **Motivation and personality.** NY: Harper & Row.

Maslow, A.H. (1968). **Toward a psychology of being** (2nd ed.). NY: D. Van Nostrand.

Maslow, A.H. (1972). **The farther reaches of human nature.** NY: Viking Press.

Matthews, D.A., Larson, D.B. & Barry, C.P. (1994). **The faith factor: An annotated bibliography of clinical research on spiritual subjects. Vol. 1.** John Templeton Foundation.

Maxmen, J.S. & Ward, N.G. (1995). **Essential psychopathology and its treatment: Second edition revised for DSM-IV.** NY: W.W. Norton & Co.

McCourt, F. (December, 1998). When you think of God what do you see? **Life,** 60-73.

McCullough, M.E. & Larson, D.R. (1999). Prayer. In W.R. Miller (Ed.) **Integrating Spirituality into Treatment: Resources for Practices.** Washington, DC: American Psychological Association, pp. 85-110.

McKay, M., Davis, M. & Fanning, P. (1981). **Thoughts and feelings: The art of cognitive stress Intervention.** Oakland, CA: New Harbinger.

McKay, M. & Fanning, P. (1991). **Prisoners of belief: Exposing & changing beliefs that control your life.** Oakland, CA: New Harbinger Publications.

McKay, M., Davis, M. & Fanning, P. (1997). **Thoughts and feelings: Taking control of your life.** Oakland, CA: New Harbinger Publications.

McNamara, J.D. (February 12, 1996). The war on drugs is lost. **National Review,** 34-48.

Meddis, S. (October 9, 1986). New Crime count differs with FBI's. **USA Today,** 1A.

Meichenbaum, D. (1977). **Cognitive behavior modification.** NY: Plenum Press.

Meichenbaum, D. (1985). **Stress inoculation training.** NY: Pergamon Press.

Mental Medicine Update. (1996). Religion, faith, and health. **4** (4), 2,7.

Metzner, R. (1990). Rebirth and the eternal child. In J. Abrams, (Ed.), **Reclaiming the inner child.** Los Angeles, CA: Jeremy P. Tarcher, Inc.

Murray, E.J. & Jacobson, L.I. (1971). The nature of learning in traditional and behavioral psychotherapy. In A.E. Bergin & S.L. Garfield (Eds.), **Handbook of psychotherapy and behavioral change.** NY:Wiley.

Myss, C. (1996). **Anatomy of the spirit: The seven stages of power and healing.** NY: Harmony Books.

Myss, C. (1997). **Why people don't heal and how they can.** NY: Three Rivers Press.

New Age Journal. Body and soul 101. (September/October, 1997). Author, 15.

New Age Journal. Life after life. (May/June, 1998). Author,19.

New Age Journal, (January/February, 1999). Religion rocks, dude. Author, 26.

The New York Times, (September 11, 1998). Vocal Clinton critic admits she had long term affair with married man. **Daily Reflector,** Greenville, NC. A4.

O'Connell, A. & O"Connell, V.F. (1980). **Choice and change: The personality of adjustment, growth, and creativity.** Englewood Cliffs, N.J.: Prentice-Hall.

O'Driscoll, P. (November 5, 1998). Bias, pot laws gain momentum. **USA Today,** 1A.

Oldham, J.M. & Morris, L.B. (1995). **The new personality self-portrait: Why you think, work, love, and act the way you do.** NY: Bantam Books.

Olness, K. (1993). Hypnosis: The power of attention. In D. Goleman & J. Gurin, (Eds.) **Mind body medicine: How to use your mind for better health.** Yonkers, NY: Consumer Reports Books.

Ornish, D. (1998). **Love & Survival: The scientific basis for the healing power of intimacy.** NY: HarperCollins Publishers.

Ostriker, R. (Spring, 1998). All you need is love. **Intuition,** 18-21, 104.

Perkins, C. & Klaus, P. (April, 1996). Criminal victimization 1994. **Bureau of Justice Statistics Bulletin.** U.S. Department of Justice, Office of Justice Programs. Washington, D.C.

Pert, C.B. (1999). **Molecules of emotion.** NY: Touchtone.

Pew Research Center. (December 22, 1997). Pew poll indicates more people believe in God. Associated Press. **The Daily Reflector,** Greenville, NC.

Piaget, P. (1954). **The construction of reality in the child.** NY: Basic Books.

Propst, L.R. (1980). The comparative efficacy of religious and nonreligious imagery for the treatment of mild depression in religious individuals. **Cognitive Therapy and Research, 4,** 167-178.

Propst, L.R., Ostrom, R., Watkins, P., Dean, T. & Mashburn, D. (1992). Comparative efficacy of religious and nonreligious cognitive-behavioral therapy for the treatment of clinical depression in religious individuals. **Journal of Consulting and Clinical Psychology, 60,** 94-103.

Psychology Today. (March/April 1999). Hot and bothered in Canada, 14.

Psychology Today. (May/June 1999). Our second brain: The stomach,16.

Rama, Swami, Ballentine, R. & Ajaya, Swami. (1976). **Yoga and psychotherapy: The evolution of consciousness.** Glenview, IL: Himalayan Institute.

Reed, P.G. (1987). Spirituality and well-being in terminally ill hospitalized adults. **Research in Nursing and Health, 10,** 335-344.

Rokeach, M. (1960). **The open and closed mind.** NY: Basic Books.

Rosenhan, D.L. & Seligman, M.E.P. (1995). **Abnormal psychology** (3rd ed.). NY: W.W. Norton & Co.

Sartre, J.P. (1957). **Existentialism and human emotions.** NY: Philosophical Library.

Satchidananda, Sri Swami, (July-August, 1998). Should you design your own religion? **Utne Reader,** 48.

Sax, J.L. (1969). Law and justice. Public Affairs Pamphlet No.433. NY: Public Affairs Committee.

Schacter, S. & Singer, J.E. (1962). Cognitive, social and physiological determinants of emotional states. **Psychological Review, 69**, 379-399.

Scott, R.O. (Fall, 1998). Survey: Adolescents accept the unexplainable. **Spirituality and Health, 19**.

Scott, R.O. (Spring, 2001). Are you religious or are you spiritual? **Spirituality and Health**, 26-31.

Shealy, C.N. (1999). **Sacred healing.** Boston: Element.

Shealy, C.N. & Myss, C.M. (1993). **The creation of health: The emotional, psychological, and spiritual responses that promote health and healing.** Walpole, NH: Stillpoint Publishing.

Shepard, S. (Cox Washington Bureau). (August 17,1998). Census report says millions were too busy to vote in '96. **Daily Reflector**, p. A1.

Sivananda, H. H. Swami. (1957). **A practical guide for students of yoga.** Hong Kong: The Divine Life Society (Yoga Institute).

Sobel, D.S. & Ornstein, R. (1996). **The healthy mind, healthy body handbook.** Los Altos,CA: DRx.

Sobel, D.S. & Ornstein, R. (1998). Healthy pleasures. **Mind/Body Health Newsletter, 7** (1), 1-2.

Sokoloff, L. (May/June, 1999). Prayer is good medicine. **Yoga Journal**, 18.

Sugrue, T. (1994). **There is a river: The story of Edgar Cayce.** (Rev. Ed.). Virginia Beach, VA: The Association for Research and Enlightenment.

Sweet, R.W. (February 12, 1996). The war on drugs is lost. **National Review**, 34-48.

Szasz, T.S. (1961). **The myth of mental illness.** NY: Hoeber-Harper.

Targ, R. & Katra, J. (2001). The scientific and spiritual implications of psychic abilities. **Alternative Therapies, 7** (3), 143-149.

Taylor, C.L. (1991). **The inner child workbook: What to do with your past when it just won't go away.** NY: G.P. Putnam's Sons.

Thomas, C. (September 17, 1998). A time for prayer. **USA Today**, A8.

Troyer, H. (1988). Review of cancer among 4 religious sects: Evidence that life-styles are distinctive sets of risk factors. **Social Science Medicine, 26**, 1007-1017.

U.S. Department of Justice. (March, 1998). **Compendium of Federal Justice Statistics, 1995. Bureau of Justice Statistics, Executive Summary**. Office of Justice Programs.

Vishnudevananda, Swami. (1960). **The complete illustrated book of Yoga.** NY: Bell Publishing Co.

Walen, S., DiGuiseppe, R. & Dryden, W. (1992). **A practitioner's guide to rational-emotive therapy** (2nd ed.). San Francisco: Jossey/Bass.

Wanberg, K.W. & Milkman, H.B. (1998). **Criminal conduct and substance abuse treatment: Strategies for self-improvement and change: The provider's guide.** Thousand Oaks, CA: SAGE.

Ware, D. & Goodwin, L.R., Jr., (1968). **DME Yoga: The drugless mind expansion yoga program for preventing drug abuse.** Miami, FL.: Unpublished manuscript.

Weil, A. (June, 1999). Hypnotherapy: The power of suggestion. **Self Healing,** 2-3.

Willing, R. (April 26, 1999). Study: Worshipers live longer than those who skip services. **USA Today,** 7A.

Whitfield, C. (1987). **Healing the child within.** Deerfield, FL: Health Communications.

Williams, W. (July 24, 1998). Does distrust of government really matter? **Daily Reflector,** Greenville, NC, A10.

Witter, R.A., Stock, R.A., Okun, M.A. & Haring, M.J. (1985). Religion and subjective well-being in adulthood: A quantitative synthesis. **Revelatory Religious Research, 26,** 332-342.

Woodward, K.L. (March 29, 1999). 2000 years of Jesus. **Newsweek,** 52-65.

Yu, W. (May, 1999). Music therapy. **Natural Health,** 40.

INDEX

Acceptance-rejection continuum, 35
Affirmations, 25, 207-216
 Guidelines for using, 211-212
Afterlife, 223, 224
AIDS, 231, 240
Amnesia, 62
Anger, 59, 93-94, 108, 130
Association for Research and Enlightenment
 (ARE), 230
Attachment, iii, 11, 36, 37, 183-184
Beliefs, 74-81
 Self-defeating core beliefs, 74-76
 Top 10 core beliefs about self (Table 8), 77
 Top 3 core beliefs about relationships (Table
  9), 77
 Top 5 core beliefs about life (Table 10), 78
 Top 4 core beliefs about illness & disability
  (Table 11), 78
 Top 10 core beliefs about alcohol & other
  drugs (Table 12), 79
Biocomputer, 26, 208-211, 216, 256
Black or white thinking, 42
Blaming, 42-43
Body/mind therapies, 33, 92-93
Buddhism, iii, 6-7, 159, 202
 Recommended readings, 269-270
Buttons
 Constructive and destructive power of
  Buttons, 129-150
 Constructive power of Buttons, 129-130
 Decision-making, 247
 Definition, 2, 26-28, 36
 Destructive power of Buttons, 130-150
 Identifying our Buttons, 36-38, 183
 Morality Buttons, 131-150
 Recognizing when your Buttons get pushed,
  30-35
 Top 10 potential Buttons (Table 13), 84
 Types of Buttons, 27-28, 38-39
 Wherever you go you take your Buttons with
  you, 244
Button-Pushers, 28, 38, 58, 96, 243-247
 Blaming, 80-81, 243, 244
 Our primary Button-Pushers, 243
 Reframing as teachers, 244-245, 246
 Stay or leave the Button-Pusher?, 245-247
Button removal and cognitive restructuring, 151-
 206
 Choosing to keep your Buttons, 151-153

 Deciding whether to keep, modify or
  eliminate your Buttons, 151-158
Button Therapy (BT)
 The Button Therapy model, 23-31
 Client criteria for utilizing BT, 14-15
 Differences between BT and CBT models,
  10
 Eclectic cognitive counseling mode2, 12
 Guidelines for mental health professionals, 5
 Humanistic, transpersonal and holistic
  characteristics, 23-25
 Holistic cognitive counseling model, 4
 How to integrate BT into the counseling
  session, 16-22
 Principles underlying BT, 12-14
 When to use BT, 14, 26
Byrd, Randolph heart study, 231
Catastrophic thinking, 43
Cayce, Edgar, 229
Centers of Consciousness Ranking Scale, 300-
 303
Chakras,101-104
 Malfunctioning chakras, 104
 Recommended readings, 276
 Seven chakras in yoga (Table 15), 103
Change and renewal, 210
Christianity
 Recommended readings, 270
Cognitions, 28
Cognitive counseling/therapy
 Applications of CBT, 10
 Historical roots, 6-10
 Primary focus of CBT, 10
 Recommended readings, 258-259
Cognitive interventions, 159-206
 Changing demands to preferences, 160, 165,
  168
 Cognitive thought-stopping, 160, 169-170
 Counting to ten, 161, 171
 Disputing troublesome cognitions, 160, 166
  168
 Empathy doubler, 161, 173-174
 Empty-chair, 161, 175-178
 Flooding, 161, 170
 Group Button pull, 163, 199-201
 Group Button Therapy empty-chair
  technique, 163, 198-199
 Here-and-now, 161, 171-172
 Inner child and reparenting work, 162, 187-192

Injunctions and redecision work, 162, 186-187
Mad director fantasy technique, 161, 172-173
Meditation, 162, 180-184
Mind cleansing, 162, 179-180
Paradoxical intention, 163, 192-194
Reframing, 163, 192, 244-245, 246
Scheduled pity pot, 162, 179
Self-hypnosis, 163, 194-198
Self-talk, 160, 165-166
Worry place, 162, 178-179
Cognitive Self-Assessment Inventory (CSAI), 19, 82-83, 277-294
Study, 304-324
Comparing, 43
Competitiveness, 114-115
Consciousness, 123, 205, 208
Centers of Consciousness Ranking Scale, 300-303
Control and power motivational state, 52-53, 172-173
Correctional officers, 42
Counting to ten, 161, 171
Crime, 44-45, 62-63, 132-137
Devil, 224
Criminal justice system, 44-45, 132-137
Defense mechanisms, 55-66
Assess your defense mechanisms, 64-65
Determining when we are using defense mechanisms, 64
Summary of twenty common defense Mechanisms (Table 5), 56-57
Attack, 58
Compensation, 58
Denial, 58-59
Displacement, 59
Fantasy, 59
Humor, 59
Idealization, 59
Identification, 59-60, 114-115
Intellectualization, 60
Isolation of affect, 60
Projection, 60-61
Rationalization, 61
Reaction formation, 61-62
Regression, 62
Sublimation, 63
Substitution, 63
Suppression, 63
Withdrawal, 63
Most frequently used, 65-66
Top 10 most used defense mechanisms (Table 6), 66
Definitions
Big monster Button, 27
Biocomputer, 26

Button, 26-28
Button-Pusher, 28
Cognition, 28
Cognitive therapy/counseling, 28
Small annoying Button, 28
Troublesome cognition, 29
Depression, 91-92
Dieting, 193
Disability, 58, 61-62, 64, 130
Prayer, 224
Spirituality and disability, 225-227, 234, 237-238, 239
Top 4 core beliefs about illness & disability (Table 11), 78
Disputing troublesome cognitions, 160, 166-168
Distance healing, 229-237
Duke University MANTRA study, 230-231
Edgar Cayce, 229-230
Maharishi effect, 235-237
Medical diagnosis at a distance, 229-230
Nonhuman studies, 232-233
Randolph Byrd heart study, 231-232
Targ study on AIDS, 231
Distorted styles of thinking, 39-54
Black or white thinking, 42
Blaming, 42-43
Catastrophic thinking, 43
Comparing, 43
Fair and just thinking, 43-47
Mind reading, 47
Negativistic thinking, 48
Overgeneralizing, 48
Pasting and futuring, 49-50
Perfectionistic thinking, 52
Right-Wrong thinking, 52-53
Should thinking, 50-52
Top 10 cognitions reflecting styles of distorted thinking, 54
Twelve styles of distorted thinking Table 2, 41
Dossey, Larry, 117, 226-227, 228-229, 232-233
Drugs and drug abuse, 58-59, 64, 104, 110, 112, 124, 133, 167, 170, 247
Drug prohibition, 132-150
Hypnosis and nicotine addiction, 194-198
Spirituality, 234, 237, 238, 240
Top 10 core beliefs about alcohol & other drugs (Table 12), 79
Duke University MANTRA study, 230-231
Dyer, Wayne, 8
Recommended readings, 259, 272-274
Eating disorders, 107
Ellis, Albert, 9, 87, 166
Emotions and feelings, 86-98, 112
Anger, 93-94
Boredom, 94

Emotions and feelings *(cont.)*
    Can emotions precede thought?, 88
    Connecting the emotions to Buttons, 97-98,
        170, 178
    Emotional amperage, 95
    Emotional games, 94-95
    Emotions vs. rational minds, 88
    Feeling avoiders, 112
    Guilt, 94-95
    Gut feeling, 90
    Hard to control emotions, 34-35
    Identify your feelings, 34-35
    Mind-body emotions, 89
    Mobile brain, 90
    Molecules of emotion, 89
    Motivational states and emotions, 121
    Recommended readings, 259-260
    Stress and the brain, 91-92
    Types of emotions, 93-94
    Welcome your feelings, 97
    What causes emotions?, 87
Empathy doubler, 161
Empowering Clients, 15-16
Empty-chair technique, 161, 175-178
    Group BT empty-chair technique, 163
Energy, 171, 177, 178, 182, 193
    Chakras,101-104
    Energy drainers, 108
    Energy healing, 33, 164, 169, 179-180, 230
        231-237, 238
    Love and acceptance energy, 117
    Recommended readings, 260-263
Fair and just thinking, 43-47
Fears, 85
    Of failure, 63
    Top 10 fears (Table 14), 85
Flooding, 161, 170
Forgetting, 62
Games people play, 48, 154-157
God, 25
    Different names for God, 25
Group BT empty-chair technique, 163
Group Button pull, 163, 199-201
Healing
    Beliefs, 238-240
    History of spirituality and healing, 225-226
    Spirituality and healing, 225-242
Here-and-now, 50, 161, 171-172
Heritage store, 230
Holistic, 221
    Holistic counseling, 4, 5, 24-25
    Recommended readings, 263-265
Hypnosis, 163, 194-198, 203
    And addiction, 194-198
    And relaxation, 194
Illness, 46, 104, 117-118, 130, 203

    Beliefs, 238-240
    Prayer, 224
    Spirituality, 234, 237-238
Injunctions, 162, 186-187
Inner child, 162, 187-192
    Recommended readings, 258, 265-266
Insecurity, 107, 108
Isolation and loneliness, 108
Job loss, 108
Ken Keyes, Jr., iii, 2, 8, 100, 118, 173, 208, 245,
    258-259, 271, 273
Love
    Love and acceptance energy, 35, 117
    Love and acceptance motivational state, 115
        118
    Love, intimacy and health, 117
Mad director fantasy technique, 161, 172-173
Magical thinking, 153
Maharishi effect, 235-237
Marital conflicts, 47-48, 60, 180, 200-201
Maslow's hierarchy of needs, 100, 117, 118, 228
Meditation, 162, 178, 180-184, 235
    How meditation differs from prayer, 181
    Maharishi effect, 235-237
    Stress management and relaxation, 227
    When to meditate, 184
Mind-body, 89-93
    Recommended readings, 266-268
Mind cleansing, 162, 179-180
Mind reading, 47
Morality
    Consequences of the Moral Control Patrol,
        132-150
    Corruption, 136
    Criminal justice system, 133
    Disrespect for the law and police, 136-137
    Diversion of law enforcement resources from
        protecting citizens from real criminals,
        135-136
    How the moral control patrol maintains
        control, 137-138
    Libertarian backlash, 139
    Moral Control Patrol, 127, 131-150
    Moral prohibition laws help make
        "criminals" rich, 134-135
    Moral rehabilitation five-step process, 142-
        147
    Moral rehabilitation in the criminal justice
        system, 147-148
    Our country's schizophrenic and hypocritical
        pleasure and morality policies, 133
    Our morality laws make criminals out of
        otherwise law-abiding citizens, 133
    Shadow, 148
    Wasting financial and manpower resources,
        135

Motivational states, 99-128
    Abraham Maslow's hierarchy of needs, 100
    Chakras,101-104
    Control and power, 104, 113-115, 172-173
    Determining the motivational states
        associated with your Buttons, 127-128
    Feelings and motivational states, 128
    Ken Keyes' Living Love system, 100
    Love and acceptance, 115-118
    Models of motivational states, 99-105
    Motivational states we spend the most time
        in (Table 17), 123
    Motivational states associated with most of
        our Buttons, 126-127
    Perception and motivational states, 124-126
    Personal growth and self-actualization, 118-
        119
    Pleasure and sensation-seeking, 109-113
    Rational-emotive behavior therapy, 99
    Safety and security, 106-109
    Six motivational states in BT model,105,
        106-128
    Six motivational states outline (Table 16),
        121
    Spiritual and transcendental, 119-120
    Transactional analysis, 99
Motivational States Inventory (MSI), 295-303
    Study, 304-324
Music, 111
Myss, Caroline, 230, 260
Near death experiences, 224
Negativistic thinking, 48
Nonhuman energy/spiritual healing, 232-233
    Implications, 233
Overgeneralizing, 48
Paradoxical intention, 163, 192-194
Paranormal events, 223
Parent messages, 186-187
Parenting, 42, 48-49, 58, 61, 129-130, 186-187
Parents, 80-81
Pasting and futuring, 49-50
Perception and motivational states, 124-126
Personal growth and self-actualization, 118-
    119
Perfection, 116, 249-255
Perfectionistic thinking, 52
Personal growth, 153, 154
    Personal growth continuum, 116-117
    Personal growth and self-actualization
        motivational state, 118-
        119
Personality traits, styles and disorders, 67-73
    Personality disorders, 68-69
    Personality traits, 67
    Recommended readings, 268
    Top 10 personality traits (Table 7), 72

Toxic and nourishing people, 70-71
Physical body
    Listen to your body, 32
    The body's wisdom, 33
Pity pot, 162, 179
Pleasure phobics, 112-113
Politics, 45-46
Prayer, 181, 222, 223-224, 227
    In healing, 227, 228-229, 230-232, 235, 241
Prednisone, 3
Preferring vs. demanding, 47, 52, 160, 165, 168
Procrastination, 52, 69
Programming, 80-81, 207-216
Questions about Button Therapy, 202-206
    Can I use any of the cognitive interventions
        described in this book?, 202-203
    Can I combine cognitive interventions?, 203
    Do I have to use all six steps of the BT
        method every time I work on a Button?,
        203
    How do I get rid of deeply rooted Buttons
        that don't want to be uprooted?, 203-
        204
    Does giving up my Buttons mean I have to
        give up my wants, desires, and goals and
        let people run over me?, 204-206
Rational-emotive behavior therapy, 9, 10, 11,
    87, 99-100, 166-168, 258
References, 325-333
Relationships
    Top 3 core beliefs about relationships (Table
        9), 77
Recommended readings, 258-276
    Cognitive therapy, 258-259
    Emotional healing, 259-260
    Energy healing, 260-263
    Guide to self-help books, 263
    Holistic health and healing, 263-265
    Inner child and reparenting work, 265-270
    Mind/body healing, 266-268
    Personality, 268
    Spiritual and personal growth, 268-274
    Stress management, 274
    Transactional analysis, 275-276
    Yoga and Chakras, 276
Redecision work, 162
Reframing, 163, 192-194, 244-245, 246
Reparenting, 162, 187-192
Ram Dass, 164, 204-205, 273
Right-Wrong thinking, 52-53
Sadhaks, 30
Sai Baba, 217
Scapegoating, 61
Self-actualizing person, 255-256
Self-esteem, 43, 50, 75-76, 152-153
    Self-defeating core beliefs, 74-76

Self-esteem (cont.)
  Top 10 core beliefs about self (Table 8), 77
Self-help, 3-4, 263
Self-hypnosis, 163, 194-198, 203
Self-talk, 160, 165-166
Sex, 110, 125-126, 133
Shadow, 148
Should thinking, 50-52
  Top 10 should messages, 51
Six-Step Button Therapy Method, 248-257
  ABE's MBA acronym and mnemonic device,
    248-249
  Illustration of applying six steps to a
    perfectionistic Button, 249-255
  Outline, 29-30, 257
  Short-cuts, 254-255
  Step one: Awareness of stress and distress,
    32-35, 249
  Step two: Identifying our Buttons, 36-39,
    250
  Step three: Emotions, 86-98, 250
  Step four: Motivational states, 106-128, 250-
    251
  Step five: Button removal and cognitive
    restructuring, 151-158, 159-206, 251-
    253
  Step six: Affirmations and cultivating your
    mind's garden, 207-212, 253-254
  Summary overview, 248-257
Smiling sufferers, 152
Sour grapes, 61
Spirit warriors, 255-256
Spirituality, 4, 178, 181, 217-242
  Assessment, 238
  Beliefs and health, 239-240
  Benefits, 225
  Buttons and spirituality, 221
  Curriculum, 240-241
  Children and spirituality, 223, 225
  Crime, 224
  Definition, 218
  Devil, 224
  Disability, 225-227, 234, 237-
    238, 239
  Distinction between religion and spirituality,
    218-219
  Dysfunctional spirituality, 238-239, 240
  Health benefits, 234, 237-238
  Health insurance, 234-235
  How do people understand God?, 219-220
  In health and mental health care, 227
  Negative effects, 233, 239-240
  New age spirituality, 223, 270
  Nonhuman studies, 232-233
  Prayer, 222, 223-224
  Recommended readings, 268-274

Spirit Warriors, 255-256
Spiritual and transcendental motivational
    state, 119-120
  Stress management and relaxation, 227
  Variety of religious groups, 222-223
  What's a spiritual act?, 219
  When prayer for healing fails, 239
  Why include a spiritual dimension in a
    cognitive counseling and psychological
    self-help model?, 220-242
Stress, 28, 32-35, 37, 42
  Recommended readings, 274
  Relaxation, 227, 230
  Stress and the brain, 91-92
  Stress junkies, 152
Students, 52, 59, 61, 62, 63, 96-97, 107, 167, 178
Sweet lemons, 61
Targ study on AIDS, 231
Teenagers, 42, 48-49
  Spirituality, 225
Thought-stopping,, 43, 50, 160, 169-170, 171
Thrill-seeking personality (T-personality), 113,
    152, 246
Touch, 92-93, 109, 230, 241
  Therapeutic touch, 33
Toxic and nourishing people, 70-71, 117
Transactional analysis, 99, 157, 189
  Recommended readings, 275-276
Universal life force, 25
Visualization, 211, 216, 230, 231
Weil, Andrew, 264, 265
Witness, 183
Work, 46-47, 108
Worry place, 162, 178-179
Yoga
  Recommended readings, 276

by
Dr. Lloyd Goodwin

The Button Therapy Book: How to Work on Your Buttons and the Button-Pushers in Your Life

A psychological self-help book for individuals and a holistic cognitive therapy manual for mental health professionals. The Six-Step Button Therapy Method includes twenty-one cognitive interventions. These cognitive interventions can be used by individuals for psychological self-help or by mental health professionals utilizing cognitive-behavioral therapy. *The Button Therapy Book* includes the *Cognitive Self-Assessment Inventory*, the *Motivational States Inventory*, and the top ten "should" messages, fears, and Buttons from a study of cognitions conducted by the author. This book is also used as a bibliotherapy resource for clients after a cognitive intervention is utilized in a counseling session. Published in 2002.

The Six-Step Button Therapy Method

A brief overview of the Six-Step Button Therapy Method. This short book is primarily used as a bibliotherapy resource for clients after a Button Therapy intervention in a counseling session. Published in 2002.

The Cognitive Self-Assessment Inventory (*CSAI*)

A self-test to help individuals identify and gain a better understanding of their core beliefs, "should messages," defense mechanisms, personality traits, thought distortions, and Buttons. Also, an assessment tool for mental health professionals. Sold in packages of twenty. Published in 2002.

Training Workshops in Cognitive-Behavioral Counseling

On-site training in cognitive-behavioral counseling (using the Button Therapy model) for mental health professionals. Contact Dr. Lloyd Goodwin at East Carolina University, School of Allied Health, Department of Rehabilitation Studies, Greenville, North Carolina 27858. 252-328-4428. GoodwinL@mail.ecu.edu.

Button Therapy Materials Available From

All of the Button Therapy materials are available from Trafford Publishing by calling toll-free (United States & Canada) 1-888-232-4444 or by contacting their internet website at *www.trafford.com*. The materials can also be ordered through other internet bookstores such as Amazon, Barnes & Noble, Borders, and Chapters.ca (in Canada) or from your local bookstore.

Lloyd R. Goodwin, Jr., Ph.D., LPC, CRC-MAC is interim chairman of the Department of Rehabilitation Studies. He is also director and professor in the Substance Abuse and Clinical Counseling program within the Department of Rehabilitation Studies, School of Allied Health Sciences at East Carolina University in Greenville, North Carolina. He teaches graduate courses in clinical, substance abuse, and rehabilitation counseling. He has maintained a full or part-time private consulting and clinical counseling practice off and on since 1968. Dr. Goodwin initiated and helped develop the first national and North Carolina master's degree level certification in substance abuse counseling. Dr. Goodwin earned his Ph.D. in Counseling, Health and Rehabilitation, with a major in Rehabilitation Counseling from Florida State University in 1974. He has been on the faculty of the State University of New York at Buffalo, Assumption College, and Emporia State University prior to his current position at East Carolina University where he has been since 1989. He has worked in the counseling field for 33 years as either a clinical counselor or counselor educator.

Dr. Goodwin is a Licensed Professional Counselor (LPC) and Certified Rehabilitation Counselor (CRC) with a specialty certification in addictions counseling (Master Addictions Counselor; MAC). Dr. Goodwin is founder and a past-president of the national *Professional Association of Rehabilitation Counselors* (PARC).

Printed in the United States
69281LVS00005B/81